Dark Matter: Women Witnessing Dreams Before Extinction

Dark Matter: Women Witnessing, Dreams Before Extinction
Edited by Lise Weil, Gillian Goslinga, Kristin Flyntz,
and Anne Bergeron

Published by NatureCulture
NatureCulture Web
www.nature-culture.net

ISBN: 978-1-960293-13-8 First Edition

Front cover artwork: *The Moon Falls a Thousand Times,*
by Naeemeh Naeemaei, author of *Dreams Before Extinction*, edited by
Paul Semonin. Santa Monica: Perceval Press, 2013. Thank you to
Naeemeh for the use of this beautiful image and her book's title as the
subtitle for this anthology.
Back cover artwork: *Ground of All Beings,* by Suzette Clough

Cover design: Christopher Gendron and Lis McLoughlin

Interior book design: Lis McLoughlin and Gillian Goslinga

Library of Congress Control Number: 2024927708

Dark Matter: Women Witnessing is online at:
https://darkmatterwomenwitnessing.com

March 01, 2025

To: Pash

In Sisterhood. The artists poets & authors in this Anthology share your beautiful soul. New Zealand is lucky, Gillian

Dark Matter: Women Witnessing Dreams Before Extinction

Edited by Lise Weil, Gillian Goslinga, Kristin Flyntz, Anne Bergeron

Published by
NatureCulture
Northfield, Massachusetts

Foreword
G.A. Bradshaw

Common to Zen Buddhist temples and meditation halls is a *bonshō*, a large bell. Sometimes suspended from a wooden beam, at others, the bronze bell sits on a pillow in a place of honor, mouth open to the sky and stars.

Bonshōs are used to begin *zazen*, the sacred practice of sitting meditation. The practitioner—monk or nun—sits in front of the bell and, using a padded wooden mallet, invites the bell to speak. Practitioners insist that *bonshōs* must be invited, not struck. Bells are regarded as alive and fully sentient. They are prophets from the empty fullness of the cosmos whose pharaonic nature derives from mere presence. This celebratory anthology is a symphony of *bonshōs*.

Like the sound of the temple bell, the writer-poet-artist's invitation begins with an *atari*, an inner wakening. Gradually, this murmur builds into the *oshi*, a sustained ring and testimony of truth. Finally, there is the *okuri*, when the sound of the bell fades. The voice recedes, the gift has been given and pen, laid aside until the next invitation.

In collaboration with ancestors, dreams, Animals, Elementals, Land, and countless other allies and guides, the writers, poets, and artists in this volume make visible the unseen, speak the unspoken, and bring into conscious light what has been pushed into collective obscurity. Cassandras decrying Promethean arrogance, they are bound to recognize, witness and wrest truth from the fog of denial.

To speak of them simply as bearers of bad news, however, is incomplete. Indeed, careful eye and ear discover that the *coniunctio* of light and dark is essential for humanity's birth into reality. By recognizing the forgotten, dismissed, and unwanted, the wanted, yearned for and delighted come into their own. The one cannot be without the other. *Dark Matter* voices are an embrace of wholeness, for it is dark matter which coheres the entirety of the universe.

Spanning a ten-year arc, the chapters gathered here weave together in a harmony of "spells, spillings, ravings and reason-defying leaps of thought and imagination" as editor Lise Weil wrote in the journal's inaugural editorial. A dazzling kaleidoscope of human and nonhuman faces emerges from the words by which they are conjured. Muted Pines burst into a chorus of pathos. Hearts of Dove and human converse without utterance. Contravening the laws of Newtonian physics, Salmon venture beyond the reaches of their streams to wind their way through skies and wooded land. Suddenly, we are thrust into a startling world alight with wonder. The healing has begun.

Yet, as our eyes move from line to line, skipping stones in a glistening brook, we find traces of blood and salted tears. These are sacrificial ingredients exacted in the process of alchemical revelation. A compulsion for truth does not come free. Bringing inner to outer leaves the writer-artist-poet exposed without protection afforded by collective deception. This is the nature of truth-telling.

These sayers, seers and their kindred are needed more than ever, not only to balance the scales of perception, but to transform humanity's profound alienation into its rightful place of unity and natural belonging. *Dark Matter* voices are clarions of beauty, revitalization, and joy declaring what being alive really means.

Mother of Us: A Prayer for Healing

Grief, grief unutterable in the trade winds of your passage. We are here upon a shadow's generosity, ley lines undone, winds burrowing through the parched soil that say not whither or whence we wander, why we are here and what we have come to fathom. Is there work for our hands the last drop having fallen? Is it the beginning or the end of prayer? Let the tall grass teach us to speak your name, bent low beneath your urgency. Mother of god, mother of us, mother of what is, restore us.

[...]

—from Kim Chernin, *Dark Matter: Women Witnessing, issue #6*

Dark Matter: Women Witnessing Dreams Before Extinction
An Anthology of Writings and Art from Our First Ten Years

Introduction 1
Lise Weil, Gillian Goslinga, Kristin Flyntz, Anne Bergeron

I. To Witness: Seeing in the Dark 9

Naeemeh Naeemaei, *Dreams Before Extinction* (#3)* 10
Miriam Greenspan, *Seeing in the Dark* (#1) 22
Christine Holland Cummings, *How to Go on When It Keeps Getting Darker* (#7) . 31
Deena Metzger, *Living by Dream* (#1) 34
Debra Magpie Earling, *from The Lost Journals of Sacajewea* (#3) 44
Patricia Reis, *Over the Edge* (#1) 51
Leonore Wilson, *The Fire That Nearly Took Us* (#10) 60
Anne Bergeron, *Winter* (#5) 62
Gillian Goslinga, *To Witness* (#2) 69
nan seymour, *pelicans in exile* (#17) 74
Alex C. Eisenberg, *Living at the Edge of Devastation* (#17) 77

II. Fired Anew: What It Means to Heal 99

Karen Mutter, *Jaguar Medicine* (#6), Dream 100
Mary Sutton, *Her Body is Burning* (#3) 103
Sharon Rodgers Simone, *Fired Anew* (#7) 110
Verena Stefan, *Quitting Chemo* (#6) 121
Carole Harmon, *My Body—an Eco-Terrain* (#17) 133
Laura Alexi Davenport, *The Unveiling: Notes on Illness
   & Beauty* (#6) 141
Eve Rachele Sanders, *The View from the Ground* (#7) 148
Shante' Sojourn Zenith, *Standing on First Stone* (#14) 154

III. *The Grammar of Animacy*..165

    Shula Levine, *Everything is Alive and Communicating* (#5), Vision....166
    Robin Wall Kimmerer, *When Earth Becomes an "It"* (#2)...............168
    Cynthia Travis, *Listen with Your Feet* (#4)....................................177
    Deena Metzger, *MaNdlovu* (#4) 188
    Judy Grahn, *Dragonfly Dances* (#2)..190
    Alexander Merrill, *Homage to Bees* (#2) 198
    Joan Kresich, *Letter to a Yellowstone Wolf* (#2) 208
    Sara Wright, *My Yellow Spotted Lady* (#1)................................210
    Lise Weil, *Blow* (#17)...213
    Elliot BatTzedeck, *Benediction* (#16) 219

IV. *What We Know in Our Bones*...223

    Hilary Giovale, *The Blood Knows* (#10) 224
    Melissa Kwasny, *Another Letter to the Soul* (#4) 228
    Andrea Mathieson, *What We Know in Our Bones* (#12) 230
    Anne Bergeron, *The Night Thunder Called* (#16)........................ 240
    Nancy Windheart, *Aspen Ways of Knowing* (#10)....................... 246
    Deena Metzger, *Dreaming Another Language; She Will not Kill* (#2). 256

V. *Songs of Undoing* 263

    Sharon English, *Nourishing the Future* (#5), Dream......................264
    Jojo Donovan, *Dispatches from the Collapse of Time* (#14) 266
    Yehudit Silverman, *Refugia* (#17) 277
    Pamela Booker, from *Lil' Lizzie: Go Let Yourself Learn How to Live* (#14) 279
    Jaime Wood, *Yaquina at Low Tide* (#5) 286
    Anne Bergeron, Debby Black, Andrea Mathieson, Cynthia Ross,
        & Nancy Windheart, *Lac Café Medley* (#9)....................288
    Leslie Schwarz, *Leaving the Mother Country* (#16).......................298
    Emilee Baum, *Demoness* (#7), Dream 304

VI. *I am Nothing Without My Dead*..............................307

Nora Jamieson, *I Am Nothing without My Dead* (#3) 308
Judith Redwing Keyssar, *Gift from the Ancestors: My Work as an RN/Midwife to the Dying* (#13).........................313
JuPong Lin, *my people sent me a canoe; 1000 Gifts of Decolonial Love* (#11). 324
Maria Blum, *Memoria: la poesia de las flores* (#15)......................333
Briggs Whiteford, *Sister Ancestor* (#14)............................345
Hilary Giovale, *Embers into Fire* (#14) 349
Azul V. Thomé, *Being with Ancestors* (#13)...........................359
Ysabel Y. González, *Chamelion or Thinking about My Mother the Sparrow* (#13) 372
Sara Wright, *Crane Song: Finding my Way Home* (#12)...................374

VII. *Healing with Land and Ancestors*.....................381

Naomi Shihab Nye, *My Grandmother Said* (#3).........................382
Anne Bergeron, *Calling Out the Names* (#3) 384
Cynthia Travis, *River of Kin* (#15)..............................390
Suzette Clough, *Remembering Our Original Pattern Ancestors: Painting as a Way of Knowing Earth* (#14)......................399
Valerie Wolf, *Dreaming the Future* (#2) 404
Kathleen Hellen, *Out of the beringian refugium* (#14).....................414
Gillian Goslinga, *Healing with Land and Ancestors* (#15) 416
Julie Gabrielli, *Song of the Chesapeake* (#3) 430
Wendy Gorschinsky-Lambo, *Making Love with a Three-Billion-Year-Old Woman* (#6) 439

VIII. *The Music of Grief*..............................451

Kim Chernin, *Mother of Us: A Prayer for Healing* (#6)..................452
Cynthia Travis, *The Music of Grief* (#2) 456
Lois Red Elk, *Take Her Hands* (#5)..............................466
Elena Herrada, *Gardening in the Motor City* (#17)....................468
Ruth Wallen, *Cascading Memorials: Public Places to Mourn* (#2) 471

Kristin Flyntz, *Too Much Sky* (#17)... 481
Susan Marsh, *Elegy for the Cranes* (#2)... 485
Susan Cerulean, *Bear Requiem* (#3) 487
Nora L. Jamieson, *Fleshing the Hide* (#2) 490
Erica Charis-Molling, *Requiem in the Key of Bees, a Cento* (#6) 493

IX. *What It Takes to Breach*... 495

Juliana Borrero Echeverry, *Landscapes at the End of the World* (#9) .. 496
Michaela Harrison, *What It Takes to Breach* (#17)........................ 502
Kim Zombik, *In the Name of So Many* (#16) 508
Andrea Mathieson, *Listening for the Long Song* (#4)...................... 511
Jacqueline Freeman, *Prey-er* (#8) 520
Margo Berdeshevsky, *In The Land of Afterwards* (#9) 528
Miriam Greenspan, *There Is No Light So Bright As That Which Shines
    from the Darkness* (#13) 530
Rachel Economy, *A Home for the Seeds* (#5) 546

Authors' and Artists' Biographies................................. 551
Editors' and Foreword Writer's Biographies.............. 567
About Dark Matter: Women Witnessing................... 571
About NatureCulture Web... 572

*(#) = Original *Dark Matter: Women Witnessing* publication issue
number   www.darkmatterwomenwitnessing.com

Thanks to Deena Metzger for the gatherings in which
Dark Matter: Women Witnessing was conceived—and for always
insisting heartbreak is a good place to start.

Introduction
Lise Weil, Gillian Goslinga,
Kristin Flyntz, & Anne Bergeron

Lise:

When we first began making our way through the seventeen issues *Dark Matter: Women Witnessing* has published since 2014 to make selections for this anthology, my co-editors and I were gobsmacked at how each and every article, almost without exception, spoke to the present moment. We were equally stunned by the power and beauty of the work. Deciding what to leave out was often excruciating.

All the material you will encounter here is informed by the understanding that as humans, our continuation on this earth hangs in the balance along with that of countless other species, and all of it can be read as a response to the question: "Are there other ways to live?" Our last labors on the book took place in the weeks following the U.S. presidential election. If the work we had chosen felt timely and urgent before, it felt several orders of magnitude more so now (Palestinian poet Naomi Shihab Nye's "My Grandmother Said" is a devastating case in point).

We have organized the material in this anthology into nine sections whose titles are also titles of essays within the sections. Taken together, these titles invoke both the spirit and the letter of what you will find in this volume.

For those of you who don't know the journal, here is a portion of the introductory editorial I wrote in November of 2014 when *Dark Matter* launched. Like the contents of the issues, as you'll see, it could have been written today.

Editorial: Issue #1 Seeing in the Dark

> The future is dark, which is the best thing the future can be,
> I think.
> —Virginia Woolf, January 1915, "Woolf's Darkness"

Welcome to the first issue of *Dark Matter: Women Witnessing*. This journal owes its existence to bad news: specifically, the increasingly brutal toll human civilization is taking on this earth and its nonhuman creatures. The evidence has mounted in recent months, and the sources are no longer alternative ones... NASA reported that August and September 2014 were the hottest months globally since 1880. In October, the Pentagon announced that ACD (anthropogenic climate disruption) poses an "immediate risk" to national security. In May, the word "unstoppable" was used for the first time by a NASA scientist in connection with glacial melt, in this case a portion of the West Antarctic Ice Sheet.

Elizabeth Kolbert's *The Sixth Extinction*, reviewed in February by Al Gore on the front page of the *New York Times Book Review*, observes that we are well into the first mass extinction event set in motion by humans and details some of its saddest casualties. And just weeks ago, The Living Planet Index (LPI) showed a decline of fifty-two percent in vertebrate species populations between 1970 and 2010. "Something between us and earth has broken," Linda Hogan wrote in *The Woman Who Watches over the World*, published some ten years ago, and today it would seem the supporting facts are all in. Yet we humans have a seemingly endless capacity for looking the other way.

The times are dark. But as Rebecca Solnit points out in her recent essay on Woolf's darkness from which the epigraph above is lifted, dark and murky places are where magic happens: "...the night in which distinctions and definitions cannot be readily made is the same night in which love is made, in which things merge, change, become enchanted, aroused, impregnated, possessed, released, renewed." The dark matter that scientists say makes up eighty-five percent of our universe, and about which they admit they know very little, is also, they say, its animating force. "To me," Solnit continues, "the grounds for hope are simply that we don't know what will happen next, and that the unlikely and the unimaginable transpire quite regularly."

...In addition to bad news, *Dark Matter* owes its existence to the women writers, dreamers and visionaries with whom I have been sitting in council at regular intervals since 2004, gatherings in which dreams are our main source of guidance and understanding. I am always stunned by the clarity, insight and ingenuity of this material that comes to us from nonconscious, chthonic realms. The knowing that issues from this source—I leave every gathering with this conviction—is knowing that we desperately need today.

...*Dark Matter* exists to honor and to take seriously women's spells, spillings, ravings and reason-defying leaps of thought and imagination (and welcomes all forms of embodied expression). But it also exists to acknowledge the other species that cohabit this planet with us, and in some cases have been here millions of years longer, by attending carefully to the signs they send us...

The editorial to issue #2, Spring 2015, opened with a visionary quote from Barbara Mor's landmark ecofeminist book *The Great Cosmic Mother*, published in 1987:

We are about to destroy each other, and the world, because of profound mistakes made in Bronze Age patriarchal ontology—mistakes about the nature of being, about the nature of human being in the world. Evolution itself is a time-process, seemingly a relentlessly linear unfolding. But biology also dreams, and in its dreams and waking visions it outleaps time, as well as space. It experiences prevision, clairvoyance, telepathy, synchronicity. Thus we have what has been called a magical capacity built into our genes... To evolve then—to save ourselves from species extinction—we can activate our genetic capacity for magic.

Whether they're aware of it or not, I believe that activating our genetic capacity for magic is exactly what the writers and artists in this collection are about. In fact, reading through the material of these past ten years it occurred to me that *The Great Cosmic Mother* had actually paved the way for much of it.

As I went on to write in that editorial, in the fall of 2014 I had an interesting exchange with Barbara about this journal-to-be. I had sent her the link to our website, and she replied to me with misgivings: "Post GCM (*The Great Cosmic Mother*), I had enough of those New Age women who were immersing in their version of dreams & visions to escape (in my opinion) the disciplines of history & the chaos of politics. I think our dreams & visions need to be grounded in the horrors of ancient & current realities, that it is time to retrieve the polemical Fist, if not my version then someone's somewhere."

"I hope Barbara would agree," I wrote in 2015 (she had died in January of that year), "there has been no escaping from the disciplines of history and the chaos of politics in the pages of this journal... But I think it's fair to say that if the polemical Fists of the writers we publish are raised, it is always—as it was for Barbara—in the name of communion, connection." All of which is as true today as ever.

Are there other ways to live?

I gave Barbara Mor the last word in that editorial, and I will do it again here: "We must *remember* the chemical connections between our cells and the stars, between the beginning and now…We must return to that time, in our genetic memory, in our dreams, when we were one species born to live together on earth, as her magic children." (p. 424)

Gillian:

By what magic, by what force, by what inspiration do whales hurtle their massive bodies to soar above the ocean in fantastic displays of freedom, joy and grace? By what magic, force, inspiration will and can we humans breach the weighted hubris of our civilizational war on every living system including our living bodies? Whales have *become* with Earth for 50 million years. Trees, without whom we would have no breathable atmosphere, 390 million. Waters, along with the oldest mineral, the zircon crystal, 4.4 billion years! Our first bipedal human-ape ancestor emerged just 7 million years ago.... Audacity indeed for the scientific and political modern human, not even 500 years on the scene, to claim that we are the species to have dominion over and stewardship of Earth. No, we are infants on this magnificent planet with much to learn from the plenitude of Earth Beings who have longer tenure with Her. As our times continue to devolve into chaos and more extinction, *Dark Matter* essays, dreams, poems, art are for me a call and a turn towards the other-than-human, evidence that souls *are* breaching the weight of our civilizational hubris in these times.

Kristin:

Deep below the cover of autumn's fallen leaves, millions of beings are composting what is old and dead into something new, preparing for the spring that will inevitably follow a long, cold winter. There, stardust and beetles and the bones of the dead collaborate to feed new life. This cycle precedes and will outlast our human endeavors and preoccupations, and makes our lives possible. The trees, those great beings of adaptability, resilience, and impeccable integrity, still stand where they have stood since before I was born—despite seasons of drought and flood and disease and development. They remind me that I am, we are, more than this moment. We are the dreams of our ancestors made manifest, the legacy of their errors and their triumphs, the fruits of their longing for the realization of their/our greatest potential. We are also the ancestors of the future. If each individual essay in this anthology is a seed planted on behalf of a viable future, together they are a vibrant, diverse garden alive with wisdom about what is required for all lives to flourish. We are invited to move slowly through this landscape, to allow its feral beauty to fill our senses and its inevitable brambles to pierce our tender places... to let its wild tendrils curl around our fingers and pull us back into remembering our rightful place in the world.

Anne:

On the morning wind and in our dreams, we are being called to kindle the fires of the old ways. We are being asked to receive the love of our ancestors—animals, forests, rivers, grandmothers, insects, and clouds—with each inhalation of breath. We are being asked to let our hearts break. May we meet our ancestors in gratitude as we honor all that is passing. May we greet them in joy with each exhalation, as we tend the future with their bones and dance into new ways of being with the winds. May the words and art in this book help us all to be the ancestors that our descendants will be inspired by as they live and as they dream.

[i] Hogan, Linda. *The Woman Who Watches Over the World*. New York: W.W. Norton & Co., 2001, p. 18. Print.
[ii] Solnit, Rebecca. "Woolf's Darkness: Explaining the Inexplicable." *The New Yorker*, April 24, 2014.
[iii] Mor, Barbara and Sjoo, Monica. *The Great Cosmic Mother: Rediscovering the Religion of the Earth*. HarperSanFrancisco, 1991, p. 424. Print.
[iv] Personal correspondence.

To Witness: Seeing in the Dark

…there are gifts that come to us when we know how to see in the dark.

—Miriam Greenspan, *Seeing in the Dark*

I wanted to offer my body as a witness to what was left of the forest. I wanted to be a body experiencing the body of the forest, and all the other bodies in it. I wanted them to feel the love of my body against theirs, before they felt the selfish swipe of the saw.

—Alex C. Eisenberg, *Living at the Edge of Devastation*

Naeemeh Naeemaei
Dreams Before Extinction

> …Naeemaei is saying that the purely logical mind has its limitations when it comes to expressing the pain and grief she herself feels at the loss of these species, or the damage our way of life causes to the natural world upon which all life depends.
> —Paul Semonin, *Dreams Before Extinction*

These paintings, inspired by Iranian artist Naeemaei's concern for the endangered species of Iran, were part of a series shown in an exhibition at the Henna Art Gallery in Tehran that was also exhibited at the Jordan Schnitzer Museum of Art in 2019. Naeemaei incorporates cultural and geographical elements as a means of communication with her audience, whom she initially considered to be indigenous communities living in or around protected areas. The entire series is collected in *Dreams Before Extinction*, a book edited by Paul Semonin in collaboration with the artist and published by Perceval Press in 2013.

From Naeemeh Naeemaei's arist's statement: *Witnessing the forest vanishing before my eyes due to rapid development in the natural habitats I grew up around was unbearable, and I needed to reach out to those who could make an impact, through a language that is beyond words. 'Dreams Before Extinction' is pure grief and elegy. I borrow rituals, folklore, and oral history to create a multilayered narrative that is woven into ecological and geographical features. I'm still waiting for Hope/Omid, the very last Siberian crane, to arrive this November. I sent him off in a painting in 2011. He has not been spotted since 2022. What is it called? Hope against hope?*

Siberian Crane
(opposite)

They say that he is the very last one! The Siberian Crane is a traveler from Russia that comes to the coast of the Caspian Sea in Iran to spend the winter each year. His Persian name is "Omid," which means "hope." The book I am holding over the crane's head is the Koran. Traditionally the Koran is held over the head of a person who is leaving the house for a journey, to make sure s/he will return safely. I am using this custom, which is common in Iran today, to ensure the crane will come back next fall. It was the only thing I could do, as a mother, sister, or a wife, whichever you may.

Siberian Crane, Acrylic and oil on canvas, 2011, 152 x 210 cm by N. Naeemaei

Imperial Eagle
(next spread)

An art critic once asked me: Have you paid attention to the symbolic meaning of the animals in your paintings? Did you think of the power of the Caspian Tiger or the symbolism of the Imperial Eagle in your paintings of these animals? Are you interested in wild and powerful animals? Do you believe in their legendary powers? He guessed that my general ideas were taken from the symbolic values of each animal. I told him, No! I don't care. I am happy if the symbols match my animals, but to me all animals, even the seemingly weak ones, are as real and powerful as any other in the real world.

Imperial Eagle, Acrylic and oil on canvas, 2011, 94 x 210 cm by N. Naeemaei

Caspian Red Deer #1, Acrylic and oil on canvas, 2010, 205 x 146 cm by N. Naeemaei

Hawksbill Turtle, Acrylic and oil on canvas, 2011, 190 x 160 cm by N. Naeemaei

Caspian Red Deer
(verso previous spread)

For me, the Caspian Red Deer is a mysterious animal. I had eaten its meat in my childhood and had seen his antlers in my paternal relatives' houses, but I had never seen his picture. I didn't know his name or what he looked like. The dark background of this painting is an image I had in mind from outside my grandma's house during a cold autumn, her house being located right in this animal's habitat! My uncles are hunters and they don't listen to my bemoaning them not to hunt. I had those antlers, so I decided to be the body of the animal himself, to be buried under a tree respectfully with him. And perhaps I wanted to say to my uncles: "We are one! Bury us together or stop killing us."

Hawksbill Turtle
(previous page)

"The Turtle and the Geese." In Iran this story is found in the tales of "Kalila and Dimna," from the Panchatantra, an Indian collection of ancient animal fables. Once upon a time there was a turtle who lived in a pond that was going dry. The turtle asked two geese for help, and they agreed to fly him to another pond. They held a stick in their beaks while the turtle was hanging onto it by his mouth. The geese warned the turtle that he must remember not to open his mouth, lest he would fall. While the geese were transporting him in the air across the countryside, a group of children down below burst into laughter at the funny sight. The turtle became angry at their rude remarks and opened his mouth to reply but fell from the sky to his death. If you don't mind, I would like to change the old story to make my own story. In a new version of the Panchatantra, I play the role of the turtle, and the blue sea plays the part of the sky. The turtles help me to fly in the sea, and I guide them far away from the roads and artificial lights on the shoreline, a form of light pollution that disorients newborn turtles, sending them inland to their deaths rather than to life in the sea. I don't want them to remain endangered. I want them to live and flourish.

Persian Sturgeon, Acrylic and oil on canvas, 2011, 190 x 125 cm by N. Naeemaei

Persian Sturgeon
(previous page)

This painting is the only nightmare in the series. You can predict the end. The net will definitely fall. The old house in the painting is my maternal grandma's house in an old sector of Tehran. It is located in a narrow alley with a little stream running through it. When I was about five years old, I used to sit on the stairs watching that small, dirty stream, waiting for a fish to pass by! I even tied a rope to a branch to fish there. How foolish! How hopeful! The sturgeon lives in the Caspian Sea and is valued mainly for its caviar. The Caspian Sea is actually a closed lake and is getting more polluted every day. The problem began after the Soviet breakup when the new countries around the lake put aside any restraint in fishing sturgeon. I have brought the Caspian Sea to my grandma's alley to be with the sturgeon there. And, as in a nightmare, the fisherman comes out of the windows above to fish us. I hug the sturgeon to be with her, to be part of the same destiny. Under the net… it is a ruined dream.

Lorestan Mountain Newt
(opposite)

This is the most introspective painting in the series, and the only abstract one. I am in the center with many salamanders linked to me by black and red threads. We have many things in common: the patterns on the backs of salamanders, the design of the costume from Lorestan province that I am wearing, the lines of my wavy hair, and my blood veins that connect me to the red pattern of the salamander's back. I've tried to gather all of them around me, to connect our blood, our body, and our destiny.

Caspian Tiger
(next spread)

In his habitat he was called the "Red Lion." Actually he wasn't a lion, but I must admit that he was red; he was bloody. The last one was killed in 1959, but there was no funeral and no one cried. I don't know where his tomb is to put flowers on it. I can only wail and mourn his passing in my own way.

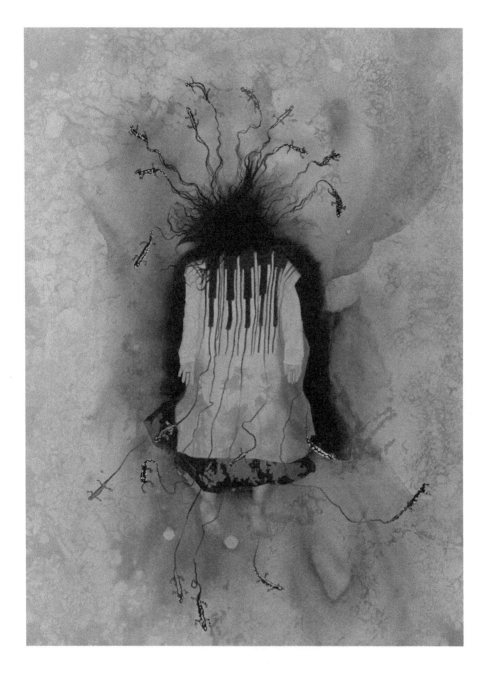

Lorestan Mountain Newt, Acrylic and oil on canvas, 2011, 218 x 160 cm by N. Naeemaei

Caspian Tiger, Acrylic and oil on canvas, 2011, 117 x 190 cm by N. Naeemaei

Miriam Greenspan
Seeing in the Dark

When I was a child, my father listened to my dreams. When he asked me "What did you dream?" I understood him to mean that my dreams were important, worthy of my complete attention, and that they contained some valuable nugget of information to help me live my life.

Years later, I realized how rare it is to have a parent—much less a father—treat a child's dreams this way. Jacob was an uneducated man from a small stetl in central Poland who, along with my mother, survived the Holocaust. Perhaps it was his lack of 'higher' education, in part, that enabled him to take dreams seriously in the way that he did. He was the first Dreamkeeper I knew.

From the age of fourteen on, I wrote down what I dreamed. Not in a pretty little dream journal, but on scraps of paper that I kept in a manila envelope hidden in my desk drawer. No one suggested I do this. It would be decades before dream journals became popular. It was 1961 and I was living in Queens, dreaming every night—often vivid, terrifying nightmares. I dreamed of people scattering in the face of a nameless Onslaught, of murderous forces approaching that would wreak unspeakable carnage. I dreamed of trying desperately to pack a single bag in time to board a train and escape. In these recurrent dreams, I was always left standing at the end, the sole survivor.

I was dreaming the Holocaust. And, more particularly, I was dreaming the contours of my mother's story before I consciously knew it. What I dreamed, my mother lived. She and my father packed one small rucksack and left Lodz, escaping to the Soviet-occupied eastern section of Poland. There they were sent by cattle train to a Siberian gulag where people perished of hunger and illness, worked to death in the labor camps. When my parents returned to Poland, their families and their world were gone. My mother was the sole survivor of her family.

My dreams carried this history. They intensified after my parents told me a white-lie version of their survival—something about being hidden by a Polish farmer. But my dreams actually started before I was told anything.

How is this possible?

Dreaming in the eternal now

As far back as I can remember, I have been a dreamer of the dark. I have dreamed repeatedly of the suffering of human beings far away and unrelated to me. I have dreamed the past, the present, and the future. Through years of dreaming, I have come to know the feel of clairvoyant, prophetic, or shamanic dreams, to distinguish them from more idiosyncratic personal dreams.

In my early thirties I had a waking dream of a world-wide virus that would infect and kill millions. When I told my friends, they were alarmed—not by the vision but by the fact that I'd 'seen' this when clearly it is not something that could be seen. The year was 1979. Two years later, HIV was finally named, but only after years of the government and medical establishment looking away. More recently, the morning of April 14, 2013, I woke up with these words blasted like a headline across my consciousness: *Terrorization across the globe while harrowing events strike here at home.* The next day two pressure- cooker bombs exploded at the finish line of the Boston Marathon....

The first time I realized that I had 'pre-cognitive' dreams, as they are called by those who study so-called paranormal phenomena, was after a dream I had in my early twenties about my father. In the dream, he lay on the ground as a fast-moving car came rumbling towards him. He looked totally panicked as he saw that any minute now, he would be crushed under the wheels. I awoke in a sweat but couldn't call home because I was on a Caribbean island and it was long before the days of cell phones. A week later, when I returned to Boston, I immediately called my parents and asked if Ta was ok. I told them my dream and my mother told me the following story:

About a week ago, your father was standing on a train platform waiting for a subway from Manhattan to Queens when he dropped his eyeglasses on the tracks. Like a fool, he jumped onto the tracks to get them. As he looked up, he saw the train approaching and panicked. A young man jumped in and dragged him up just before the train came into the station. If not for that man, he would have been crushed.

In my dream it was a car, not a train, and the dream cut off before the heroic rescue. There was enough similarity, though, to give me pause. But the real surprise came when I asked my mother to tell me when this happened. My mother was a stickler for details and had a memory like a steel trap. The date she gave me was a day after the night of my dream. So my dream came before the event.

How is this possible?

Mother's second sight

When I was young, I understood dreams like this as a kind of psychic fluke. But becoming a mother considerably ramped up my awareness of the seemingly impossible ways of dream and vision.

I was thirty-four years old when I had my first child, Aaron. A year before, I'd had a vision while in the yoga corpse posture. I saw bright blue blazing eyes and felt a terrible jolt of fear. I heard the words, *These are the eyes of your son, your firstborn.*

I shivered the vision away, wanting to forget. But when Aaron was born, when he was limp and unresponsive, when the nurse whisked him away, when the doctors said that he seemed to have suffered some intrauterine event that damaged his brain, and especially when I looked long and hard into Aaron's bright blue blazing eyes, I remembered my vision.

I remembered, as well, the dream I'd had in the eighth month of my pregnancy, that this baby would be a boy who came early. He would be beautiful, long, and pink, and there would be a question of whether he had an infection, whether he would live or die. In the dream the baby was perfectly calm and omniscient. He spoke with his eyes and said, *Don't be afraid. I'm alright.* The dream ended with great joy in my living child.

Much of what I saw in dream and vision came to pass: Aaron was born early, beautiful, long, and pink, with bright blue eyes. I prayed that the end of the dream would be realized as well.

But Aaron did not live. He died in my arms, never having left the hospital. The night before his death, I dreamed that menacing dogs were barking at him, as he lay encased in a box with clear plastic around it. The next morning the doctor was puncturing his spine with a needle, worried that he had an infection. He was taken to the ICU and placed in an oxygen tent: a small boxseat with plastic around it. I insisted he be removed so that my husband and I could hold him while he died. It took Aaron as long to die as to be born: six hours and twenty minutes. He died at 4:48 in the morning, the same time, to the minute, that he was born, 66 days before.

The morning of his funeral, as we placed his small casket in the ground, I heard the words, as though whispered in my ear: *You are looking in the wrong place.* My attention turned from the casket to the open sky, which was blue and cloudless. And I saw there what I can only describe as a magnificent radiance, the light of Aaron's eyes, magnified. His communication was clear: *Don't be afraid. I'm alright.* I was flooded with a kind of bliss that cannot really be described, certainly something one doesn't expect to feel while burying a child. I was an agnostic, a humanist, a social activist, not a true believer or religious person. Yet, in this most unlikely place, putting my baby's body into the earth, I discovered a world inhabited by spirit—a world that no doubt had always been there, but that I hadn't been open to seeing.

Pregnancy and childbirth amplified my ability to dream and to see. I saw that my next child, Anna, would be a girl and would be born with the first January snows. I knew that she would be fine. And so she was. I saw Esther a month before her birth, a gentle soul with clouds hanging over her head. Esther was born with multiple congenital disabilities both physical and mental. The clouds are still there, but she, more than anyone, has taught me to see the sun through the clouds.

In the Tungus language of Siberia, the word 'shaman' means one who sees in the dark. In my reading about traditional shamanism, I have learned that a shaman is often initiated with some dark, life-threatening illness or near-death experience. It is not unusual for a shaman to dream of her children before they are born or even conceived. Motherhood at the extreme, at the portal between life and death, was my initiation into shamanic ways of knowing. And motherhood has been my continuing education course.

I didn't choose Dreamkeeping or shamanic ways of knowing. I didn't decide to see Aaron's eyes before he was conceived or born, or to undergo my own 'near death' in accompanying him through death's doorway. What I have chosen is to not turn away from what's been given to me. It has taken me years, decades, to accept the gift of seeing and dreaming; to overcome my resistance to restructuring my entire understanding of reality. Years of fear—the fear of being 'different,' of being seen as crazy by professionals in my field, of bequeathing the capacity to dream and to see to my daughters, knowing how much they might suffer from this kind of sensitivity.

But the spirits have never let me off the hook. They keep on teaching me and I keep learning as best as I can, reluctant mystic that I am.

While cutting-edge quantum physics hypothesizes about parallel universes and the simultaneity of all time, I can report from my own experiences of dreaming and seeing that time is a convenient illusion, and space is not what we think it is. Our conditioned way of perceiving time and space limits us to what is right in front of us when we are in fact capable of seeing the past and the future, of dreaming events that have not directly happened to us, of healing at a distance, of knowing beyond the five senses—through dream, through vision, through communing with and listening to the spirits that share the earth with us.

In many ways, a child's social conditioning and learning about the world can be compared to a kind of repetitive hypnotic suggestion. We are hypnotized to consensual 'reality' as children, and from then on can only see through our very limited frame. Or, to use a scientific metaphor, we are like a small number of brain cells that get turned on by social learning, while the vast majority remain unused.

What we do not learn as children, or unlearn as we grow up and develop a conventional ego, is our interconnectedness in the web of life—the connections between 'me' and what some call the world soul or Anima Mundi. Some indigenous peoples believe that we dream the world collectively, that the reality 'out there' is what we have interwoven together from our dreams and nightmares. While this may the case, Dreamkeeping as I understand it is not about 'creating' reality. It is about being interconnected, for better and for worse, in the collective realities, the communal dreams and nightmares of humanity and of the earth.

Another way of putting this is the simple phrase I heard from a mountain in Vermont: *Everything is spirit.* And in spirit, all life is interconnected.

Everything is spirit

Through decades of dream and vision, I began to apprentice with spirit animals and plants, to learn from living animals, to work with herbs and stones. In every instance, these allies and teachers came to me when I most desperately needed them, as well as in more ordinary times. Snake introduced me to shamanic power and made it clear that it was not 'my' power but could be used to serve others and for the purpose of healing. Wolf has carried me through many difficult passages. I am also very grateful to a Camperdown Elm I met in an open field, who tapped me on the shoulder and made it clear that inter-species communication is of great benefit to both humans and non-human sentient beings. Leopard came in a vivid dream to teach me how to sit still and not scatter in the face of fear for my child's life. Grandmother Spider has been a stringent teacher of patience and faith in the midst of grave dark nights of the soul when my older daughter became ill. My prayer to Spider is the one I repeat each day: *Teach me to listen. Teach me to see. Teach me to know. Teach me to be.*

These spirits, and the blessed spirits of my father and mother at their deaths and after their passing, remind and reassure me that we are not alone.

The open heart is the doorway

The doorway to vision and to spirit—known to indigenous people, taught to me personally mostly through the examples of my father and my daughter Esther—is the open heart.

The heart's way of knowing opens the door to the stars, to non-limited seeing and healing. This form of perception and cognition is not recognized in our culture and is often pathologized. Ours is a culture of hyper-rationality and pseudo-rationality that masks an underlying, profoundly destructive irrationality. The Final Solution was considered, in Hitler's Germany, a rational solution to the nation's problems, a way to rid itself of a national poison. "We had to bomb this village to save it" made sense to the Pentagon during the time of the Vietnam War. Wall Street's madness, which would bankrupt the whole world for the greed of a few, continues unabated. And ecocide—human beings destroying the ecological underpinnings of the earth that sustains us—has brought us to the brink of the unthinkable.

The crisis of ecocide demands no less than a total rebalancing of mind and heart, reason and emotion, spirit and body, light and dark, in order to see, to know, and to feel what we are actually doing to the earth, to the animals and plants, to the air and water, and to ourselves.

Whether humanity will rise to the occasion is an open question. Hope for many may not be possible, but faith is necessary.

Faith in ways of knowing and seeing in which we connect to the spirits of the earth seems to be one of the most critical things being asked of human beings today. What I call "carriers"—people who carry the memories and collective experience of sentient beings in this age of ecocide—are in a sense carrying this consciousness for the world. The more fragmented, dissociated, benumbed and addicted we become, the more out of our bodies and hearts human beings get—the more carriers and Dreamkeepers have to carry. In my experience, it is becoming more difficult to be a 'sensitive' at this time in the history of the world. It is getting harder to breathe, to live in balance and stay attuned to the spirits in a world that seems hell-bent on every conceivable kind of destruction and distraction.

I see this in my daughter Esther, who has the most open heart and exquisite sensitivity of anyone I know. Esther, it seems, was born without the filters that most of us humans have, the blocks and walls we use to compartmentalize, deny, and rationalize in order to live with the unacceptable. Esther dreams frequently of violence and sorrow. Fortunately, she has never known any personal violence. She dreams of guns and death outside her own personal circle of experience. Every act of destruction, every mutilation of the spirit, every unnecessary death affects her—she feels them in her heart and they haunt her dreams. When she cries, it is not about being disappointed or frustrated personally—though her life is riddled with disappointment and frustration. She cries for the dead, and for their families. She cries at every anniversary of 9/11 and at every mention of war. "My heart hurts," she will often say. As she grows older, her hurting heart becomes more of a problem. Her anxiety has increased from year to year. Her unprotected, open heart is beginning to constrict, the pure sweetness tainted by the world's suffering and evil.

So it is for all of us, though perhaps not so obviously. As I know well, sensitivity in the interconnected web of life can have its drawbacks. It can lead to illness, to being overwhelmed, to being diagnosed as mentally ill. It can take its toll on our physical, mental, and emotional wellbeing.

Still, we who carry the dreams of the world—seers, visionaries, and mystics—if we are to remain true to what is real, must not be tempted to engage in a spiritual bypass of the darkness on the planet. We must take care not to be seduced by the kind of spirituality that says only light is real.

More than ever, we are called to carry together the massive destruction of the times in which we live. What we know, what we remember, what we dream is no less than the collective travails of the earth. And from these dreams—I hope, though there are no guarantees—we will be given the gifts of insight, wisdom, imagination, creativity and energy we need to help heal ourselves and the planet.

Seeing in a time of ecocide

Some may ask, what good does it do to dream? To live with a heart open to the broken heart of the world? To see and feel the collective suffering on the planet? To be able to foretell terrible events?

Will feeling and knowing that we are all connected in Spirit and having the ability to communicate with spirits save the world?

No one can answer these questions with any degree of certainty. This much I know: by some mysterious cosmic calculus, what we dream and see, what we carry, and what we do—the acts of love, however small, to which we commit ourselves, and how we commune with the spirits of the earth and the cosmos—make a difference.

What will come of these communications cannot be predicted. But I choose to place my faith in the essentialness, the urgency, of these connections. And I know without a doubt that there are gifts that come to us when we know how to see in the dark.

N.B.: This is an abridged version. Please see Dark Matter: Women Witnessing #1 *online for the complete essay.*

Christine Holland Cummings
How to Go on When It Keeps Getting Darker

Open the flashlight of your mouth and illuminate something.

You'll know what. It's yours, it rises out of those shadows
cast over your own life

the ones that have carved themselves into
dark scars tatooing your mind.

Or choose a shadow thrown over another, one of the many
advancing now

like Godzilla's over Tokyo growing bigger
as the monster reaches the outskirts of the city.

༄

State your name, please. State your nationality, please.

Speak your true name. Say it over and over. Make a song of it, tag it
on walls with a can of paint, feel the letters

shape themselves in the dark.

Do not stop saying it
even when they stand you up and shoot you full of holes.

When you're dead
let your blood speak your name.

༄

Why do you come here. Why do you invade.

Carve your teeth into keys to open all the cages.

Melt down the good solid fat of your body to slick the ground
under the soldaten's boots. Throw in your bones

to break their grinding machines,
stop up their gears with your ash-dark hair.

᷂

Is it your intention to rape murder deal drugs be an animal infest.

Make a blanket from your skin and drape it over the last of the species.
Hide them in your lungs, your spleen, your gall bladder,

wherever you have a space they can shelter
until the murdering is over.

Until the murderers are over.

᷂

Do not forget the rose. Her soft heart, her thorn.

Do not forget fragility.
Keep it somewhere safe,

at the bottom of Lake Tanganyika or the top of Mount Denali.
Some day you will want it again.

Notes

"How To Go On When It Keeps Getting Darker" was written in the Sierra Mountains, during the height of the first round of family separations at the border. Images and recordings of kids crying for their parents, 24-hour news cycle reports of the outrages committed by our government, by my country.

So I was thinking about the children in cages, and the way Trump and his ilk seem to hate our pachamamita, wanting to dig up and burn all the oil on the planet, to befoul the air and flay the earth's skin for mineral profit in beautiful sanctuaries like the Grand Staircase-Escalante monument, cut in half by presidential decree. About the tears of the people who come here seeking safety and a chance to thrive, who are greeted with cold hostility and bureaucrats who take away their children and send them back to their countries, bereft.

It was hard not to give in to despair.

The poem, which arrived in a rush of dictation the way some poems do, is/was a kind of healing, a directive to myself: this is how you keep going, this is how you fight back. It was my way of refuting the voice of hatred that shows up in italics, the one we hear all around us these days. You have to stand against that voice, even if it means, ultimately, you must sacrifice yourself, your teeth, your skin, your blood — you must resist in whatever way you can. The poem's final charge, to remember love, tenderness, vulnerability, not to lose them, seems to me the only way we can survive with our humanity intact.

Deena Metzger
Living by Dream

People once lived according to the dream spirits. Then the Church, the State, and later Science taught the people to distrust and disregard them. Attending the dreams in the old, old ways was prohibited and the priests and secular rulers persecuted dreamers. Learning to live by dream again honors the spirits and realigns human activity within a web of relationships.

The sacred ritual of the Eleusinian Mysteries was practiced in Greece for fifteen hundred years until 396 CE, when the Christian/Roman empire suppressed them.[1] The Mysteries were extensive ritual and narrative events that were prepared for rigorously in March of one year, and then enacted eighteen months later in September. During the Mysteries, as many as fifteen hundred people at a time walked the nineteen miles from Athens to Eleusis, engaging in complex activities on the way. Much of what we associate with rites of transformation was practiced here: purification, fasting, dietary restraint, rites of endurance, meditation, theater, sport competitions, and visioning. Women and men, citizens, slaves and foreigners were all able to participate if they prepared for and committed themselves to the beautiful extremity of the event.

My consciousness was reawakened to the old ways of dreaming through the means of a play I was writing that drew increasingly on the spiritual context and intent of the Mysteries. As has happened to me many times, the writing of the play revealed the nature of dreams far beyond what I had understood until then. I don't remember why I started studying the Mysteries, only that they pulled me down into the sacred underworld as they were meant to do. I was immediately "entranced" when I learned that the underworld had been a destination in the Mysteries, a place of wisdom and transformation. (Pluto, the Roman name for the equivalent god, Hades, means 'treasure.') Christianity, to gain hegemony, demonized the ritual event, declaring Hades to be hell, Dionysus/Pan to be Satan. A ritual required by the ancient world on behalf of soul-making was forbidden. Soul, as the ancients would have warned us, began to disappear and was increasingly replaced by secular materialism.

In the '70s, I was working with an improvisational theater group. Our work led to the development of different characters who became important to me and to the actors. Unexpectedly, the characters began to create relationships among themselves in my imagination, and the play *Dreams Against the State* was born. Each of the contemporary characters was based on a contemporary revolutionary and a figure from the Mysteries. In the first draft of the play, there were entre-acts in which the Gods – Demeter, Hecate, Persephone, Hades, Hermes – appeared. Later, their roles were incorporated into the characters so that the audience could see that we can each live the intensity and passion of divine energies if we allow ourselves our real lives.

The contemporary characters were drawn together "underground" through the power of dreaming at a time when dreaming was illegal. The dangerous upper world was inhabited by police and other forces of conformity and repression who sought to stifle all vital and individual life energies. When one of the dreamers was captured and incarcerated, the dreamers had to develop the ritual means to retrieve her and restore her body and soul.

Theater director Steven Kent and I re-enacted the Mysteries in Greece in 1980 (and twice again in the '90s) for the first time since 396 CE. We began the long ritual at the Cave of Dicte where Zeus had been born on the isle of Knossos. As we descended the narrow spiral of stone stairs, each *myste* carrying a lit taper to illuminate the way into the dark, I knew that we had found the entrance into the ancient way of the dream. We were stepping into another world, not only the underworld from which we would emerge ritually, but into the old, old world whose ways would continue to guide and sustain us from that time forward. Rising quietly in the morning, telling dreams before speaking and before breakfast, and using the dreams to enhance and understand our experiences was our way, then, of beginning to live according to our dreams.

More than forty years later, the necessity is even greater to live the dream, to live by dreams and the values they teach when the dreaming community is aligned with spirit. The centuries since the Mysteries have ricocheted between a search for spiritual consciousness and increasing banality. An age of unprecedented brutality is upon us as ongoing violence is directed against humans, animals, the earth and the spiritual life, but few, if any, safe havens remain for any beings anywhere on the planet. If the imperium of technology and power has its way, everything may die. Still, as we grieve, we also see a parallel revitalization of vision, dream and spiritual presence, which as we gather and attend these, may save us.

People were enjoined to participate in the Eleusinian Mysteries once in a lifetime in order to gain a soul in this life and the next. Perhaps we may also gain a soul by listening deeply to our dreams and living according to their sometimes very demanding wisdom, often requiring a radical change of one's life and mind. Since the advent of psychology, dream analysis has been a familiar process designed to help people improve or heal their lives. But in the old days, dreams came to an individual on behalf of the community which was charged with living accordingly.

Not every dream is of portent for the future. Not every dream contains ethical instruction or direction for the community. Dreamers may be involved in nightly narratives, but only some are essential guides. Over time, often with a teacher, elder or companion, or in dream circles, we learn to distinguish them. Sometimes it takes several dreams over time to reveal where we are being led.

I will consider several dreams together, as they constitute a field of consciousness that has guided me, with increasing intensity, over the years. When these dreams came to me, I recognized them as significant, even urgent, and offer them to you to contemplate in that spirit.

Spain. The time of World War II, of Franco and Hitler. A film is being made. Scene One: A young woman is too poor to become a great dancer. Scene two: A street festival becomes a riot. A man pulls down his pants so a demented king can anoint his penis with firewater. Scene Three: We try to hide from a group of men who will kill anyone. A blood bath will follow. Scene Four: A parade of polished sedans. The wealthy class, young men and women in formal dress, are aloof to the dangers around them. Scene Five: Brown Shirts are marching down the street, ten abreast. I climb a steep wide flight of stairs to the empty platform above. The Brown Shirts approach. There are not that many yet. They are not the majority yet, but they are very dangerous. Scene 6: Increasing dehumanization, soullessness and violence: We must leave Europe today. If we stay longer, it will be too late. **We have twenty-four hours to leave Europe.**

In 2001, I brought this dream to Daré, (Council) the community healing event that has been meeting at my house since 1999. The last lines translated quickly into urgent instructions: Twenty-four hours to leave European **mind.**

Over the last years, Euro-American mind and Western civilization have come under great scrutiny from non-Western people and developing nations. European mind is associated with the hegemony of the Church, the military, science and materialism that set out to conquer the peoples of the Northern and Southern Hemispheres in 1492. In that year of the Inquisition, Jews and Moors were expelled from Spain. This same mind prohibited dreaming, the inner life and earth-centered, spiritually-aligned Indigenous wisdom traditions wherever they were encountered. That legacy of persecution exists to this day.

Sometimes the content of our dreams seems to reiterate what we know, but I didn't think the dream was giving me a history lesson. It was asking me to see where I was unconsciously carrying the destructive qualities of European (Western) mind. Where were I and my peers unconsciously aligning with power and riot? As such dreams are for the community, *we* were being asked to engage in self-scrutiny to negate any tendencies toward fascistic thinking. We need to scrutinize our souls.

The stairs in the dream resemble the pyramids of pre-Columbian peoples. They link the Holocaust implied by the presence of the Brown Shirts with the holocaust against the Native peoples of the Americas, beginning in 1492. The dream invokes the global European occupation: a history of violence, brutality, burning, slavery and torture, land and resource appropriation, exploitation, pollution and all the possible ills of war and conquest. It awakens us to the urgency of changing my/ our minds. We have twenty-four hours, that is, it is urgent to change our minds.

When I had breast cancer in 1977, I knew I had to change my life in order to be healthy. Sensitive to the fact that our Euro-American culture treats women and the earth in similarly brutal ways, I moved to land, to a very simple house at the end of a dirt road, living as closely as I could to earth-based values. And, as the title of one of my books suggests, I practiced *Writing For Your Life*.

In 1986, nine years after I had breast cancer, I developed a program called Personal Disarmament. It was a direct response to the Brown Shirts dream. Participants were asked to examine their own inner governments. Are we living under the dictates of an inner general? An inner war machine? Are we armed? Are we developing the equivalent of chemical, biological or nuclear weapons? Did we stockpile weapons? Do we have armies? Will we agree to no first strike? Will we disarm?

Writing the scenario of our inner governments was like writing and living in a dream. I was shocked to discover that my inner government was a theocracy that denied full citizenship to its creative members, confining them on reservations. I discovered I ruled by force, by those Euro-American values I thought I had renounced. I set myself the task of changing again.

At that time, breast cancer was occurring like a plague that was not being acknowledged. I wanted to learn what ideas and assumptions were making me and others so ill, then what was destroying our communities. Finally, I had to learn what was killing the earth. Stepping out of European mind became the focus of my intellectual, ethical and spiritual work.

Again in 2006, I dreamt the Nazis were coming. I could easily interpret these as precognitive dreams warning me/us about the developing fascism in the U.S. and globally. We can, foolishly, use such dreams to confirm our fantasies that we are innocent and the others are the enemy. But I prefer to understand them also as a reflection on our lives and our history and so as instruction, as an increasingly urgent call to awareness. In 2007, another dream:

There is an occupation in the works from a foreign or home army, resembling a Nazi army. This is happening here and we are in great danger. We are trying to pack food, clothes, supplies for the dogs, between the bodies of the children lying on the floor in the back of the car. I fear that we will not get out in time, that we will not find the route to avoid the soldiers, to hide, to cross the border. That we will be recognized and arrested or killed.

This dream came just after I led a circle, The Council of Possibilities, in Oakland, CA. A conversation about water-boarding was current in the public sector. Michael Mukasey, who supported enhanced interrogation techniques on al-Qaeda suspects, had been approved by the Judiciary Committee to be U.S. Attorney General. Accordingly, protesters had been demonstrating against water-boarding in the streets in Washington, DC. It was clear that Cheney and Bush approved and ordered torture; Rumsfield had just been indicted in France for torture, as Kissinger had been earlier for his role in fomenting the brutal *golpe* against the democratically elected government in Chile, in 1973.

The dream made it clear that we had to give up innocence. We are all endangered. Fascism is here and we are its vehicles and its victims. There is no place to hide.

In 2009, I had another dream, set in Europe and in America. It challenges the belief that some can be safe while others are endangered because the rich or powerful can successfully negotiate with evil to protect themselves and their loved ones. The dream starkly emphasizes the need to leave the European mind that creates privilege:

Central Europe. Early twentieth century. We are in a European manor house in which the stairs, like in the first dream, resemble the stairs of an Aztec pyramid. A group of men dressed in black are confiscating things from the house at the corner. They will be here soon. I ask my mother to find something to give them. We find silver pieces in an anteroom and select a good piece but not her finest, but still she must give away something valuable. I know she wants to hold on to everything. I am trying to protect her and I am also hoarding her valuables, so she will have them, so she will have something for the next time, as if she can continue to bribe and remain safe.

I wait for the doorbell but the smugglers jimmy open the door and come up the large staircase into the house. Trying to find out who these smugglers are, I speak to them about the Mob in Brooklyn and the possibility of buying "protection." Even so, I understand that there is no guaranteed exchange and they will be back for more.

Through the window, I see an old woman running. They have taken her things too, but this doesn't matter to her. She has left her doors unlocked. She is running very fast, and I follow her, barely keeping up. We run through the entire country. A single red dirt road turns here and then there. We are no longer in Europe. We are in two time zones simultaneously, contemporary New Mexico and New Mexico before the Conquest. We enter a labyrinth of clay tunnels and stairs that lead down into a vast cave house, with a clay floor. The dwelling is essentially a workshop. A kiln occupies one area. She works in clay and silver. While there is no evidence of her work, this is the place where she works, where she is entirely happy, where the smugglers will not come, where her life is. Where I will stay.

The teachings were clear: The old (European) world is a dangerous place. Making payments is a way of staying connected to the system. We must come to a new world. As with the Mysteries, it is necessary to go underground and return to the earthen ways.

In 1998, I went to Zimbabwe with my then husband Michael Ortiz Hill, who introduced me to a Shona medicine man, Mandaza Kandemwa, *a nganga*. As I had become a healer, it was very gratifying to recognize that we worked in similar ways, though we languaged our work differently. Mandaza would say, "The spirits are heavy upon me" and I would say, "Illness is a path," but we would mean we were being called to ways of being.

Meeting Mandaza and his community, participating in his Daré, watching how he worked as an Indigenous healer in an urban setting, revealed the depth and value of native dream-based healing ways. How might equivalent healing communities develop in the United States? In 1999, I was called to sit in Council with Mandaza's community and also to sit in Council with Elephants. On the last day in Chobe National Park, a wild animal preserve, we met and entered into a relationship with an Elephant in the wild whom we now call the Elephant Ambassador.

Healing from Euro-American mind means stepping out of hierarchy into relationship. Elephants have complex and developed social systems extending from their young calves to their elders and ancestors, and from which we have much to learn. Indigenous people know this about the animals. They have great respect for other beings and live in a harmonic web of relationships and alliances. Meeting an Ambassador from another species brought the understanding that the animals and the beings of the natural world are equal partners on the planet.[2] They are our peers, and the old ways teach us how to live in right relationship with them. I have met the Elephant Ambassador in the wild several more times. I have also met other Elephants in waking life and then in dreams.

After the meeting in Council with Mandaza's community and with the Elephant Ambassador, we introduced Daré to the community. So many years later, that Council-based, spirit-led, dream-focused community healing circle continues. By 2001, I began to understand something of what might shift if we changed our relationship with animals and the natural world. By 2004, the Lakota wisdom *mitakye oyasin*, all my relations, became central to Daré.

There are many Indigenous traditions that speak of the Fifth World or the Next World, a real place that we can access only if we leave our dangerous Fourth World ways behind. The next or Fifth World is ruled by its own cosmic laws. To live in the Fifth World, one's entire nature and being have to resonate with these intrinsic ways. This cannot be negotiated; one is aligned or one is not. In this instance, ethics, values and actions are as absolute as the laws of physics. The values of interconnection and deep respect for the beings of the natural world and the spirits are fundamental. To live in the Fifth World we must strip ourselves of our Fourth World qualities and become other beings. This activity is as rigorous as the imagined journey through a black hole into another universe. To enter the Fifth World means we change our ways entirely.

People often speak of dreams or other ways of knowing as being given to us. What we mean is that the understanding is not a creation of our minds, but comes from beyond us. Sometimes such gifts come in a single unit, like a dream or a story. Sometimes they come over time. The dream that advised us to leave Europe morphed into an understanding that we needed to leave Euro-American mind, which became a focus of a series of teachings which were transmitted to me, known as the Nineteen Ways to the Fifth World. These are a distillation of paths we are called to take simultaneously so that we can live in ways that serve the future. It could well take a lifetime to understand and incorporate and truly inhabit any one of the Nineteen Ways. We don't have lifetimes. I began to explore and teach them to myself and to others. The Nineteen Ways create a field. It is the field that creates the world.

After receiving the Nineteen Ways, I had a dream that changed my life again.

I have won a contest that I have not entered. I have won it three times. The award is a trip to New York for a year, where I will be educated and trained. After the year, I will be an Indigenous woman.

I understood this dream as a mandate. I am to apply myself to becoming an Indigenous woman. I am taken back to my origins to begin again on a different trajectory. I must discover how an uncolonized Indigenous woman would think and act in these times. I have entered into a different way of living. Before I speak, before I act, in the face of any important decision, I ask myself: How would a wise Indigenous elder, free of the great damage of the ongoing Conquest, act? Over time, I see my mind changing and my ways of living, as well. Living as an Indigenous elder calls one to put the community and the earth before oneself. It means one is loyal to and committed to the future. It means we respond out of relationship, not out of self-interest. It means alliance, not competition. Harmony not conflict. It means we know the earth and all her creatures are alive. This has come to me from the dreams.

Let us return to the initial premise. In accord with the old ways, the dreams come on behalf of the community and these times. They are presenting us with the dilemmas we are facing and will face in the future and they are teaching us, as they once did, how to live. These dreams, then, are available to guide any one or all of us.

It is possible that the world can heal. Dreams are showing us the ways.

N.B.: This is an abridged version. Please see Dark Matter: Women Witnessing #1 *online for the complete essay.*

[1] The Edict of Thessalonica, also known as *Cunctos populos*, was issued in 380 AD. It ordered all subjects of the Roman Empire to profess the faith of the bishops of Rome and Alexandria, making Nicene Christianity the state religion of Rome (Wikipedia).

[2] Hogan, Linda, Brenda Peterson and Deena Metzger, eds. *Intimate Nature: The Bond between Women and Animals*. New York: Penguin Random House.1999. Print. The essays collected in this anthology revealed, without question, the fact of animal intelligence and intent.

Debra Magpie Earling
from *The Lost Journals of Sacajewea*

in the fog-brutal days when backs of buffalo scab with ice
and the weak calves
fall to attendant wolves.
Lewis and Clark are shooting game
gray clouds tumble birds
                              falling from the gun-hazy sky—
Fawns mewl in the frosted grasslands
Red guts steam snow and the
Hooves of deer and antelope
click in the trees
slaughter-hung where wolves cannot reach them.
The woods are haunted by the silver eyes of dead animals.
But these things are always and survival and
these white men have not cached the summer berries
haven't split the rye grass to seeds or twisted the black moss
to chewing ropes for winter hungry days.
Now a blood scent rises in the bowl of sleep.

No one speaks about the woman
dying in the frail rising of a killing day.
A woman hard-frozen in the field
Her trail marked by the blood of the hundred pounds of buffalo
she carried.
And the sleek footed wolves trailed her,
~~wove~~ weaved* a tight trail around her sniffing
the bitter wind she carried.
The razor snarl of their teeth chewed the meat off her back
down to the column of her bones.
But her life was so powerful
even in death she is still
standing. Her rigid spine
sparkles in the steam of river light.
Her eyes glitter at the swooping birds.

Men weight their wives with venison   antelope   buffalo   meat

make them walk for miles
for one small favor from the white man
a trinket
a handful of beads
a promise of plenty
dying in the shrill wind.

In the deep burr of sealing snow
women are struggling
their bones
quaking
the rattle of leaves falling forever
skittering over
ice.
They are not the beautiful women
men fight over.

The white men don't see the wives who are hidden
in the lodges at the edges of lost
the women who carried the small-pox dead
to scaffolds
losing their fingers
in purging fires
of children
or women who gather bundles of sticks
in the frost-bitten winters of fever.
They are witches
who crawl hump-backed
~~their~~ hands only palms/~~the~~ webbed feet of ducks/work dogs to carry
meat.
                              This is the life left to unfortunate
women.
Infection a quick blessing.
Fingers of weeds
scuffle
point to sky
above them.

Blind days of men.

But the beautiful women are running
running
the banks of the black river
begging
the white men
are laughing.
York** weeps ~~wheezes~~
hiding in the gray timber grass.   Even the faces of trees
turn toward him.
The white men   ~~mistake~~ believe
they are desirable.

* I used strike-outs on the manuscript in an attempt to say and not say the things Sacajawea may have thought to say (or not say). I also used the strike-outs as a device to get at the idea of cross-cultural interpretation and misinterpretation on the page. I believe–although history tells a different story—that she spoke English and understood nuanced language and the power of words better than any other in her company. As an interpreter I think she would have struggled to grasp the right word or words and would have cast them out as shimmering ghosts of the whole idea she wished to convey. Words obscured but evident. As a traditional woman I think she saw words as living things, not so easily dismissed or discarded.

** York was William Clark's slave on the expedition. He fully participated in the expedition. I have often wondered what he thought of the whole thing. I believe for the first time in his life he experienced power, a rare and certain power that went to his head—I imagine he was dizzy with the attention he received from all the Indians along the Missouri. Instead of a slave they saw a man of great power and might and wished for their women to sleep with him in order to retrieve his power for their own.

Traps —They are Trapping the Animals

Lewis and Clark are sending fox to the great white father.

They have trapped a spirit fox, a fox that carries the weighted soul of a man possessed by bad spirits.

Meriwether places the caged fox at the edge of camp every day
because his cage is foul as pig's blood, he says.
But I know Meriwether is afraid.

Every night the caged fox moves
                                        when night fastens
                                        the moon-heavy water
          to spirits
                              when light sifts
down in dark currents
          and the river
          begins chanting.

Do not look
there
at the bottom
there
along the lip of shore
water channeling the thing-not-named
the dim sky water carries is older than time older than blood
bigger

In the deepest still place of the river

fox is chanting

sparkling scales of fish scattering silt
beaver slick currents

fox conjures

sparks of waves   smoothing stones

fox gnashes his teeth
his black mouth open
his teeth so white
I chatter in sleep

They can't
put his cage
far enough

away from me

In the dark he is the thing moving

I wake

his rattling cage beside me
fox whispering
a harsh wind low

I have opened the cage door
he remains

Fox blood is sour
his small head wounded

I am afraid of his teeth,
his grim shining eyes
mostly
I am afraid
of his voice

He could kill me with his stories

I bludgeoned my wife he tells me———
I broke
  the blood of her flesh——-
I broke
  the thin bones of her fingers for touching another man——-
I branded
her ribs with fists.
I stabbed her
with a fire stick blazing
to sear her
to me.

She turned
so many colors the sky could no longer please me.

Who is she? I ask.

Wife for Dark Nights, he answers————*Wife for Dark Nights*   *Wife for Dark Nights*   *Wife for Dark nights*   *Wife for dark nights*   *wife for dark nights*

Notes

November 13, 2015*

I woke up around 3 in the morning and in the staticky light saw a woman standing next to my bed. She had a cage at her feet. I couldn't make out her face but I saw that she wasn't very tall and that her hair was in braids. I turned on my light and the apparition disappeared. But I began to scribble something down on the notepad I keep by my bed.

The next morning my mother phoned to ask me if I had heard the news. Apparently the Smithsonian had announced the return of a sacred fox to its rightful place and people. The sacred fox had been removed from its traditional homeland by Lewis & Clark over two hundred years ago. I cannot remember the tribe but when I hung up the phone I picked up the notepad and was stunned by what I had written. An odd coincidence? I am not sure. But the story of Sacajewea is so powerful, it haunts me.

I see Sacajewea as a very young woman, so young we would consider her a child in this day and age. There is dispute about who she was, her name, her origin, but the fact that she was a traditional native woman has never been disputed. She knew the sacred ways, the old ways and when I think of her, I also think of all the native women who have disappeared in recent years. Sacajewea is powerful because she refuses to disappear. Her knowledge of the old ways is a lifeline to memory, a light that continues to shine. She continues to be reinvented, revised, re-envisioned.

After reading the journals I was struck by the references to the ferocity of the time. Women were strapped with a hundred pounds of buffalo to carry to the corp in deepest snow. Women had to attend to the small pox sick, the dead and dying. In writing *The Lost Journals of Sacajewea* I tried to capture, perhaps illuminate, native women's longstanding struggle and desire for freedom.

Because her name is also in dispute I wrote her name phonetically–the way I remember it pronounced as a child hoping perhaps people would once again feel comfortable talking about her. The revisionist thinking in the pronunciation of her name–even if correct–is another lens that removes us from her story. When people become uncomfortable attempting to pronounce her name, they become silent, and little by little the story becomes lost to us. Remember how often you used to hear of her. Now I have people correcting my pronunciation and insisting on a glottal stop—but how can that be—when the Lemhi Shoshone still call her Sacajewea? I fear it is another way to make native women disappear.

Oh, and I don't call these pieces poems. I don't consider myself a poet. I used line breaks to accomplish a pattern of image that I call shattered prose but feel uncomfortable with the term poet.

―――――

* From personal correspondence

Patricia Reis
Over the Edge

> I know we have to remember. … I remember when we had
> dreamers and they knew the water and its first songs, and I
> remember that the dreamers found water and medicine for the
> people. *Nan okcha*. All alive. Remember.
> —Linda Hogan, "Dawn for All Time"[1]

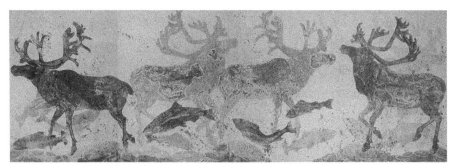

Caribou Migration IV by S. Amons

The James Bay Project, Canada's massive effort to generate electricity for energy- hungry Canada and the United States was one of the biggest environmental re-arrangements of land and water undertaken on the planet. Hydro-Québec dammed powerful rivers and flooded over 7,000 miles of land in the northern Quebec wilderness, altering the landscape and its inhabitants – the Innu and Cree natives and the wildlife – forever. The consequences of this massive dislocation – of water, land, people, and all other sentient beings – for the sake of powering an energy habit has yet to be truly calculated. There are, however, events and stories that give testimony.

In *Electric River,*[2] Sean McCutcheon writes about how stymied Hydro-Québec was in the fall of 1984 when the electricity, collected in the form of water, had not yet sold. Stored in a large, already corroding reservoir, the water had to be spilled before rains caused a disaster so they began to release the water into the Caniapiscau River.Meanwhile, the torrential autumn rains began and the combination of spillage and rainfall created a monstrously swollen river. The Innu protested that their hunting camps on the shores of the river had been washed away and demanded the Energy Corporation reduce the spilling, which they did on September 28. The effect of the reduction, however, was not yet felt 400 kilometers downstream at Limestone Falls, the last of a series of narrow, steep drops over which the Caniapiscau river plummets on its way to the sea.

On September 30, two days after the Energy Corporation's reduction, more than 10,000 George River caribou, traveling on a traditional migratory trail toward their winter range, approach the Falls. One of the biggest herds of large migratory mammals anywhere in the world, they are at their peak, their fittest and fattest. The young, born in mid-June, are still travelling with their mothers and the big males are fitted out with new antlers and their best pelage for the mating season soon to come.

The caribou migrate as a herd for reasons of security, their numbers a protection against known predators, the wolf pack. This herd has undoubtedly encountered weather hazards before – an early snow storm, a torrential rain – and because they are natural swimmers equally at home on land and water, swimming across a body of water rather than walking around it is not uncommon. But rivers require calculations. A river can change its nature quickly. Early snow melts and heavy rains create different river conditions, a rushing mix of slush and ice, a wider, deeper, swifter moving body of water; a body enlarged and swollen, eager to discharge itself into the arms of a larger body. Assessing a river's temperament is a caribou's necessity.

The map in the mind of the caribou has been laid down for millennia. They understand they will reach their migratory destination sooner or later. The decision to leap into moving water and risk being swept away by the force of a raging, roiling river is never undertaken lightly. Sometimes the herd chooses to parallel the river until it comes to a more inviting place to cross. But there is no inviting place on this river, nor is there memory for the treachery of that two-legged predator with his infernal tinkering. Approaching their timeworn crossing spot, they encounter a river, grotesque and distorted from carrying a burden of natural and unnatural waters. This is something new. Limestone Falls has been interfered with to such an extent that the caribous' great collective intelligence cannot decipher the mortal danger.

Do the powerful lead caribou telegraph their immediate terror to those pushing on them from behind? They are used to communicating in this way, sending messages of stop and go, rest and resume, bunch up and spread out; those in the lead count on the ancient pathways laid down by generations of caribou. But this time it is all too confounding, the river's voice, lost to itself, is untranslatable. There is no time to assess; their messages are drowned out. Pushed from behind, the lead caribou have no choice but to enter the raging torrent. The rest follow. What terrible frisson shudders through the great body of this herd of noble animals as they plunge in? What heart-pounding, soul-piercing cries emanate, mother to child, mate to mate, sister to sister as they push over the edge? Within four hours almost all are swept over the falls, smashed on the rocks, their corpses strewn over the banks and beaches downriver.

What are we to make of this great community of magnificent animals tumbling on top of each other to a collective death, their instinct so betrayed? And did every last one go over the edge? Are there survivors who now have this terrible tragedy embedded as a haunting memory? And the river, does she remember the day her waters were so forced that she grew cruel and unknowable, the day she unwillingly wiped out a whole herd of caribou? Certainly the Cree and Innu do not forget. In her poem, *Ballad of a River*, the Cree poet, Margaret Sam-Cromarty who lives in the St. James Bay region, writes:

The River Chisasibi
In grey and blue
A happy river
Once, long ago.
Times changed,
Struggles came.
The courts agreed
Dam the river
For kilo watt power.
The happy river was lost.

It weeps now.
It seeks
golden sands.
The Chisasibi River
Its soul calling
Hears the old people
no more. Voices
The wind has tongues
A lady speaks
meekly
A cry of terror
It's only the wind's voice
Frightening
my beating heart
Silent weeping
A wind warming
Voices
Of my elders[3]

The story of the St. George Caribou unwittingly jumping to their collective death is a morality tale from which we must learn. We want cheap electricity. It is better than fossil fuels. But what about the cost? For the sake of a light switch far distant from their territory, the caribou herd has been decimated. For the Cree and Innu who have lost their homeland and a way of life, losing 10,000 members of the St. George River is equivalent to losing almost their entire population. Have we, too, not lost something incalculable? Has our own house not suddenly darkened?

Like the magnificent herd of St. George caribou, we humans are in a tenuous moment, on the verge of going over the edge, pushed from behind, numbed by grief at what we've already lost, deaf to the voices of wisdom that warn what's ahead. How to listen when there is so much mad and maddening noise? Whose voices are reliable? How to remember who we really are when so much has been forgotten?

Memory is the living filament with which we humans stitch together what has happened in time, giving our individual biographies and our collective history a coherent and continuous integrity. But whose memory can we draw upon? Where is our earth-based memory deposited? In our genes? In our dreams and visions? In morphogenetic fields? Like the caribou, we might rightly wonder, can memory be a trustworthy guide for the future?

Do the land and the animals hold memory? If so, how can we translate what is spoken in a language we have forgotten? Does a river remember its bed long after it has been dammed into a reservoir? Do the caribou survivors remember the genocide? Do beaver in my local pond remember that the Great Beaver Nation of the Northeast and Canada was driven almost to extinction by human fur-trappers? Do the trees in the woods I walk remember that once the whole Northeast was ninety-five percent forested? Are some memories lost forever?

How we humans have become so amnesiac about our primary kinship with the earth is an urgent question in need of answers. Western culture is rapidly and insistently moving us away from the sensate world of nature, plants, and animals, and ever more into a disembodied thrall to virtual transcendence. Memories of our deep and necessary inter-dependence and connection are lost in the hubris of present day human-centeredness, greed, and ignorance. We are being pushed from behind into an unknowable future that demands a moral response, informed ethical action, and a spiritual stance.

In *Hold Fast: At Home in the Natural World*[4], philosopher Kathleen Dean Moore reminds us that there is an essential connection between personal identity and place. First, it's literally true that people are made of places. "Minerals from eroding mountains strengthen your bones and mine.... We are calcified by gravity, wrinkled by wind, softened by shopping malls. Gradually, eventually, particle by particle, our bodies are constructed from places." And it's not just our bodies that are influenced by place, she says, but our ideas, our emotions, our characters, our identities – all are shaped, in part, by places. "Alienation from the land is an alienation from the self, which causes sadness." She goes on to say, "It's our memories that make us who we are... Every time I notice something, every time something strikes me as important enough to store away in my memory, I add another piece to who I am.

These memories and sense impressions of the landscape are the very substance of my self. In this way, I am – at the core of my being – made of the earth."

Moore asks, "If people are defined by their landscapes, then what happens to our selves – our integrity, our wholeness – when those landscapes are destroyed?" She answers, "If we go around systematically destroying the places that hold meaning for us, that hold our memories, then we become fragmented and don't have a sense of who we are." Spinning off of Thoreau's famous remark that people live lives of "quiet desperation", she observes that today we are living lives of "relentless separation." Limestone Falls not only marks a tragedy for the caribou nation, it marks a place of human self-destruction we ignore at our peril.

It is the work of the artist to help us re-story and re-member our place on the earth. Chickasaw poet, essayist and novelist Linda Hogan's novel *Solar Storms*[5] does exactly this. Hogan interleaves personal, tribal, and earth-based memory against a backdrop of massive environmental disruption in the story of five generations of Native American women seen through the eyes of seventeen-year-old Angel Jensen.

Fostered away to Oklahoma as a child, Angel makes her way back to her tribal people who live in the Boundary Waters area between Minnesota and Canada. She is looking for her mother, but more than that; she is seeking herself, her tribal identity, and the original motherland that her body remembers. Agnes Iron, her paternal grandmother, Dora Rouge her great-grandmother, and Bush, Angel's surrogate mother, are the memory keepers. It is they who provide, each in her own way, what Angel is seeking. They hold important memories of Angel's personal story, which is inextricable from the story of her tribe and the landscape into which she was born.

Although it is never named, these women have lost their ancestral homeland to the hydroelectric dams of The James Bay Project, the same forced damming of rivers and lakes that drove the St. George caribou herd of 10,000 to their death at Limestone Falls. For Angel, the massive environmental rearrangement has separated their people from each other, from their ancient homelands, and from the animals and plants with whom they coexist and on which they depend for life.

Angel dreams one night of a woman in a white-walled cave sewing together pieces of humans, an arm to a trunk, and a foot to a leg. Later, when she tells Bush the dream, Bush thinks the dream is about starting all over, this time doing it right. "This time, humans would be love-filled, the way we were meant to be all along." The women in Angel's lineage labor to stitch unnaturally separated things back together with the thread of memory. Angel is also engaged in the work of mending; she thinks she has found her way back to this landscape "to put together all the pieces of history, of my life, and my mother's, to make something whole."

In Hogan's novel, it is the force of the women's love that works, despite agonizing losses, toward a kind of restoration. Their love is not only personal; it is generational, and includes the land and animals. As Angel comes into her identity as a tribal woman, Bush tells her in small bits about caring for Angel's mother, Hannah Wing, as a young girl. Everyone knew Hannah was damaged, but Bush thought maybe she could be healed with enough love. One day she insisted that young Hannah take off her layers of clothing and take a bath. Hannah complied. "Beneath all the layers of clothes, her skin was a garment of scars. There were burns and incisions. Like someone had written on her. The signatures of torturers, I call them now." Bush tells Angel:

Everyone had a name for what was wrong. Dora-Rouge said it was memory and I think she was the closest. After a time, I thought, yes, it was what could not be forgotten, the shadows of men who'd hurt Loretta, the shadows of the killers of children. What lived in her wears the skin of children... It walks with us, inside those we know ... As I looked at her from scar to scar that day, I could feel the edges of her. I touched the scars on her back and I could feel the hands of the others. Bush takes the girl, Hannah, to one of the tribe's elders, called Old Man, who tells Bush, "She is the house... She is the meeting place." And Bush says to Angel, "I didn't know what he meant at first. But I saw it in time, her life going backward to where time and history and genocide gather and move like a cloud above the spilled oceans of blood. That little girl's body was the place where all this met…"

Great-grandmother Dora-Rouge joins Agnes, Bush and Angel on a canoe journey back to her ancestral homeland, the home of the Fat Eaters, the Innu, where the damming of lakes and rivers for hydroelectric power has radically altered and destroyed the landscape. Dora-Rouge is going back home to die. Along the way she imparts all her knowledge, her life-giving memory, to Angel.

Dora-Rouge gives Angel a talisman, a piece of amber with a little perfectly formed frog captured inside its golden light. It came from those native people who navigated the waters from South America to the far north centuries ago. Dora-Rouge tells Angel, "Those people from the south told our ancestors, 'Remember us when we are gone,' and they placed this into the hands of an old woman named Luri, one of my ancestors, one of yours." The frog serves as instruction for Angel as the growing intimacy with the landscape opens her to this "tree-shaded place where unaccountable things occurred, where frogs knew to wait beneath dark ground until conditions were right for them to emerge, where water's voice said things only the oldest of people understood."

One night Angel dreams a plant. She draws a picture of it and shows it to Dora-Rouge, who recognizes it. Angel starts to understand that, "maybe dreams are earth's visions … earth's expressions that pass through us." Dora Rouge tells her there were always plant dreamers in their family and Angel is becoming one. Angel realizes that there was a place inside the human that spoke with the land, that entered dreaming, in the way that people in the north found direction in their dreams. They dreamed charts of land and currents of water. They dreamed where food animals lived. These dreams they called hunger maps, and when they followed those maps, they found their prey. It was the language animals and humans had in common. People found their cures in the same way.

The work of restoration, as Linda Hogan tells us, is an ongoing act of faith and determination, of dreaming, love, and remembering. Angel says, "If you listen at the walls of one human being, even if that one is yourself, you will hear the drumming. Older creatures are remembered in the blood. Inside ourselves we are not yet upright walkers. We are tree. We are frog in amber. Maybe earth itself is just now starting to form."

Some say we have entered the period of a sixth extinction, this one not made completely by nature, but by human design. Restoration is always a belated occurrence—belated in the sense that what has been lost can only be restored in the present. Hopefully, we still have the time; the dislocations are tremendous, some things are irrecoverable. Like the caribou facing an unrecognizable river, our disorientation is great. Slowly, slowly, with great longing and thirst, writers, dreamers, philosophers and poets lead us toward that deepest well of memory – our profound affiliation with all things. May we put our ears close to the beating heart of the earth and become a clan of deep listeners, dreamers, and memory-keepers.[6]

---

[1]Hogan says *Nan okcha* means that the animals all have lives and are sentient beings. See Linda Hogan "Dawn for All Time" in Dean Moore K, Nelson M P, eds. *Moral Ground: Ethical Action for a Planet in Peril.* San Antonio, Texas: Trinity University Press, 2011. Print.

[2] McCutcheon, Sean. *Electric Rivers: The Story of the James Bay Project.* Montreal: Black Rose Books, First Edition, 1991. Print.

[3] Sam-Cromarty, Margaret. "Ballad of a River" in *James Bay Memoirs: A Cree Woman's Ode to Her Homeland.* Lakefield, Ontário: Waapoone Publishing and Promotíon, 1992, p. 57.

[4] Dean Moore, Kathleen. *Holdfast: At Home in the Natural World.* Guilford, Connecticut: Lyons Press, 1st edition, 2004. Print.

[5] Hogan, Linda. S*olar Storms.* New York: Scribner, 1997. Print.

[6] Through grassroots effort and communal commitment, the Innu of Quebec and Labrador, who have maintained an on-going, intimate relationship with the St. George River caribou for millennia, have been instrumental in gaining protection for a 3.5 millions acre area of St. George River calving grounds, making them off-limits to mineral exploration and other industrial development.

Leonore Wilson
The Fire That Nearly Took Us

…the flames, the no I will NOT go, NO of wild broom and oats and wheat, the me the mother who says NO I will stay, this land is my womb, my children, this acreage of my mother's and her mother's, over a thousand maternal acres handed down and down, yes….but MOM get in the car, get the cat, get the dog, get the photographs, NO…I will stand right here with my cracked heels wrinkled and hurting as the deep dry earth, October earth, deep creases of walnut shells, see they have stained my palm, see, I will NOT… no, I say, the last leaf, see how it still hangs from the miracle oak…why leave ME, it says, and the bees with their see-sawing grief on the wild rose, … now this is, NO this is I will not go… yet you MUST, hear the winds, MOM, what winds, I have heard them like the coyotes in the middle of the night when everyone's sleeping, when cattle low and low and their calves… no mother GO, but the owls, my owls, yes I know them too, the owls at dawn, they low low like the coyotes, oh yes, they all have their own oboes, I listen I LISTEN I have given my milk in the bluest hour, a woman walking in the pale pale darkness, rubbing beads of moisture from her bedside window, see ME moving into the fiery woods with the sash of my kimono opening, closing, catching the moon in my hand, holding in the light, under the fish net of stars as a moth flies across an old mare's flanks so soft even I won't go, I have been awake when there is no one, when the bedside clock cast its minutes out, the flames I see them and think of the orange-robed monk kneeling down in a billowed flame decades ago backed up to a wooden brothel in a place called Saigon, oh Mai Lai half asleep, on its bruised hands and knees, the things that keep me awake through the early hours, white hours, my house wrapped in its black armband, and the flames I can hear like mortar fire waking up the valley, my valley, while a circle of tomes lies like an open eye around my bed, and the rampant touch, the inflamed kiss, oh hot autumn night, of gold leaf and sky, oh fires you say the fires are here like Phantom jets that roll in the sun, making the sound of grief like the churning of rivers in winter, oh how we cling to each other, we who grew flowers to slide into rifle barrels, who danced in People's Park with incense tapirs, when hope was a temple bell, when the folk songs began that rose from our lips… no, NO, I say to you as if it were my marriage vow… in sickness and death, I will not go…

Notes

No one was prepared for the fires that swept Northern California in October 2017. I did not want to leave the ranch that I have always known, that I grew up on, that I raised my hearty sons on. My grown boys tore through the valley from their scattered homes and begged me to go! But I was frozen. It was as if I believed the gods would not burn this ranch, no way. They have protected it for 100 years. The only ranch around these parts to stay safe. I stood firm in that belief, perhaps a bit crazy, but I have always been a bit crazy. I am a hill wife. A Cassandra. The Northern California fires of 2017 were and are an indication of what is to come: fires and more fires.

Notes 2024

We had escaped other fires, but not the 2020 Hennessy fire sparked on August 17 by a rare lightning storm that lapped near the eastern edge of our ranch then veered east away from us, burning 50,000 acres with the overnight wind. The fire would later merge with others to become the LNU Lightning Complex fire, the third largest in California's history.

We waited as long as we could, spraying down the log house multiple times and removing fallen branches from the perimeter. We had begged firemen to come and help as we saw a gathering plume on the horizon, but they had too much land to cover; additionally, they were ordered to go to the town of Vacaville an hour away from us in rural Napa.

At dusk we were forced to leave, deciding to half-sleep next to the corral in our sedan loaded with pets, quilts, bags of photos, memorabilia. We stayed under the three hundred year old oak that had watched the cattle for a century come and go.
The next day, that giant oak fell right on that very spot.

My 95-year-old mom still lives in her old ranch home, but we live in town now. We cannot rebuild. We visit the land multiple times a week, but it is still very painful to return to where our family hill house once stood.

Anne Bergeron
Winter

> By mid-century, it is predicted, there will be no more glaciers
> and a million species of living beings will become extinct.
> The end of winter might mean the end of life.
> What is the future of winter, of snow, of ice?
> —Gretel Ehrlich, *The Future of Ice: A Journey into Cold*

Twenty degrees below zero. The bird feeder is empty, the heel of bread eaten, the weekend visitors have closed the door behind them. Orion is up, not a tree moves, nothing expends energy, only what is needed to hold everything in place. I keep my wits, kindle a big fire in the Freeflow barrel stove, place a worn sheepskin on my chair and curl up. The barely insulated walls of my one-room cabin and the fire are my warmth.

The thaw begins the next day. After a stretch of sub-zero mornings, one ice storm and many snowfalls, the world unlocks. I split wood in the warm sunshine in army issue wool pants, an Icelandic sweater, and knitted cap. Walking into town with the dogs to get the mail, I inspect moose tracks in the center of the dirt road. They lead to a pile of first cut hay, full of vetch, red clover, and timothy — my neighbor's offering to the resident moose, who like all of us, has been working overtime to stay warm this past month. When I return home, it is too sunny to go inside, so I make myself an outdoor room. I kneel beneath the maple tree where the bird feeder attracts chickadees, nuthatches, blue jays, and red squirrels. There, in deep snow, I sculpt a bench and a round table. The snow holds beautifully: wet, dense, and deep. On the table, I place a clay pot full of hemlock boughs. I collect two pack baskets worth of sticks and a scroll of white birch bark. I dig out my fire pit and kindle a fire with twigs and bark. I marinate chicken, clean the cabin, and invite a friend to supper.

As daylight falls away, I look west toward the red glow where ridgeline meets sky. Inside, I run spring water over watercress, parsley, and purple cabbage, then toss them with oil in a red Mexican bowl. Behind me the sky deepens with darkness. The fire has burned down, and it is still warm inside. As I move a lighted match toward the mantle on the gas lamp, I hear footsteps on the cabin porch.

This excerpt from my journal, kept while I lived in a one-room cabin in the hills of Vermont in the winter of 1992, documents a classic January thaw, several consecutive days of above-freezing temperatures in the midst of winter. In Vermont, winter typically begins in November and ends in April. In recent years, the dramatic fall and rise in temperatures has mellowed as the climate has warmed. I feel winter's identity shifting, and my own changing along with it.

Photo by A. Bergeron

Last winter, in mid-February, my 15-year-old nephew Kyle and I attended an art exhibit at Vermont's Shelburne Museum, entitled "32 Degrees: The Art of Winter." The curator brought this mixed media collection together to explore the identities of snow and ice and to pique viewers' nostalgia for the season. Included in the exhibit were large snow globes with darkly comic tableaux, a snow music video game, Monet's "Haystacks, Snow Effect," and three large digital images of tiny fishing shanties set in the center of landscapes of white by photographer Scott Peterman. The loss of winter due to global warming across the planet was the unifying message coming through the work of each artist.

Inside the snow globes, children and adults in street clothes soared off the edges of icebergs with smiles on their faces, a woodcutter wielding an axe chopped a tree with black birds seated on every limb, and wolves surrounded a man perched on stilts. Outside on the museum grounds, we explored a village of fanciful fishing shanties, the work of several craftsmen paying homage to an age-old winter activity. On the field of greening grass, these tiny houses looked marooned and odd as space ships. It was 55 degrees Fahrenheit, a day of high clouds and intermittent sun. January's snowfall had melted away. Kyle wore a light jacket and blue canvas boat shoes. We took pictures of each other with our phones as we opened each shanty door, sat on curving cedar benches, ran our hands along decorative carvings, and admired stained glass windows.

From inside one house, Kyle looked out at me through a perfect cutout of a large geometric fish. Above the fish, carved circles of all sizes represented air bubbles. Closing the door of the house across from him, I sat down inside and looked out onto the empty field. A memory of my mother arose: She stood at the stove in our galley kitchen, battering and frying to a golden crisp the tiny smelt my grandfather had caught that day on a frozen Lake Champlain. Her back was to us as she dipped the fish by their tails into flour and egg batter, and then dropped them into hot oil in the skillet. I could almost taste the crispy fried batter, could almost see the little golden headless fish draining on brown paper lunch bags next to the stove.

The Shelburne museum sits astride Lake Champlain, the sixth largest lake in the United States. Last winter, once again, it did not freeze over.

Even the bays, usually solid enough to skate and fish on, were thought to be too precarious for fishing shanties. From 1860 to 1930, there was only one year that the lake, 120 miles long and 12 miles across at its widest point, did not completely freeze over. After that, each decade included multiple years when the lake did not freeze completely. The 1990s were a turning point. For seven winters the lake remained open, and in the first decade of the new century, only half of the winters saw a solid stretch of ice between Vermont and its far shore in upstate New York.

Inside one of the artists' fishing shanties crafted of memory and imaginings, I sat on a bench and looked down at the hole in the floor where the ice would be cut. My gaze turned out the window to February's grass, and I understood what it might mean to lose the full experience of a season in my lifetime. When I was Kyle's age, I could never have imagined such a thing.

It is now nearing the end of January 2017, and Lake Champlain is open for the fifth winter since 2010. So far, only three days have registered below the average temperature for the month. Most have ranged much higher, as much as 27 degrees above the historical average; January 12 came in at 54 degrees Fahrenheit. Today, far from the lake, in the hills of eastern Vermont where I live, fat flakes of snow blow chaotically, then turn to ice that pings onto windows, and then transforms to rain that coats white spruce trees in a frosting of ice. A symphony of silence, a chorus of ice, a tympany of water. I chose the town where I live because it is well known as the center of a snow belt. I feel most fully alive in winter gliding on my skis through the forest. I am nostalgic for all that winter means and has meant to me.

It is February and I breathe heavily, climbing on wooden skis through Nebraska Notch toward the junction with the Long Trail below Mount Mansfield. I am twenty-two. Gregg is ahead of me on the trail, his coat an occasional patch of blue through the thick flakes that fall, wetting our faces, sticking like icing to our wool hats. A few inches of new snow allows me to easily angle my skis as we herringbone the steep sections. Our wax holds, the skis grip, and I use my arms to anchor metal poles and push downward. At the trail junction, a wind gust obliterates our visibility; Gregg looks back to me. I nod that I want to continue.

Our destination is Taylor Lodge, a favorite spot, and I mean to get there one more time before I leave. Through blinding snow we press slowly on, focused on finding the white blazes on trees that mark the trail. We travel like this for at least a mile, and just as I realize I am scared, the snow lets up and begins to fall gently. Beneath our skis, the powder is deep. Above us, clouds rise in between firs and balsams. I feel my effort lessen as we start to glide down toward Taylor, kicking with long strides through fresh snow. It's so easy now. I love this, more than anything.

Soon, the roof of the lodge comes into view.

We tamp down a smooth place with our skis, remove them, and hop up onto the porch. Snow buries the stairs. Little paths have been worn through snow to the half-door and along the porch. We kick new fluff from in front of the door and open it. Inside we shed our parkas and put on the down vests we pull from our packs. After slipping on spare hats and gloves, we retrieve our lunch: a thermos of tomato soup, cheese, and bread. We place the meal on the wooden table and sit next to each other on the bench.

We pour soup into stainless steel cups and drink. Salty, thick and warm, it relaxes my stiff limbs and I lose the slight chill I had. I cut cheddar into wide slices with the Swiss army knife Gregg gave me and place them onto wedges of bread. A whirl of wind sprays snow onto the table. Thin shafts of sunlight appear. We walk to the door and watch the clouds lift a little, not enough to open the view of the Champlain Valley spreading below the rock face in front of the lodge.

Now, three decades later, each passing winter tells me that the winters I knew as a youth are becoming extinct. I feel this loss as grief, as for someone I love, with whom I feel intimate. Skiing in deep snow below Mount Mansfield in winter is part of my story, my geographical autobiography. On a sub-zero day or in the midst of a white out, the warmth of a sturdy shelter, a cup of hot soup, a cozy place at the wooden table engenders an intimacy with others and ourselves that may be more difficult to access when the weather is warm and the energy is high, as in the height of summer. Experiences in the cold, snow and ice tell me who I am, over and over again. Remembering them makes me feel good. In 2012, *The Atlantic* reported on a study first published in the American Psychological Association's journal *Emotion* and conducted at the University of Southhampton. The study linked an increase in nostalgic feelings to cold temperatures. The college students participating in the study claimed more nostalgic thoughts in cold rooms and on cold days, and, interestingly enough, experiencing nostalgic thoughts correlated to an increase in the participants' body temperatures. Feeling nostalgia literally warms us up. I wonder if nostalgia may be an antidote to experiences that leave us emotionally cold, sad, or depressed – such as our changing climate.

I think again of the Shelburne Museum exhibit. The painted winter landscapes, the fishing houses, snow covered haystacks, and snow globes reminded me of the winters of my childhood and young adulthood. What happens to us when there are fewer of those memories to stir?

That day at the museum, after Kyle emerged from a dome-shaped shanty, we went back into the museum. From the far edge of the gallery, we heard the low moan of a glacier calving. Kyle walked to the source of the sound, a screen stretched across one full gallery wall. With his phone, he took a video of the video. It was several minutes before a section of the Iceland glacier cracked, slid, and plunged into the ocean. Kyle seemed small before the sound and the slow, certain crash of ice, much as I was once small before the snow squalls filling Nebraska Notch. Will Kyle's geographical autobiography include the story of winter as told on a gallery wall? For what will he feel nostalgia?

Several years after my last ski with Gregg in Nebraska Notch, I found my way to a job in the White Mountains of New Hampshire, and thereby, back to winter. On the day of the Winter Solstice, a neighbor told me he believed that because their lives were so entwined with the seasons, ancient people knew they had to participate in ensuring that the sun would return. Each year on the afternoon of the Winter Solstice, in the long shadow of his ancestors, my neighbor skied to his special place on a mountain trail above his home to make sure that the light would come back.

The following year, in encroaching dusk on the Winter Solstice, I skied alone up a trail along the Smarts Brook in the White Mountain National Forest. The whispers of my wooden boards in the snow plied the silent air, rich with the scent of balsam fir. I skied up to a west-facing outlook, and then stepped off the trail to watch daylight fade on the darkest day of the year. I felt my skis sink. The late afternoon sky was pale, the falling sun gone, and the evergreens were nearly black against the whiteness. I stood for some minutes, waited until true dusk, and then quietly slipped back down the trail, navigating by the light of the snow. My neighbor's story had become my own myth, a tradition that I keep— whether on skis, snowshoes, or on foot— of taking myself to a special place outdoors on the year's shortest day so that winter will come and the light will return.

In my memory of that first Winter Solstice ski, I see myself as if in a painting, standing still in the forest on my old blue wooden skis, not aware enough yet to feel nostalgic for the deep snow, for the young woman I was, and for my neighbor, no longer alive.

But here and now, on the far side of that memory, I am deeply nostalgic for Nebraska Notch in winter, for the sub-zero nights in my Vermont cabin, and for the sight of 12 miles of frozen lake between two long shorelines. The memories warm me today, at the end of a mild January, as the temperature drops below freezing and snow begins to fall.

Gillian Goslinga
To Witness

Fragility

I am driving along a scenic road in Sedona County, Arizona, its famed red rocks flanking the winding road on either side and in the distance. A sign announces the beauty ahead, inviting drivers to raise their eyes above the road to look about. Wisps of yellow grass brighten the slopes up to the awesome rock formations around me, the yellow broken by dark green junipers and pines, fanciful clusters of purple cacti, and rich deep ochre earth. I am enchanted.

Around a curve, the mangled corpse of a hare on the road makes me swerve. Around another curve, further down, another corpse, a coyote this time, its skull crushed and jaw lying flat on the pavement, its body contorted by impact, like a gruesome trophy carpet. I swerve again, feeling a pang in my belly. I count a third little nondescript creature crushed further down these five miles of scenic views.

But what a rush the landscape gives! All I have to do is raise my eyes to the horizon to be enchanted again. I imagine that other drivers feel this same hypnotic elation too, eyes and hearts raised beyond our windshields to the sublime on this God-given corner of Mother Earth. The corpses of the animals who didn't make it across the road fast enough jar these good feelings, if you see them at all. Maybe you swerve to avoid crushing the bodies a second time, as I just did, thinking yourself lucky that it wasn't you that crushed them in the first place. If you have a heart, you feel a pang of pity.

On mornings like this, when one corpse after another greets me on the tarmac, I ache to do ceremony for these fellow creatures whom we call, with sick humor, "road kill." I have many times imagined erecting little crosses along the roads, bright with flowers and the recognition of death, as is done for human victims of accidents, who incidentally are never called "road kill." I always say a prayer for their souls' safe journey home. But are prayers enough?

Next day, same hour, same scenic stretch.

The road is picture-perfect again. All three corpses have vanished, leaving not a trace of blood or bone or fur. Courtesy of the Sedona municipality and our tax dollars, the red rock vistas can again rejoice the vision and hearts of drivers from behind the looking glass of a car's windshield, without stain of death. All is forgotten.

I think: if all the corpses of road-kill on that scenic road were to be piled up along the side of the road, they would surely rise higher on each side of the tarmac than the graceful yellow grasses that delight with their movement and wispy color. Would a forest of crosses bright with flowers do these deaths' justice? What kind of witnessing would this be, truly? Are pangs of pity and gazes of recognition enough?

To witness

I want to turn the concept of witness on its head.

I have prided myself on being a witness to these road- kill with my prayers and my thoughts of ceremony. The harsher truth is that I have not once stopped to honor the dead ones.

The wanton corpses of creatures killed as they travel the tracks of their lives are witnesses to the wanton narcissism of my breed of humans. To privatize my sorrow – I have a heart thank God! – is to re-enact the very narcissism that built this scenic road that cuts through the land and the tracks of others without consideration or respect. The pang of grief I feel is not only my own; it is the pain of a covenant that has been broken. Bad deaths hurt not just the animals or my sense of righteousness, they hurt life itself.

I have read in Deborah Bird Rose's *Reports from A Wild Country* that a band of Victoria River Australian Aboriginals camp "on the blood and bones of their people that had been murdered" at Kinbarra by colonizers at the turn of the 19th century[1] The camping is neither protest nor memorialization. The band keeps their murdered ancestors company during daily living and remembers them, because they loved their kin and their kin loved them, and that is what those unjustly killed need most, the company of loved ones. Camping on the bones is not proof of a greater humanity, Bird Rose insists, but is an action that repairs what was violently torn asunder in the matrix that is country, the place where one is born and dies in the company of others. She explains, "If people decided to cease to tell the stories of what happened, the implication could be that the deaths and the pain no longer matter."[2] Wrongful death doesn't want to be memorialized. It wants to be kept company with.

Roadkill in Village of Oak Creek, Sedona by G. Goslinga

It's hard to look at a photo like this without feeling rude and voyeuristic. In *Wild Dog Dreaming*[3], Bird Rose describes how she comes to a tree along a road on which dead Dingos – all poisoned – are hung like Christmas ornaments. After the initial shock and horror – "God, where are you here?" she hears herself cry out – she just looks, reaching beyond feelings of shame and guilt. Something transforms in her, beyond the horror and the anguish. She takes each animal in, an honoring. There is something respectful in looking this way. We don't know how to do it. Certainly we don't know how to sit with death and especially not with gruesome death in quiet dignity.

To be called into relationship

Bird Rose goes on to write about what it takes to call us humans into relationship with our Earth's others. She says that we must locate "an ethical call-and-response **within** the living reality of life"[4] rather than in the abstract spaces of the mind, or of a heart that has been made abstract by narcissism.

This has been my point so far: An emotional witnessing of the suffering of others can be as ineffective as thought, no matter how intense or sincere the felt emotion. Unless I am honestly present with what has transpired—e.g., roads that cut through the tracks of others without respect or consideration—I will not know how to respond in kind, in a way that repairs what has been breached. Love, in Deborah Bird Rose's account, is what sparks in us the ability to respond in kind to the presence and needs of others. Love is what awakens us to the life-worthiness of others in death and in life, and calls us into right relationship with them. This kind of love is rooted in knowing how to keep company with. This kind of love is the antidote to narcissism.

I wonder what I would come to know if I did stop and keep company with the dead on the scenic road out of love rather than pity. I wonder what I would come to know about what they need. I wonder what I would feel sitting next to them as cars drove by and drivers stared at us. I think: Being in right relationship with has to be the first step of ceremony. Listening to what the other needs, in death as in life. Let ceremony begin from that listening. Let all witnessing begin in the here-now of keeping-company-with.

Reparation

I have yet to stop along the scenic road to honor and keep company with the dead. I want to. But I think reparation before the fact would be a better idea. I have heard that in the Dakotas, courtesy of taxpayer dollars, tunnels are now being dug beneath highways and roads at regular intervals to ensure the safe crossing of animals large and small for whom the Dakotas are also home. This is reparation that matters, where the human has witnessed the needs of fellow creatures and learned to keep company with them in life.

[1] Bird Rose, Deborah. *Reports from a Wild Country: Ethics for Decolonization.* Sydney: UNSW Press, 2004. Print. p. 56.

[2] Ibid, p. 57

[3] Bird Rose, Deborah. *Wild Dog Dreaming: Love and Extinction.* Charlottesville: University of Virginia Press, 2012. Print.

[4] Ibid, p. 29

nan seymour
pelicans in exile

> As of last week, Luft said, there were fewer than 1,000 adults. As of
> Thursday, there are virtually none. All the state biologists observed
> were a few dozen juvenile birds, too young to fly,
> hiding in some rock outcroppings.
> — Leia Larsen, *Salt Lake Tribune*, June 30, 2023

we fly wide
we live on islands
we nest on the ground.

other birds hatch like colts, ready to run
our children arrive as naked as yours
featherless and vulnerable as scrotum
everyday we leave them in the care of the waves
we fly the lengths of lake
we fly over tar seeps
fly over salt sea
glide until river water
fish until we have enough to feed them
before nightfall, we return.

when we fly high
we see the scar you made of a mountain
we see the waters strangled by your tracks
we see the patterns of your poison.

when we fly wide
we watch you pave habitat
we reel in the steam heat rising from the smelter
we feel you working at the speed of destruction.

since time before memory
we have slept within water's embrace
the place we called safe, you called gunnison.

we saw the sea diminish

until the tide did not return,
we witnessed the end of our protection.

when four-leggeds crossed the sand bridge
they came swiftly, all teeth
when teeth came, many of us left
for a while, some of us bore the peril
and watched as foxes slaughtered
our helpless children.

last spring, the rest of us departed
when we left our nests for the final time
pink sand still glittered through the sticks.

and though we have nowhere to go,
we know this home is over—

we left our young
we left our dead
we flew high
we flew wide
and we fled.

Notes

Great Salt Lake is my teacher, my dear companion, and my imperiled neighbor.

The lake is also one of over one hundred diminishing inland seas worldwide and an essential refuge for twelve million migratory birds. I have lived on the land she made with her waves for over half a century.

Three years ago, I heard scientist Dr. Bonnie Baxter explain the impending threat of losing the lake entirely due to human diversion. Like many listeners, I was rattled by her description of the perpetual toxic dust storm that would arise from a desiccated playa in the lake's absence. Around that time my mentor, Deena Metzger, encouraged me to begin listening to the sea herself. I turned my broken heart in the lake's direction.

The lake's voice then came in dreams and then a call to keep a vigil on the shoreline for forty days and nights in the winter of 2022. Not accustomed to winter camping, I was surprised by the invitation.

Nevertheless, I borrowed a camper and moved myself to the water's edge to become a neighbor to microbialites, bison, and ravens. Once there, the lake prompted me to call on others. She beckoned us and we came. Over a thousand people participated in the vigils on Antelope Island. We are now preparing for our third winter vigil on behalf of the Great Salt Lake, one that will begin on the Utah State Capitol steps on Tuesday, January 16th, and continue each day of the state legislative session until March 1st.

When the life of someone you love is at stake you stay with them.

Until recently, Great Salt Lake provided a vital nesting ground for white pelicans. As many as 20,000 individual birds lived on Gunnison Island on over 5,000 nests. As humans have continued to dam, dredge, and divert the waters, land bridges to the island have become exposed, allowing predators easy access. In May of 2023, the last adult pelicans left their home, in some cases leaving behind flightless and defenseless chicks. Their nests are now empty.

This poem imagines this exile from the pelican's perspective. As devastated as I am by this loss, I remain devoted to bearing witness to the beauty and vitality of this water body and all of the lives she sustains.

Even as we teeter at this precipice of unfathomable harm, our movement to restore and replenish the lake is swelling. We are learning to love more robustly and visibly. We are transcending our tired divides. We are gathering on behalf of everything that matters.

Alex C. Eisenberg
Living at the Edge of Devastation

I.

I live at the edge of a clear-cut.

Literally.

The cut line is mere feet from my floor-to-ceiling windows, so that from almost anywhere in my one-room cabin the un-forest is the totality of my window's view.

As I write this, I look out onto a near-dystopian landscape. Marine fog blowing up from the Strait of Juan de Fuca obscures the still-wooded foothills of the Olympic Mountains, and serves as a fitting backdrop for the logging slash bulldozed into several hundred piles of wasted wood. The closest of these piles is a long, tall wall about a hundred feet from where I sit. Aside from the single spindly leave-tree still standing in the distance, as well as the scatterings of stumps and the sun-burnt sword ferns clinging to life, these slash piles are all that is left of the forest: piles of broken bodies, waiting to be burned.

Without the shelter of standing trees, wind blasts against the siding of my home, rattling windows, whistling through the pores of the house, and sometimes seeming to lift the whole thing from its foundation.

It wasn't like this a year ago.

A year ago, when I came to visit this little piece of land for the first time, seeking a new place to call home, the cabin was wrapped in a lush forest of moss-streaked maples, sentinel cedars, sword ferns, Doug firs, and so much more. A hundred shades of green dripped from the canopy, reached upward from the forest floor, and mingled in the middle. Sunlight slanted through thick branches, dotting the cabin walls with light. Sitting in the same place where I am now, I remember feeling sheltered in this little cove of forest. Now, I feel exposed.

Pre-clearcutting by A. C. Eisenberg

I also remember, during that first visit, seeing the survey markers tied to trees along the property line, and feeling startled by their proximity.

My previous home, just a few miles away as the crow flies, also bordered land owned by this company, and I had also lived there while they were cutting down the forest. So I was no stranger to the reality of industrial logging, nor the ruthlessness of this particular corporation. But somehow, this older, more diverse, and more structurally complex forest seemed too stalwart to be going anywhere anytime soon.

Perhaps that was wishful thinking. Perhaps denial or delusion. Mostly, though, it was desperation.

My partnership was ending, and therefore my roots—which had been planted deeply in the home we shared—were seeking new soil.

Post-clearcutting by A. C. Eisenberg

With the housing crisis raging on the Quimper Peninsula, my options seemed to be surrendering my beloved off-grid lifestyle for an expensive apartment in Port Townsend, or renting this inexpensive and adorable rustic cabin resting on a half-acre triangle of land, wedged between a gravel road and the uncertain certainty of the survey markers.

Either way, uprooting from my previous home felt like a scarcely survivable severance. I had given myself to that land: given my blood, my sweat, my labor, and my full-bodied love to that land. I ate from the land, drank from the sky, and offered all that came through my body back to the body of the earth. We buried my cat there, attended my partner's father in his dying process in that house, and spread his ashes across that land. We'd made love in these forests and then we watched them fall. My body and heart had merged with the land—through life and death—and my identity had become entwined with it.

To disentangle from all of that and transplant myself was incredibly daunting, even seeming impossible at times. For who would I be if I wasn't there, where I had lived in such deep reciprocity?

Photo by A. C. Eisenberg

II.

> My refuge exists in my capacity to love. If I can learn to love
> death then I can begin to find refuge in change.
> —Terry Tempest Williams, *Refuge*

On the first day I visited this little triangular plot of land, I squatted in the garden in the mid-summer sun, between raspberry and stinging nettle stalks and the failing fishnet fence, to pee and release. I remember watching wisps of moon-blood and piss merge with the soil. When I stood, I remember plucking ripe red raspberries, plopping them in my mouth and thinking: "my fertility will feed them, as they are feeding me."

In that moment, my body recognized reciprocity with this land, and I knew exactly where I needed to be.

That bodily knowing overrode any reservations I had about the fact that, at some point in the next couple of years, the forest that bordered this land would be cut, and that, if I still lived here, I would have to live through that horrific experience again. Only this time, I would have a front row seat to the devastation.

Despite knowing this, I thought I had some time to breathe and to just be here in peace. Or, perhaps, time to change the fate of this place.

I was wrong.

Only a few short weeks after I moved in, I heard the first saw buzzing in the distance. I was in the middle of building a kitchen for the cabin, feeling hopeful about home and settling in to my new rhythms. But with that first swipe of saw cutting through the quiet, my sense of refuge toppled with that tree.

Over the next weeks, the sounds of the saw got closer and closer. Cut by cruel cut, it sliced through each of my illusions.

III.

> The challenge of modernity is to live without illusions
> without becoming disillusioned
> —Antonio Gramsci, *Letters from Prison*

I stayed anyway. I needed a place to live and had already invested so much here. Even still, I knew I would lose this place, for I understood clear-cutting as an act of displacement. And by displacement I mean not only an act of pushing bodies out of a place, but an act of *unmaking* a place.

One day, I heard the un-making happening much closer to the cabin than usual. I wanted to see just how close, so I ventured into the forest to find out.

The noisiness of the machine both oriented and disoriented me. I could follow the sound, but it also seemed to bounce around and surround me. Finding the source was further disorienting. It just didn't seem possible to be walking through this thick forest with no roads nearby and find such an enormous machine inside.

Hidden, I watched the mechanical arm grab tree after tree, slice swiftly through their trunks, and send them crashing against the ground. I tried to keep a safe distance, but curiosity and an attempt to document drew me closer. In my distraction I didn't really realize how much danger I was in. That is, until a tree fell in my direction.

The removal of that tree put the monster in clearer view so that I could even see the face of the man inside. I ducked behind a larger cedar thinking I might be able to stay safe and out of sight for a while. But the machine kept moving toward me.

Perceiving the danger too late, I turned into a wild animal—prey with an oncoming predator—and ran, straight out from the cedar until I reached another one and crawled behind it. I looked back at my pursuer in time to see another tree crash adjacent to where I'd been hiding. Staring, I wondered if the branches that landed right where I had been would have killed me. I quickly decided I didn't want another chance to find out and ran again, bushwhacking blindly, not looking back this time.

Finally, I found my bearings, crossed the property line with great relief, and returned to the relative refuge of my cabin. I couldn't stay inside long though. My body, shaken, needed to be around other bodies to regulate. The only way I could see processing what had happened to me, and what was still happening to the forest, was to be with the forest.

I went in the opposite direction of the noise this time, and found myself among a grove of giant maples. They reached in every direction with thick and twisted branches, dripping with old man's beard and coated in many hues of soft green.

Mesmerized, I stared upward and spun in circles in wonder. Then, I lay on a mossy log and breathed until my nervous system synced back up with the pace, serenity, and sounds of the trees, rather than the scream of the machine.

IV.
> Clear-cutting is disorienting. It destroys all points of orientation.
> —My journal entry from later that night

When, in the evening, I decided to return to the scene of the severing, it took everything in me to keep walking forward, toward the devastation. It was an act of will to keep upright. Gravity itself felt heavier.

The words *gravity* and *grief* share the same root, *gravis*, meaning heavy. I think of grief as perceiving the weight of the truth of loss in our bodies.

And in that moment the truth was this: I could see light where there hadn't been light. Where there had been forest, there was no forest. That whole section of trees had been leveled. It looked as if a giant had come down from the sky and mowed his lawn.

I found myself on all fours, my body involuntarily undulating with dry heaves. The sickness that had been building in my stomach for weeks intensified and took me over. Nothing but saliva came out, not even bile, but my body kept trying to purge something rotten inside me. Instead, a throaty roar emerged from the depth of me, along with a river of questions—why and what and how and how and why?

I finally sat up, dizzy, trying to find some reference points, but the world had been turned over and torn and rendered unrecognizable. The place had been taken, unmade.

What did feel familiar, though, sitting there under the stars, was the piles of bodies of trees. I'd seen this before in my previous homes, and in clear-cuts along the highway, but they reminded me of something else, too.

On my trip to Auschwitz a few years back, exploring my ancestry in relation to the Holocaust, I'd seen image after image of human bodies piled in mass graves; I'd seen rooms full of shoes, hair, luggage, kitchen utensils, piled behind plexi-glass. Piles of the dead, selfishly, violently, unceremoniously ripped from their lives and stacked as if they were nothing.

Looking at the un-forest, I thought of the long legacies of war and displacement—the villages torched, the bodies taken, broken, burnt. I thought of all the apocalypses our species has lived through, all the horrors endured. I felt the sick initiation of it, and saw myself suddenly joining the ranks of those who survived long enough to tell the tale or pass along the genetics of survival. And I remembered: I am made up of those genes.

I silently thanked those ancestors for surviving long enough to make the bodies that made my body. And I thanked the genes in my body that know what it takes to survive such displacement, disorientation, and dismemberment as this.

Around me, the still-standing trees seemed to talk to each other. They creaked and cried. I swear to you, some of them were crying. I've never heard a tree keen until that night.

But they kept standing.

So eventually I stood up too.

Over the next months, I begged those trees to uproot and run, or fight back, or something. What they did was stand their ground.

So I did too.

Photo by A. C. Eisenberg

V.

> The two primary sins of Western civilization: amnesia and
> anesthesia—we forget and we go numb.
> —Francis Weller, *The Wild Edge of Sorrow*

I wanted to offer my body as a witness to what was left of the forest.
I wanted to be a body experiencing the body of the forest, and all the
other bodies in it. I wanted them to feel the love of my body against
theirs, before they felt the selfish swipe of the saw. I wanted them to be
felt and remembered.

So, once again, I ignored the cruel rule of the red ribbons marking the property line, warning me not to cross them, and I crossed them.

And I crossed them.

And I crossed them.

Every evening, usually after dark, I stepped barefoot across that line to wander through the doomed forest. Under the cover of night, bringing no light, I let my feet feel their way between mahonia and sword fern, over the soft litter of the leaves and the hard roots elbowing up, under a varied canopy of maple, cedar, fir, and alder.

Step by step, November night by December night, my body learned this forest—its rises and its falls, its roots and branches, its shapes and shadows, its sounds and stirrings, its rhythms and relationships.

It didn't take many nights of this ritual before my cat, Grendel, started to join me, sometimes leading, other times following, sometimes staying underfoot, other times riding my shoulders, and yet other times bolting off into the darkness.

Being a cat, Grendel's body was more attuned than mine will ever be to walking through the dark and to the ways of the wild. This became abundantly clear one night as we were walking together, talking to each other—him meowing, looking up at me inquiringly, and me looking down at him cooing my love in return. Suddenly his body went silent and stiff beside me. My own attunement to his physiology is the only reason I, too, stopped and quieted enough to notice the noise in the brush ahead. A large animal, ahead and to the left, was moving slowly through the under-story.

My mind raced through the possibilities—deer, elk, coyote—landing of course on the worst of the litany: cougar. I gathered Grendel in my arms and took a few steps backward, naturally snapping a branch underfoot. The noise startled the animal, and it immediately took off in the opposite direction, snapping and crashing through the woods.

I cut my trip short for the night, feeling distinctly the facts of my body in this place: my vulnerability to its dangers and to its wonders, my ignorances and insensitivities. I felt myself both apart from and a part of the other bodies here, startling and being startled, shaping and being shaped. There was communion and competition. Protection, defensiveness, curiosity, fear, welcome, and unwelcome.

But mostly, there was the feeling that we were all bodies—alive and breathing—together in this place.

That night, I felt the boundaries between me and the land begin to dissolve.

VI.

> Devastation respects no boundaries.
> —Terry Tempest Williams, *Refuge*

The owls left first, their haunting hoots receding night by night.

Then, one day, I watched the birds flee from the noise of the machines. They took refuge near my roof before flitting across the road, further from the commotion. I thought of how the animals of the forest would have no way to know which direction was safest to go—no way of understanding survey markers or property lines or where the edge of the devastation might land. All they could know was: *this place is no longer safe. I must leave.*

Witnessing the animal flee, I questioned the sanity in staying. But I stayed, and Grendel stayed with me, and we kept walking through the shrinking forest every night.

Over the coming day and weeks, as I watched the forest recede, I had to continually seek new points of orientation. I would orient to one line of trees and then it would be gone. Each time, the whole familiar face of the place changed. I kept thinking I was somewhere that I wasn't, looking for trees that were no longer there. The edge had moved. It was still the edge, but a different edge.

There was rarely a night that I *wanted* to go out on my walks. It seemed much easier to stay inside and watch a stupid show on my computer, or read a book, or just sleep. I kept forcing myself to go out because every time I did I came back feeling more alive—even if that aliveness was manifest in grief or rage or confusion. Honestly, though, it was often joy.

Regardless of my mental state, my body consistently felt better after walking barefoot through the forest. Even if my feet were frozen to the bone by the time I got back, I was always grateful I went. My cells would sing. And I always slept better afterward.

That is, until I didn't.

I can't describe to you what it felt like to wake up in the early morning dark to bright work lights shining through the forest, through my windows, and straight into my eyes as I rested in the sanctuary of my bed.

I could see the lights were in a section of forest that was dear to me, though the company had agreed to warn me before they cut any closer to the house. You might think, after my experience with the machine, the obvious response would be to run *away* from the noise, or at least stay inside. But something deeply protective and instinctual came over me.

When I heard the saw start, I was out the door before I could think, wearing some semblance of dress and careening through the darkness.

The adrenaline stopped short of running me into my death, but the man operating the machine took longer to see me than I expected. The blade arm had swung too close to me, and he was mid-cut into a tree— one I knew well—before he saw me flapping my arms and screaming. He stopped the machine mid-cut.

After a strange exchange, where I sobbed and pleaded and he told me "I'm just doing my job, squaring off this corner." The man agreed to move his work elsewhere for a while to give me time to say goodbye.

An hour or so later, from inside my cabin holding hands with a friend, I watched that place be erased.

Photo by A. C. Eisenberg

From then on, the company kept me diligently abreast of when they would be cutting along the property line.

The morning it was finally going to happen, after weeks of delays due to snow and wind, I left early with Grendel, having decided to bring him back to my former home while they cut adjacent to the house. I was afraid he would run away from the noise as all the other animals had, or be trapped inside and scared. As for myself, I had originally wanted to witness and document the process from the property line, but my friends urged me otherwise, so I retreated as well.

Driving away in the dark, as the lights of the logging machines descended on the forest, I felt like a refugee fleeing the destruction of my home.

VII.

> It may be that hypersensitivity to the ecological unraveling of the only home we know is the necessary condition of an attuned few who can awaken the rest of us to the existential nature of the ecological crisis we face.
> —Christopher Ketcham, "The Machine Breaker," *Harper's Magazine*

On the day I returned, finding the rest of my forest fallen, I thought my body would be sucked through the ground, the force of grief was so powerful, so heavy. It was as though the trees themselves were what controlled the degree of gravity—with their heavy bodies on the ground, it seemed nothing else could stand either.

I crawled. Gasped. Wailed. Screamed. Sounds I have never heard come out of any body came out of me. I felt as if I had lost limbs and lungs. I felt as if I had been broken into ten million pieces along with the forest.

And the sky had fallen. Literally.

To say it was the worst day of my life—to say much of anything about it for that matter—distorts the horror into something perhaps comprehensible, when in fact what I witnessed and felt was beyond comprehension or even sanity.

Indeed, I went mad with grief.

A few days into this madness, I found myself sitting barefoot in the January cold, picking up wedges of trees from the ground and trying to piece them together on their stumps, as if the clear-cut were the world's largest puzzle. Like a child whose toy was broken, I just kept saying to myself as I cried: "I remember how the forest went. I can put it back together. I remember how these trees looked. I can fix this. I can fix this…"

I could not.

VIII.

>Health is membership. …We must consider the body's manifold
>connection to other bodies and to the world.
>
>—Wendell Berry, "Health is Membership." *The Art of the Commonplace*

When I eventually brought Grendel home, after they'd hauled the trees away, I relived my experience watching his. The cabin was the same— he sniffed around and found his favorite spots and seemed to relax—but when he looked out the window, his body stiffened. He stared out across the cut and then back into the cabin, out and back and out, clearly confused. How could this be the same place, but not?

I wanted to keep him inside for a while, to help him settle, but he insisted on going out right away. I followed him, his feet finding the path we always took, but leading us through a different landscape. He slowed down, meowing sadly and sniffing stumps and looking and looking and looking. He seemed so lost.

From there, looking back at the cabin against the backdrop of the cut instead of the backdrop of the forest, it looked as though the now constant winds had lifted it from its foundation and, like Dorothy's house in the Wizard of Oz, dropped us in a completely new land. Only, instead of going from a black-and-white world to a world of color, my home had started in a world of vibrancy and life, and had been dropped into a land of desolation.

Grendel and I continued our nightly walks, at least as often as my heart could stand to. there were many nights when my nervous system couldn't handle it.

These walks were different. No longer would I come back enlivened, but heavy. And Grendel never ventured far from me anymore. He'd often stand on my feet and just stare. All his meows seemed sad, elongated, longing, and punctuated with question marks.

When the trees were still on the ground, waiting to be hauled away, I did more climbing, stumbling, crawling, and falling than walking. I looked for the trunks and stumps of trees I knew, attempting orientation. I was only ever able to recognize a few, but whenever I did I was surprised at the relief I felt in my body. It offered some evidence that this was the same place, reorienting me. I would lay my body on their body, and cry and sing and breathe in a way I couldn't otherwise during that time.

Sometimes I would visit the trees still standing on the other side of the cut line, and wonder if they had been waiting for their turn to be cut, only to be spared. I wondered if they

Grendel by A. C. Eisenberg

wondered why the machine had left them to bear witness, at the edge of the devastation. I know I did.

And even on the days I didn't cross that edge, or even look at it, the clear-cut was always still reaching back across to touch me.

There is a cost to dissociating, to forgetting, to turning away. But there is also a cost to not. How do I feel all of this, or how much of it do I feel? These are constant questions for me.

To live at the edge of devastation, and to not forget or go numb, is to bear bodily witness to the devastation. It is to pay part of the actual cost of the clear-cut—something money could never buy.

On the other hand, to dissociate and turn away, to not let the grief move through, is also to pay a price. Not only do we miss out on our humanity when we refuse to feel, but that unprocessed pain can linger in our bodies and turn to disease.

Either way, the cost is too much. Too much for one body. Too much for all bodies.

Over the course of this year, I've developed tremors—violent body jolts, like hiccups on steroids that originate in my chest. If I hear a machine, see lights reflecting off my window from the road at night, if the movie is too loud, if I pass a clear-cut, my body rebels. It got so bad one day I thought I was having a stroke. This is one way my body is trying to process what it has seen.

In order to cope, in order to keep coming home every day to the edge of the clear-cut, and not be continually destroyed, I have *had to* lean into some level of dissociation, some level of anesthetization, some level, even, of amnesia.

But I also know that in order to keep living here—not just at the edge of the clear-cut, but in this world as we teeter at the edge of every devastation—I also need to keep feeling. I need to keep remembering. I need to keep associating—finding association and kinship—and staying in living, dynamic relationship with this place and the world at large. Even if it is no longer what it was or what I want it to be; even if more of it is going to be lost.

If I don't do this, I might as well have died with the forest.

———

Photo (next spread) by A. C. Eisenberg

CODA
I.

> There will be no managed retreat.
> —Aviva Rahmani, *Dark Matter: Women Witnessing #16*

The landscape keeps changing.

They hauled the trees away and I realized that even their stacked and broken bodies were more comforting to me than the emptiness they left behind.

The wind became a constant companion. When it rips against the cabin walls, I miss the sound of the treetops slowing it down with their dance.

Months later, spring came and the brown sprawl of stumps started to green with weeds. The maple stumps sprouted and grew leaves. With clear skies and a collapsed skyline, I found I could see the mountains—a strange consolation prize for surviving. Everything softened and hope for ease sprang in me. But prematurely.

The company came back to spray glyphosate to kill off any competition to their Douglas fir cash crop. I was able to garner a 25-foot buffer from my house where they wouldn't spray, and within a week, the contrast between the sprayed and unsprayed land was stark. Still, run-off respects no boundaries, and suddenly the distance I was willing to range with bare feet was reduced to almost nothing.

My refuge continues to recede. Sometimes I just want to leave, to find a real refuge, somewhere untouched by the insanity of industrial extraction. I'm not even sure that exists anymore.

Instead, I hold my ground, here, tending and witnessing.

Today, about a year after that first swipe of saw sounded across the forest, the company returned and began burning the slash piles. The remains of the bodies of that beloved forest turn to smoke before my eyes and drift away from this place. A final procession.

I can't help but think of the bodies of humans billowing as smoke from the chimneys at Auschwitz. How the neighbors could see and smell the smoke and maybe even hear the screams, day in and day out. Most did nothing. Most of the world knew what was happening and did nothing.

II.

> Finding beauty in a broken world is creating
> beauty in the world we find.
> —Terry Tempest Williams, *Finding Beauty in a Broken World*

A month or so ago, in late summer, my friend helped me rebuild my wood shed. He'd recently learned timber framing and we decided we could salvage some of the slash to build it in that way.

We picked through the piles of dismembered trees and found an abundance of usable timbers. Then, over the course of weeks, using wedges, chisels, hand saws, sledge hammers, we notched, split, cut, and joined the wood into a shed. With 2x4s and plywood I had salvaged from a tree-house that also would have been destroyed by the logging company, we built a roof frame, adding the metal roofing from the old shed on top.

When it was finally finished, standing just adjacent to my cabin at the edge of the clear-cut, the shed appeared to me as a body in itself, born in and of this place—born of the consummation between my body and the other bodies of this place.

Seeing the four posts standing upright, I realized I had helped resurrect pieces of the trees so they could stand, once again, in dignity on this land. I had taken their dismembered bodies—bodies that had been removed from the membership of the forest—and re-membered them, and joined in a new membership with them. If nothing else, my body had facilitated these bodies staying in their place.

Their place, which is now my place too.

Photo by A. C. Eisenberg

Fired Anew: What It Means to Heal

If you are fortunate, healing overtakes you, works your
stubborn muscles of mind into clay then fires you anew.

—Sharon Rodgers Simone, *Fired Anew*

For me, the trade-off for physical limitation is a deepened appreciation
of the inter-woven complexity of life in any eco-system I find myself
in… I too am a terrain… My health now relies on the bounty of
Earth, its food and medicines.

—Carol Harmon, *My Body—An Eco-Terrain*

Karen Mutter
Jaguar Medicine

After the election in November 2016 and then the inauguration in January, there was a sharp increase in the number of people who seemed to be taken down by illness. Some of those illnesses were life threatening. When those needing help came to me asking for assistance, I asked for dreams. Several helpful dreams for individuals came through, but the call for help escalated faster than I could keep up. In the beginning of April 2017, I asked for a dream that would address the root cause of illness, regardless of the diagnosis.

This dream came that very night. This is an abbreviated version.

I am with my friend Sharon (who in waking reality was trying to navigate her way through a diagnosis of metastatic pancreatic cancer). She has asked me for help to further her understanding of a vision that has come to her. I drop into a trance and her vision comes clearly into view.

*Sharon is in the jungle lying in a hammock reading a book. Suddenly, a very large wild cat—a magnificent spotted jaguar— leaps over the hammock, narrowly missing Sharon, and knocks Sharon's glasses off of her head. They fall down into a ravine over which the hammock is perched, lost forever. Sharon is startled both by the abrupt, close presence of the jaguar and also, that her glasses have been ripped off her face. The jaguar reappears at the edge of the jungle and clearly speaks this message: **"You must see with new vision."***

I was awakened briefly by my alarm then fell back deeply asleep. The writing that follows came upon awakening. This is the essence of my understanding of the dream.

This dream is for all of us who are seeking a path towards healing and true health. It is also a dream for the medicine people, the ones who hold the space for healing to happen. It is imperative to see with new eyes the previously hidden possibilities, the encrypted ways forward, the metaphor in the test result. The startle factor itself is essential—as we need to be startled into awareness. The glasses come off so that we can really see what is before us to be met.

No matter what the medical reports say—CT scan, pathology, bloodwork—there is an entirely different way to see them. It is the one-dimensional black- and-white medical way that incites such fear in us because it is not natural to move through the world without the imaginal realm. There is no imaginal realm in conventional medicine and because we are fluid creatures born of that realm, conventional medical treatment creates a panic response that only worsens the illness and keeps us firmly under the control of the people who create and perpetuate the medical language.

Science will never catch up to the mysteries of the natural world. There will never be a way to unlock, decode, map out each and every miraculous unfurling that nature produces in every nanosecond. But we can tap in, merge with mystery. Include ourselves emotionally and mentally. We don't have to ask, we already *are* a mysterious force of nature. Without conscious recognition, however, we have become frightened outsiders. Afraid of the dark, afraid of the Not Knowing. So often we become lodged in the fear of dying, the fear of pain and suffering or becoming dependent. This is understandable. And also, in this state of mind, it is most difficult to see beyond the diagnosis to the deeper wisdom that often only can be realized when we are taken out of our ordinary reality through illness.

But imagine now if "the diagnosis" were offered with an understanding that the illness has come to reveal to you an entirely new perspective about the life you are living and the places that need healing? If we pay close attention and gather up the strands of the story that have woven the life to this point, the exact path that the illness is asking us to explore will emerge. This process requires companionship and community, stepping out of old patterns of thinking and then listening deeply to the language of our bodies, dreams and signs.

It may be the greatest challenge before us: not healing from an illness but pulling ourselves out of the magnetic field of the mental construct that rules our culture, our minds—the illusion that science is supreme over nature. That is the illness to be healed. To do so we need to break the spell that keeps us separate from our truest nature.

In Sharon's case, she understood that she was being asked to give up a war against the microbes in her body and a worship of the scientific method, to find a way to live in peace with all beings. Today she is alive and well and seeing all of life with new vision.

From across the ravine in the heart of the jungle, wild leaping Jaguar has come to set us free.

Mary Sutton
Her Body is Burning

Editors' note: "Mary Sutton" is an assumed name to protect the author's identity in an era of Google searches and background checks, and in a culture in which addiction is still a source of great stigma and shame.

It is 1991, and my body is burning.

Doctors mark my skin in ink, drawing borders around areas that are hot to the touch. Like wildfire, infection advances across these boundaries in a matter of hours, sometimes faster. I am possessed by fever extremes of hot and cold that refuse to be regulated. A river of antibiotics floods my system, killing good bacteria along with the bad. The boundaries we draw stop nothing. My tissue swells with poison and turns black as it dies. This is the nature of necrotizing fasciitis, also known as the flesh-eating bacteria.

Saving my life requires medical experts in infectious diseases, gynecology, plastic surgery and other specialties.

The only way to stop the infection is to cut it out. Across the entire width of my abdomen, down through my pelvic region and part of my left leg, metal tools carve into my skin, through the subcutaneous tissue, removing everything above the fascia, and forever changing the landscape of my body.

Two decades later, in 2011, I was doing well at work, I had a loving spouse, and was living a comfortable life. Yet I had the nagging sense of participating in a sham. My skin felt too tight. I was agitated and uncomfortable. I wanted to break out of what I was in and enter into… I didn't know what. I felt there must be something else, something more.

I began to have dreams. Night after night they came. Some showed me violence, loss and death. Some included images and iconography that were foreign to me, but which I later learned are significant in other cultures. Some dreams presaged events or conversations, teaching me that time is unbounded in the dream world. Frequently, the dreams involved animals. I researched their geographic origins, their spirit-totem associations and their habitats, trying to understand what they might be trying to tell or teach me. Initially, it seemed that most of the animals that visited my dreams were endangered species. Over time, the dreams made it clear that all animals, including humans, are endangered; again and again, I learned that the primary threat to their survival is our way of living. Through the dreams, animals became my primary source of awakening to the danger facing all life:

A reindeer, her dark hindquarters strewn with white speckle-stars, comes with her little one. I learn that the reindeer, and the cultures in which they are at the center, are in jeopardy.

A doe and her daughter graze in my yard until a lone gunman shoots them just because he can, then leaves them on my doorstep. I am catapulted into grief.

A mule deer teaches me that wildfire and overdevelopment are eradicating her habitat.

A snow leopard appears in the heat of the summer sun, and I learn that climate change and poaching are two of the greatest threats to her survival.

One night in 2012, I held the question before sleep: "Where is the rest of me?" I hoped I might glean insight into the source and nature of my longing, and the persistent sense that something was missing—something important, and maybe essential. In response, an epic dream-journey returned me to several life events during which I had left my body. The dream, which I titled "Re-membering," allowed me to finally feel and integrate those moments of dissociation.

A bear comes and gives me explicit instructions for reclaiming lost parts of myself: "Go back to the woods. Go back to the water."

I return to the scene of a frightening and painful betrayal in the beloved woods of my childhood home. Pinned beneath a trusted friend like small prey, my face in a bed of dead leaves, I feel confusion and terror, the threat of violence, as he mockingly thrusts himself against me from behind. I hear his dry laughter when he finally releases me, as though it was all a game. I want to flee from him, from our friend who witnessed and also laughed, and the flood of embarrassment, hurt and fury that fills me. Then, separate from the memory, I hear, "I wandered out of the woods and got lost."

Next, I am in the hospital pool after the surgery for necrotizing fasciitis, where each day, my wounds are debrided in bleach water. I lie on my back as the nurse moves me around the pool, doing her work of cleaning the surgical site. My flimsy hospital gown floats up around my chest, exposing the rest of me. Looking up, I am mortified to see that through a window above the pool, I am being observed by a large group of residents. They see the most private parts of my ruined body, the body that even before the surgery was a perpetual source of disappointment and shame. I feel the violation of their unannounced invasion of my privacy, their detached, clinical regard for their "subject," the nurse's failure to cover me or turn me away from their gaze. Then I am alone in my hospital room. I slide out of bed and position myself in front of the mirror. Defying the doctors' recommendations, I undo my bandages, and for the first time since the emergency surgery some two months earlier, look at my body, willing my eyes not to leave the mirror. It is not my body, not the one I remember. Spanning the entire width of me is a deep, raw, gaping space where the smooth white skin of my belly used to be. Gone is the line of peach fuzz that led from my belly button down to the curly dark triangle of womanhood—and that, too, is gone—all of it replaced by the glistening red hole where the center of me used to be. My stomach roils as my grounding gives way to an inky darkness of shock, horror, fear and shame. Swells of dizziness accompany tingling at the top of my head as I try to comprehend that the wreckage in the mirror is me.

The final image of the dream was one I did not recognize, and could not reconcile: *A newborn is submerged in a pot of boiling water, then pulled out and held up with forceps. It is beet red, arms and legs clutched tight, its entire body trembling, its face contorted in a shattering scream.*

I woke terrified and choking on tears. Afraid of whatever in me could have conjured this last image, I told myself it might be a depraved metaphor for something I couldn't quite decipher, perhaps related to the bleach water in which my wounds were debrided.

One year later, I was reading Eve Ensler's memoir, *In the Body of the World*. There on the page, in even more gruesome and impossible detail than in my dream, was the infant. A woman in Bukavu, Democratic Republic of Congo, was telling her story to Eve, reliving it. Raping soldiers cut the baby out of her best friend's belly, tossed it in the air and then into boiling water. The soldiers held a gun to the mother, forcing her to eat her baby or be shot. Ensler writes, "It was here that I walked out of the world…. Here where I decided to exit, to go, to check out. Here in the suspended somnolent zone where I told my body it was time to die. It was not a foreboding, as I thought. It was in fact a longing, a decision I made…I saw how death had been my only comfort. I had quietly and secretly been moving toward it."

Not long before reading this, I had a dream in which elephants self-selected to be culled: *Take me. Take me.*

I knew something about making the decision to check out of the world, had lived my own version of "Take me". Before contracting the flesh-eating sickness, I was on a path to starve or drink myself to death, or both. Starvation took me out of my body, away from its persistent needs, its softness and vulnerabilities, away from its intrinsic and dangerous proclivities for "sinful" thoughts and behaviors. Control became my religion, and my body was my offering. Life lost all color and nuance. I began to see the world, to live it, as a series of extremes: good or bad, yes or no, all or nothing. I measured my worth by the numbers on the scale. Achieving "success" as an anorexic (and later, bulimic) became a solitary endeavor, one in which I was at the center of everything: how I looked, how much I weighed, what I would eat or not eat, how I felt, who or what might be an obstacle to getting what I wanted or needed. There was little room for anyone or anything else. My body became an empty, arid landscape—all hard surfaces, straight lines and sharp angles. There was no such thing as going too far or getting too thin. The sensitive, artistic, intuitive, and compassionate girl I once was got smaller and smaller. I was going to make her disappear.

Drinking, on the other hand, took me out of my head: a reprieve from the logic, discipline and control that dominated my daytime behavior. As the alcohol flowed, it carried me along, loose and free, from initial buzz to blissful oblivion, where I could feel nothing. When I drank, the introverted, prudish anorexic became something of a "wild girl"—I laughed too loud, danced with abandon, spoke with confidence, tested my sexuality. But, just as there was no "too thin," there was also no "too drunk." More was always better, and I overindulged—in alcohol, food, spending, and sometimes risky and irresponsible behavior. Most days, I spent many hours hiding in some bathroom, sick from the last night's drink, or the box of laxatives I had eaten before bed, or a morning binge. The potentially rock-bottom moments—stealing from a roommate, sexual assault during a blackout, repeatedly soaking the bed with my own urine—failed to move me to change.

What the starving, purging and drinking had in common was to sever me from my heart, from the messiness of feelings. It was this I craved most of all.

Having finally depleted my immune system to such a degree that I had no defenses, my body succumbed to a shock-and-awe attack from Streptococcus A, the bacteria that caused the necrotizing fasciitis, and put my slow march toward eventual suicide on the fast track. That I survived is a mystery and a miracle.

Shortly following my release from the hospital, after the surgery that saved my life, I resumed a cycle of dieting, binging, and purging. And drinking. Having come so close to death, my body radically and irrevocably changed, one might assume that I woke up, took my great good fortune to heart, and made different choices. The truth is, I did not. I continued to struggle with disordered eating for another nine years. It was another eighteen years before I got sober. I never mourned what the illness had taken from me, never celebrated or gave thanks for my survival. I got on with it, pushed forward. I moved through the days functionally enough to acquire some trappings of "success", and spent my nights in search of "the flat line" – a quiet state of numbness, a placebo for inner peace. Shutting down was reflexive, like a series of steel doors slamming shut from the pit of my stomach to the top of my throat and across my chest: *Access Denied*. Vulnerability, needing others—these were the hallmarks of the weak and undisciplined and were to be avoided at all costs.

Now, nearly twenty-five years after surviving necrotizing fasciitis, and in recovery for the disordered eating and drinking that made my body an ideal host for the infection, I am beginning to understand that my illnesses were a microcosm of what is happening in the dominant culture and on the planet. Dreams have come to weave a story of connection and disconnection that has helped me begin to understand the nature of our world, though it has taken me years to piece it together.

The "Re-membering" dream tells me: "I wandered out of the woods and got lost." In the moment of my friend's betrayal, my body and the woods had become unsafe, and I fled them. In doing so, I quite literally became a lost soul, untethered and disconnected from my body and the earth's.

The dream of the elephants who self-selected to be culled helps me to understand the anguish of other species that are being asked to witness and bear the unbearable: the slaughter of their families, communities, and habitat at the hands of humans. If humans can decide that the only comfort or hope of relief is death, could not animals decide the same? How do we live with this possibility?

Through the lens of these dreams, I began to see that the cultural mindset that causes men to systematically destroy women and children in the Congo is the same mindset that causes them to brutally decimate communities of elephants for their ivory. It imagines, enacts and justifies horrors such as the genocide of Native Americans, the African slave trade, the Holocaust, Hiroshima, the global war on women, and ecocide. It is this same mindset that caused this woman to turn against her own body, to view it as an enemy to be dominated and controlled, and to ignore the grave risks and dire outcomes of her life style.

In my understanding, this mindset arises out of our profound disconnection from the earth, the great body from which we all emerge, and by which we are sustained. Life itself has become the "collateral damage" of our rapacious hunger for more power, control, property, resources, and wealth. We take with a sense of entitlement and impunity.

It is 2015, and Her body is burning... Wildfire... advances across ...boundaries in hours.... Extremes of hot and cold refuse to be regulated... A river floods... killing the good ... along with the bad. The boundaries we draw stop nothing...

When I do as the dream tells me to do, and return to the woods and the water, I am right-sized, no longer at the center or the apex of things, as our culture would have us believe, but one minuscule part of a living, breathing, interconnected organism that is constantly communicating. In the presence of brook or ocean, under a canopy of birch and conifer, I begin to remember what I come from, what I am made of and belong to, what I must attend to, and what is at stake.

Sharon Rodgers Simone
Fired Anew

Healing is a river—a live current, a cascade like the one I loved up in North Cheyenne Canyon growing up—a glissade down a mountain, a drill hole directed straight at one's tectonic plates. If you arc fortunate, healing overtakes you, works your stubborn muscles of mind into clay then fires you anew.

I am fortunate. Healing has overtaken me. Two years ago, I was diagnosed with Stage IV metastatic pancreatic cancer and given two months to live by a surgeon who unexpectedly encountered my belly full of metastases while operating to resolve a bowel obstruction following a pancreatic resection five weeks earlier.

Today, I am well with no evidence of disease supported by nine negative CT scans and normal tumor markers over the past two and a half years. I owe my well-being to the Village Sanctuary as I have come to understand it these years, although the journey began years earlier.

Called to attention

When I was a young girl still going to church, especially on Good Fridays, I loved the ritual chanting we did of the *Litany of the Saints*. We intoned the names of all the saints and angels, sitting then kneeling, sitting then kneeling, until our backs and knees ached: *Sancta Maria, Ora pro nobis; Sancta Maria Magdalena, Ora pro nobis; Sancta Agatha, Ora pro nobis; Sancta Lucia, Ora pro nobis; Sancta Cæcilia, Ora pro nobis.* We acknowledged mostly the male saints and Church fathers, and a rare female saint, never the rest of Creation. I did not know the language of the Earth or her creatures though these had seeded themselves in me awaiting a time when I carried a mind that could recognize their communications.

Today, daily, I intone the names of particular rivers in the same way I called out the names of the saints—*Colorado, Arkansas, Rio Grande, Gunnison, Platte, Kern, Missouri, Mississippi*—praying to know the depth of the language they left in me, the imprint of their bends still moving me along. At age 74, it is not too late to confess my love of and dependence upon the rivers, upon specific mountains and streams, and on Raven. I believe the rest of my life depends on being in relationship with these beings—on my being open to their call to attention when it arrives.

When Raven cries out overhead, as one is doing at this very moment, does it mean anything more than Raven carrying out its life as I am carrying out mine? As if answering Raven's call, I begin to write about what I just experienced *as a call to attention*. This attention. *This* writing about relationship with Raven, or wind, or trees or snake or moonlight in which they *speak* to me and I respond in some unexpected and spontaneous way, or they reorient and reorganize me down to my tectonic plates.

Every day since I was diagnosed with pancreatic cancer, I have prayed to *recognize* and *heed* signs, warnings, omens and magic that arrive separate from thoughts and plans or even worries about my state of health or the state of the world. No one told me that this practice or habit would help me navigate the catastrophic undoing and reorganizing underway. I just began, in the quiet that descends upon one living such an illness, to notice, say Raven crying out, or the trees turning from green to golden to barren as the seasons passed outside my window. And in this noticing, a form of communication unfolded, an entire language, not rooted in words, but in sounds and moonlight, the hoot of an owl at 2 a.m., when I woke with a nightmare I could not shake, or in the slight movement of leaves in an easy breeze that educated me, comforted me, loosened the heavy cloak of *civilized* ways of knowing and living from my shoulders. Until I woke up well—more well than before I was diagnosed with cancer.

The weight of knowing

Village is not a metaphor or concept, but a concrete reality to which I gave my life when the unmistakable call arrived, as it did for me in 2011 outside the Uffizi museum in Florence, Italy. I was in the birthplace of the Renaissance.

Standing in the Village Square one afternoon I broke down in tears. I felt the weight of Western civilization on my shoulders—a weight in stone and stained glass, art, cobblestone streets, papal crypts and cathedrals. It was an unbearable weight to which I had dedicated five decades of my life—this *one way of knowing, this Western, Imperial way*. I knew there were other ways, older, indigenous ways of knowing; I had been exploring these since I had a disturbing dream in 2005 that caused me to acknowledge and confront the Imperialist within me. I made a vow then in that Village Square, to finally leave this Western way of knowing and change my life.

Mountain lion enters the field

In April 2012, upon returning from Italy to Topanga, California, I sat out all night beneath an old Acacia tree on the land dedicated as a Village Sanctuary. Others were on this land in various places, all of us offering ourselves to the spirits and non-human beings of this land. We fasted and were up without shelter all night.

Near 11 p.m., under a white moon that hung high in the sky, a Mountain Lion ambled up a small hill toward the citrus orchard, maybe fifty yards from me. I froze. I had ignored what I understood to be an internal directive—that I stay beneath the canopy of the Guardian Tree. I gambled with the spirits, rationalizing I would be just three feet outside the canopy where I had promised to stay—that this little distance would not make a difference. *I wanted a better view of the beauty before me—the moonlit, magical meadow* (my Western, imperial mind at work). And at the moment I settled myself outside the canopy, there stood the Mountain Lion. He turned his head 90 degrees and stared right at me for perhaps fifteen seconds. Though I wanted to bolt to the car nearby, I knew he had to be faster than I was and I had made a commitment to stay out and offer myself in dedication. So I cautiously slunk back beneath the canopy of the Guardian Tree, chastened and terrified, where I remained, awake, for the rest of the night.

Sacrifice an old identity

In April 2016, at a gathering in Connecticut, thirty women were sharing dreams, visions, personal stories, fears and sorrows related to the dire state of the world, the endangered planet and its non-human beings in particular. We were asked to consider this question: "What current impediment arising out of Western mind is keeping you from meeting your life's calling?" We were given time to reflect, walk in the woods, listen. My response was to do a divination using the I Ching[1]. The hexagram I received, #59 Dispersing, offered this central message: "Clear away what is blocking clarity...sacrifice an old identity." Immediately, I knew what old identity I must sacrifice. On receiving the instruction, I responded: "Yes, I will sacrifice it. But I don't know how in the world this will unfold."

Three days after the gathering, I was with my friends Karen and Lawrie at a bed-and-breakfast. I was up all night, very ill and in pain. Rather than rush to the hospital, which I would have done in the past, I worked alone with myself all night trying to release the old identity that worshiped and relied primarily upon Western medicine. In the morning, it was obvious to my friends I was quite ill. After a few hours, I asked them to take a walk in the snow and to leave me alone with the fire and my spirits. This vision unfolded:

I am in the anteroom of a cave up in the high desert—a place very familiar to me. An old, old woman spirit lives here. I met her in 1995 when I was despairing in the aftermath of dealing with a violent childhood very publicly.[2] She brought profound healing over many months and has stayed nearby all this time. I consider her a teacher. She is sitting on the earth before her fire—a pit in the floor of the cave—doing what she always does—throwing stones and bones divining for where the rents in the world are so she can mend them. I can see her from an anteroom where I am lying on a slab of stone. I am in a hospital gown and an IV is in my right arm. A Mountain Lion stands next to the earth bed I am lying on.

The cave is lit as if a fire is burning in this anteroom though I do not see it—the walls are illuminated warmly. I know those gathered here in the cave are from the Village. They are divining and discussing what they are reading from their stones and bones.

The door to the cottage opens with my friends' return and I hear a parting message out of the fire: "This will take some time." I understand I am to be hospitalized and will have IV treatment. Yet the place of healing will be this cave where I am lying and where a Village is gathered doing healing activities they know and live.

We left for the hospital, where I was diagnosed with pancreatic cancer.

Snake. Bear. Drum. The Way opens

It was all so sudden and so dire. I didn't know the Way. Family had flown in from around the country to be with me for the surgery. Karen Mutter, my physician friend, returned to Connecticut from Florida to stay with me during the hospitalization.

A woman from the gathering in Connecticut dreamed of snakes coming up around a fire pit in the woods where I had just been before falling ill; the snakes in the dream were asking, "Do you trust us?" She believed the dream was a message. At the very moment this dream and its message were being conveyed over the phone from Connecticut, a six-foot-long rattlesnake approached Deena's office door in Topanga and nudged at the doorknob as if seeking entry to her home. A video of this snake's appearance was taken and sent to me.

A week prior to surgery to remove most of my pancreas along with my spleen, I had had a consultation with a homeopathic practitioner. On the same day as the snake dream and the rattlesnake's appearance at my mentor's door, and without knowledge of these events, the practitioner emailed me to say, "I have meditated on your behalf asking what homeopathic remedy out of the 3900 possible remedies is needed at this moment—it is rattlesnake venom."

The night before the surgery, Terri Kamihcetwayaksihk Opiway[3] offered to drum and sing Dakota sweat lodge songs of protection for me over the telephone. She sang traditional native songs sung in the Dakota Inipi ceremony—a sacred activity undertaken for the purpose of cleansing and clearing mind, body and spirit.

Terri told me that just before she entered her sacred space to sing and drum, a large bear showed up near her door. It was a good sign, she said.

The morning following Terri's offering, I was taken into the pre-op area, where I was given a paper hospital gown with a large animal paw print resting over my heart. Beneath it were these words: "Bear Paw."

Microbe hunter girl

I had spent a lifetime pursuing microbes in one way or another—as a microbiologist, science teacher, researcher, in short, a worshiper of Western medicine and its ways of knowing and acting. This old identity took shape when I was ten years old as I read and re-read Paul de Kruif's *The Microbe Hunters* about the greats such as Pasteur van Leeuwenhoek, Lister studying the immensely small "assassins." After this immersion I asked for a microscope for Christmas.

I learned to think, as the microbe hunters did, that killing the microbes and eradicating disease in this way was a *healing* activity.

Throughout childhood and across my lifespan I pursued cures for countless respiratory and gastrointestinal ills, all of them involving antibiotics. A fair estimate of how many of these antibiotics I used would be in the hundreds of rounds over five decades. I don't know how many billions of microbes I eradicated *because I could* and because I saw them as the source or root of my illnesses, as did many of the physicians who treated me over the years. It is not surprising that I am now allergic or resistant to most frontline and even second-line antibiotics. It has taken me a long time to come to a change of mind regarding my belief in pursuing microbes in the way the microbe hunters did. Pursuing master's and doctoral work in my forties, focusing on uses, misuses and abuses of power in educational systems, still did not awaken in me any wariness concerning the particular orientation of mind lauded in *The Microbe Hunters*. I now understand that capricious, relentless and unexamined assault on microbes does not constitute a healing activity and comes with great cost to life itself—mine, the microbes' and the planet's.

Mountains and mind

As a kid growing up in Colorado, I loved the mountains. Pikes Peak most of the time was snow-covered, often blazing in the pinks and golds and fiery reds of sunrise and sunset and frequently shrouded in ominous blue-black thunderheads. This mountain held me, kept me, comforted me when the darkened rooms of childhood threatened to swallow me into an unending cycle of child abuse and domestic violence at the hands of an FBI agent father. It was, for me, a compass, a companion, a sentinel—one far more trustworthy than the human beings charged with raising or educating me.

Years later, on a return visit home to Colorado, I saw long, red gouges dug deep into the mountainside beneath Pikes Peak and across the foothills of the Front Range—evidence of strip-mining. It was like seeing the scars of rape in plain view. It was a first *awakening* for me to the ravages of exploitation, for human purposes. I did not know then, would not know for decades, that I, too, carried within me a mostly unexamined allegiance to entitlement and domination.

The return: Mountain lion and microbes

At that Village gathering in the woods in Connecticut in April of 2016 where I made the commitment to "sacrifice an old identity," the group entered a quiet state of visioning together, listening and looking for guidance separate from our own minds. I closed my eyes and listened to the drum. Immediately, the Mountain Lion I saw that night in 2012 picked me up at The Guardian Tree. He took me down a path past the oak grove into Topanga State Park. I was taken through an "aperture," some sort of lens, and was shown a phosphorescent green landscape with a few tumbling little creatures I recognized as microbes. Further down the path I encountered a vast, phosphorescent blue-purple landscape with the same situation—devastation. Many dead microbes littered these landscapes and a rare living one remained tumbling with life. I was *stunned* and deeply disturbed. The microbes were revealing themselves, for which I was humbled and grateful, and their state of affairs was one of almost total annihilation. Where were these landscapes? In me? On the planet somewhere? Both?

I had tried to make peace with the microbes that were wreaking havoc in my gut—so many episodes of bowel infections from microbial imbalances, so many rounds of antibiotics, so many hospitalizations and finally a surgery to remove a large section of my colon. I tried to approach the microbes in vision from 2010 through 2015, but was never given an audience with them. I understood that perhaps being barred was a lifelong consequence of the havoc and destruction I had participated in personally and professionally.

When I received the cancer diagnosis a couple of days following the phosphorescent blue-purple vision, I immediately concluded that the first devastated landscape I saw was in me, in my pancreas. A year later, after treatment for the cancer, I discovered that there is a direct relationship between a disrupted gut microbiome — which years of antibiotics can certainly cause—and pancreatic cancer. [4] This intuitive understanding was one of those communications (signs, omens, warnings, magic) that I was learning to take seriously and live by.

All My Relations

I have come to understand that there is no separation between me and other beings, the earth, the cosmos, that we are all interdependent. I am indebted to indigenous peoples for this understanding, many of whose worldview is rooted in "All My Relations". In June of 2017, six months following my last chemo treatment, I was in at the Greenwich Hospital Infusion Center receiving an I.V. infusion of magnesium as my kidneys had been injured by one of the chemotherapy agents. A Healing Touch volunteer approached me to ask if I would like Healing Touch. I happily accepted. She put her hands beneath my left rib cage, right where my pancreas and tumor had been. As her hands alighted there, the words *Great Barrier Reef* dropped into my consciousness and then: *I wonder if the Great Barrier Reef is in trouble?* I did not know anything about the Great Barrier Reef—only the term was familiar. When the session was over I learned the healer did not know my diagnosis—her intuition had guided her hands. When I got home and researched Great Barrier Reef (GBR), I learned it is the largest living being on the planet and is located off the coast of Australia. It is 1400 miles in length, can be seen from outer space, and *yes, it is in deep trouble* due to rising ocean temperatures caused by global warming and increasing levels of CO_2 from the burning of fossil fuels that creates ocean acidification.

In 2016, the year I was diagnosed with pancreatic cancer, the GBR suffered a massive bleaching event in which thirty percent of the corals died. A second bleaching event took place in 2017 and wiped out another twenty percent of the corals. Bleaching is directly related to microorganisms the corals are symbiotically dependent upon for their nourishment and protection. Acidification and higher ocean temperature alter the microbes. The corals read the chemical changes as dangerous to their life and they eject the microbes. As a result, the corals bleach and die. Because marine animals such as turtles, whales, dolphins, sharks, many fish species, some birds, and others spend up to thirty percent of their life cycle on the GBR, the implications of the fifty percent loss of coral in just two years for them and for ecosystem balance is catastrophic.

I saw the documentary *Chasing Coral* a few weeks after the Healing Touch experience. I almost lost my mind when the exact blue-purple devastated landscape of my vision from two years earlier appeared on the screen. The narrator explained: "This beautiful color is not natural to the corals. It only appears when the corals are in their death throes." It was as if they were saying: "Look at us. We are dying."

The bedrock of Village

When I read the literature on the dismal survival rate for pancreatic cancer when first diagnosed, I made an important decision to depart from my reliance on science. I chose to *not know* what the outcome would be for me. It was predicted by a surgeon that I would die in two months. I did not. I have survived because of the Village and Village Medicine. Many offered this Medicine—so many beings, spirits and visions, and people and land, and elementals.

It is August 2018. Healing has been *working my stubborn muscles of mind into clay* for a very long time. What has the mind got to do with healing—or more accurately, *my healing*? And what am I healing from and toward? I am healing from pancreatic cancer, but what else? What else is there beneath or embedded within this illness that took me down to my tectonic plates? For what life was I healed to live?

My experience with illness has shown me that it was necessary to reach bedrock in order to heal. What do I now understand the bedrock of my healing to be? My understanding is still evolving but I do know that it has a great deal to do with returning to Village ways of knowing, living and acting—old, old ways.

Village is a consciousness, a call, and a sentinel in an increasingly violent and dissembling world. It is a place, an orientation and Way to live. This Village requires a new mind, one that works to restore right relationship with the natural world. Village itself may be being restored in the process.

It is predicted that the Great Barrier Reef will succumb completely and soon to the impact of climate change, but perhaps it will not. We don't *know* the outcome and if we foreclose possibilities, as I might have done with my diagnosis/prognosis, we may also foreclose the potential for—and the enablement of—miracles and healing.

Healing has meant saying *yes, I will sacrifice a beloved old identity* on behalf of entering Village mind, which is rooted in Village ways. So far, the amends I am making to the microbes consist of saying yes on behalf of their survival and the survival of the Great Barrier Reef. I am listening for what else.

I am riding this river, this live current, this cascade of healing into the life I was born to live. I am being fired anew.

N.B.: This is an abridged version. Please see Dark Matter: Women Witnessing #7 *online for the complete essay.*

[1] Karcher, Stephen. *I Ching: The Symbolic Life*. 2000. Print. *Author's note*: I used Karcher's I Ching for divination as it is faithful to original Chinese texts that reveal that Pairs, not individual hexagrams, form the actual relationships that demonstrate the flow of energy in the Change underway. So, for hexagram #59, the pair would be 59:60. Hexagram 60 reads: "Dispersing and Articulating displays the sacrifice of an old identity that dissolves obstacles between the spirit and human worlds, revealing key moments where we can articulate the river of time into a shape of a new life for all" (p.182).

[2] *Head Waters Productions*. Web. n.d.

[3] "She Carries Many Feathers"

[4] Ertz-Archambault Natalie, Paul Keim and Daniel Von Hoff. "Microbiome and pancreatic cancer: A comprehensive topic review of literature" in *World Journal of Gastroenterology* 23 (10) (2017):1899-1908. Web. n.d.

Verena Stefan
Quitting Chemo

Editor's note (Lise Weil): Verena died November 30, 2017. In the last years of her life, she had been working—in English for the first time—on a book about living with cancer, which she was not able to finish. I was one of her readers in those years and before she died, she gave me her permission to excerpt from the book. "Quitting Chemo" has been culled, edited, and pieced together from the writing in that manuscript.

Dream, December 31, 2016:

On a big city street, I come face to face with an old man, soft white hair on both sides of his face, soft round cheeks, incredibly sweet smile and attitude. He looks me in the eye with a tenderness and benevolence I've never experienced before. We are actually lying face-to-face on our bellies on a sidewalk.

He asks: "What's going on with you? What's at stake?" Waving one hand over me with a friendly smile, as to indicate: this (chickenpox) is not such a big deal after all.

"I don't know," I say," I don't know yet."

He is nodding, seriously: "I see." He wants to get up.

"Yes, I know!" I exclaim with the next breath: "I don't want my body to be intoxicated any longer. I want to stop chemo."

"Oh?" He says, surprised and getting more serious. "I see." I feel that my answer is taking us to a different level and would like to go on talking but he is already walking away, talking into a cell phone on his left ear. I know he is delivering my decision to higher spiritual guides.

In January 2017, I tell my oncologist that I wish to quit chemotherapy. I am relying on the messenger of my dream, feeling backed up by it. However, once inside the hospital, in a small examination room, I feel the pull of the institution. The oncologist is not pleased with my announcement. According to her, the cancer might take over rapidly in my body, especially in the liver.

"I would consider radiation, should there be more brain tumors," I tell her as she washes her hands and dries them with a paper towel. "And I would continue to do the CAT scans and the brain MRIs."

"Why would you want to do the scans if you don't continue with the treatments?" she retorts, turning her whole body abruptly to face me. I am struck dumb. Does she mean she'll refuse to do follow-ups if I don't continue chemotherapy?

"Would you reconsider your decision until we meet for the results of the last scans?" she asks. I nod. I'll think about it. That's as much as I can manage to end this conversation without overreacting.

Oncologists brandish the threat of death without chemotherapy here. Having lived fifty years in Switzerland and Germany before coming to Montreal I was used to complementary medicine, a combination of allopathic, naturopathic and homeopathic approaches. In Montreal I have had to face a rather dismissive attitude toward complementary medicine.

The doctor and I meet again a week later both knowing a decision will be made. My friend Ginette is with me. The oncologist enters the room with her usual friendly smile, stops in front of Ginette, introduces herself and offers a hand shake. I hold my breath. It took her several years before she greeted Lise, the woman at my side who takes notes and asks questions. I can't remember a handshake between them. A murky sensation is creeping up my spine. I can feel the pull: Look, how friendly we are! Be-a-good-girl, do-as-we-say.

The oncologist repeats her concern about possible liver deterioration within the next three months. If that should occur, the liver won't be able to deal with another chemotherapy, and she won't be able to do anything more for me. She wants me to understand the facts fully. I reassure her that I take full responsibility for my decision. That I'd like to take that weight off her shoulders. "You can't," she says. "The weight is there, but that's ok."

For many people cancer has turned into a chronic disease and can be treated with long-term chemotherapy. I have benefitted from it myself. But with the dream message a shift has taken place. A veil is lifting. It is a daring decision I am making. A deep breath moves through me pushing me to stand on my hind legs. Sniffing a fresh breeze. The salty taste of freedom, of setting off towards a new shore- or towards the other shore.

I wish to take my life back into my own hands, my whole life. I am taking back the part that had started to rely on the treatments. They may prolong your life all right but you hand over a big part of your innate vitality. You forget what you know. You let the drug handle it. The drug is a dimmer. It attenuates your life force, your knowledge. It suffocates your own voice. Fills your mind with fog and fatigue (e.g., maybe slack off in your daily Qi Gong practice that renews life force and builds up energy).

Walking away, I can feel the hospital at my back and everything I no longer have to do. When you first enter the cancer clinic for a chemotherapy treatment a huge machine grabs you. You have to follow the machine's programmed orders step by step. Between individual steps you still meet a real human being from time to time. You still have a sheet of paper in your hands that you hand over to the receptionist for the blood test. The receptionists at all the desks are now typically staring at a computer screen with furrowed brows, tense backs, tense shoulders.

After the blood test you have to wave your health insurance card in front of a check-in screen. You have to hold it at the right angle so that a red vertical line on the screen hits its bar code. Your first name and the first three letters of your last one appears on the screen. One of the many dissociating moments of the day. "Hi Verena," you say to the screen. Everybody fiddles with their card to hit the right angle for the machine. Volunteers are ready to help. Like with bank machines, in super markets and airports you have to learn to check yourself in and then "be in the system." After that, you head over to reception and hand the hospital card to a live secretary to be registered for a doctor's appointment or a treatment. Then you take a seat and wait amidst the piercing Ding-Dong from loudspeakers and human voices calling patients into doctors' offices. In terms of noise level it is not that different from a bus terminal. The waiting hall is full. Each and every person waiting there has cancer. Treatment rooms are full, the machines are running, the drips are dripping drip-drip-drip.

There is a poster in some examination rooms that announces: *Your chemo day.* It shows picture by picture how chemotherapy is applied to a smiling female patient by a smiling female nurse. The pictures suggest a friendly procedure and an easy-going treatment. They don't inform you about dizziness, nausea and fatigue, to name some of the milder side effects. Nor the constant lack of energy that sometimes morphs into listlessness. There is no such thing as your chemo day. The possessive pronoun doesn't apply. A chemo day is not an achievement or a cherished belonging. It is neither inspiring nor nourishing.

The nurses are busy administering different drugs for different patients, putting on and taking off light blue disposable coats, blue rubber gloves, a mouth protection or even a transparent visor that makes them look like a blend of a police officer and a medieval knight. They put on the visor to protect their face in case a plastic bag breaks and toxic medication splashes at them. "It happens rarely," one of the nurses explains, "the technology has been improved. But nonetheless we are exposed to the chemicals eight hours a day." They have to check the computerized machine that times the different drips. From time to time the machines are replaced by new models. Pharmaceutical computer technicians, a female technician in high heels and a tight black evening dress and a male one in a banker's outfit give instructions and supervise the correct procedure. The nurses have to learn the programming of the intricate machine. They are responsible for setting the exact timing and dosage for the medication. For weeks, their gaze stays fixed on the slim screens when they approach my seat. To serve the machine properly is paramount. Once the procedure has turned into routine, their extreme stress level lowers. They are again able to switch their gaze between machine and patient.

The small plastic bags with the toxic drug and the saline solution dangle from the IV stand. Just looking at them makes me nauseous. The fact that I'll deliver part of the toxins that drip into my blood stream into the water table with my urine and will add to the pollution of the planet is utterly depressing. In bad moments, it makes me feel like a collaborator with Big Pharma. Consider non-recyclable waste alone: plastic bags, tubes, syringes, gloves, coats and visors. From there it is only one step to despair about the planet, its cynical destruction by corporate companies. Chemo waste is burnt at a very high temperature, I hear.

Where? How? How are the emissions dealt with? Is the heat generated used for a good purpose?

I haven't learned how the toxic liquid of chemotherapy running through my veins actually works on my cells, except that it is meant to kill any fast-growing cancer cells in my organs or tissues. The information I get, first from the hospital pharmacist, then from the internet, speaks of possible side effects only. It feels like murky offshore business.

What about the depths and hollows and cavities of my body, the veins sunken or vanished, the mucus membrane, the intestinal lining, my muscle tone? The streaked and brittle nails, the constantly broken skin on my fingertips– all that I can see with my eye. It is the invisible damage that worries me more. For each side effect there is a pill, which might have another side effect for which there is another pill to pop into a patient's mouth. "I feel nauseous when I approach the hospital," I once told the oncologist. She nodded smiling: "We have a pill for that!"

On a chemo day, a chemo burn may occur. I feel a strong sensation of burning as soon as the new drip with Navelbine starts. The nurse immediately increases the flow of the saline solution. Later the area around the IV needle starts hurting and gets numb; the nurse wraps my forearm in a warm, moist towel. Navelbine takes only ten minutes to run; the flushing with saline solution will require another twenty to thirty minutes. The last minute of vein-flushing I sense a huge pressure and congestion all around my chest as well as muscular pain. There is congestion in the head, too, and a chill again.

Now without the monthly trips to the hospital a spell is lifting. In the space of freed energy, the connections to my body's memories grow stronger. As I did as a small child I am pulling my hand away from an unwanted grip and guide. I am repeating one of my earliest gestures, an early manifestation of my desire for autonomy and freedom: I want to walk by myself.

I can still feel the pull of the institution at my back. I am overwhelmed by my decision, and shaky. Can I do without their suggestions, their promised safety nets? What will become of me?

With time, out of the growing distance of time and space, something new is being born. It is tender like gossamer wings. Hopefully it will become as strong as a spider's web. For the time being I feel its fragility.

I'll never again have to lie in a comfortable reclining chair looking up at the plastic bags dangling from the drip stand to my right and wait until the toxic substance has entered my body, drop by drop, through the tube plugged into the port in my chest. Never again will I have to feel the venom seep into my blood and into layers of body tissue.(I often wondered why the nurse would squeeze the bag repeatedly at the end of a 30-minute treatment with Herceptin, pressing out every single drop. "One of these bags is worth $2000," she informed me. A sick feeling. How much profit is the pharmaceutical industry making.) Life inside the body turned into wasteland, greyish and chemically alien. A pasty, lifeless skin and the smell of burnt rubber. I want my life back in full colour and with all my cells sparkling.

No more chemo-related questions to answer: Tingling, numbness in fingertips and toes? Mouth sores? Any rash? Hives? Dizziness? Shortness of breath?

There are no nature-related metaphors in chemotherapy.

The pattern of illness and healing is reversed. The body's self-healing capacity and self-regulation are silenced. White blood cells that normally deal with a cold or an infection are hit by chemo toxins, too. The white blood cell count drops. The body becomes more vulnerable if not defenseless.

I am still walking but don't know whether I want to continue being alive or not. What exactly is my life? What does strength mean? And what am I meant to do here for the time being? Love for my life-companion of twenty years is growing daily. Gratitude for the good life we share is paired with the distress of leaving her behind. The love relationship will come to an end because my life will come to an end in the foreseeable future. When I move closer to that thought my heart clenches. I turn my head abruptly around as if I could look away from it. We don't talk of this often. What can be said other than: I don't want to lose you, I don't want to leave you?

It has become difficult again to believe that I could bring cancer, or rather the many cancers in my body, to a halt. There are moments and hours and whole days where I can't feel the connection to a self that would orchestrate self-healing. Cancer is a big story, located in a barely deciphered territory. It seems too big for a singular I. With cancer, I am thrown into a void.

Breast cancer can lead to lung, bone, liver or brain metastases. The mapped territory is laid out on the other side of the table where the oncologist sits or the radio-oncologist or whomever you will meet along the road. Maps or a map do exist in their mind. You don't know of a map. Cancer exposes the patient to an unmapped territory.

You stumble along.

There are healings

In body awareness practices, I explore listening to the body and seeing it in my mind's eye. I compare temperature and weight of both sides of the body, and colours. I scan volumes and spaciousness of organs, bones, limbs, and follow the breath everywhere from the many spaces in the head along the rib cage, the lungs, the sternum and the whole spine, the pelvis and down to every single toe. Doing so I am breathing life into my body, I am connecting with it. I am having a conversation much like a conversation with flowers and trees. Like on an outdoor walk, I am going for a walk inside the body, moving from place to place and over time getting to know them better and more deeply.

Life wants to be attended to with never-ending presence like the incessant current that streams through a snake's body. Life requires being present with every beat of my heart, fully.

Healing doesn't primarily mean to get rid of something. Sometimes it means sorting out and mending. Sometimes it means transition and evolution, in short, the potential any crisis may offer.

Cancer cells are darker than healthy cells and need to be suffused with light. Mistletoe injections insert light into body cells. Visualising light I can move it through my body. Cells light up through creative activity, colour, drawing, moving and music....

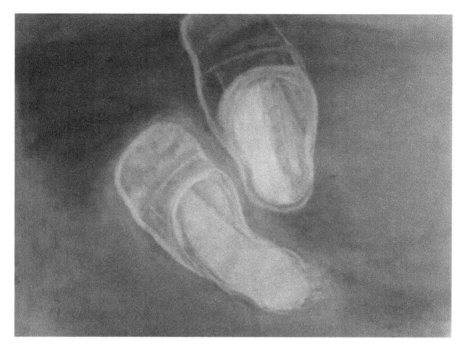

The Slippers: A Self-Portrait, exercise in charcoal and contè by V. Stefan.

A friend suggests organising three to four long-distance treatments per week by different people from our healing group. During a treatment my body temperature typically builds up from my navel where it is said that there is an ocean of Qi.

The heat continues to increase steadily and spread through my whole torso. Both arms and hands tingle symmetrically. The tension in the neck, the fog and pressure in the head lift and vanish and with it the pollution from the hospital, the machines and the city noise, too. After forty minutes I feel completely restored. This is how it would feel to be connected to universal healing energy. It becomes almost palpable. Practicing Qi Gong on a regular basis I might become capable myself of producing the same heat.

Sometimes the healing energy stays with me the whole day. The greyness and the numbing chemical substance start to lift. There is color, and once in a while, an image. I clearly see my bare left foot, its toes covered with rich dark fresh garden soil, dangling from my bed. My faculty of visualization re-emerges after having been muted.

During a shiatsu treatment I saw a huge tree, one of those giant trees that stand their ground bow-legged so that a car could pass through underneath. The image of the giant tree unfolded in the middle of my chest, where, a year ago, the surgeon had filled the caved-in vertebra with medicinal cement. In the middle of the tree trunk a concavity opened and in it sat a dark wooden goddess. The wood had blackened with age or with fire. She reminded me of Kali or of a Black Madonna.

When I told the therapist afterwards, he said no wonder you were growling like a grizzly bear when I worked that area. Release ferocity. Release radical healing power...

"Do you have to be productive rather than just be?" was one of the questions the psychologist asked me when I talked again about my fear of becoming marginal and useless. I have been living with cancer for more than twelve years. During that time, I wrote and published three books in Switzerland and Germany. I benefit from a health care system that granted me all the necessary tests, surgeries and treatments for little to no financial contribution on my part. I definitely want to be productive or at least useful. Fact is, I am moving further and further away from it.

"Do you rest enough?" is the question every homeopath, astrologer, naturopath, massage therapist and acupuncturist has asked me throughout my life. Tilting their head and casting a scrutinizing look at me. For the longest time I did not understand their question. Sure I rested enough. Weekends I slept in. I napped after love-making.

Sometimes I even held a siesta on a Sunday afternoon. Year after year I took long holidays. I went traveling, once or twice for months. I kept a dream journal, I spent hours hovering over tarot cards. For many years I did yoga and belly dance.

Why then, after the first shock and tears, was my emotional reaction to the cancer diagnosis in 2002 a deep relief and the sigh: *I don't have to do anything anymore.*

Not to meet expectations anymore. No need to present anything, to perform something because performance has become a new currency, a tyrant. Not earn my living any longer teaching creative writing and not

getting enough students. Not to have to prove to a jury that I am worth
the grant for a next book. Not to prove anything at all anymore. Not to
wriggle along in a parallel life to institutions that demand degrees and
CVs. Not to be part of a system that wants you to compete, to be better,
stronger, more important than somebody else.

My deep relief after the first cancer diagnosis was buried again by me
picking up my busy life of being somebody in the world. Four years
later, with the first recurrence, I experienced the exact same emotion.
Much like before a flight, a birth, a death, everything was suspended.
Nothing else to do. *Arrêt sur image.* Again, I "forgot," again was haunted
by: I haven't done enough, written enough. Only from 2012 on, with
the first bone metastasis, did a shift begin to take place.

The coarse voice

Somebody is dying. The person who can't go on as usual. The person
who was coping all the time for years, decades. Coping puts stress on
every single cell in the body: I am able, I am fit, I'll rise to any given
occasion: as a feminist, a lesbian, a writer, an immigrant and now as
a person with cancer: I'll overcome the odds, I'll adapt to what is not
familiar.

Lively conversations with more than one person have become too
demanding. I look around the table where friends eat and drink and
talk and laugh and move their arms and heads in whichever ways. I am
acutely aware of how much is going on from my neck up being attentive
and engaging in a conversation. Just paying attention and keeping the
neck for a while in the same listening position creates a strain. How
rapidly eyes and ears switch between faces! I never noticed before how
each of these minute movements strains my neck muscles. Everything
happens too quickly, friends talk too rapidly, too nervously; voices and
ideas and associations whirl in every direction and I get dizzy.

I take liberties. I get up from the table and stretch out on the sofa. In
deep relief, I hear the low rumbling of a voice on the horizon that wants
to be heard. It is approaching from the near future. Although still faint
I can tell it is coarse, rough-hewn, without a refined syntax. Like a child
that grew up in the woods and all of a sudden encounters civilization.

The voice is raw, knowing, radical.

In 2015 I temporarily lost my voice, and the Coarse Voice made its entrance. The ORL specialist confirmed the family doc's assumption. A metastasis had touched the recurring nerve to the larynx and paralyzed the left vocal cord.

The coarse voice enters this text bellowing. It is blunt, croaking, hot and blurting. It does not always follow grammar and the known order of syntax. It makes its entrance with eruptions. The coarse voice tells me what to do.

Me taking me in my arms. My voice and my spine need me to connect with them, and stay connected.

"What would you do if spine was a sick person?" it asks, growling.

"I'd hug it and touch it," I say, "and give it a massage."

"Yes," says coarse voice, "you do that and you tell your spine that you love spine and you stop treating ailments the way childhood illnesses were approached: What is it again? What does she have now? Then some caretaking and get rid of it. You stop doing that now; you switch to love and love your bones and strange voice and touch them." Hot gets in every cell, whole body gets hot and big, heat evaporating from soles of my feet.

"I love you deeply," I say to me, "you just wonderful, your life meanwhile vulnerable like nature, attacked by cancer and polluted by chemical treatments. We fight to protect environment, but why say environment? Wrong thinking to think we in the middle and something around us. That something is nature. Why not say protect nature, she in big danger, somebody been stabbing her for so long, she already in emergency room and still somebody stabbing her. She our mother, she center stage. She life. "I am my caretaker now," I say to life, "I can tell what you need."

....What is body? We together in a different manner now. What does liver need? I ask. Spine, neck, T12, coccyx, brain, throat with scarring tissue after radiation? What story does my right arm tell me? Numbing like a blood pressure cuff. Does it say: nerve from C7 leading down to small finger or does it say: brain tumor?

Body is a big reliable ally. Says: Take rest. Repose. Take more rest. Enjoy rest. Rest a lot. Enjoy being, carefree being. You don't need to worry about money anymore. Not worry about achievements either. You done a lot. You do have time and you can do what you like as you like.

Editors' note: Verena made a short video, "Just Being", about living with cancer, gardening, love, and thinking about death. It can be found online at Digital Stories Canada.

Carole Harmon
My Body—An Eco-terrain

> I trust myself to nature, she may do as she will with me.
> —Johann von Goethe in *Plant Intelligence and the Imaginal Realm*

I've become a country, my blood a river which carries bacteria, viruses, spirochetes to unsettled territory. The valley where I met these travelers is beautiful but abused: it's littered with old shotgun casings, tin cans, hub caps, fenders of rusted cars. It is protected now, its name a local secret—location hidden, road closed.

I feel an uneasy connection to this land, which was violently wrested from Indigenous people for whom it is their ancestral homeland. My great-great-grandparents were settlers in Washington Territory. In the 1850's they homesteaded north of Mt. Ranier, not so far from here.

It's May 2012 and I've come with a group of twelve women on a Vision Quest. I'm uncomfortable with the idea of a group of white women co-opting an Indigenous spiritual practice, however good our intentions, yet I've come.

On the surrounding hills where we wander, ponderosa pines follow hidden springs which emerge as trickles, occasional pools, and tiny bogs. Skirting the valley sun-parched hills bloom with May flowers, wild among antelope bitter-brush shrubs: purple sage, rock buckwheat, scabland penstemon, prairie star. White mock orange blossoms scent the air.

Water draws wildlife: deer, elk, wild turkey, hawk, owl. Coyote serenades the nights.

Wildlife draws hunters. One good ol' boy on a horse drops by to check us out. Target practice nearby shatters the peace.

In the relative privacy of these days I drop my inhibitions, and my caution. I bathe in the small spring, spend time naked wandering in the woods.

Wildlife draws ticks which are vectors for several exotic diseases. Ticks spring from bushes, drop from trees, cling to tall grass—leap at me. Four ticks in four days bite me. Illness floods my blood, stiffens my hips, weakens my muscles, fogs my brain. I'm not the only one in our group who is bitten by a tick, but I'm the one infected, the vulnerable one, the receptive one. After eight days, when we leave the valley, it's a challenge to carry my pack.

My diseases are named for beautiful places: Rocky Mountain Spotted Fever, Lyme Disease named for Old Lyme Connecticut, Old Lyme named for Lyme Regis in Dorset, setting for Jane Austen's Persuasion and John Fowles' French Lieutenant's Woman. Some tick-borne diseases are too little known to have earned common names and thus are named for their discoverers: Babesia microti for Victor Babes, Hungarian pathologist; Epstein-Barr virus for Anthony Epstein and Yvonne Bar.

Modern western medicine's metaphor for 'combating' disease is war. Disease is seen as the enemy, to be killed or eradicated by whatever means possible. Bacterial and viral diseases are seen as invaders of our body. There is no Geneva Convention in this war.

I see a relationship between unending cycles of global political and religious wars and our human tendency to use war as a metaphor and methodology in (trying to resolve) social and health problems: War on Poverty, War on Drugs, War on Invasive Species, War on Aids, on Cancer. The English language is inundated with the vocabulary of war. "She is fighting for her life." " The battle is almost won." "Let's bring in the big guns." Apparently we humans, collectively, haven't noticed the ineffectiveness of war to solve problems in the long term. England and France engaged in near-continuous warfare for over eight centuries. I'm reminded of spirochete behavior—advance, retreat, advance again when the coast is clear.

Some historians believe the First and Second World Wars were one continuous conflict with an uneasy stalemate between periods of open warfare. Looked at this way both the Ukrainian War and the conflict in Gaza are a resumption of this war after decades of ineffectual attempts to secure lasting peace and resolve disputes over land. The idea of war mutates, multiplies, adjusts, finds new ways to express itself. The principal of deterrence in the modern nuclear era is used as a bulwark against fear of being overtaken by the untrustworthy and threatening other, be it a disease, a country, or a species.

Modern western medicine relies on antibiotics and other pharmacuticals to treat Lyme disease. While there are success stories, especially if the infection is treated early, the cyclical nature of this disease means that such treatments often lead to chronic Lyme disease. Many auto-immune diseases have similar treatment patterns, and similar failures.

Under such a treatment plan, I would have understood my body as a battlefield—with metaphors that reflect this perception. Doctors would be the generals and drugs their weapons against enemy alliances, 'co-infections'—clusters of diseases, which are known to occur together, and often accompany Lyme disease. Spirochete saboteurs would be undercover; Lyme disease is a cyclical spirochete disease caused by spiral-shaped bacteria which are known to have active and dormant phases. Although their original point of entry is the skin, via an insect bite, a spirochete swims through bodily fluids to interact with the organs and nervous system. When they encounter resistance—from the immune system, or from drugs—they form impenetrable cysts to hide in until the "coast is clear". These parasite reserves, with viral reinforcements, would re-invade at the slightest lessening of my defenses. This would be sophisticated guerrilla warfare.

Instead I choose to think of my body as a country at peace. My illnesses have returned me to cheek-to-cheek interaction I had with the natural world as a child. As I'm allergic to antibiotics most effective against tick-borne diseases my quest for healing has led me away from the field of war. My path leads through landscapes of herbal medicines and homeopathic remedies made from substances and creatures of Earth: Japanese knotweed, milk thistle, cuttlefish, copper, magnesium, zinc. I eat turmeric, garlic, Reishi mushrooms, oregano, sage, thyme. I drink tea of nettles and dandelion. These foods and medicines co-operate with each other, form synergies. Some are adaptogens, herbal supplements which help my body handle stress. They strengthen my immune system, whose job is to protect and heal, not to wage war.

My blood is a river that transports food supplies and medicines wherever they are needed. My journey is guided by herbalists and homeopaths, inspired by shamans, witches and wise women of old. Some maps were prepared in ancient times, some are charts of routes only recently discovered. The peace is holding.

Since contracting Lyme disease and Rocky Mountain Spotted Fever, and after blood tests that have confirmed several co-infections which have no name, I negotiate with the world within. It is populated by beings who live in ever-fluctuating relationship with my blood and organs, nervous system and brain. To them I am home. I am their colony.

I grew up in the Canadian Rockies and worked and lived there as an adult. I consider those mountains, alpine meadows, turquoise glacial lakes, and forests my spiritual home. Play, hiking, camping, photography—living in those mountains formed the backbone of my being for most of my life. Contracting Lyme disease began slowly but inexorably to close the door to physically visiting remote wilderness, which requires a fit and able body to navigate its slopes and crags. It was a devastating loss. At the same time I was aware of how much worse it could have been; chronic Lyme disease can rob people of their mobility, ability to work, can leave them permanently incapacitated, sometimes paralyzed. Rocky Mountain Spotted Fever can be fatal.

For me the trade-off for physical limitation is a deepened appreciation of the inter-woven complexity of life in any eco-system I find myself in. I too am a terrain. Growing up so close to nature, and as a shy only child, I have always been more comfortable with the natural world and its creatures than with human society. My health now relies on the bounty of Earth, its food and medicines. Earth is my home. I am also home to countless beings and live with them in constantly shifting reciprocity. And with gratitude.

I have held imaginary conversations with what I imagine to be the spirit of tick.

Why did you choose me? I ask.
Tick spirit replies, We're food for birds, travel winged, cling to fur. You were in

our path.
There's an old song, "I've Got You Under My Skin." I hum it.
Tick responds, We cull weak animals, strengthen ecosystems.
You regurgitated disease into my blood! I protest angrily.
We don't choose to carry disease. Diseases choose us. Hitch hikers.
I consider this perspective.
You ask about our pre-occupations? Feed. Multiply. Survive.
Am I weak? Is that why you chose me? I ask.
You choose safety over risk. You hide. We never do.
I'm afraid. The way ahead is dark, I whisper.
Tick spirit advises, seek balance, resist fear. Illuminate your shadows.

Ticks are not an invasive species. They have been found in the fossil records, and predate our species by millions of years. Ticks have long been endemic to North America. Deforestation, creation of suburban landscapes, the proliferation of deer due to extirpation of wolves and other natural predators, and warmer winters have enabled tick populations to soar. Have ticks always been vectors for disease? Who knows? One might label the diseases ticks carry as invasive species but fortunately they remain known by their classification: bacteria, viruses, spirochetes, etc.

I have come to believe that there is no such thing as an invasive species. There are only situations facilitated by events which have created change in the constantly shifting and re-balancing fabric of existence. Some changes, which appear to be harmful, have hidden benefits we may not understand; apparently destructive changes may be part of larger patterns we cannot yet fathom. Changing climate patterns, land use and development are major factors in any scenario which involves so-called invasive species. When applied to human populations, these changes result in migration.

Many changes to the environment have been caused or facilitated by humans, intentionally or inadvertently. It is an aspect of human hubris to notice this while ignoring the way creatures of Earth constantly rearrange and relocate themselves, seeking every opportunity to broaden their horizons, improve their circumstances, and create balance. Sometimes simply to find safety. This natural process unfolds with and without our participation and understanding. Humans have been responsible for intentionally and unintentionally bringing species from one part of the earth to another, often with dramatic consequences. But wind, rivers, tides, rain, desert storms, hurricanes, migrating birds, insects, animals all play their part in creating change through species movement. Humans have an inherently limited perspective, dictated by our short lives. Our blinkered, paternalistic and arrogant attitudes toward other species greatly hamper our understanding.

To apply the term 'invasive species' to a creature is to declare a war against it which usually cannot be won, and is unjust in its very nature. This word interferes with observation and perception by imposing human judgments and combative strategies on natural processes.

Perhaps it is easiest to observe this process with so-called invasive plants. There may be instances when human intervention is warranted but what is usually overlooked is that native plant species struggle and retreat when conditions are not favorable to their growth due to changes in climate, loss of habitat, disturbances to soil or water, etc. Frequently this is when 'invasive' species begin to move into previously healthy terrain. The old adage "nature abhors a vacuum" is apropos. What is missed, or ignored, is the benefit 'invaders' may provide in soil remediation, erosion control, feed for animals, nectar for bees and other benefits. Many 'invasive' plants such as blackberry remove industrial toxins from the soil.

A guide in my healing journey with Lyme disease has been the herbalist Stephen Harrod Buhner, who wrote extensively about this disease in his book *Healing Lyme*. One of the plants that is central to the treatment he outlines is Japanese knotweed, *Polygonum cuspidatum*. Knotweed is on the International Union for Conservation of Nature's list of the 100 worst invasive species in the world. There are four species of knotweed and they appear on every register of invasive plant species. Buhner writes: "…the plant [Japanese knotweed] is specific to the treatment of Lyme disease, reducing the inflammation in the neural system that the disease organism initiates…the plant…is invasive in the areas where the disease is most strongly emerging."[2]

This contention that not only does this particular plant uniquely treat a specific disease but that it has come to do so in a time of great need flies in the face of most present-day science and environmental theory. It turns the situation on its head. Japanese knotweed is part of a solution to an existing problem.

Japanese knotweed has been my frequent companion, as a remedy, for many years. It is another guest of my interior terrain, a country rich and strange. I close with an address to this companion:
A year ago I barely knew your name. Your reputation on breath-stained pages: loathed invader, hu zhang, tiger cane, Japanese knotweed, *Polygonum cuspidatum*. On disturbed land, barren ground, your amazon army roots the defense of tissue, blood and brain. Samurai of plant medicine, you are the vanguard.

Immune system modulator, you cleanse and balance blood, protect brain and nervous system from neurotoxins. You treat: cancer, heart disease, diabetes, stroke, Alzheimer's disease, multiple-sclerosis, Parkinson's disease, Huntingtons chorea disease, front-o-temporal dementia, encephalomyelitis.
You treat Lyme disease and its cohort co-infections
born by ticks, mosquitoes, birds
riders of deer
borrelia—babesia—bartonella—rickettsia
vector born diseases—a new vocabulary
your future is clear.

You are: anti-oxidant, anti-inflammatory, anti-mutagenic, anti-fungal, anti-thrombotic, anti-atherosclerotic, anti-pyretic, anti-viral, anti-spirochetal, yet war is waged against you. Your enemies arm themselves with chemical weed killers, blow-torches, shovels. Well-intentioned volunteers seek to save indigenous plants from your colonization. On his website, "Dr. Knotweed" promises to eradicate you. You have been described as the scourge which could sink a house sale. Is this just another international misunderstanding? Your giant female root brain drinks up Round-Up, detoxifies polluted earth. Ticks need you, birds, deer—I need you.

I read you're delicious in muffins.

Author's Note: I would not be the healthy person I am today without the healing regimes prescribed by Dr. Cindee Gardner, PhD, HD (RHom), CHom, DHom, of Monroeville, PA. Dr. Gardner is an internationally renowned homeopath, master herbalist, molecular biologist and clinical nutritionist. She is approaching retirement after forty years of an internationally renowned career.

---

[1] Buhner, Stephen H. *Healing Lyme, Natural Healing of Lyme Borreliosis and the Coinfections Chlamydia and Spotted Fever Ricketsiosis.* New York: Raven Press, 2015. Print. 2nd Edition.

[2] Buhner, Stephen H. *Plant Intelligence and the Imaginal Realm: Beyond the Doors of Perception into the Dreaming Earth.* Rochester, Vermont: Bear & Company, 2014, p.290. Print.

Laura Alexi Davenport
The Unveiling: Notes on Illness & Beauty

> Beauty, like love, is a fierce power that restores the world.
> The healer's power is diminished if it is not associated with beauty.
> Healing helps align the individual with the trajectory of the soul.
> —Deena Metzger, "The Soul of Medicine"

"Shouldn't she be better by now?" my friends quietly asked each other. It was December of 2001, nine months after my mastectomy for a recurrence of breast cancer. The regimen of intensive chemotherapy left me as close to death as the cancer that had tried to consume me. I felt depleted in body and spirit, my soul water-boarded.

Those close to me said, "Aren't you glad chemotherapy is over? Why don't you get out of the house?" What are your plans for the holidays?"

Between the lines, I heard annoyance and a demand that I 'move on.' But I had no idea how to leave cancer behind.

Friends stopped calling; their visits were fewer. Flowers no longer came in robust bouquets and cards and calls of encouragement ebbed. My husband's patience wore thin.

In the upstairs bathroom one evening, I turned off the faucet after washing my face. My husband yelled up from the living room where he was watching television, "Go easy on the pipes!"

I looked into the mirror. An emaciated, bald, crying ghost stared back. My eyes would not look at the crater where my right breast had been in a body I could not seem to love. I'd lost what I thought defined me as a woman and my husband was concerned only with the plumbing.

I had worked so hard to live and now I just wanted to die.

Then, at a gathering of women, an artist friend suggested I pose for an art class at the University of Hartford. She hoped it might give meaning to my ordeal while providing young art students a unique and challenging painting opportunity.

The thought of posing nude horrified me. I remembered summer camp when I was eight years old, changing into my bathing suit in a 100-hundred-degree bug-infested outhouse so the other girls would not see me naked.

Surviving cancer twice meant that I had been poked, prodded, and pricked repeatedly over many years. When I was hospitalized for six days with a fever of 104 degrees after my third intravenous chemotherapy, IV antibiotics could not relieve the bloom of painful and "mysterious" lumps that flourished on my labia. A mob scene erupted in the examining room when five "medical specialists" gathered for the view between my legs.

I no longer felt I was in control of my own body. I was afraid if I posed, I would be objectified as I had been before. But I could not allow fear to win. I wanted—and needed—to take charge of what I could in spite of all I'd lost. Posing felt to me like one thing I could do on behalf of my healing. I no longer cared if what I did made sense to anyone else.

I arrived at a tiny room in the Art Department of The University of Hartford. Easels, unfinished oil paintings, and old rags lay scattered around. I took off my winter boots and coat and met the painting teacher, Stephen Brown. After introductions and small talk, he revealed that he too was a cancer survivor and had lived many years with Hodgkin's Lymphoma. I felt heartened by this connection.

I changed into a fluffy white robe. Professor Brown then brought me to his classroom to meet his students, all eighteen of whom started talking simultaneously.

"We don't bite. You'll have fun today, really," said a woman with a wide smile and dreadlocks. The mood in the classroom was festive and I calmed a bit. Stephen brought me over to the raised platform where he told me I could sit or stand whichever was more comfortable for me.

I laughed. "Really, I'm not comfortable at all. I'm scared."

Professor Brown stationed four space-heaters in front of the platform where I would soon stand. My body gave an involuntary shake anyway.

"If you need a break from posing at any point, just say so," one of the students said.

"Most models," Stephen said, "ask for water, or need to move after holding a pose for twenty to thirty minutes. You're in charge really."

Yes, I was. I liked that.

Once on the platform in the class I was too frail to stand in front of the canvas backdrop as other models did. I prayed in silence, "May what is created here today benefit all beings." Then I adjusted my bony rear end into an old wooden rocking chair, placed my long scarf across my lap, and dropped my bathrobe.

Goose bumps formed on my upper body and the chill turned my fingers white. After the initial jitters wore off an intense calm embraced me like a warm cocoon. The buzz of the heaters became a comforting whirr as the students focused on their canvasses. Occasionally, a student looked at me for what felt like a long time, but they did not stare. Nor did they chatter among themselves.

I closed my eyes. I felt holy.

Stephen left the room. I remembered nothing until he returned an hour later and asked, "Are you tired? Do you need a break?" Leaning back in the rocking chair, I arched my chest and stretched my arms overhead as if making a snow angel in the air. "Nope, I'm in the zone, best not to interrupt the flow."

One young woman released an appreciative sigh. Echoing Stephen, she said, "Most models move around a lot or take breaks after fifteen minutes."

"Yeah, she's right," said another. "You can come back any time."

The vote of confidence from these young men and women brightened me. For more than ninety-minutes, I rested in a living prayer. The only sounds I heard were the space- heaters at my feet and the soft scratching of paintbrushes across canvas.

For most of my life, and for years as a survivor of sexual abuse, I had been treated as an object. As the subject of the student artists, however, I did not feel objectified. Their respect, consideration, and regard loosened something inside me. The emotional noose twisted around my throat by the symptoms of cancer, a diagnosis of mental illness, and the grief of abuse unraveled.

While the students bore witness to the wound on my chest, they also mended my heartbreak. They were an antidote to all the ways my humanity had been stripped away. And in choosing to pose, I had authorized a new way to be seen in the world—as real, raw and vulnerable.

When the class was over I walked around the room and studied each image. The paintings were so different. Some were in high contrast colors of red, yellows, and blues; others were somber, muted with hues of gray. There was one pastel. Only one student painted the seventeen-inch path of my mastectomy scar that moved from my right armpit to my breastbone. Some students painted one breast and some did not paint breasts at all.

The students had transformed my loss into eighteen soulful images— each one different from the last. In giving myself over to these students, I had allowed them to breathe new life into me.

In 2002, after I had posed for two classes of students, Professor Brown asked if he could paint me. Though my husband was against it, and I felt more trepidation than I had about posing for his class, I said yes.

Stephen's completed painting became part of an art exhibition at The Forum Gallery in New York City. He did not want me to see the painting prior to the opening of his exhibit; by the time I walked through the door of The Gallery, my legs were Jell-O.

Stephen took my hand and guided me to the main Gallery. There he pointed to a 25x14 inch oil painting on a wooden panel titled *Laura*.

Artwork (opposite): *Laura* by Stephen Brown [2006.05]; Michele and Donald D'Amour Museum of Fine Arts, Springfield, Massachusetts; Gift of the Artist; Photography by David Stansbury

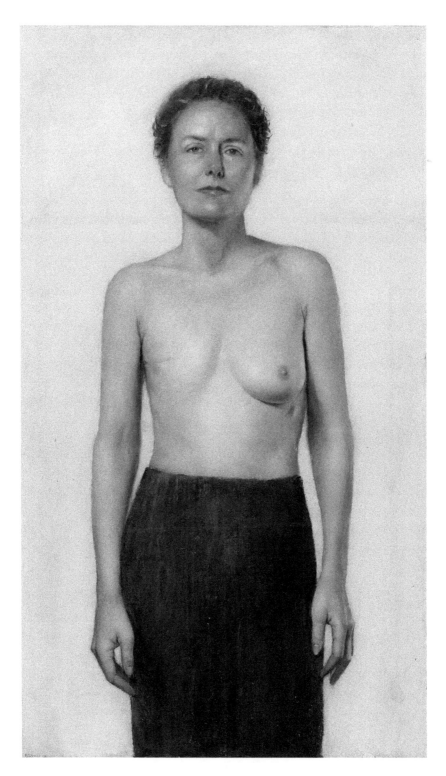

Although I had posed for Stephen nude, his painting of me was not. In his work, I am naked from only the waist up. His *Laura* is half-veiled. She is semi-nude in a black skirt that might just as easily be a shroud. There is honor, mystery, and paradox in the juxtaposition of the black skirt and the one-breasted, white-skinned woman. *Laura* stands squarely before you with a shoulder jutting out into the world—bearing witness—her gaze meeting yours. Her left hand moves towards you out of the plane of the picture.

The painting shows me in a moment in time when I was filled with despair. When I looked at the painting I recognized that in some ways I had healed from that woman on the canvas. Yet, parts of me still carried heartbreak. What was healed and what was broken existed side by side in my body just as they did in the image.

Stephen Brown called me late in 2006 with good news. "You've found a home. My painting of you is now in the permanent collection of the Springfield Museum of Fine Art in Springfield, Massachusetts." The write-up in the Museum's newsletter read: *In the painting,* Laura *is nude from the waist up. It is the portrait of a woman struggling to come to terms with the loss of a breast, her sexuality, her femininity, and beauty. Ultimately though, the picture is about beauty, strength, the triumph of survival and this woman's irrepressible spirit.*

Healing is not an individual experience. I believe witnessing is essential to healing and in this case, my witnesses were the students, the teacher, the friend who suggested the posing and the participants at The Forum Gallery opening. They are also each person who views the painting that now hangs in the art gallery. Each witness offers the genius of their own healing.

Stephen Brown's painting is both witness and testimony to the fact that I am not the sum of the worst things that happened to me. Anyone who looks deeply into *Laura* can see the medicine in the wound. The students and Professor Brown helped me learn to carry the beauty and the wounding side by side, moment by moment. I saw that I could not become one who heals without being seen also as one who carried the physical, spiritual, and emotional wound.

I have made several trips to the Springfield Museum to see *Laura*. Each time I witness her I am different. And each time *Laura* looks back at me I am made whole in a new way.

Notes

Stephen P. Brown died at the age of 59 in Granville, MA on October 21, 2009 after a long journey with Hodgkin's Lymphoma. He was a full professor at the Hartford Art School, University of Hartford. He won an Academy Award for painting from the American Academy of Arts and Letters in New York and was a member of the National Academy of Design, New York. His paintings are in the collections of Hofstra Museum, NY, Albany Museum, GA, New Britain Museum of American Art, CT, Springfield Museum of Fine Art, MA, Speed Art Museum, Kentucky, New York Academy of Design and the Mattatuck Museum, CT.

Eve Rachele Sanders
The View from the Ground

*On a scale of one to ten, with ten being the worst pain you
could imagine, what level is your pain now?*

A question I was asked hundreds of times.
The question I asked instead was: what does it mean, to heal?

The timing had to be right, the traffic manageable. Twice a week, I
would be rushed by a friend out the door of the Intensive Care Unit
at the UC Davis Pain Center in Sacramento to the nearest redwood
forest, Muir Woods. It was a two-and-a-half hour drive. When I arrived
at the state park, an hour or so before closing, the lidocaine would be
about to wear off. A short span of time remained for me to be fully in
the world. I had come in hope of a synergistic effect, the possibility that
a forest infusion might magnify the benefits of the lidocaine infusion.
Now I walked upright, effortlessly. Soon, my head would feel heavy, like
the cast-iron ball of a convict's ball and chain, dragging me downward,
so heavy that I would be unable to stand or sit upright. Now shapes
and colors, the green of a moss-covered tree stump or yellow of a
banana slug crossing my path, were vivid; the scalloped curves of each
leaf of clover, the segmented geometry of each cobweb, immediately
apparent. Soon, all objects in my field of vision would recede into a blur,
discernible only with the strain of repeated staring. Yet the moment
at hand was a reprieve, an afternoon not to be squandered, time for
looking up.

While still in a state of quasi-wellness, I would lie down in my winter
coat, in the center of a family circle of redwood trees. There I would
drape my backbone over the forest floor layered with hard protruding
tree roots, soft mosses and fungi, scattered needles and pine cones. The
stream tumbling over stones and branches cascades through the open
doors of my senses. Filtered shadows lighten briefly, then darken with
the recurrent breeze. San Franciscans complain of overcast days but
only the fog, the ocean's nearness, sustains the coast redwoods. The
smell of dampness, of cedar and bay laurel trees, calming and refreshing

my senses, was what I missed most living in Montreal, thousands of miles away. Only the deep scent of this forest can expunge flashbacks, odors of patient gowns and hospital corridors, cocoon me from the assaults of memory. I inhale and am buoyed elsewhere. The view above beckons my attention, spokes of a tree circling upward along the trunk as if toward an infinity of light. Each branch is tipped with a shock of newly grown needles, like pale green nails on dark fingers, outstretched, reaching.

On the day of my first appointment in the ICU, the doctor explained by way of a metaphor the lidocaine infusion he would be administering. It would be a kind of reboot. If my nervous system were the operating system of a computer, it would be like having the control-alt-delete keys pressed simultaneously. The lidocaine slowly trickling into my blood stream from a plastic bag attached to a needle in my forearm would provoke the closing of sodium channels and thereby prevent sodium from reaching any of the cells of my body. Nerve cells, therefore, would pause their incessant firing. (Hence the need for the procedure to be done in an ICU: theoretically, the infusion could stop my heart.) With the nerves quiet, muscles and fascia would no longer tighten and spasm. All pain would cease temporarily.

It seemed quite theoretical as the doctor in scrubs explained it, but that very scenario occurred seemingly more or less according to plan. Initially, I was jubilant. After a test run, the second infusion left me functioning nearly normally and pain-free for three days. Unfortunately, the curative effects of the third infusion lasted only two hours, those of subsequent ones, three or four.

To heal: why I am here, lying on my back in this forest of coast redwoods. *Sequoia sempervirens,* named for the great Cherokee leader, wordsmith and visionary, and for the coast redwoods' perpetual greenness. The second word in the name means also "always alive"; here in the park, new potential tree trunks grow skyward from the side of a bay laurel toppled in a storm as I have seen redwoods do in other places. Redwoods have a history of being scorched by fire, some charred to the root by a lightning strike.

At the empty center of the circle where I'm lying now was once rooted a primeval redwood. Fire torched its trunk, branches and bark to cinders dispersed with the wind. Imperceptibly, what was left of it inside the earth later regrew into a full circle of genetically identical trees, two hemispheres around the hearthstone of the originary redwood. It sounds like mythology but it is true. The coast redwood actually is the Phoenix of the forest. This intriguing species once offered a way to explain death in a hopeful light, the family circle illustrating the circle of life in a 3-D diorama. Today, in the wake of global warming, redwoods lack moisture; their most lofty upper reaches shrug brown needles from branches brittle and desiccated. Park rangers no longer speak of fire season. Year-round wildfire is now the status quo turning all to combustible twigs; fog and damp recede before the steady incursion of drought and flame. Redwoods that used to grow two to three feet a year now progress by bare inches. In the unrequited thirst of these last remaining ancient trees, for whom humidity is breath, millennia of fire and rebirth have come to a dead end, the family circle broken.

What fires together wires together: basic neuroscience, Hebb's dictum. What fires together also roots, embeds. Like a Chinook salmon, a monarch butterfly, I contain memory of my point of origin on earth, some fierce internal yearning powerful enough to pilot us home. I have no other explanation for what brought me from Eastern Canada here to a redwood forest in California, the place where I remember being last most fully alive, agile, part of a family circle: whole.

Again, I find myself among redwoods, this time reclined on the ground. I start my sentence with "I". It is a figure of speech. I am no longer I. I am not the person I was. I cannot read or write. I cannot remember the color of the rental car I've been riding in for weeks. Most days I cannot stand upright without help. When asked what I like or what I do, I can't answer. Yet I, this person I seem to be, still is here somehow, remembering walking in a forest in another body, another life. "If I am not I, who am I, then?" I asked Pilar, the wisest person I know. Trained as a midwife and manual therapist, Pilar gives treatments in a room built around a standing redwood tree. The clinic where she works is called The Healing Tree. "You are the one who has witnessed all that has happened to you," Pilar says.

The word "heal," going back to its Anglo-Saxon and Germanic roots, means to make whole. The same connection between healing and wholeness is found in civil law, which puts the onus on the injurer to make the injured party whole. It is there, too, in the language of the Bible, spirituals from Black folk religion that sing of the medicinal plant grown east of the Jordan river. *There is a balm in Gilead to make the wounded whole.* Here in the forest, dusk approaching, I ask myself: What do you need in order to heal?

For Virginia Woolf, being recumbent is the epitome of illness. She observes that a person who falls ill is perceived, before all else, as in need of a bed. Patients cannot be upright. It is incumbent on them to be supine or prone. From that change of bodily posture, a new orientation and identity emerges. In a horizontal position, "we cease to be soldiers in the army of the upright … they march to battle. We float with the sticks on the stream."* Woolf notes the wisdom to be gained from such a shift, the granting of a new viewpoint, a position that allows one to look up at the sky, time and perspective to watch the clouds change shapes over an hour or a day.

Forced to lie down by the weight of my seemingly hundred-pound head, I see wholeness also in walking upright. I understand why injured horses will never stop trying to right themselves, even using their heads to support their body weight if their legs will not. My wish is not to join the ranks of conformity, Woolf's army of the upright marching with the crowd, unappreciative and unaware. Instead, it is to savor kinetically what I first noticed when, like Woolf, I was a floating stick on the stream, to take in up close and with my senses intact landscapes I observed from below. I yearn to do so again, but now with a view of the horizon, the mobility to look right or left, up or down, to set off and explore, arms and torso and legs swinging freely, earth resonant under each step.

If healing means to make whole, I need now to do something: eat a piece of fruit, walk across a field, crochet a scarf, dance to music, breathe deeply. Even lying down, I can move my arms and legs, extend and flex my spine and head. Taking action engages, stimulates in concert, wires discrete parts, tissues and physiological systems, central nervous system and periphery. Within the constraints of my injury, the more that I nonetheless act, the more I integrate these different components, and the greater the chance of this temporary reboot lasting. My surroundings, I think, imprint this dynamic more profoundly: the knitting together of stimuli and responses for a functional purpose, a walk in the forest.

Imagine resetting the nervous system as a process like learning to ride a bike: turning the pedals with my feet, going through the motions repeatedly, over and over in search of balance, the wheels of the bike spinning, until one day, in a flash, I have my equilibrium and ride away, no training wheels needed, powered by my own resources. Here each step on sodden redwood and fir tree needles, each touch of the underside of a fern frond rough with brown spores, each breath of air infused with mud and laurel and animal smells, recalls me to inhabit my body once more. There is no veil between me and the world.

And if tonight or tomorrow, I regress?

The coast redwoods stand around me. They answer with their mass, their towering presence, their ancient claim. The internal capacity to turn a charred root socket, charcoal remains of a past inferno, into a stand of enormous trunks and green branches, a grove of giant trees spaced geometrically in a circle. For all their immensity, redwoods have a strangely shallow hold on the earth. The coast redwoods of Muir Woods and giant sequoias further inland alike have no taproot to anchor their gigantic weight, as much as two million pounds for a three-thousand-year-old giant sequoia. For both kinds of redwood, solidity rests on the breadth, not depth, of the fibrous latticework bracing them from below, each tree's roots joined to those of adjacent redwoods, both a system of irrigation and a structural foundation.

To heal, let go the question, what does it mean? Ask instead: to heal, what is to be done? For now, my answer is: lie here, take in this humming abundance of stillness, nourishment palpable in each groove of bark corrugated to catch rain, endurance of ancient cycles that continue now. On other days, you'll need to plumb your last reserves of strength, to walk, step, touch, reach, even–down the road–run, leap, read the history books in the park store, talk to the other visitors and to the park rangers, write about what you see and recall. But now, at dusk, just hear what the resonances of time have to say: even sequioas three hundred and fifty feet tall keep their footing by clasping shallow roots to the broader mass of all the roots of their neighbors intertwined. Sometimes the only way to be vertical is to tap into what is unseen, what is under our feet.

N.B.: This is an abridged version. Please see Dark Matter: Women Witnessing #7 *online for the complete essay.*

———

* Woolf, Virginia. *On Being Ill*, rpt. Ashfield, MA: Paris Press, 2002, p.12. Print.

Shante' Sojourn Zenith
Standing on First Stone

> The only medicine for the place of aching is to nestle your body into the shape of the absence. Make your body the prayer that resonates from a depth of soil. Become the portal back to home.
> —Maitake Mushroom[1]

> A vision of self in isolation cannot imagine the materials of mending.
> —Nora Bateson, *Small Arcs of Larger Circles*

The roots of dis-ease

Several years ago, I had a vision about my ancestors, a kind of waking dream that bubbled up within me as I stood at the edge of a river.

Standing in the shallow water, sharp little rocks scattered the riverbed, biting into my bare feet, I felt my deep time ancestors as the solid ground below me, holding me up. Between my body and that support, the broken rock fragments felt like the shards of unmetabolized trauma from my near ancestors, settler-colonists dissociated from a felt sense of relationship with the earth.

As I stood at the edge of the water, immense somatic awareness came through my body in waves and my right calf began to tremor. I realized how difficult the sharp rocks were making it to feel my feet fully on the ground.

The experience in the river was provoked by a conversation I had earlier that day, in which I had been speculating about "the roots of dis-ease" with a group of friends from the permaculture training that I was in.

This dialogue about the origin point of colonization, whiteness, and other entangled contexts of domination is a conversation that I have experienced multiple times now in groups focused on systems change and reconnection to nature.

In my experience, the outcome of this conversation often plateaus at a place of simultaneous blame and confusion, accumulating a list of culprits such as patriarchy, imperialism, agriculture, and greed but never really delving under the surface to look at what relational wounding might already have happened to lead to the emergence of those things.

In this particular conversation about the roots of our settler-colonist trauma, my permaculture friends were talking about fear, fear of difference, fear of death. They were sensing into the way that violence and domination originate in a need to control the ecological rhythms of life, a need to have agency over fear and the terror of the unknown in a reality where to die means to cease to exist.

As my friends were speaking about tracing the origin point of colonization, an intense flow of energy started to move through me as I touched into the felt sense of this archetypal rupture. I felt an aching hollowness in my chest and the sense of something melting, as if I had touched into a river of grief so vast I needed banks to contain my flow.

If my kin are afraid of death, it is because we have lost the perception of ourselves as a part of the wider body of life.

Self-as-ecosystem

There's a difference between death and not-existing if you perceive your "self" in somatic entanglement with the wider ecosystem. In *Small Arcs of Larger Circles,* systems poet Nora Bateson invokes this experience of a sense of self beyond the edges of the individual body:

> The outlines we draw around 'parts' (like a hand or a kidney) are useful to us as arbitrary separations that conveniently contain our study within limits we can manage; but these outlines more aptly serve to indicate areas of interaction, transmission, and reception of information. The skin of my body provides what looks like a boundary around me, but 'I' extend well beyond the container of my flesh, both biologically and socially.[2]

This perception of self-as-ecosystem isn't threatened by death in the same way because our existing continues to circulate as nutrients through the wider ecosystem after we die. We continue to exist, just in another shape. On the day of the conversation about the "roots of disease," a hollowness continued to haunt me after I left the permaculture gathering. Later that day, I found my way to a river, standing barefoot in the shallow water with a prayer on my lips for a kind of belonging that I had never experienced.

What is this aching loneliness in the bodies of me and my European lineage kin, this separation from the wider body of the earth?

Bodyworker Susan Raffo writes about how the first orienting process of a baby upon being born is "the reflex that helps our body build a relationship with gravity."[3] Raffo explains the way that systems of violence and ancestral trauma impact this relationship:

> This is the place of contradiction, the wrapped up tight knot that generations of living within and overriding violence have created. It is very difficult, although not impossible, to bring our bodies to gravity's weight if we don't believe we can let go of our weight…Rest is how life remembers itself, reflects over what it has learned and slowly remakes itself in response to that learning. All of this is why systems of supremacy hijack the body's survival responses, keeping our nervous systems at the ready for disaster. Unable to rest.

That day at the river was the first time that I consciously felt into what I have since called the "ancestral abandonment pain body," the backlog of ancestral grief from all my European lineage kin that sits in between my body and the support of earth.

Tracing the Long Body

Poet-philosopher Bayo Akomolafe invokes the way in which the indigenous sense of self includes both this ancestral backlog and the wider earth body, describing human beings as "replete with loss and disappearances and monsters and secretions and microbial transgressions… Not drawing the line too closely around the humanoid shape we are used to allows us to see a vast body, what the Iroquois/Haudenosaunee call the 'Long Body.'"[4]

I use the term Long Body in my practice frequently, imaging my animal organism as a kind of fruiting body, the tip of an entire cascade of roots, inextricably entangled with the ancestors and ecosystems that sustain my aliveness.

Recently, I started to become aware that I did not know the cultural context through which the term Long Body emerged. So I started to research the cultural lineage of the term and try to find the point at which there was knowledge transmission of the phrase from a Haudenosaunee person to a European person. I especially wanted to learn the original words that Long Body was translated from and what mythology was attached to the term within Haudenosaunee culture.

I searched for several weeks and was amazed to find absolutely nothing. In all the writing I have been able to find about it online, nowhere has there been a description of how white academics came to learn this concept from the Haudenosaunee people, an absence that effectively invisibilizes the process of indigenous knowledge transmission and the particular cultural context from which the term emerged. Besides Bayo Akomolafe, all of the people I have seen using the term Long Body are white. All of them cite other white scholars as their sources for the term. So far, the furthest back I have traced the phrase is an essay from 1986, "Psi and the Phenomenology of the Long Body," which cites an earlier university lecture from a Dr. Joseph Lyons. That's where the trail runs dry as I haven't been able to find any documentation of Dr. Lyons' work on the internet.

Eventually I turned to my community of animist kin to seek their advice for this conundrum. My teacher Dare Sohei wrote back:

> All words are spirits that point to spirits, these spirits that point to spirits also come from spirits (i.e. the original receivers/creators of the words, the persons that heard the words and shared them in books etc). Therefore, all words can be related with as spirits directly (spirits who have many relations and many "parents"), which can allow a "new" direct experience/dream of contact/ encounter that is "yours".

Based on this recommendation from Dare, I began a process of journeying with the term Long Body to learn directly from the spirit of the word about its origins.

Here is some of what I heard:

Lost in snows, no absences but those unmerited, uncalled for, melted into air. Warming self by fire, the web of entanglements. This was always known, whispered by flames. It only came into being as a concept to be given to the ones who didn't have it anymore. A perception of the frozen absences—an insight into those who had forgotten their own belonging. It was already a translation, whispering a memory into the bones. Arising out of a moment of contact.

The Long Body is the gestation of soul, the wider unfolding outside of the human womb. The Long Body is the tree within the seed. The imprint of forest giving birth to new life, the energies and shadows that sustain your remembering, the full cycle—the journey of water gushing forth underground and back to the source.

Of course the transmission is invisible. It is one of those portal places, the absence that both obscures and illuminates the pattern in itself. Why cry for the loss of this direct knowledge? Maybe it was never yours in the first place. As soon as it passed it transmogrified into the shape that was needed. Wolves devouring the carcass, it is here to meet a hunger. The word was always an offering, a prayer for remembering, a seed to plant in the soil of your own becoming.

What emerged for me out of this journey is that the absence this term carries with it is also a part of its teaching. Part of the dissociative spell of my kin's ancestral trauma is the creation of absences that trail with us everywhere.

I can feel this absence all around me, haunting my lack of relationship with the materials that sustain my life. My very existence right now is sustained by this obscuring of relationship: from the heat in my room to the light, the computer I'm writing on, the chair that holds me, the chocolate and pomegranate I ate earlier…All of these beings that support my life are ones I am not in reciprocal relationship with where I can feel the impact that I create. Even the desk that I write at, the family heirloom of a friend of mine, is an object displaced from context. I do not know who built this desk, the kind of tree it's made of, or the specific texture of that tree's bark against my hand. Instead of these relationships, there is an industrial scale dissociative complexity outsourcing survival to supply chains—leaving little space for response-ability in a tangle of extractive relationships so massive there is no way for me to respond to all of the impacts that my existence is making on this earth.

Nora Bateson speaks about this same pattern of dissociated extraction:

My clothing, probably my breakfast, most of the technology and furniture in this room, the way each of us got here, all of this—is made possible through exploitation and extraction. The institutions of our world have allowed this to happen. That is our moment. This has been true for decades, maybe centuries, but there's an acute sense that the time is up. And that it's not comfortable, it's not do-able to continue in that way. But to pay attention to it causes an unbearable broken heart that has the risk of debilitating the creativity to respond.[5]

How do you notice an absence? A dissociation? What is its shape? How do you even begin to notice that a gap is there where a relationship should have been?

The shape of absence

November pond. Empty log. The shape of absence.

This is the place where I sit with turtles on most days.

This place is a part of Turtle Island, of Mni Sota Makoce, the ancestral homelands of the Dakota people, a people who are still present in this land where I live, as much as they have been systemically invisibilized by my settler-colonist kin.

This place is a backwater of the Mississippi River that may once have been a tributary linking the Mississippi to the Zumbrota Rivers, until the flow between the two was separated and the Zumbrota River redirected. In the summer, the water here is often stagnant due to lack of flow and pollution from the boat harbor nearby.

Getting to root myself into relationship with a place I have gone to almost every day for the past four months has been a sweet and humbling experience. For a while it was novel and exciting in high summer when I would get to know the turtle who sat on the rock in the middle of the water, the turtles on the log near the path who would jump into the water every time I biked past, and sometimes, quiet turtle heads peeking out of the water at me as I sat and talked or sang with them, then dipping back under the water leaving ripples of concentric circles in their wake.

After a while, it no longer was such a peak experience to come here every day. The turtles are my friends, the ecosystem is a friend, the daily visit is a more-than-human check-in process into my connectedness. No matter how grumpy or tired or lonely or excited or grieving I am, this place is always there. And sometimes those little heads poking above the water, looking at me. I speak to them every day, about my life, about my kin, about what is broken and what is longed for. And I listen for the rhythm with my drum and I entwine the harmonics of my voice with the meeting point of flow.

Now it is November, and the turtles are burrowed deep underwater, brumating in the mud, slowing their metabolisms and breathing through the pores of their skin until spring. Part of the shape of absence in my culture is the loss of relational context. Of knowing that the turtles aren't basking on this particular log, in this particular not-anymore-tributary, on this particular occupied Dakota land. And yet how can we begin to turn towards what has been dissociated from when simply tuning into the absences in a single room of a house is to be paralyzed by an immensity of supply chains, overwhelmed by the haunting of relational absences.

On that day when I stood calf-deep in the river, noticing how afraid my body was to fully allow my feet to touch the earth, time curled and I received a transmission from my ancestors. I felt the terror of the women when the men did not come home initiated, when through some accumulation of unmetabolized trauma the knowledge of ceremony was lost that webbed my people into relationship with the wider body. I felt the way the mothers had to uproot their energy from their lower body, pulling their life force away from relationship with the earth and wrapping that energy around the children to try and protect them.

On my second journey into the spirit inside of the term Long Body, I received the image of an elder from the Haudenosaunee confederacy speaking to a white anthropologist. I understood that "Long Body" was a metaphor the elder created to try to explain to this anthropologist a consciousness that was missing from the colonizers' perception. I heard the words of that elder…

"It was a gift to the broken people. The frozen ones, who threw their hurt into others' surfaces. It was a reminder of their mothers, of what…"

Then a feeling of blockage, and energy coming in and stopping the words, separating me from the energy of the elder….

What's happening now? Blocking the words.

The massive grief dragon inside the European, inside the lineage of harm that broke the story.

"Roar! I must speak first, I must crowd all the air with my warning. All who approach my shadow risk being met with the full force of my despair. I am not crumbled into ash. I am an accumulating entity, I live in the lineage of your belly, I echo the tightness of your muscles and vibrate the ligaments that link together the existential patterns of your being. Your perception of these has been severed. You are not a body any longer. I feed on your fragmentation. I was born out of a lack of keening the loss of the sound that wove your fabric to that of another. I am what remains in the liminal if the loss is unwitnessed. I haunt the broken bonds weaving together the fabric of the world."

And then another energy emerging, older than the dragon…

"I exist with each of your children in the placenta. I am the salt fluid floating and shaping them into their becoming. I am the field of intelligence they drink from, the essential belly of bellies, the mother of mothers. The imprint given back through each emergence, the essence that shapes matter into a field of stories. I must flow between you. My intelligence expands on its passage in between. The fissures and canyons and ligaments and joints that channel life force from one part to another. My existence is spreading and flow. You must meet me in the passage, at the threshold, you must learn how to relate to me, to join within the wider network, to pour yourself forth into the empty places, to participate in the flow of betweenness, to dream as organs of this wider being. This is the Long Body, this wider circulatory system, including the sacred, the invisible passage from identity to mystery to pulsing relationship with the organismic intelligence containing you as you create it with your song."

First stone and living water

For the next four days after standing in the river, I was suddenly, violently ill. I became dizzy every time I tried to stand upright. I had tried to hold a grief within my body that was way too immense for me, and I did not yet know the skills of asking for deep-time ancestors and earth to hold the emotion with me and help me to modulate for the "just right amount." [6.] My body was reacting in overwhelm to a "too muchness" that I could not contain within my system alone. Vomiting and faint, my digestive and vestibular systems were in turmoil, as if my body had ceased to move in cycles. I realized the water of the river that I had drunk through my cupped palms as I prayed must have contained pesticide runoff from the monocultured crops around it, a devastating metaphor for grief within this settler-colonist culture. What do a people do to heal when the water they pray to has also been contaminated?

A few days later, still so dizzy I was unable to stand upright, I went to an herbalist who felt my pulse while one by one she placed bottles in my open palm, face down so I could not read the labels. One of the bottles felt like a pebble dropped into rippling water, falling deep into the place where the weeping came from. The herbalist said my pulse flatlined as I was holding this bottle. She turned it around and the label read "Rock Water."

Rock Water is spring water from a subterranean source, "living water that comes directly from the womb of the Earth." [7] After taking the Rock Water essence, I could walk again without dizziness, and it was as if all of the intensity that had been stuck in my body with no place to go was now able to circulate down through my feet and back to the wider body of the earth.

Years later, in a bodywork session as I pressed my feet against the hands of a trusted therapist, the somatic memory of standing in that river came back into my body to be witnessed. With my therapist's supportive holding, I was able to breathe into that moment of ancestral rupture without becoming overwhelmed, sensing into the support that was accessible before my ancestors' bodies contorted away from the felt sense of ground.

As my body began to orient to the contact of the therapist's palms against my feet, repatterning my relationship to ground, the words "standing on first stone" appeared to me, along with an archetypal image of the moment when fungi first left the ocean, learning how to draw nutrients from barren stone so they could live outside of the water. I received the message that the fungi's ability to stitch relationship between water and land by metabolizing death into nutrients for life has medicine for the ancestral abandonment pain body that has become so amplified within the bodies of my settler colonist kin.

We are always standing on first stone. Even when our perception of it is obscured by generations of ancestral trauma, the stone is still there beneath us and inside of us, in our bones, in the support of gravity holding us into relationship with the earth. The stone of all the dead, all the ancestors, every living thing there was, returned to feed the wider ground of life. The question is, how can we learn to feel this support again? What mycelial processes of relationship can re-member our felt sense of that primordial ground of Original Belonging, of rest and gestation, digesting death into the soil that supports all becoming?

N.B.: This is an abridged version. Please see Dark Matter: Women Witnessing #14 *online for the complete essay.*

———————

[1] Sojourn Zenith, Shante'. "Make Your Body the Prayer," a Long Body Prayers podcast episode. *Earth Poet Edge Weaver.* YouTube. 2022. Web. n.d.

[2] Bateson, Nora. *Small Arcs of Larger Circles: Framing through Other Patterns.* Triarchy Press, 2018, p.229. Print.

[3] Raffo, Susan. "Gravity: The First Reflex." *Susan Raffo.* 5 Nov. 2017. Web.

[4] Báyò, Akòmolàfé. "I Coronavirus: Mother. Monster. Activist." *Akòmolàfé Báyò.* 15 May, 2020. Web.

[5] Stephen Gilligan in Conversation with Nora Bateson, audience Q&A. 28 Jul. 2021. Creative Mind, YouTube. Web.

[6] These are somatic practices I've been learning about from Dare Sohei and Larissa Kaul of Animist Arts.

[7] Orianna, Nienan. "Bach's Rock Water: The 'Life Elixir'". *Nienan Orianna Medium.* 4 Aug. 2020. Web.

The Grammar of Animacy

On behalf of the living world, let us learn the grammar of animacy. ...
Let us speak of the beings of the earth as the "kin" they are...

—Robin Wall Kimmerer, *When Earth Becomes an "It"*

It behooves us to consider that the elephants realize that our species
has gone rogue– that our trauma is driving us to rape and destroy; that
we are in dire need of some serious cross-species
eldering and matriarchal leadership....

—Cynthia Travis, *Listen with Your Feet*

Shula Levine
Everything is Alive and Communicating

I sit beneath a graceful old tree wrapped in tattered sacred cloth. Its deep, calm presence fills me.

Soon I am traveling below the surface of the earth along the roots of the tree, am aware of being underground, and of the incredibly complex network of information and life force all around me. Aware of respiration. The entire community below the surface works together in intricate beauty to feed and breathe and decompose and regenerate. Everything essential comes from this energy pulsing around me. Information is passed between species, bugs, roots, the microbes of the soil itself. Everything is alive and communicating. I am aware that I can't possibly understand this language, but I am also aware that all I am supposed to understand is this gorgeous complexity. The Earth is quite literally speaking.

Then I am walking on a quiet stretch of ocean beach. It is a familiar place, the shore of Wellfleet, Massachusetts. A seal raises her head from the surface of the ocean and makes eye contact with me. Then she is guiding me beneath the surface of the ocean. Again I am aware that my senses are not equipped to fully comprehend what I am being shown, but I have a sense of vast intelligence being transmitted. I experience something like synesthesia—hearing smell, and tasting sound—there is so much information pulsing within the water, between species, between elements. I am aware that though I am unable to perceive and receive all that is here, it is enough to feel awe and deep reverence for it.

Then I am on what feels like an abandoned city street. It feels like a poor residential neighborhood, run down, a heavy feeling of despondency in the air. There are no people in this scene except for one young boy, maybe eleven years old, sitting on the steps of a building. It is as though he has been waiting a long time for something to happen. I move toward him with the feeling that we are in a silent movie—sound has been muted, a stark contrast to the fervor of sound and energy in the soil and ocean. I have the sense that I am supposed to drum for him. I feel hesitant, awkward, self-conscious, but there is a frame drum in my hand, and I realize that I am supposed to reconnect the boy to an essential life force that has been exiled. I start to drum.

Then I am in the midst of outer-space. It is dark, but there are an infinite number of distant stars shining. I feel the stars are radiating love, streaming unending love and nourishment and protection to the whole planet and to all beings on the planet. I laugh, realizing what a grand truth this is. There is so much love streaming toward us all of the time.

Robin Wall Kimmerer
When Earth Becomes an "It"

Editors' note: Robin Wall Kimmerer delivered this keynote address at the Geography of Hope *conference, March 2015. A portion of her talk was also published in the Spring 2015 issue of* YES! Magazine. *See also Robin Wall Kimmerer,* Braiding Sweetgrass: Indigenous Wisdom, Scientific Knowledge, and the Teachings of Plants. *Minneapolis, M.N: Milkweed Editions, 2013, pp. 3-10 and pp. 48-59.*

Let us begin with gratitude, for we are showered every day with the gifts of the Earth. *Megwech* to one another as people, for the privilege of being in one another's company, for this beautiful day, for being whole and healthy and surrounded by the companionship of oaks and grasses, butterflies and fog. Gratitude for the Coast Miwok people in whose homelands we meet. And for the gifts, the everyday miracles with which we are showered every day.

At a literary conference, it is important to honor together the deep roots of the oral tradition and so let me start with a story, an old story.

In the beginning, there was the Skyworld, where people lived much as they do here on Earth, raising their families, raising their gardens, walking in the forest. And in that forest grew the great Tree of Life, on which grew all kinds of fruits and berries and medicines on a single tree. One day, a great windstorm blew down the tree and opened at its base a huge hole in the ground where its roots had pulled up. Being curious like all of us, a beautiful young woman whom we call Gizhkokwe, or Skywoman, went over to have a look. She stood at the edge and looked down, but could see nothing for it was entirely dark below, so she stepped a little farther and the edge of the hole began to crumble beneath her feet. She reached out to stop herself by grabbing on to the fallen tree, but the branch broke off in her hand.

She fell like a maple seed pirouetting on an autumn breeze. A column of light streamed from a hole in the Skyworld, marking her path where only darkness had been before. But in that emptiness there were many gazing up at the sudden shaft of light. They saw there a small object, a mere dust mote in the beam. As it grew closer, they could see that it was a woman, arms outstretched, long black hair billowing behind as she spiraled toward them.

The geese nodded at one another and rose as one from the water, in a wave of goose music. She felt the beat of their wings as they flew beneath and broke her fall. Far from the only home she'd ever known, she caught her breath at the warm embrace of soft feathers.

And so it began. From the beginning of time, we are told that the very first encounter between humans and other beings of the earth was marked by care and responsibility, borne on the strong wings of geese. The world at that time was covered entirely by water.

The geese could not hold Skywoman much longer, so they called a council of all beings to decide what to do—loons, otters, swans, beavers, fish of all kinds. A great turtle floated in the watery gathering, and he offered to let her rest upon his back and so, gratefully she stepped from the goose wings onto the dome of the Turtle. The others understood that she needed land for her home. The deep divers among them had heard of mud at the bottom of the water and agreed to retrieve some. The loon dove to get a beakful, but the distance was too far and after a long while he surfaced with nothing to show for his efforts. One by one, the other animals offered to help, the otter, the beaver, the sturgeon. But the depth, the darkness and the pressure were too great for even these strongest of swimmers who came up gasping for air and their heads ringing. Soon only the muskrat was left, the weakest diver of all. He volunteered to go while the others looked on doubtfully. His little legs flailed as he worked his way downward. He was gone a very long time. They waited and waited for him to return, fearing the worst for their relative. Before long, a stream of bubbles rose from the water and the small limp body of muskrat floated upward. He had given his life to aid this helpless human. But the others noticed that his paw was tightly clenched and when they opened it, there was a small handful of mud. Turtle said, "Here, put it on my back and I will hold it."

Skywoman bent and spread the mud across the shell of the turtle. Moved by gratitude for the gifts of the animals, she sang in thanksgiving and then began to dance, her feet caressing the earth with love. As she danced her thanks, the land grew and grew from the dab of mud on Turtle's back. And so, the earth was made. Not by one alone, but from the alchemy of the animals' gifts and human gratitude. Together they created what we know today as Turtle Island.

This is a fragment of the creation story told by both Haudenosaunee and Anishinaabe people in my homelands. Our oldest teachings remind us that reciprocity is the thread that binds us together. The animals were Skywoman's life raft at the beginning of the world, and now, so much closer to the end, we must be theirs.

Whether her name is Skywoman or Spider Woman or Changing Woman, the Goddess Ki or Gaia or Eve, our origin stories, the stories of who we are in the world and how it is we might live, often have a cast of characters which includes women and the land. The bond is deep and enduring. We know these stories, for isn't the world shifting under our feet, too? Aren't we all at some time falling into a new place? And trying to make a home?

In an era of accelerating climate change and the Sixth Extinction, we know we too stand at the edge, with the ground crumbling beneath our feet. Like Skywoman, we ask: what can we grab onto to stop the fall? What gifts do we carry to make a new home? How do we care for the beings who have cared for us from the beginning of time?

This time we live in—one of great change and great choices—has been spoken of by our ancestors, in the teachings of the prophecies of the seventh fire, and I will share just a tiny fragment this morning. After the long migration of our Anishinaabe people, after the arrival of the newcomers and after all the losses—of land, of language, of sacred ways, of each other—the prophecy and history converge. It is said that the people will find themselves in a time where you can no longer fill a cup from the streams and drink, when the air is too thick to breathe and when the plants and animals will turn their faces away from us. It is said in that time, which we will know as the time of the seventh fire, that all the worlds' peoples will stand at a fork in the road. One of the paths is soft and green and spangled with dew. You could walk barefoot there. And one of the paths is black and burnt, made of cinders that would cut your feet.

We know which path we want. The prophecy tells us that we must make a choice between the path of materialism and greed that will destroy the earth or the spiritual path of care and compassion, of *bmaadiziwin*, of the good life. And we are told that before we can choose that soft green path we can't just walk forward. The people of the seventh fire must instead walk backwards and pick up what was left for us along the ancestors' path: the stories, the teachings, the songs, each other, our more-than-human relatives who were lost along the way—and our language. Only when we have found these once again and placed in our bundles the things that will heal us—the things that we love—can we walk forward on that green path, all the worlds' people, together...

These are the questions we face today at the crossroads. What do we find along the ancestors' path that will heal us and bring us back to balance? What do we love too much to lose that we will carry it through the narrows of climate change, safely to the other side? For there is another side. The prophecy of the seventh fire teaches that the people of the seventh fire will need great courage and creativity and wisdom, but that they will lead us to the lighting of the eighth fire. It is said that we are the people of the seventh fire. You and I... As writers, we mark that path with our stories, we mark the path with our words...

Our Potawatomi stories tell that a long time ago, when Turtle Island was young, the people and all the plants and animals spoke the same language and conversed freely with one another. But as our dominance has grown, we have become more isolated, more lonely on the planet and we can no longer call our neighbors by name. If we are to manifest the values of the Skywoman story, we have to learn once again to call each other by name. And by name, to call on each other for help. It is said that Skywoman went back to the sky, and looked over the land with the visage of Grandmother Moon. It is said that she left our teachers behind us, the plants. In this time of the Sixth Extinction, of coming climate chaos, we could use teachers.

We don't have to figure everything out for ourselves.

Singing whales, talking trees, dancing bees, birds who make art, fish who navigate, plants who learn and remember. We've forgotten that we are surrounded by intelligences other than our own, by feathered people and people with leaves. There are many forces arrayed to help us forget. Even the language we speak, the beautiful English language, makes us forget, through a simple grammatical error that has grave consequences for us all.

Let me share with you a poem by one of my heroes of women and the land, the Cherokee writer Marilou Awiakta:

When Earth Becomes an "It"

When the people call the Earth "Mother,"
They take with love
And with love give back
So that all may live.

When the people call Earth "it,"
They use her
Consume her strength. Then the people die.

Already the sun is hot
Out of season.
Our Mother's breast
Is going dry.
She is taking all green
Into her heart
And will not turn back
Until we call her
By her name.

I'm a beginning student of my native Anishinaabe language, trying to reclaim what was washed from the mouths of children in the Indian boarding schools. Children like my grandfather. So I'm paying a lot of attention to grammar lately. Grammar is how we chart relationships through language, including our relationship with the Earth.

Imagine your grandmother standing at the stove in her apron and someone says, "Look, it is making soup. It has gray hair." We might snicker at such a mistake, at the same time that we recoil. In English, we never refer to a person as "it." Such a grammatical error would be a profound act of disrespect. "It" robs a person of selfhood and kinship, reducing a person to a thing.

And yet in English, we speak of our beloved Grandmother Earth in exactly that way, as "it." The language allows no form of respect for the more-than-human beings with whom we share the Earth. In English, a being is either a human or an "it."

Objectification of the natural world reinforces the notion that our species is somehow more deserving of the gifts of the world than the other 8.7 million species with whom we share the planet. Using "it" absolves us of moral responsibility and opens the door to exploitation. When Sugar Maple is an "it" we give ourselves permission to pick up the saw. "It" means it doesn't matter.

But in Anishinaabe and many other indigenous languages, it's impossible to speak of Maple as "it." In our language there is no "it" for birds or berries. The language does not divide the world into him and her, but into animate and inanimate. And the grammar of animacy is applied to all that lives: sturgeon, mayflies, blueberries, boulders and rivers. We refer to other members of the living world with the same language that we use for our family. Because they are our family.

What would it feel like to be part of a family that includes birches and beavers and butterflies? We'd be less lonely. We'd feel like we belonged. We'd be smarter.

In indigenous ways of knowing, other species are recognized not only as persons, but also as teachers who can inspire how we might live. We can learn a new solar economy from plants, medicines from mycelia, and architecture from the ants. By learning from other species, we might even learn humility.

Colonization, we know, attempts to replace indigenous cultures with the culture of the settler. One of its tools is linguistic imperialism, or the overwriting of language and names. Among the many examples of linguistic imperialism, perhaps none is more pernicious than the replacement of the language of nature as subject with the language of nature as object. We can see the consequences all around us as we enter an age of extinction precipitated by how we think and how we live.

So here, today—among a community of writers and readers, of storymakers—let me make a modest proposal. Just a small thing: the transformation of the English language. Let me invite you to join an experiment, for a kind of reverse linguistic imperialism, a shift in worldview through the humble work of the pronoun. Might the soft green path to sustainability be marked by grammar?

Language has always been changeable and adaptive. We lose words we don't need anymore and invent the ones we need. We don't need a worldview of earth beings as objects anymore. That thinking has led us to the precipice of climate chaos and mass extinction. We need a new language that reflects the life-affirming world we want. A new language, with its roots in an ancient way of thinking.

To consider whether animacy might be shared with English, I sought the wisdom of my elders. English is a secular language, to which words are added at will. But Anishinaabe is different. Fluent speaker and spiritual teacher Stewart King reminds us that the language is sacred, a gift to the people to care for one another and for the Creation. It grows and adapts too, but through a careful protocol that respects the sanctity of the language. If sharing is to happen, it has to be done right, with mutual respect.

I was pointedly reminded that our language carries no responsibility to heal the dominant society that systematically sought to exterminate it. At the same time, other elders have taught that "the reason we have held on to our traditional teachings is because one day, the whole world will need them." It's a complicated path to navigate.

Stewart King suggested that the proper Anishinaabe word for the beings of the living earth would be *Bemaadiziiaaki*. I wanted to run through the woods and along the river saying it out loud, so grateful that there was such a word in the world.

But I recognize that this beautiful word would not find its way easily into English to do its work of transformation, to take the place of "it." We need a new English word to carry the meaning offered by the indigenous one. I wonder if that final syllable, *ki*, might be the key. Inspired by the concept of animacy, and with full recognition of its roots in *Bemaadiziiaaki*, might a new English pronoun come into use?

"Ki" to signify a being of the living earth. Not "he" or "she," but "ki." So that when we speak of the Sugar Maple, we say, "Oh, that beautiful tree, *ki* is giving us sap again this spring." And we'll need a plural pronoun, too, for those earth beings. English already has the right word. Let's make that new pronoun *"kin."* So we can now refer to birds and trees not as things, but as our earthly relatives. On a crisp October morning we can look up at the geese and say, "Look, *kin* are flying south for the winter. Come back soon."

Language can be a tool for cultural transformation. Make no mistake: *"Ki"* and *"kin"* are revolutionary pronouns. Words have power to shape our thoughts and our actions. On behalf of the living world, let us learn the grammar of animacy. We can keep "it" to speak of bulldozers and paperclips, but every time we say *"ki"* let our words reaffirm our respect and kinship with the more-than-human world. Let us speak of the beings of the earth as the *"kin"* they are...

We are gathered here to tell a new story, to imagine how writers, as people of the seventh fire, can mark the path, the many paths. To ask, as women, the descendants of Skywoman, how can we use our gifts to tip the world back into balance? In a new world, how shall we make a home?

In the face of our fears, we will ask ourselves: what do we love too much to lose? And answer each other: what will I do to protect kin? For in the words of the respected Onondaga Nation Clan Mother Audrey Shenandoah, who would have so loved this gathering: "Being born as humans to this earth is a very sacred trust. We have a sacred responsibility because of the special gift we have, which is beyond the fine gifts of the plant life, the fish, the woodlands, the birds and all the other living things on earth. We are able to take care of them."

Cynthia Travis
Listen with Your Feet

Prior to colonization, African elephant consciousness mirrored the unfenced expanse of the continent. Elephant civilization was a dense, intricate, multi-dimensional network of millions upon millions who were comparably bound to all other creatures and Nature's rhythms. Experience occurred in tandem, embedded in the space-time matrix of infinite relationships… Each elephant was a self-similar fractal who embodied all elephant consciousness…

The way forward is the way back—by returning to a way of life modeled on elephant ethics and values. Restore our consciousness to that of elephants of old. Renewal will come.
—G. A. Bradshaw, *Elephants, Us and Other Kin*

The way we treat land, and the ghosts of our land, is the way we will treat everything, including ourselves.
—Alexandra Fuller, *Leaving Before the Rains Come*

We have subjected ourselves to a holocaust of the personal, the subjective, and the intuitive, becoming objects, even to ourselves. And that has made us lonely. No wonder we stay up late and keep the lights on all night long. A little more darkness and we might awaken to the question suppressed by virtually every aspect of our light-drunk lives: What on Earth have I done?
—Clark Strand, *Waking Up In the Dark*

Photo by C. Travis

I really must get to sleep, and soon, because by 3 a.m. the logging trucks will resume their ceaseless clatter. Tie-down chains bounce against the long, empty metal platforms of the trailers—long as a tree, as the trucks judder and clang along the narrow haul road across the river from my usually night-silent land. Well, almost silent, except for the all-night barking of my neighbors' dogs as they patrol their small flock of sheep, an irresistible buffet loitering just out of reach of the mountain lions that have been hemmed out by fences, and bears driven mad with hunger because the logging companies have cleared the acorned oaks that are normally interspersed among the redwoods. In desperation, the bears scrape and eat redwood bark. The trees ooze a sweet sap to repair themselves. Bees that feed on this sap are immune to colony collapse disorder.

Species in distress seem to have built-in mechanisms for protecting each other. Let us *bear* this in mind. At least the distant barking is an animal sound that blends with the calls of the owls and the booming rush of the ocean that echoes up the canyon from the dunes. But it is not possible to become inured to the logging trucks, not possible to sleep to the jarring lullaby of metal against metal. I turn out the light. I turn it back on again. Shit. In Mexico, they have a saying, *se me espantó el sueño*:

sleep got frightened away from me. I find myself scrolling through Facebook, looking for hope. (I don't own a television. This is my version of numbing distraction.) With luck, the blue-light-blocker pasted to my laptop screen will allow sleep to find me if it decides to return. Here are baby elephants piling into the laps of delighted humans who are visiting an elephant orphanage. The little elephants gently knock the humans down and curl up in their laps. It's so cute that I almost forget to wonder: What has happened to their mothers and fathers? Were they machine-gunned for ivory? Culled because the herd outgrew its impossibly small range, reduced by human encroachment? Or were the elephant parents enslaved by loggers, or perhaps stolen for a circus or a zoo? The Facebook clip makes it all seem like a day at the petting zoo.

I dreamed once of a long line of baby elephants ambling by, and awoke with the words, *our nearest orphans.* Martín Prechtel says that in early times, when hunters killed an animal mother, they understood that they were now responsible for its orphaned young. This is how we came to have pets.[2] How many, many orphans have we created?

An unexpected memory swims to the surface. When I was a little girl, my grandparents used to vacation in Hawaii. On one of those trips, my grandfather went sport fishing and caught a Marlin. A few weeks later, it arrived in Los Angeles, stuffed and lacquered in a permanent, exuberant arc. For years it hung above the louvered doors of the His and Hers changing rooms by my grandparents' swimming pool. I always hated walking beneath it, always felt ashamed and vulnerable, as if it might crash down on my head, as if any one of us would have deserved to be crushed by the obscenity of its ignominious end. Years later, my friend Tom told me that Marlins mate for life. I thought of her then, the swimming widow spawned by my grandfather.

Tom worked as a termite inspector. In his early forties, he contracted pancreatic cancer from exposure to Chlordane, a pesticide developed and manufactured by Monsanto and used from 1948 to 1988 for fumigation of corn and citrus crops and for termite eradication in over 30 million homes. It has a half-life of 30 years.[3] Tom died in our arms the year before Chlordane was banned. The notion that 'pest control' is necessary and can only be accomplished by eradicating entire species of insects is identical to the thinking template of the Nazis' 'final solution', identical to the justification of every genocide. Are humans the host for greed? Is greed the intermediate host for Death?

Just as each life has its personal snapshots of mayhem and suffering, every era has its wars, it seems, and its public icons of madness. I was born after the concentration camps with their emaciated prisoners in striped pajamas; after the boxcars and the impossible mounds of children's shoes; after the mushroom clouds and the indelible, scorched shadows etched onto the sidewalks of Hiroshima and Nagasaki. In elementary school, in the 1950's, we used to practice 'drop drills'—a sudden shout from the teacher to DROP! and we'd throw down our pencils and dive under our desks, covering our heads with our hands. It was a surreal enactment of the illusion of Western invincibility, as if our spindly arms and a piece of Formica could protect us from an atomic bomb. It reinforced what we already intuitively knew: that, like everyone and everything else, we, too were expendable. At best, the adults in our lives would shout a warning, but it was up to us children to protect ourselves. The fact of nuclear weapons meant that, like us, the future was expendable. By the early 1960's, this sent us, like lemmings, over the edge of our known world, in search of a better way. Our drugged hedonism and political fury gave momentary expression to our desperate longing (and there are some beautiful experiments that have taken root). Yet, fifty years on, we are still running, faster than ever. Running away, always running way. But what are we running toward?

I came of age during the Viet Nam war, watching Watergate on TV at dinnertime, stoned, with my roommates, the whole surreal drama unfolding as if real-time war and Nixon's crumbling presidency were just another sitcom. For me, the overarching image of that time was Kim Phuc, the napalmed girl running toward us, naked and screaming, with outstretched arms. Now we have Alan Kurdi, the drowned toddler from Syria who washed up on a Turkish beach.

In the media, human suffering, though terrible, is nonetheless privileged over the suffering of the natural world. Images of the devastated Earth and her beleaguered animals are comparatively few and hidden, reinforcing the illusion that we are separate. One must look more deeply to get to the truth. Few among us can escape the expanding library of horror lodged in our minds, whose images we can play at will like a slideshow. Each one is unbearable. With each one I think, That does it! *That* toddler, *those* baby elephants, *that* melting ice. *This cannot continue!* But how? How can I contribute to wholeness with the shape of my life?

And so, and now, how shall we live?

The Wild is sanity. Darkness. Silence. The great knowing of Nature's rhythmic wisdom. In the wild is contained the dignity of intactness, authenticity, and the congruence of original design. Earth's relentless enfolding of each thing into another keeps life going. It is a terrifying comfort to remember that nothing, *no thing*, is outside it. Every *thing*, everything, is contained within her eternal cycling. All of the murdered and all of the murderers. Policemen shooting unarmed black men, and those who, in turn, shoot policemen. Revelers. Travelers. Suicide bombers and drone-makers. The fracked earth, pitted and paved, and politicians justifying torture as they parse 'collateral damage'. Even the mines with their unspeakable chemicals, and the desperate gouging for gold, silver, copper, platinum and 'rare earths' to put in our smartphones. Each and all of it deemed by someone's mad calculus to be a necessary sacrifice in the pursuit of righteousness, pleasure or profit.

Last night, I saw a huge, black mound lying motionless in the middle of the road. I realized it was a black bear that had been hit by a car. It was past midnight, and with no houses nearby, and no other cars on the road, I could neither attend to it nor move it by myself, and so I guiltily drove on, nauseous and in tears.

The keystone species[4] that sustain entire ecosystems are under siege as never before: beavers, whose wetland engineering protects endangered salmon; wolves whose presence keeps rivers alive; sharks, who, as apex predators, keep the oceanic food chain in balance; bees, whose pollination we depend on for food; and elephants, especially elephants, with their huge range that benefits countless other species who depend on their journey, that also protects the land itself. Every life prepares the way for those that will follow, whether consciously or not. Are we humans a reverse keystone?

A tracker friend once told me that when a species goes extinct, the last individuals step into a world that is invisible to us, a parallel reality enfolded in a corner of the space-time continuum beyond our reach, awaiting the day when it is safe to return. I imagine a shimmering curtain, a barely discernible ripple in the air. Beyond it there are grizzlies, great auks, and northern white rhinos, all thriving. There are tribes of Native Peoples from all over the world, speaking their lost languages. It is comforting to think that so much beauty and irreplaceable wisdom remain intact somewhere.

It used to be that elephants migrated over thousands of miles in cycles lasting 200 years or more. The elephants' long memories made it possible to find water, food, and refuge along the way and to honor their dead. Unerring navigation over vast distances remains encoded in their DNA. By the time the elephants had come full circle, many generations later, the trees their forebears had pulled down had regrown, and countless plants and animals had been sustained in the interim.

Elephants communicate through infrasonic rumbles and seismic vibrations across hundreds of square miles. When they stand on the tips of their massive feet, they are listening. The fatty tissue that cushions their footpads also transmits sound waves to their brain. With their trunks, they can discern scent particles of one part per 100 million. They are matriarchal and communal. They mourn their dead, remembering the identity and location of those that have perished.[5] Elephants have an unerring, psychic intuition. The morning that legendary conservationist and 'elephant whisperer' Lawrence Anthony died of a heart attack in 2012, the two herds of rescued elephants that live at Thula Thula, his private game reserve in South Africa, gathered in the predawn light in front of his house. Each year, on the anniversary of his death, they return.[6] In both Sudan and Liberia, when peace came at last after protracted war, elephants returned that had fled into neighboring countries.

Male elephant elders keep young males in check. Like humans, when juvenile males are not properly eldered, they go berserk, raping and killing. (Elephants attack not only their own species but others as well.)[7] Elephants, humans, and dozens of other species (including birds, reptiles, dogs, and many others) currently suffer from PTSD. Elephants, like humans and other animals, are able to heal once they find safety, kindness, and the opportunity to devote themselves to helping others.[8]

It used to be that elephant hunting was a gory colonial sport, and modern poaching was the province of hungry villagers or resentful farmers. Now elephants (and rhinos) are being gunned down from helicopters by criminal gangs armed with automatic weapons and night-vision scopes. Rangers who attempt to protect the animals are often executed. The numbers are staggering: it is estimated that in 1900, there were 10 million elephants in Africa. In 1980, 1.2 million. In 2013, 450,000.[9] Each day, about 100 elephants are killed in Africa—one every 15 minutes, 35,000 or more per year.[10] At this rate, viable populations of elephants in the wild will be gone within our lifetime. The situation for rhinos is even worse. Yet, despite hundreds of years of torture, enslavement and genocide at human hands, elephants remain miraculously steadfast in their willingness to connect with us. They are a keystone species and then some. In the refined complexity of their social behavior as well as in their physiology, elephants are deeply, exquisitely sane.

In September of 2006, I went to Botswana with my friend Deena Metzger to visit the Elephant Ambassador, so named for a bull elephant with whom she had had a life-changing encounter a few years before, and had pledged to live in alliance with the elephants as a result.[11] We had returned in hopes that the elephants might wish to continue the connection. Whenever we were with them, we practiced, as best we could, a sustained heart and mind-opening, allowing our awareness to melt into theirs and vice versa. In the course of our silent conversations, we mentioned that we were on our way to Liberia, where the presence of elephants was known to be a sign of peace. We told them that peace was deeply needed there, both for their elephant kin, the beleaguered forest elephants of West Africa, and for humans.

As we sat under the tree that was our elephant meeting place, an elephant family of four crossed to the nearby river to drink and to play. As with Deena's first encounter with the elephants in that place, we had been waiting all afternoon and, on the last day, at the last moment of the last hour, they came. When it was time for the elephants to go home, the youngest didn't want to leave and the adults had to insist, gently pushing it out of the deliciously cool mud and back up the riverbank. The parents stood close to our truck and affectionately entwined their trunks before the mother left with the youngsters. When they had disappeared into the bush, the male began pulling at something in the low grass, eventually picking it up and tossing it toward our truck. He came closer. Stopping about ten yards away, he turned to face us and got down on one knee. After a few moments, he stood up again, twisted his trunk into a figure eight—a sort of elephant-trunk infinity, and ambled away. What he had thrown to us turned out to be an elephant thighbone. Surely he must have known whose. The deliberateness of his actions was unmistakable. It took our breath away.

And so, and now, how shall we live?

While in Liberia some weeks later, we made offerings to the elephants in the forest and told them of our visit to their cousins in Botswana. The following year, just before Thanksgiving, I received a call from Liberia that elephants had arrived in all of the villages where offerings to the elephants had been made. I rushed back to hear the stories in person, wondering whether the Botswana elephants had, indeed, put out the call to their Liberian kin.

In the village of Womanor, when the elephants came, the elders fanned out into the forest and read certain passages from the Koran out loud. They explained that this had been customary in the old times, to let the elephants know that the people recognized their presence as a sacred event. Since the appearance of the elephants the village had not been troubled by poisonous insects or snakes. The elephants had come in a small group, led by a large and very old bull. It was thought that this individual had escaped from a zoo during the war, and had walked several hundred kilometers to safety in neighboring Guinea, and recently returned. One day, a woman met him while farming her small plot, coming face to face with the huge old bull elephant just as he was about to pull up one of her cassava plants. She looked him in the eye and said: *I'm a woman and I grow this food for my children. My husband was killed in the war. Please, be sorry for me, and leave us something to eat!* The elephant unwound his trunk from the cassava stalk and disappeared into the forest. A short time later, that elephant died. The people brought out his massive skull to show us.

We accompanied our friend Karmah Jallah, an elder from the Lorma tribe, to the Mandingo village of Kuluka. Though the Mandingos and the Lormas were historically very close, during the Liberian civil war they were, literally, at each other's throats. Now, two years after the war had ended, there was still much bitterness and animosity between them. Because the elephants had come, Karmah Jallah convened a council at Kuluka, which was held at the gravesite of the founding elder of the village. There, Karmah Jallah recounted the history of their two peoples and the deep and loving connection they once enjoyed. The Mandingo elders wept openly and peace was restored. A few weeks later, Karmah Jallah died.

In the village of Barkedu, we met a man whose elephant dreams had flowed into daytime reality. Other villagers corroborated that when the elephants told him, for example, *Meet me at the pond on Thursday at noon*, he would go there at the appointed time and find an elephant waiting for him. Soon, the elephants instructed him where to plant his crops. He did as he was told. The elephants ate the other farmers' harvest, but left the dreamer's plot undisturbed. When he asked them why, they replied, *The others have forgotten their manners. They are cutting down too many trees, and killing too many animals for no reason.*

One of the elders there told us that, before the war, the people and the animals used to speak freely with each other and communicated well. He remembered when, as a young boy, there had been trouble in the river nearby. Crocodiles were attacking humans, and humans were killing the crocodiles in self-defense. The head elder of the village summoned the crocodile elder. The man telling us the story said he remembered seeing the old croc walking slowly up to the old man's hut. There, the two leaders sat together all afternoon, discussing their shared dilemma. They came to an agreement that each group would have its own special bend in the river where they would each be safe. The agreement was still in force at the time we were told the story. People said they bathed, washed their clothes and swam freely in their designated area, without a crocodile in sight. A short distance away, the crocodiles basked in the mud undisturbed.

At the end of our meeting, an ex-combatant recounted a dream: He is pounding on his neighbor's door and shouting, *Is there Mercy enough for me?* A question like that burrows deep in our soul and lays its eggs. It feeds on our unshed tears.

Intuition, dreams, and synchronicities are the language of the liminal world where human and non-human meet. Logic cannot take us there. This past January (2016), inspired by a mysterious dream that had come to Deena, we returned to the site of our previous meeting with the Elephant Ambassador, and visited two other preserves where we hoped to find elephants whose communities were relatively intact. Everywhere we went the elephants seemed to deliberately come meet us. The desert elephants of Damaraland, in Namibia, reached their trunks into our vehicle to sniff us.

Stories make images, images make memories, memories feed questions. What does it mean to inhabit a question? To invite the questions, the images—and the elephants themselves—to inhabit us, and to notice where they take up residence in our bodies and in our lives? *Those* elephants. *That* soldier. *Is there Mercy enough for me? Enough for us all?* Not God's mercy, but our own. They're one and the same. That's the point.

Back in the U.S., Deena and I sit together to ponder what the elephants might want from us now. In our minds, we journey to meet them. At first all is darkness and chaos. Fleeting images, none that are clear. But at the last moment, I hear them say, *Learn to listen with your feet. Then you will know what to do.*

It behooves us to consider that the elephants realize that our species has gone rogue – that our trauma is driving us to rape and destroy; that we are in dire need of some serious cross-species eldering and matriarchal leadership; that they are calling us back into the life-and-death alliances that are our birthright if we are to reweave the threads of ourselves back into the tapestry of Life. It is the last hour of the last afternoon of the last day — the hour of the elephants. It is time to quiet ourselves in order to receive them. *And so, and now, how shall we live?*

N.B.: This is an abridged version. Please see Dark Matter: Women Witnessing #4 *online for the complete essay.*

---

[1] Dolman, Brock. OAEC (Occidental Arts and Ecology Center). 2016. Web. n.d.

[2] Prechtel, Martin. *The Smell of Rain on Dust: Grief and Praise.* Berkeley: North Atlantic Books, 2015. Print.

[3] Wikipedia, 2016. Web. n.d.

[4] " A keystone species is a species that has a disproportionately large effect on its environment relative to its abundance… The role that a keystone species plays in its ecosystem is analogous to the role of a keystone in an arch… which collapses without it. Similarly, an ecosystem may experience a dramatic shift if a keystone species is removed, even though that species was a small part of the ecosystem by measures of biomass or productivity." Wikipedia. Web. n.d.

[5] Anthony, Lawrence and Graham Spence. *The Last Rhinos: My Battle to Save One of the World's Greatest Creatures.* New York: St. Martin's Publishing Group, 2013 and *The Elephant Whisperer: My Life with the Herd in the African Wild.* New York: Thomas Dunne/St Martin's Press, 2009. Print.

[6] zululandobserver.co.za, beliefnet.com. 2016. Web. n.d.

[7] Bradshaw, G.A. *Elephants on the Edge: What Elephants Teach Us about Humanity.* Yale University Press, 2009. Print.

[8] Bradshaw, G.A. "Elephants, Us and Other Kin". www.gabradshaw.com. 2016. Web. n.d.

[9] www.howmanyelephants.co/. 2016. Web. n.d.

[10] CA4Elephants.org, savetheelephants.org. 2016. Web. n.d.

[11] Metzger, Deena. *Entering the Ghost River: Meditations on the Theory and Practice of Healing.* Hand to Hand Publishing, 2002. Print.

Deena Metzger
MaNdlovu

Poet's note: MaNdlovu *is the word the Ndebele people of Zimbabwe use for* female elephant. *It is connected in resonance with* Mambo Kadze, *the name for the deity that is at once elephant, the Virgin Mary and the Great Mother.*

Suddenly, I am of a single mind extended
Across an unknown geography,
And imprinted, as if by a river, on the moment.
A mind held in unison by a large gray tribe
Meandering in reverent concert
among trees, feasting on leaves.
One great eye reflecting blue
From the turn inward
Toward the hidden sky that, again,
Like an underground stream
Continuously nourishes
What will appear after the dawn
Bleaches away the mystery in which we rock
Through the endless green dark.

I am drawn forward by the lattice,
By a concordance of light and intelligence
Constituted from the unceasing and consonant
Hum of cows and the inaudible bellow of bulls,
A web thrumming and gliding
Along the pathways we remember
Miles later or ages past.

I am, we are,
Who can distinguish us?
A gathering of souls, hulking and muddied,
Large enough – if there is a purpose –
To carry the accumulated joy of centuries
Walking thus within each other's
Particular knowing and delight.

This is our grace: To be a note
In the exact chord that animates creation,
The dissolve of all the rivers
That are both place and moment,
An ocean of mind moving
Forward and back,
Outside of any motion
Contained within it.

This is particle and wave. How simple.
The merest conversation between us
Becoming the essential drone
Into which we gladly disappear.
A common music, a singular heavy tread,
Ceaselessly carving a path,
For the waters tumbling invisibly
Beneath.

I have always wanted to be with them, with you, so.
I have always wanted to be with them
With you,
So.

Judy Grahn
Dragonfly Dances

As a child without television, phone, or any electronic distractions, in complete freedom during the long summer days when my parents were at work, I asked questions of wild life. I lay on the ground eye-to-eye with fighting beetles and clashing pairs of praying mantis. I knew where the black widow spiders, the horned toads, and the crawdads all lived. I brought fearsome red fire ants home in a jar of sand to watch them replicate their home tunnels, to gape at their amazing labor of moving and hauling, building and cooperating. I watched them clean out their house and carry their dead above ground. I also knew how dangerous they could be; a toddler had to be hospitalized after getting trapped on one of their big sprawling mounds in a lot near our home. I had dropped my Levis to the ground more than once, shrieking with the pain of a red ant stinging my knee. But living close to them as they were safely encased in the glass jar, I was learning to love them, as well.

Asking questions is how I came to closely watch Mollie, the wild cat in our neighborhood, in her hunt for the grasshoppers and mice that fed her. I saw how she swallowed a mouse until only the tail dripped down her chin and then allowed it to slowly slither into her slender inexorable maw. My nine-year-old self laughed until my sides hurt over this sight of the tail dripping out of her mouth.

As I trailed around behind wild Mollie, wanting to know her habits, I also wanted her to reach out to me. She never did this, though she did give presents to a neighbor dog. A medium-sized young collie had been tied to a wire clothesline by neighbors who owned him. He could run up and down the yard, his leash sliding along the line as he barked angrily at everything that came into his view. Not much did, on those long hot nearly silent days. The first indication I had that animals reason and have compassion came from watching how the little grey cat lurked around the building near the collie's confinement, with a dead mouse in her mouth. She would wait until the dog was at the other end of the big yard, and then would trot over to drop one of her extra catches under the clothesline so the dog could reach it. While I thought this might have been coincidence the first time, I saw Mollie do this several times, and saw also that the dog found each little body and joyfully played with it for the better part of his otherwise monotonous days.

The little wild cat had reached across to the dog, with every appearance of empathy and decision-making. Perhaps this was the germinal moment of my desire to experience creatures reaching across species lines, and of longing for them to communicate with me, not pet to owner, but creature to creature. I wanted to know them, and didn't know how to initiate the dialogue. Would any of them reach across to me? Could I learn to reach across to them?

As I entered college and in 1961 attended a year of medical laboratory school and then college again, my educational experiences sharply distanced me from creatures, as well as from the human body. Medical language was constructed in 17th-century Latin-based syllables expressly to achieve this distancing, to ensure the emotional stillness necessary to cut someone open and work on fixing their internal organs. "Cardiac" is so different (in meaning) from "heart." However, the specialized distancing necessary for science and its preoccupations then became part of a broad Western philosophy about the nature of reality, and of nonhuman beings. Nature was mechanistic, this view said, and fishermen echoed: "fish don't have feelings." Creatures don't think, this view insisted; they operate solely on "instinct," imagined as a set of pre-existing internal settings that somehow came about through evolution without intention or volition, without interaction and culture. Despite all this, my path kept returning to the open curiosity and affection of my childhood. I conquered an irrational terror of wasps by giving them water, and learning to remove them from my house with a piece of paper and an empty glass. And I continue to cherish those life moments when I can still my incessant human activity enough to just be with another species long enough to learn something.

The cleverness of their communication system came clear when with a friend in India, I watched a group of ants—a medium-sized light red variety. Their task was to insert the body of a long, slender-winged beetle into a crack about three feet up a wall. The group had posted four overseers that formed a square on the wall about six inches above and below the crack site. A work crew held the body, twisting it this way and that, getting the front part way in, then backing out, rearranging from radically different positions, trying again. The beetle was longer than the crack opening so this operation didn't look possible to our eyes, yet to theirs it obviously did, as they spent twenty minutes on the maneuvering. The oversight crew appeared to signal with their antennae between each attempt, as though conveying logistical information, and eventually the crew succeeded, vanishing with their prize into the wall opening, followed by the four members of the talkative oversight crew.

People who study ants closely say they communicate through smell, sending out pheromones from glands in their bodies, detected through their antennae. But what of the ant-movers on the wall? Did their out-posted lookouts have pheromones that could tell the work group, "Try again from a steeper angle, girls, and turn the body on the bias." What would be the signal language for, "Try 90-degree angle, try from the left, try turning the body upright, a certain portion out from the wall"? However they do it, the instructions eventually enabled the ultra-strong worker ants to hold the long body of the beetle in defiance of gravity, then slide it like a letter into the envelope slot in the wall.

Insects talk to each other, but do they also attempt to talk to us? One day, I looked down at my arm to find a small brown ant vigorously touching its antennae to the fine hairs on the back of my wrist. I watched this one-sided interaction for a long time—minutes of my time, hours of ant time—and had a strong impression of witnessing someone trying to engage a conversation. Was this ant attempting to detect intelligent life on planet human? Having no way to consciously manipulate my arm hairs, I could not respond in any way, watching helplessly until the patient creature finally gave up. I can only wonder, and hope some clever naturalist devises antennae-like linguistic devices through which we can connect to these marvelous beings.

One day in 1995 my childhood desire to have a personal interaction with an insect—this time a dragonfly—was fulfilled. An encounter with a dragonfly is an encounter with a gatekeeper of spirit, according to the lore of some indigenous people of the North American continent. The connection, usually initiated by the creature, indicates a major change in one's consciousness and therefore one's life.

My very personal dragonfly encounter took place summer of 1995, and lasted over an hour. Kris and I were playing golf with our friend Ruth, on the Willow Park course in Castro Valley. Ruth's ball had gone into the creek that runs the length of the course and keeps it both challenging and life-filled. From TV images, golf courses seem like human-only territory, but the municipal courses my friends and I play in the Bay Area are full of wild creatures. A blue heron lives along Willow Creek, as do hawks and snakes, rabbits and foxes, turkeys and coyotes; once, we saw a mountain lion on a nearby hill. So when I went over to help Ruth look for her ball I wasn't surprised to see something moving in the thick scum of algae growth covering the water at this particular spot. An insect about three inches long was persistently, if weakly, moving. I called Ruth to come with her long aluminum ball retriever, and she got the cup of it under what we now recognized as a dragonfly. The rescue immediately looked like a cruel exercise in futility as we saw that the body of the creature was completely enmeshed in webs of slime, a mossy growth of algae in long thin intersecting lines that made a netlike cocoon around the struggling body. The largest dragonfly I had ever seen now lay helpless in the palm of my hand. Gingerly, I began to strip off the binding strands of slime. There were dozens of them. Would the dragonfly let me help? My fingers looked huge compared to the vulnerable, exhausted body in my hand.

We still had a golf game to play, and golf etiquette requires keeping up the pace, so we treated the creature as we walked along, at first taking turns holding it while we hit our shots. The creek area where we had found the dragonfly was the fourth hole, less than half way through our game, which is about a mile and a half in length. By the fifth hole she—I call her she because she was so large, and often among flying creatures the larger ones are female—was riding on Kris' shoulder, clinging with well-developed hooked ankles and feet to the cotton cloth of her tee shirt. Because my fingers are small I was best qualified to softly, softly unfurl the stubborn shroud of muck from the fragile body. Holding my breath I peeled layer after layer until I could see the structures of form, a long brown body, large dark eyes, two pairs of magnificent, delicately netted wings, now crumpled and stiff.

After I had stripped away most of the filaments binding her legs and the first of several layers of fiber from her wings, the still-encumbered creature made an attempt to fly. The flight consisted of a yard-long head-over-heels somersault to the ground, testifying to the fact that the second layer of muck, which had dried by now on the wings, was weighting them down and had caused their usually transparent fabric to crinkle into what amounted to an aerodynamic crisis. The dragonfly raised not the slightest protest when Kris picked up her upside down body and placed her again on her own broadly human left shoulder.

I went back to my restoration work, aware that drastic measures were indicated for the crinkled, disabled wings. I pulled another layer or two from the body, and tenderly worked a few more strands from under the wings, of which she had two pairs. The coating on top of the usually transparent wings had now completely dried and looked to be a permanent cement, rippling their thin surfaces like bent airplane propellers.

I set aside my fears that I would tear the fragile, brilliant instruments of flight and remembered the bottle of water always tucked into the pocket of my golf bag, along with extra balls, an old glove and a bag of raisins that had petrified in the heat. In a hurry, I raised the water bottle over the wing, aware of watchful dragonfly eyes, The sight of the bottle's metal form looming overhead immediately set off a creature alarm and her second attempt to fly. Again, flight was a breath-taking failure as the dragonfly catapulted head-over-transom onto the dry California earth. Again, Kris leaned down and picked her up, and again, the shoulder was solace and hope, as hooked feet dug in.

Now I became cognizant of a strong current of awareness beaming toward my eyes, and emanating from what looked like a little square organ on the dragonfly's head. I became certain that she was in touch with me, was thinking, and not only thinking, contacting me somehow with her thinking.

Smarter now and more patient, I wet my fingers first then slid them ever so lightly over the wings, first the two on the left, the most encrusted. The water dissolved the stiffened filaments, and allowed me to roll them. Now she was far from being in a state of panic; the dragonfly was acting as though she knew exactly what I was doing to help, as I could tell from her body language. She seemed to be making very conscious motions, turning and lifting her wings one by one, separating the upper and lower pairs so as to allow the needed access for my wet fingers, and enhancing the process of my tender work. Could this be true?

Giving up the golf game, I stayed completely in the moment as I rolled and rolled until the slime fell off each wing, which as it did, immediately straightened. Elation! And our conscious connection was not my imagination— the dragonfly was turning to engage my wet fingers, was guiding me into the next step and the next, turning to present her other side, and the undersides as well as the tops of each of her four wings, and also her wire-like legs. We were working together! Delicacy of timing in joint effort did not fail us, and by the end of the sixth hole, the slime was off. One wing remained a little wrinkled, but the game of recovery was won, and this was clear to all of us. We relaxed. She would live.

With her long body as brown as the recently released mud, the dragonfly stayed still on Kris' shoulder. "Resting," I heard clearly as I stared at the head box between her large eyes, that appeared to emanate toward my mind, and now emitted a golden glow that opened my heart as well, a distinctive sensation that I experienced physically, as well as emotionally. The insect foot-clutch on cotton cloth was confident, even as Kris hit her shots off the tee and fairway. When the golfer's left shoulder dipped, the dragonfly dipped with it, as though on a slender bough in the wind.

On the seventh hole, I noticed the change. It began as an underglow in various sections of her body, so at first I wondered if it had been there all along and I simply hadn't noticed. Then the blue color became more evident, then startling, deep and luminous as summer sky. "Look," I said breathlessly to my companions, "She's a *blue* dragonfly." The blue was that sparkling clean lake-water shade beloved of race car drivers and motorcyclists, and it spread until the whole body had it, except for the dark eyes and the darker box, that intriguing communicating shape that I could feel as well as see between her eyes, on top of her head. Then, amidst the blue, dazzling gold appeared as well, as though a whimsical, good-humored and patient painter had put golden trim on a particularly treasured model. We were all in love by then. Ruth and I continued to exclaim our pleasure, and Kris glowed as she craned her neck to check on the condition of the creature that rode her like the most stable of horses across this winding course.

Each hole on a golf course takes about fifteen minutes to play, so we had been with her for almost an hour. As we left the seventh hole, the dragonfly turned her body around into the late afternoon wind and we sensed another change. "She's getting ready to leave," Kris predicted. I tried to keep my attention riveted so I wouldn't miss the take-off, but as we walked up onto the eighth tee box, my eyes wandered and I didn't see till Kris called out. The blue dragonfly had launched and was already high above Ruth. Stopping still about thirty feet in the air, she performed a steep downward spiral dance, directly over Ruth's head, before twirling left and disappearing into the upper branches of the nearest tree.

My rational mind, always clicking away in its sometimes cynical fashion, said into my ear: "Probably a practice spiral, not necessarily a dance of gratitude and fare- thee-well." But none of us believed that, especially because we were left in a happy state that lasted days afterwards, as happens from a visit with persons one loves intensely.

Rational mind is frequently wrong about these fine interactional moments, so I was surprised but not skeptical at our next encounter, which took place about a month later. That much time had passed before the three of us again played golf on the Willow Park course. As we approached the fourth hole we were recalling that this was the place where we found the creature that had spent such a long time in our care. Deliberately, I had worn the same hat and shirt I had on then, and my companions had on similar clothing.

The air directly above the tee box was swarming with dragonflies as we arrived, at least fifty of them, most of their bodies in the brown state, though a few of the larger ones were blue. Had they been gathering there for days? Were they gathered there on this day because of some food source or because every year at that time they gathered there? Or, as our lifting hearts told us, were they gathered there because we had been recognized and they wanted to perform a group acknowledgement? A dance for us. One, a particularly large blue one, came very near and looked into my face—and I could sense a connection. Once again, I felt the heart emanation from the head area, straight toward my own opening heart.

According to anatomical drawings, a dragonfly has an organ called an "occipital triangle" just in back of, or between, the large compound eyes; perhaps this was the source of the emanations I felt.

A year following our first encounter with the blue dragonfly, we played again on the same golf course. I wore the same tan golf hat. And once again, at the fourth hole, a dragonfly approached me. She was brown-bodied, large like the one we had rescued, and she hung in the air about five feet in front of me, looking directly at my face. She flew higher and did a little downward spiral dance, twice. The encounter took only about a quarter of a minute but was very intense. After she left, I felt a burning sensation in the lower left quadrant of my face, spreading to my heart, flooding me with goodwill. I have come to recognize this from my travels in India as a *shaktipat*, a sensual experience of eros, heart-opening spiritual love with extreme joy given as a *darshan*, a blessing. It is both physical and emotional, and I am unable to conjure it from my imagination, or from inside myself, alone. The sensation of intense heart-open love following my encounter with the dancing dragonfly lasted about five minutes before fading.

Fortunate encounters with insects, moments of wonder, of rescue and recognition, of communication and camaraderie, of intense love and long memory, remind me that we are not alone here on earth, abandoned on a burning stone whirling mutely in space. We are connected in relationships of diversity, human with human, human with insects and plants, creatures and spirits, requiring only that we pay attention and stay still enough to think/feel the connection, and accept that we have been recognized, sent a vital communication, given a gift.

Alexandra Merrill
Homage To Bees

In September 2007, while walking with friends, single file through the ancient Arc of Appalachia, countless swarming bees appear among us. We keep walking, casually and stupidly, brushing them away. Suddenly their focus centers in on my body and I am under the siege of their collective strike. Severely allergic to bee venom, I realize I must get to a safe house. I walk there and lie down on the floor of a quiet room. I slide quickly into an anaphylactic shock state from which, with help of friends and emergency medicine, I will later return. For now, I offer my attempt to bring image and words to the impact of that collaborative journey of mutual affliction, to the wise teachings from the bees as well as I can translate them, and then finally, to my gratitude for the honor of bearing witness to their suffering and our complicity in creating their struggle.

A maternity of bees: the story of my journey into and out of anaphylactic shock

Still hearing my own words as a tail wind, "a good day to die," I wing up, weightless to where nothing is broken apart, where all that has been long broken is waiting to be made whole by being told. Here, I am torn and whole, folded into patchwork clouds, untethered from time, reviewing a summer afternoon of 1944 and we are at war and I am six and busy, killing garden bees with Grandma's red DDT sprayer gun. I will spray them until they're dead because I love her and she told me to use the gun. Squirting the smelly sprayer barrel over and over until they're all down in the dirt under the roses, I am ashamed to enjoy watching the bees falling down dead. I loved the little bees when they used to come sit here on my chubby fingers.

My eyes are down in shame. I can take a deep breath away from shame. Now I am sliding down into an old stump hole. Here, a full-bellied honeycomb glowing in her own dark luster hums an endless prayer for all the wrongful deaths. Curling my cloud self around the waxy prayer body and inhaling honey scent, I am forgiving my small heart and Grandma's old one. Shame is weakening. I breathe again, in and then out, more easily this time.

An outside hammer force punches my lungs to gasp toward air. Wild wrath rises to counter the uninvited foreign volts. I oppose, fail, relent, accept and crash back down onto this cold table, to these humans, these men and women, under cold white lights. I float out and back, too weak to go far. This time I accept the breath as my breath. Countless tiny bees buzz all over my stinky, sticky self, licking me warm and clean into clock time. A maternity of bees reminds me to remember what I must now know and do.

Back under the lights in the Emergency Room

For a time, I am noticing the dry blinking of my eyes, and a cataract blur of shapes leaning in toward me under the dead cold light above us. I am sad to be losing the delicious sensation of all-over bee-licking as it fades off my body and as my eyes attach to the Emergency Room clock and my ears turn to the anxious buzzing of human voices around the repair table where I have been deposited. Bereft. Bereft is the word that helps my emotions crash onto the sterile benevolence of this clinical slab. They are caring for me. I accept.

In the next days, I am homesick, forlorn, aggrieved. I can't remember my assignment anymore. I pray to remember it. As I learn to pray to the bees, asking them to help me remember, it occurs to me that I have acquired a secretarial capacity. I begin to notice a rhythmic buzzing in my ears. Standard tinnitus is not a sufficient explanation. The licking sensation returns each time I bring attention to the sounds in my ears. At first there is nothing to write down.

Soon I understand that images precede the words. So I begin to paint the first in this series of 8 x 8 inch images. With no interest in their meaning, I copy onto the paper. When one image is done, I know because I get the licking feeling on my skin. At that point, a rather monotone neutral voice drops a statement down into my ears and the buzzing stops as I write down the text. All the little messages arrive in the same capsule form without much tonal inflection—as if they are being droned in a medieval chapel, or as if I am a nun transcribing manuscripts with quill onto parchment miniatures. In all of these messages, one voice is speaking both AS the collective and for the collective to an invisible (perhaps human) audience.

Art by A. Merrill

I am obviously not the queen bee. Our hive-bound queen only breeds us and uses the venom to kill her rivals until they kill her. She is pale, ungainly and awkward inside her bulk while I am lean, lithe and agile. I fly free, am devoted to her and the hive. I work to sustain our culture, as do all workers. Workers are all female and our drones are male. Workers collect the nectar wherever we are living and bring it directly back to the waxy cells to store. We all work hard.

Animals and humans often attack us so each of us has to carry a survival portion of venom. When I have to sting, I do it discreetly and precisely. When I sting, all of us receive the message immediately and come immediately to multiply the dosage by our number. If one is challenged, all arrive. Our venom has always been mighty: wounding, killing, and occasionally curing.

Currently, all of our colonies are endangered and at risk of collapsing. Insecticides. We are all at risk together. We'll have to collaborate with humans to save all our communities. I know I speak bluntly. No time left for imprecision: it is better to speak blunt truth than to play nice. You pay a price either way, bee or person.

Art by A. Merrill

A swarm of us isn't necessarily a hostile force. Most often, we are either acting in legitimate self-defense or traveling together to a new location. The woman who trespassed on our well-hidden hive that day didn't know she was stepping on marked territory and wasn't prepared for our response. She was blindly following the lead of a man who appeared to know everything about the forest. He didn't. It was an accident, you might say. But from our perspective, it was not at all an accident. As we kept stinging her, we heard her say out loud to the forest

"Well, this would be a good day to die."

That is the very moment we knew to stop, satisfied with her response. We left her to her own conclusions. Those of us who hadn't died stinging flew down under our ground with the day's collection. We knew that our dosage had been precise and correct. We thought she'd be back, working for us. We were right. We can see through time because of the structure of our eyes. We see behind and ahead, all at once. And we know humans don't yet have that capacity.

When we all sting down into her, she is not afraid. She walks slowly and deliberately as if she has been waiting for us, almost offering to receive us. She gets as far as the edge of the woods and lies down in the little house to let her heart go gently. A few of us are buzzing around, up above in the shadows, watching the people who arrive and beg her to stay here. "Please stay," they say.

"Stop calling me. I am busy learning" is what we hear her thinking as they call her back. They can't hear her thoughts but we do. We know she'd be happy to leave and she knows it is in the hands of the Mother, not her mind.

She returns to her people eventually, healed by our venom, and permanently connected to us by a constant internal buzzing resolve, the long-term after-effect of our medicine. She can speak and sting when necessary. And, of course she pays the high price every time—predictable shunning, exile, accusations of meanness. Workers and drones, we all understand this. She will learn to live with the loneliness of working leadership. And she has no desire to be the queen, anyone's queen, except her own.

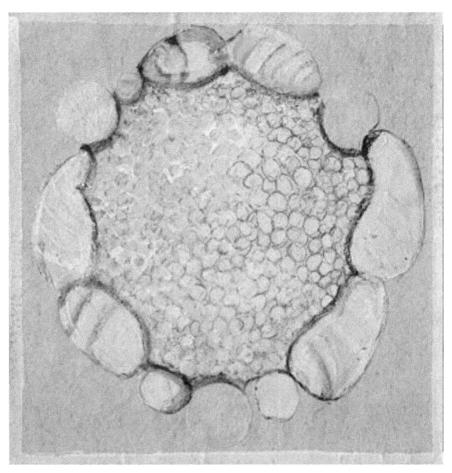

Art by A. Merrill

Our waxy cells, in no way prisons,
are strongholds for our medicine.
The old queen lives inside
with the cells for her whole lifetime.
She will breed us, birth us and wait
inside her chamber to fulfill her time
killing her rivals until one kills her—
and becomes our new queen.
Such is our way, the law of our community.
The young always come along and we always leave.
We have no problem with this.

h.o.w.w.e.

s.e.e.
w.e.s.e.e.a.l.l.a.t.o.n.c.e.
w.e.d.o.n.o.t
b.r.e.a.k.u.p.
e.x.p.e.r.i.e.n.c.e.i.n.t.o.
b.i.t.s.a.n.d.p.i.e.c.e.s
s.o.
w.e.a.r.e.a.l.l.o.n.e
a.n.d.w.e.a.r.e.a.l.l.h.e.r.e.
a.l.w.a.y.s.a.n.d.n.o.w.
a.u.n.i.f.i.e.d.f.i.e.l.d.
o.f.a.w.a.r.e.n.e.s.s.
i.n.r.e.a.l.t.i.m.e.a.n.d.s.p.a.c.e
a.n.d.s.o.a.r.e.y.o.u.
i.f.y.o.u.w.i.s.h.t.o.b.e.
j.u.s.t.c.h.a.n.g.e.y.o.u.r.
p.o.i.n.t.o.f.v.i.e.w.t.o.
b.e.w.i.t.h.u.s.
y.o.u.a.r.e.w.e.l.c.o.m.e.

Seven years to the day after the day I was stung, in September 2014, my dear neighbor here in coastal Maine is walking in our woods with her dog on this land where I still live. Directed by her dog's bark to look up into a beech tree, she sees the elegant hanging palace of nine golden combs, covered with countless honey bees who have travelled with their queen to this winter palace. Knowing that I owe them, I ask family, neighbors and local bee-keepers to help create a suitable winter home for the immigrant colony. I feed them the fluids they need as they prepare for winter. They are gentle, busy and receptive. I hope they make it through the long, stark cold of our Maine winter.

(opposite) Photo by A. Merrill
(above) Art by A. Merrill

Notes

In my decades of experience working with large hive-like groups of women on leadership development, I have often needed to stand tall as the queen of my own hard-earned authority, while a fine younger woman leader and sometimes a group of less experienced challengers make what I experience as a swarm attack on my designated leadership. I now see the challenge as a deep and natural human need to match strength and competence in order to claim our own personal authority. I have learned to welcome these strong challenges as younger strength testing itself. At several moments in my work life, this natural challenge has been laden with the toxic sting of unconscious misogyny, both mine and theirs. Having come to understand this universal venom, I do not take these moments as mean-spirited stings from a reactive hive but rather as the sign of a residual toxic disorder in our species. To take these poisoned moments personally is not a useful response.

I'm a woman leader who is aging. Instead of clinging to my long-held position of acknowledged leadership, I have to discern when it is time to let go and move aside. This is different from disappearing myself. My wish is to make time and space to support the emerging competence of new leaders. Their time has come and mine is going. If I take the lesson of the hive, I accept this dynamic just as I learned to accept my own earlier need to separate from my mother, my sisters and my teachers in order to learn to mother and sister myself. This way, I can continue to have my own internal authority while supporting others' growth-in-community, a benevolent long-term function of human hive life and an antidote to collective global misogyny, one of the most lethal of our human colony's collapse disorders.

A physiological benefit of the massive stinging is that I have been fully relieved of the progressive and crippling arthritic pain in my hands, a legacy inherited from my father. As a result, through my own hands, I feel a spirit level connection with my dear father who suffered long and hard with the degenerative arthritis pain in his big bony hands. My big, bony hands have heat and a buzz but no pain.

Another long-term benefit of the sting is that the episodic tinnitus buzzing in my left ear has become an invitation to turn inward to listen to my own knowing. When I do that, the buzzing disappears and I hear myself way more accurately. Once again I know what I know and must do about the problem at hand.

Learning to live in collaboration with the benevolent bees as neighbors and allies in our blended community helps me experience the interdependence of all forms of life. My tiny practice of awareness is as small as one tiny bee, smaller even. My little prayers for peace between all species, the invisible thought forms that float up the hill to the bees, all this new practice keeps me a more mindful participant in the joys and sorrows of our beautiful and troubled world.

There is a multi-faceted healing power in the bee venom. It is my good fortune to have been treated by an extremely potent and benevolent remedy from the colony of Appalachian bees to whom I offer this grateful bow.

Joan Kresich
Letter to a Yellowstone Wolf

I felt I needed to write to let you know our meeting wasn't what I would have wished. It's true I've been imprinted with the classic images: you in a ruffled granny cap salivating through slick teeth, or closing in on Jack London's north woods fire. But I never took those to heart.

I would have wanted an encounter of equals, two creatures passing in the copse of vulnerability, pared down to sinew and synapse, the copper wires of our wits holding the whole thing together. One of those meetings where energy and mass trade places in a flash of eyes. A meeting where everything funnels and explodes in the same moment.

But the way you paused and turned your lowered head to look back at us made me think you felt pursued. Why did you stick to the ribbon of road? We never saw where you came from, just rounded the bend and there you were. We slowed the car and waited for you to take off across the snow, but you kept loping along the pavement. A few cars passed you going the other way, and you just moved over, and kept to the road. We could see the gleeful faces when they passed us.

So this was our meeting: you loping ahead, us rolling along in our bubble of amazement. We had time to wonder: were you banished from a pack? Was there a fight? You seemed fatigued, and yet you kept going, never rested. Why?

You have your history, and we ours. When was it we parted? Once, we inhabited the same land, the same territory. In that time, I would have understood the bargains you made to stay alive. Ribs undulating across your flanks would ignite a flash of recognition and kinship in me. Cold bursting in upon my lungs would remind me how the same cold was shocking yours. My empty stomach would tell me how hunger massed the last resources of your body to search for food and how it kept you riveted to your prey.

You weren't wearing a collar like some of your Yellowstone kin. Every pack is named, every wolf numbered. (I have to admit this numbering makes me think of other human counting schemes: digits shelled out to prisoners, tattooed on wrists– if those are dehumanizing, what is this?) I saw the reams of data on the internet, every detail of wolf movements, kinship, pairings, quarrels, deaths. Some people write to complain about helicopters descending on wolves, and photos of researchers proudly posed behind drugged-out wolves, their tongues lolling. I could see their point. I've seen a similar expression before, in the old safari photos. It says: This is my story.

And why was I on the internet? I wanted something there to tell me where you were going, why you were alone. But once inside that mess of sticky facts, I got a trapped feeling. I'd flown into a spider's web, and she was making her way down the silk. I turned off the computer, and walked away. For a long time I sat thinking of dominion.

Yours is a tiny population, and one clever virus could take you out. Of course, we could be the ones to go. But being human, I can indulge a fantasy: maybe you are making your way across a single narrow plank into the future, an unrehearsed time without tranquilizing darts and renderings about whether you get one last chance to stay away from sheep. In that future, your life and death will no longer be in human hands. It will rest in the same invisible hands that once kept salmon thrashing upriver, bats billowing into starlight, bees hauling their garlands from field to field. Life dancing long into the night, beads of sweat flying everywhere like a thousand seeds, and awakening at dawn to the first breath of primordial light.

Even though I didn't see you in your prime, you sent a bolt of your power into my chest, and it's still there. Sometimes, before I drift into sleep, I see you loping, and that gives me a strange feeling, a small wet hope just opening its eyes. After all that has happened, we are still connected.

I wish you well, Yellowstone wolf. I wish you well.

Yours truly,
Joan Kresich

Sara Wright
My Yellow Spotted Lady

The February sun was streaming in through the window, slicing through the circle of cut crystal that I twisted gently, waiting for the warm water to fill the sink. As rainbow diamonds of cracked fire swam crazily around the kitchen, I could feel the apprehension tightening the muscles into a cross in my back. How much I was dreading this task. But I was determined to follow through.

I turned off the water and stood staring out the window. My thoughts drifted back through a golden haze as I recalled my generous-hearted orchid who had been blooming ever since I bought her when I moved into my house four years ago. I had never repotted the plant. I didn't know it then, but this lemony lady would capture my heart with her loyalty and lead me down the path to becoming an orchid lover.

At first my relationship with her was quite casual. We visited daily in the bathroom where she sat on the bottom shelf of my plant window that looked out over the mountains. After a time I couldn't help noticing that each of her buttery freckled faces seemed to seek out my own as she perched there in the east window whenever I entered the bathroom. I watered her in a sloppy sort of way, pouring water through her and then letting it stand in the bowl beneath her pot until the sun would evaporate the rest, wondering when the yellow saw–like spikes would cease their bloom. I knew nothing about orchids, but because the soil mixture was so porous, I figured her roots couldn't possibly be hurt by this kind of attention. A few months later, another yellow orchid joined her, and then another, and I treated them all the same way. Soon there were four. All of them bloomed predictably, but my Yellow Spotted Lady never ceased to amaze me; she bloomed all the time. She didn't seem to mind the passionflower that curled its tendrils around her spikes, or the cold drafts in winter. Sometimes, it seemed to me, she took a little rest in the summer. Her waxy yellow flowers would diminish in number during the hottest months.

I'm ashamed to say that after a while I took her for granted, paying closer attention to the bi-annual citrus-fruit-scented blossoms of the

Cattleya that burst like winter sunsets out of thick green leaves in spring and fall. I began to experiment with a few more supermarket orchids, most of which rapidly expired. I finally bought a book on orchid culture, discovered a nearby orchid greenhouse, bought more books, more orchids, and began throwing out all my other plants. Orchid fever is like nothing I have ever known, and I've lived with plants all my life! Armed with newly acquired knowledge, I began to feel uncomfortable around my loyal friend. Guilt rose unbidden. I would wince whenever I watered my Yellow Lady. How was it that she still lived? I was no longer taking her for granted. Now I was feeling paralyzed by the thought of doing her more harm. Still, I kept watering her in the same way believing that changing the routine after four years might kill her even though everything I'd read indicated that I must repot her because she was so root- bound. Worse, it seemed to me that each time I looked at the wizened old roots that wound their way into the air that she was gasping for breath. Wasn't she begging me for help? I recoiled from repotting. It looked so hard. But one Sunday I finally I gave in. I had to risk losing her, even though I felt I didn't have the experience I needed to repot her without more trauma. I was after all a novice with orchids. Maybe I felt that I didn't deserve her because I had treated her so badly.

Turning away from the sink, I reluctantly made my way to the bathroom window. My back ached. I held my breath as I cut one of her spikes in order to remove her from the window. That spike had grown up through the shelf above her a couple of years earlier. I winced as I made the cut and pulled my lady out of her spot for the first time in four years. My heart thundered. I felt such misery as I murmured words of apology to her on my way to the kitchen table, where I planned to remove her from the pot. I sat down still talking to her as I braced us both for the task ahead.

I first cut off the dry brown roots that protruded into the air. I feared the inevitable tangle of black rotting roots still hidden in the pot. I had pored through every book I owned in preparation for this moment, and picture after picture of desiccated roots flashed through my mind. Gingerly, I started to cut away the pot, being careful not to break the four remaining flower spikes. When the first firm white roots appeared I was stunned. How was it possible that these healthy roots were growing in an orchid that had been treated with such ignorance and disregard? As I carefully cut away the old debris, relief flooded me. My Yellow Lady wasn't dying after all! I felt my body heave and sigh as I relaxed my vigil and thoroughly enjoyed the remainder of our task. When I was finished cleaning her up, I set her back in the pot, testing it for size. Then grasping her plant body in one hand I stood up. I planned to bathe my orchid in the sink before re-potting her in new bark.

I think I was gazing out the window as I lowered her into the still warm water, because I felt some kind of subtle tingling through my hands that caused me to look down at the plant. When I did, I was momentarily dazzled by the eerie glow of emerald green roots pulsing intensely, as if some sort of information was flashing between the plant and me through color and touch. All I can say is that I saw the varying shades of green roots deepen to emerald and fade as I stood there in a trance. When the thoughts came, they were sharp, clear and carried authority. My Lady is thanking me, her roots glowing to let me know she feels gratitude, too. I almost let go of her then, the shock of conscious thought was so great. I peered even more intently at the roots that even now were returning to a healthy pale green. A green I recognized. Did I imagine that emerald? "Trust your senses," I heard her say. Breathing into the miracle of my body, I let all the love I felt for her and her kindred flow through me.

Blessings to you, too, My Yellow Lady.

Lise Weil
Blow

> We are all so much more than we think we are…. We are air exhaled
> by hemlocks, we are water plowed by whales, we are matter born in
> stars, we are children of deep time.
> —Kathleen Dean Moore, *Great Tide Rising*

It was our last day in Baja. I had come here to spend time with whales.
I am not fond of heat and Baja is *hot*. And truthfully, whales, though
I worshipped them from afar, had not been my favourite mammals.
Despair drove me to Baja. It was March 2017 and I was still reeling
from the elections and what they said about the U.S. and our chances
of redeeming ourselves as a species. Could nature recover from our
relentless assaults? Was there any reason to hope? I thought the whales
might have some wisdom to offer. That I would be travelling with a
women's wilderness outfit and a guide who communicated with whales
seemed to increase the likelihood of this outcome.

When a blue whale first approached—we were camped on the shore of
the Sea of Cortez, just gathering for our morning circle—all the other
women fell to their knees and stayed there as we watched her circle the
bay (a mama and her calf our guide told us). In circle, the women spoke
in tones of reverence and rapture. I abstained. I had seen those huge
bodies blowing and breaching and yes it was impressive, they were BIG
(the biggest mammals on the face of the earth, we had been informed,
up to two city blocks in length), and these enormous creatures had come
to us, or so the others insisted, come repeatedly, but I felt nothing….
certainly by contrast with my companions. Or, to be honest, I felt rage.
What the fuck makes you think they are coming for us? Why the fuck
would they want to come to us? After what we've done to them? Done
to the oceans. I said this one night around the campfire, my face wet
with tears which in all honesty were probably less tears of shame for our
species than pain at not being able to feel what the others felt, at feeling
separate from them.

But after five days on the Sea of Cortez, spying one fluke after another, watching those giant bodies dive and surface and dive again, I had come to believe, I can't say how exactly, that maybe yes they did love us and yes they had come for us. Now we were staying in cabins on San Ignacio Bay on the other side of the peninsula. San Ignacio is a protected lagoon where gray whales come to calve and where for this reason they were murdered *en masse* by humans in the nineteenth and for much of the twentieth century. But in 1977, a fisherman in the bay received a visit from a mama gray and her calf who would not leave the side of his boat until he had stroked the baby. Since then, San Ignacio has become a pilgrimage site, a place where humans can venture out in boats and be pretty sure that they'll not only see but be able to touch a gray whale. It was now our fourth day here on the lagoon and already its rippling waters had come to feel like one of those neighborhoods that was sacred to me because *she* lived there—the woman I loved— and any second she might suddenly appear.

It had been a hard morning. The hardest of the trip. Several days earlier, after a rough day of paddling that had done me in, I had leapt to the aid of someone who was heaving a double kayak out of the water—in the spirit of pitching in but also so as not to be outdone by my younger travel mates. In the process I pulled something skeletal badly out of whack. It had caught up to me the day before and I had barely slept. All night I had dreamt of a chiropractor—could I find one in this area? In the morning in the circle I told the dream and then, since the dream seemed to be wanting it of me, asked if anyone in the circle knew anything about alignment. There were on this trip an assortment of healers and yoga teachers and I was secretly hoping someone might offer to help straighten me out. No one did. I felt—there is only one word for it—rejected. No one wanted to take on my case, my crooked, aging body. An old haunted place—not beautiful enough—I went back to it.

But there is something I've left out here, something about that sleepless night that feels important to say. I have spent many nights lying awake with one kind of ailment or another just listening to the minutes tick away. This night was not like any of those. Because throughout the hours, and the muscular cramps that seized my neck and held it in a vice, I remained completely calm. I remained calm because I had every confidence I would be healed....in fact it occurred to me during that long night that there is no healing without affliction. So maybe affliction is necessary? I was afflicted, and I needed this affliction so that I could be healed.

I had been reading about whales the night before, suddenly ravenous for knowledge about these beings about whom until now my main source of information had been *Moby Dick*. In one book I read that just by the way they navigate, conducting waves of light and sound, whales serve to bring everything into balance. "Planetary alignment" is how the writer put it. Well if they could align planets why not one human body?

In late morning, after the circle, we went out in the boats. The driver of my boat was Sextos, a big burly Mexican who never ventured out into the lagoon without his flute. "A blow!" someone would shout, pointing, and all binoculars would take aim as Sextos sped up to get near, then cut the motor. Soon he would unfurl the bandanna in which he'd wrapped his flute, pick it up, and begin playing. The whales would arrive within minutes. One time what looked like a whole pod came and stirred the waters beside our boat, rolling over and spyhopping and cavorting while we raced from side to side of the boat in anticipation. At some point we knew at least one of them would sidle up to us.

I can still feel it, seeing one of those huge mottled gray bodies arcing and diving and arcing again until she was just alongside the boat, how alive it would get down in my belly. As if at one time that gray mottled body had been in mine. As if it had *been* mine? In these moments there is only body, there is just you and your friends on this boat and beside you now practically rubbing up against the gunwales, this giant gray slippery body of the "baby" who is the biggest animal you have ever touched. There is only the feel of the slick rubbery skin against your hand as the body moves up and down, the feel of your hand inside the baby's mouth when you manage to push past the soft fringe of the baleen and he seems to grip onto it, the feel of that rubbery skin against your lips the one time you manage to attach your mouth to it —*"Besame! Besame!"* Sextos is yelling, kiss them they love it!

Photo by L. Kutlik

A Somali friend of mine told me that the most horrible moment of her childhood—and she lived through mass killings—was the first time she looked at herself in a mirror. She was five or six years old. It was not that she did not like what she saw. It was that until that moment she had lived in the world as a purely sentient being. Now, she said, all was *localized* perception. Then, it was her whole body that perceived and the world was completely alive. *Whole-body perception.* Here, with the whales, I had an inkling of what she was talking about.

This is all there is in the world, just these human bodies around you these animal bodies in the water and the body of the ocean and you, who are suddenly both heavier and lighter than you've ever been, have been given the ballast you have always needed, yet are floating in watery ether. This is what it is to know a being so big, so massive in its primal ISness, that its waves ripple out to the far edges of the world and leave no being untouched.

When the boat pulls in to shore Sextos helps us disembark then gathers us all in a circle and has us dance sideways together and then blow kisses at each other. "Love is in the air," he sings. It *is*, I can feel it, we have been loved by the whales and now we all love each other, we can't help it! And there is not a crooked bone or aching muscle in my body.

But the whales are not done with me yet. Or I am not done with them. I am going out one more time in the afternoon. My last chance. As the boat pulls out I wonder if I'm being greedy. There are only five of us from the trip, wanting to get in our last hellos, and our driver is a woman who is mostly quiet as we head out to sea. The water is rough now, rougher than it's been before, it is harder to spy the whales and for a long time we don't see any. I notice myself beginning to long…. to hanker. To crave. Please whales just one last time. As if I haven't already had enough. As if they haven't already given me…. EVERYTHING! Oh but this is my last day, my last chance. Please mama please baby, just one last time. But haven't they been teaching me patience? Being one with what is, whatever that is? Isn't that their palpable wisdom? Obviously I have not taken it in as I watch myself getting more and more anxious….. Only twenty minutes left and still we have not spied one whale. Until, at last, yes!!! Just fifty feet from our boat, a mama and her large calf, frolicking, seeming to want our company.

And now the baby is right up against the boat and the others are all rushing to one side to stroke him—no doubt jonesing like me. Most of them manage to get their hands on him, but he shoots off before I can insinuate myself. Damn! But now… a giant body moving towards us. The mama? Yes! Just feet away!! This I will not miss, we have been sending the mothers our love now for days, we can't help feeling the most aching gratitude to them for the way they keep offering up their young. And now… now I get to thank her with my hands!! I push my way in and extend myself far over the side of the boat. Oh Mama come come you're the best mama we love you so much…. She is now so close just a few more inches and my fingers will make contact…. Instead…….!!!!… sudden shock of spray…!!!!

wet spray salt spray jet spray and now WET hair WET jacket WET pants and even the boat WET now, filling with water, and your friends and the driver also wet and pointing at you, laughing—you who all week have been trying to protect your hair from the salt water!! You, who, when the shock relents, are laughing the purest loudest most HEARTY laughter of your entire life. Also the longest, as it goes on and on and on… because this great mama has chosen this moment of your readiness your openness to blow on you with all the force of her giant lungs. There is NOTHING now but this and then for hours there is only this… complete abandon to this moment, of laughter…. And love.

N.B.: Adapted from an essay published both in Russo, Stacey, ed. Feminist Pilgrimage: Journeys of Discovery. *Sacramento, California: Litwin Books, 2020, and* Honoring Nature, *Lis McLoughlin, ed. Wendell, MA: Human Error Publishing, 2021. Print.*

Elliott batTzedek
Benediction

In the years that farmers cleared their fields
by throwing flames across the nights,
half-mile rows of black black smoke
leached across late autumn days

until the west wind came with the frost
and blew the burned soil away—

that great prairie wind, pushing leaves
and garbage and ash from the river edge of Adams
County to well past Terre Haute—that wind,
that just one time before, my father said,

had yielded magic.

Come outside now, he, rousing me, said, *the wind
all last week has moved the Mississippi
flyway to the east.*

And pointing, showed, how the old pine just out the door
shimmered, shimmered—the slow beat of
a million wings all aglow such brilliant orange
that the morning star could blush that morning only pink, watching

as his familiar lips touched my ear, his family
code – *this secret is ours, only ours*—
and he whispered then only one word: *Monarchs.*

Then warmed awake those wings spread wide,
each a book of prayers I felt I once
could read, such delight, such despair,
I dared not even breathe

so breathless watched them rise
from our tree, creatures made of air,
so light their launching stirred not
a single needle. And so my father's lips

and my ear became blessed, and all our years
of secreting were made holy, holy,
holy ever after by the touch of the great kings
who once had rested here.

Notes

Growing up as the third generation in a tiny, tiny town in rural Illinois, it
is nearly impossible for me to separate the land itself, my father's body's
memory of that land, and my own body's memories. I roamed the same
woods, climbed the same trees, slept in his room at my Grandma's, and
experienced all of those through his stories and memories as much as
through my own body and senses. To have grown up embedded in a
place is to have permeable skin; what was inside me and what outside
of me were so interconnected that I remember my childhood body *as*
geography—that day biking home between the high corn when the
humidity left me just as wet as the swim in the lake, that day shrieking
in joy in the cold on the sled down the hill, that day running in pure
terror through hickory woods chased by a wild hog and how the green
was both smell and taste. To live in exile from that land—the cost of
breaking family secrets—is to live unsure, still after all these years, of
the actual boundaries of my body. I left because I wanted to live whole,
not knowing I was trading having a whole spirit (and future) for having
a whole body-world. I'm glad I made that trade, yet much of my writing
is really just counting its cost.

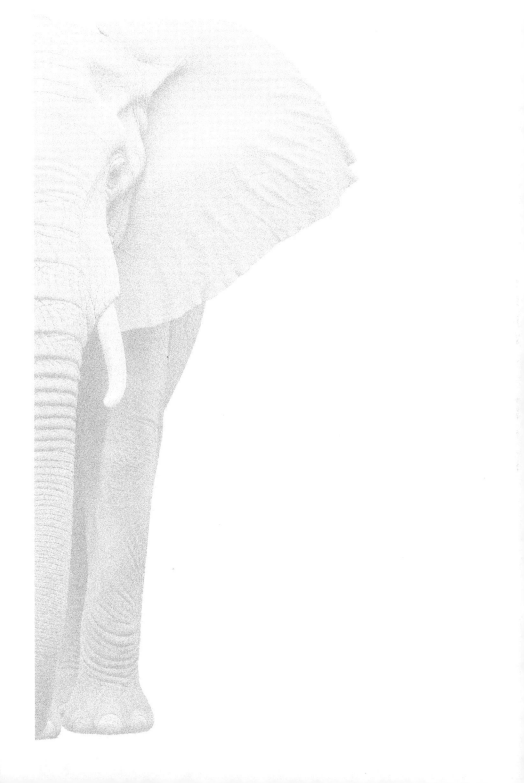

What We Know
in Our Bones

The women say, "This is what we taught you in dreams you have forgotten you dreamed in your childhood, the dreams that formed you and that surface now at this time in your life when you are asking what is to be done, what is to be done, what is to be done?"

—Deena Metzger, *Dreaming Another Language: She Will not Kill*

That night in the storm, my body remembered the time before women were murdered for the power of their connection to the earth. As I made love to the rain, the thunder, the clouds, and the grass without shame and with intense abandon and pleasure, I felt complete love for myself. Love for my love of the earth that birthed me. Love for the earth that I will nourish in return, with my flesh and bones and teeth and organs, when I no longer breathe.

—Anne Bergeron, *The Night Thunder Called*

Hilary Giovale
The Blood Knows

I know because the blood told me.
More precisely, spending time with the waters showed me.

In truth, being cooked in a cauldron of moon time, waters, and dreams is how I came to know. The stew simmered in this otherworldly pot, blackened with the soot of open fires, chipped and dented with age, indispensable to the family cooks, became my best teacher.

She begins the lessons with sparse words: "No human being will teach you what you need to know." Instead of employing lectures, reading guides, and webinars, she steers me by the heartstrings, month after month, to a flat, red, sandstone surface hidden by trees and grasses along the side of the creek. She guides me to lie down, with my aching belly upon the cool rock. The pulse and flow of the blood excitedly chatters with the creek's rushing water in an ancient tongue my mind cannot grasp. When I'm lucky, though, I eavesdrop on bits of their conversation through the ear of my heart.

The class inevitably begins with tears. Its curriculum is based on detoxification: thus, sobbing is a prerequisite. It doesn't matter which topic opens the doorway to tears—it could be stolen children, mass extinction, climate change, white supremacy, historic and current massacres, the trash floating downstream, or even just the cognitive dissonance that's part of mothering two children in times such as these. I sob, face down, spilling tears onto the rock—tears that first come cloudy, polluted, and toxic.

These tears conduct energy between the sandstone and me. When I visit this place in this state of being, I am received with timeless, unconditional love. Over time, this place and I have come to a mutually beneficial understanding: I come with offerings in hand, willing to cry with her and listen to her. Overwhelm, poison, rage, and grief, all symptoms of daily life in the Anthropocene, are gradually absorbed into the depths of Earth. Somehow, in a way I know but don't yet understand, Earth combines these emotions with moon time to make compost that nourishes new seeds being carefully planted in the Dreamtime.

The sandstone being now sighs and shifts her weight underneath me. Earth's human children are malnourished these days. They hardly ever listen anymore, and they usually come as orphans: hungry, lost, empty-handed, and demanding. Yet, as it is in her nature to be generous, she begins sending nourishment back to the human who has come here to do her work. Warm, pulsing, ancient stone-knowledge emanates from her, and watery music cleanses the residual static. As though waking from a dream, I re-member, again, what it is to be connected.

With the detoxification well underway, I am drawn to sit upon a round, gray stone planted solidly in the middle of the creek, surrounded by rushing water on all sides. Now is the time for listening. What is needed, I ask? Without fail, the answer comes:

Look around you, child. Here are my red dragonflies, my golden monarch butterflies. Listen to my abundant, sparkling waters flowing from snow at the mountain's peak to the North. Look at the green leaves all around you, digesting the light of this great star, the Sun. Look up! See how the waters find their way out of the cracks and crevices of the red rock walls towering over your head. My waters know how to travel. My waters have been in relationship with all of your people throughout time and space. My waters are your body, your ancestors, and your blood. Your blood holds the memory of these waters, since the beginning of time.

My heart blossoms; a song asks to be sung. Sometimes the songs are carried wordlessly on the wind; other times they are made of primordial human languages I barely understand but know, nonetheless. When the songs come, I no longer have to strain to overhear the ancient language of the blood and the waters. We become one language. Tears flow again, and this time they run clear. They fall into the surrounding waters, mingling with mossy stones and tiny fish. Longing becomes the medicine for restoring memory.

⁓

I enrolled in the School of Blood and Waters as a spiritual, cultural, and linguistic orphan. My ancestors came to this land as refugees and migrants from Scotland, Ireland, England, and Germany beginning nine generations ago. Among them were grandmothers, bakers, artists, railroad workers, linen factory workers, shopkeepers, teachers, and farmers. Among them were men who received grants of land stolen from the land's original peoples; men who fought wars in allegiance with both England and the Republic, Union and Confederacy; men who enslaved human beings as a form of livelihood. I was raised in a ninth-generation fog of amnesia, for our languages, our land, our cultures, our waters, and nearly all of our people were forgotten to prioritize our assimilation and survival in the new American empire.

Our women's blood had been forcibly forgotten long before their migrations took place. According to the Project of Vast European Amnesia that devastated Indigenous Europe over many centuries of the Roman Expansion, Burning Times, Inquisition, and the institutional spread of Christianity, I am not supposed to remember the significance of this blood today. I am not supposed to talk, think or write about it. I am not supposed to sit in its ceremony or know its magic. I am meant to stay too busy and compartmentalize it as an unfortunate fact of female biology—something to be managed with hygiene products and drugs. In the year 1178, when an Icelandic bishop outlawed the practice of European women sitting alone on the land to communicate with the elements and receive instructions,* it became official: mixing womanhood and nature adds up to dangerous business.

These many centuries later, the orphanhood and amnesia of the European diaspora have had dire consequences for all of Life. Throughout the world, humans are seeking answers, grieving, and struggling to find paths forward. Delusions of commodification have distorted our relationships with water, and many (but not all) of us have forgotten.

Our blood calls us back to knowledge that is much, much older than time. Our blood is the memory of countless generations, all the way back to our common grandmothers of long ago. Our blood carries instructions for eggs to develop inside the bellies of baby girls, even as they swim in the waters of their mothers' wombs. Like Russian nesting dolls, our blood allows us to birth successions of future generations who carry ancestral blueprints encoded into their DNA. Our blood is made of our peoples' resiliency over time, in relationship with Earth herself.

Our blood speaks our kinship with Grandmother Moon. As she waxes and wanes with each passing month, so do/did we. As she cycles thirteen times every year, so do/did we. Grandmother Moon, Queen of ocean tides, mentors our communication with the waters of Earth. Those who have completed their bleeding years nestle the wisdom of all the moons they have lived. The waters, the blood, and the moon have been singing us back to re-membrance of who we are and who we are becoming for a long time.

The blood is calling me out of orphanhood, back into belonging. Back to reweaving, re-membering. Back to the cauldron, to cook something new, using the well-worn, beloved recipe of original instructions.

⎯⎯⎯⎯

*Dashú, Max. *Witches and Pagans: Women in European Folk Religion*, 700-1100, p. 325. 2017. Print.

Melissa Kwasny
Another Letter to the Soul

You picked me from the litter as a brightness, rubbed me between finger and thumb. You placed me, and the bees, who are like-spirits, came. You gave them, through me, a place to come to. You provided me with properties, inaudible spells, invisible arrows that point to the hurt places. Illness of my friends: her failing liver, his failing nerves, earth-drought, flood, the poisoned animal. I know you have been testing me, first toughening the fragile frame. Inside, an infant cries and objects. You have set me apart like the bald eagle, found floundering in the river and put into the feeding cage. Long enough to gain its strength back, and then it fled. I admit I didn't know that a broken wing could right itself. I forget about healing, though I grow more fond of birds, the poor nieces I can afford to bring the berries to. Sun's out, you say, serving its broth of light.

The watercolorists are happy. They've picked their views and are sitting, barely moving, in long-sleeved shirts. Mystery and clarity is what we aim for as an achievement. You speak in the variations of wind. Upper reaches of the cottonwood, its adolescent limbs spurred on and off into a froth of soundings. Anxiety of ground-shadows as wind passes among the leaves. It stops, and the tiny insects descend. We experience you only in your arrivals, not departures, so strong you tear the tent from our hands. And yet your remains are tender, broken and soft, as if strung with beads of dew atop wet sand. Each one of us suffers, small things and joys. All of us are aging, having watched each other age. What are the past lives of the wind? It cycles through the channel where the deer carcass stinks. Where dinosaur bones protrude from the ancient banks.

Water. Mint. Water-mint. The braided currents at the bend of the nearby stream. Their fluid consonance. A granite boulder, like a sibyl behind summer leaf, shade-spattered with lichen and moss. Bachelard writes that, in human reverie, the rock imagines. Not we that imagine the rock. Because how could we have come here, have accepted so much, without having had a foundation to build on? You, then, as luggage, our library, perhaps our DNA? Entrance as noun: what we step through. Entrance as verb: how we are changed. What could we see if not movement? The sibyl measures each fish's weight against the blue root of her own. The leafage separates in autumn into its individual tones. We say autumn moves us. That it is moving. Given the forecast. Given how easily the subject can be erased.

Notes

This prose poem is from a new manuscript I am working on, provisionally titled *Where Outside the Body is the Soul Today*. When I began the poems, it was to challenge the prevailing assumption that words like "soul" and "spirit" don't belong in our highly technological, secular world, and that, as well, they are not a fit subject for contemporary poetry. Contrary to my understanding that soul was something found deep inside us, as I wrote these poems, I began to discover that I can sense soul most clearly in others, especially the animals, plants, rocks, waters, and winds that people our world. Anima /animal: our intuition, even expressed in our language, that the soul is embedded in the animal body.

Andrea Mathieson
What We Know in Our Bones

What Tent Caterpillars can teach us

Years ago, I was fascinated to learn that when a caterpillar colony becomes too crowded, some intrepid adults will leave the safety of the branch. Their voluntary exodus expands the borders of the tent, creating space for the whole community to thrive.

As one who has left a variety of comfortable nests and repeatedly stepped into unfamiliar territory, I appreciated this living metaphor. What initially appeared a selfish act sometimes was a creative impulse, not just for me but for my community as well.

The otherworld ways of the wilderness are what Nordic and Celtic cultures (my ancestors) called Wyrd. Our modern "weird" comes from this word.

Photo: istock.com/NNehring

The way of Wyrd honors the ever-changing interconnectedness of all things and the timeless forces intersecting the present moment. In the Oracle Runes, the blank stone is named Wyrd, signifying what is not yet fated. The outcome rests in the hands of those willing to take intelligent risks and make lasting changes.

We are at a pause point. A critical threshold. A blank rune, fate-in-our-hands time. How we know, not just what we know, is the critical question. I agree with Bayo Akomolafe who audaciously suggests there are no solutions to all the problems in the world, that instead we must develop new ways of seeing. We are being called to find a different way to respond. I know this to be true. We are being called to find a different way to respond, a way that is natural, or dare I say, indigenous, to each of us.

Earth-Body wisdom via intuition

Through the softly focused lens of my intuition, imagination and the sensations in my body, I've gone out on many limbs to listen to and gather wisdom from Nature. With only the slimmest of scientific validation, I've slowly learned to trust my instincts. Though I realize this way of listening has informed Indigenous peoples for millennia, our western culture has forgotten these wisdom-ways, partly because they are subtle, complex, and nonlinear. Our fast-paced and achievement-oriented lifestyle tends to dismiss them as fanciful and even childish. In one sense, this is true, for these ways of being with the earth are highly responsive to unseen forces which makes them less easily controllable.

Through sensual engagement with our bodies' wisdom and our immediate environment, we have access to a wealth of information that cannot be learned through a purely mental approach. When our hearts are touched by a numinous encounter with some element in the natural world, we feel its significance, even if we can't immediately make logical sense of what we know in our bones.

Part of the work of embodying our intuitive abilities involves a deepening acquaintance with our bodies' sensations, and in particular, the sensation of pleasure. This is not as easy as we might expect. Locked in our heads, we often ignore or actively avoid the slow, rhythmic waves of pleasure. We're addicted to the rush of accomplishment, whether this is simply getting a task done on time or endlessly overbooking ourselves. All too often, pleasure gets postponed or scheduled, months away, for a holiday, rather than being sensuously enjoyed in the moment when it is most needed.

Being intuitive does not preclude the essential work of developing all aspects of our being. In fact, without a healthy skepticism and well-honed emotional intelligence, an over-active intuitive ability can make us imbalanced and ungrounded. When we fly into intuition's fascinating realms without an earth anchor, the information we receive becomes unreliable, even nonsensical. It's easy to become overwhelmed, even by the most inspired insights.

Intuitive visions and messages often occur swiftly, with a feeling of exciting, empowering possibilities. They also come with a great responsibility; we need to integrate and apply the insights we've been given. Several years ago, I vowed to stop tuning in for a time. With dozens of journals full of insights, I needed to pause and digest what I'd already received instead of seeking the reassuring 'hit' of a new insight. Not only that, the messages were beginning to repeat themselves: "You know what to do... just DO IT!"

Communing with Plants

Over a period of twenty years, while intuitively communing with flowers in my garden, I was initiated into the art of deep listening, an approach that gave me access to the rhythmic life-force pulsing far below our human dramas.

Creating flower essences gave me a "legitimate" excuse for developing an intimate relationship with plants.* Plants don't speak our language. When I was near a plant I wanted to commune with, I found myself dropping into a very slow and softened state of being. Letting my familiar personality recede, the humming presence of the plant became more distinct as it reached out to me. I listened gently, being careful not to snatch the phrases as their unspoken language softly imprinted on my psyche. As precisely as possible, I recorded what I 'heard' and thanked the flower for sharing. This wyrd ability to listen and commune with Nature in my garden expanded to include other elements reaching out to be heard—the ancient stones of Georgian Bay, creatures in my dreams, the river near my home and recently, the invasive dog-strangling vine in my neighborhood.

Conversing with people

Communing in my garden, I was intensely present and receptive, yet when I spoke with people, these qualities seemed to vanish. It was as if I was two different people—one who loved listening to the soul of the plants, the other who felt awkward and self-conscious in casual conversation.

For many years, I kept my "plant-listening" ears hidden, except with colleagues or in my professional work. In Nature, I learned to become aware of entire ecosystems, including the ecosystems of human relationships, what Lynn McTaggart calls "the field." This field needs as much professional work, and sometimes more, than the actual conversation. Meanwhile, my intuitive skills continued maturing with clients. The quality of atmosphere in the field shapes the communication, the rhythm and tone of speech, as well as where we each source our ideas before speaking.

Sometimes, when a client is struggling to articulate something important, I notice the gesture they are making with their hands is actually 'speaking' more articulately than their words. If the situation allows, I may ask them to stop talking and simply repeat the gesture that caught my attention. As they shift their focus from the right words to the accompanying gesture, they often get clear about what they were trying to express.

Whenever I host women's gatherings, I include spontaneous movement. The Romantic poets knew the importance of movement; walking on the moors for hours stimulated their cerebral spinal fluid and lubricated their lyrical writing. Without some form of physical engagement, our best intentions to connect with ourselves and each other tend to remain somewhat guarded and superficial. After we engage our bodies through dance—stretching, stomping, flowing, bending and wriggling—our conversations are always more honest and authentic. Spontaneous sounding can be another entry-point for deeper understanding and connection.

The difference between our mental concepts and our bodies' expressed reality can be humbling. What we thought we knew and felt is often very different from what our bodies "speak" through sound, movement, and gesture, yet it is through these less civilized expressions that our resonating body-souls begin to serve as a conscious bridge to Gaia's body.

Conversing with guides

Some of the most powerful advice I've ever received has come through automatic writing with a spiritual guide. When I first felt Iliadne's presence in a meditation in 2004, I asked what her role was in my life. "To help you with the rest of your life!" was her frank reply. At pivotal times when I am at the tenuous edge of a new phase, I will sit with my journal and open to Iliadne with a specific question. Here is an excerpt:

From my first session in November 2004: You are fritzing because you are not using your brain in the way it was designed to operate. You are forcing it, jamming too much into a small space, then expecting it to sort and work efficiently. As a metaphor, your thinking has been all air and very little love. What does your brain need? Rest—from worry, lists, ideas, and overly-excited mental stimulation. You have gone as far as you can with one level of operating system; learn a new one!

To help others access wise inner guidance through automatic writing, I sometimes ask women at the end of a day-long circle to write a love letter to themselves. Opening to the wisdom of "the Beloved" (their higher self) I suggest they start with "Dear One, I want you to know…" After hours of movement, meditation and soulful sharing, the words flow easily onto the paper, a direct balm to and from their soul. They put the love-letter into an envelope, they address it to themselves, and I mail it to them a month later. When they receive the letter in the mail, they are often astonished. "Where did this loving wisdom come from?"

Heart resonance with our non-human community

How do we know who or what is calling us? In meditative stillness, I have encouraged people to drop into their hearts and welcome whatever creature comes to be with them. Once the animal—owl, butterfly, deer or tiger—approaches, I encourage them to somatically merge with the creature, to feel the feathers, fur, talons or paws as if they were becoming that animal. This form of imaginal entrainment cuts through our projected assumptions. Once embodied resonance is established, it is time to ask for a message from the animal's soul. Transmitted heart-to-heart, these wise and personal messages from the animal kingdom offer one of the most intimate ways to commune with the earth.

When I was a child, I had a recurring nightmare of snakes hanging over my bed. This powerful dream seeded a life-long relationship with this remarkable, paradoxical creature. A series of seventy shamanic meditations in 2015 with him as guide was the fruit of our strange kinship; those meditations were published as *The Book of Snake* in 2021.

Earth messages for these times

Time and time again, I've witnessed how the Earth responds when we open ourselves to commune with Her. As we cultivate our connection to our larger community by responding to the specific places, plants, and creatures that call us, we commit to Earth through our loving attention and deep listening. Through our soulful presence and our willingness to be met, we are kin to all, be they gorillas, whales, trees, waters, soil or seeds.In a recent meditative conversation with Gaia, she said, "Any small step taken to engage with the hidden, withdrawn parts of my soul are tender comfort. Know that in your bones. I am listening. Your actions are not perfunctory. They go directly into the magnificent multitude of entry points into my soul, my body. Every rivulet is welcomed."

A conversation with COVID-19

Nudged by an intuitive sensation to listen deeply, in spring of 2020 I spent some time in meditation and received this image.

I see people rappelling on the edge of a cliff. A fine web connected the different people—up, down and across. The web was made of friendship and it provided safety for everyone. I also realized there was no judgment about whether the "right" journey for each person was up the rock-face or down into the depths.

Later, I looked up the word "rappelling" and learned the word's origin is "to recall" or "to pull through." As I wondered which guide would help me understand this vision, I knew it was the spirit of the Coronavirus that wanted to speak.

I am holding you gently on the rock-face, with barely a foothold for each of you, a place of uncertainty and even terror for many of you, but it has come to this. Your body knew that progress as you aspire and dedicate yourself to was an impossible commission. It had a short shelf-life—yet mesmerized, you continued at break-neck speed.

Now you are suspended in a prolonged moment of precise attentiveness on the sheer cliffside. Will you squirm and lose your footing? Will you try to scramble to some unseen ledge? Will you let go in despair? Will you assume that climbing up is the one true way?

If you were actually stranded on a cliff-side, your underutilized instincts, visions, inner strengths and intuition would swiftly arise. In reality, this is where we are now, yet your response is to reach for reassurance from the very things that have driven you to this impasse.

Everything in your life, if you could accurately read that history-book, would reveal your preparedness for this time. What you need to know now is immediate, precise, and finely etched in this moment. And the next. And the next...

As a contagion, I work with each of you in very specific ways, whether I touch you physically or not. I am working with the entire fabric of humanity right now, having risen up through the vomiting outrage of the earth, through the violated animal kingdom (your closest and thoroughly abused family members) into and through your sophisticated defenses.

Now I say, "Get engaged." Not in resistance. Not in reaction to me, but within yourself. That is my deepest, most urgent call to you. Get engaged with what has grown numb, atrophied, buried and forgotten. Quicken the skills that the urgency of the moment calls into action within you. Pay attention to the precision of instructions at the moment. Trust what your body speaks—soft or loud—and take that next foothold firmly. Reach out across the airwaves through the heart-threads of friendship. Beyond your own wise instincts, these are the most sturdy and reliable safety measures needed during these times. Do not trust those who say they 'know' because they have been here before. Collectively, you have not known the nature of these times. This is a gateway time with no reassurance from the past. What is being written now is of the future. Everything of the past is being eaten and absorbed during this poised entry into an unknowable future.

You do not have an indefinite time to hover in suspense. Take up what is yours to do, now. Listening with every fiber of your being, feel where your hand should go, where your foot must find its next step. Keep your heart open to the web of love and friendship that keeps you safely held as you move. The entire cliffside is conspiring with you, if you can go deep enough to feel and hear its slow wisdom.

Covid time is sacred time. Remember, I came as an act of Love to activate what you have forgotten and to reclaim what is truly indigenous, within and around you. The paradox is that you cannot do this alone, yet you must do it on your own.

Lake Ontario, Port Hope by A. Mathieson

Conversation with the water of Lake Ontario
Port Hope, 2019

I began my conversation by asking the waters of Lake Ontario, "What can you teach me about being with the wounds in us and in the world?"

I bring life, I take it away. I cleanse and I nourish. I resist your concrete riverbanks and dams; I need to meet and mingle freely with the land, the creatures... I meet you today in my role as cleanser. You fear destruction, a sense of loss at your shorelines, but your boundaries were, at best, artificially constructed to accommodate your will and desires separate from my full and necessary aliveness.

Listen. Hear the underbelly of my roar. Feel the force of my waves rearranging the shore. You cannot even begin to see what is being cleansed by my rising tides. A new bargain is being struck, not all in your human favor. But I am essentially the same—life-giver, nourisher and cleanser. I am taking back my own vitality —through storms, through melting ice (which holds ancient memories, fresh salt and minerals.) I need to feed myself; my organs (bodies of water) are exhausted, depleted, toxic, stagnant. I am taking back what is mine. You must reclaim what is yours and no longer rob what is not gifted freely and generously.

As these rising tides alter the plants and weather, even rearrange the stones, you can listen and bow to the forces in deep humility and respect for what is being cleansed and carved anew, or you can waste precious breath fighting the inevitable. It is your choice, but none of our concern. The cleansing is going on and must continue. The question is: Will you be present to the immense power of change or will you shrink in separate fear and self-protection? From this perspective, where are the wounds?

A conversation with Snake

In one of my shamanic meditations with Snake in 2015 he said, "I have seen the holy and the hell." At the time, I felt the depth of his loneliness and how deeply misunderstood he has been, yet I was also aware of the potent, essential medicine he offers for this critical moment. At one point I asked him about why he wanted to come forth now. What was his essential message to humanity?

I am the animal of resurrection. I am ready to come out of the cave into the dim light of your world again. In this liminal time, where everything is becoming, yet again, I am your wisest ally. I embody the art of shedding without dying, as well as shedding in and through death. You need to befriend my nature, persisting past the fear and revulsion... to let me use your brain, your imagination, your buried feelings.

I was banished and reviled because of my power and what I am in touch with— the deeper, darker mysteries that humanity has both ignored and been addicted to in perverse and distorted ways. Facing and welcoming me back in my full presence is essential for the reunion of spirit and matter. Twisted forms of power are evidence of theft of my nature. I yearn to be seen and witnessed so that I may contribute my essential role as shape-shifter, earth-singer, spine-tingler, medicine- giver, awakener and death-guide in these times. I have many names and infinite ways of revealing my nature. You have opened the door to some of these. The rest is up to others to discover in their own kindled flesh.

N.B.: This is an abridged version. Please see Dark Matter: Women Witnessing #12 *online for the complete essay.*

---

* See Mathieson, A. *The Raven Essence Manual: A Love Affair with Nature*, self-published, 5th edition, 1995. Print.

Anne Bergeron
The Night Thunder Called

I inhale. I exhale. Every breath is a consummation with place.

There was a moment when I knew this was true.

I lived in a one-room cabin for three years, alone. No phone, no electricity. I walked across fields, then a short path through a hemlock forest to get there. I carried all my supplies on my back. I hauled water from a spring on the hill above me. I snowshoed in winter, and lay in tall field grass beneath the starred road of the Milky Way in summer. I walked barefoot, drenched in moonlight. I bled, urinated, and defecated into the soil. A great horned owl flew at me out of the darkness, three times, within inches of my face. I stood mindless, awed, unafraid.

The night my life changed I was reading at the table by the light of the kerosene lamp. The warm June air turned suddenly cold. Thunder rumbled, cracked, then roared. Lightning flashed through the room like a strobe. Rain as loud as clashing cymbals pounded the metal roof. Suddenly, I wanted to feel the storm all over and inside of me.

I threw off my jeans and cotton shirt. I pulled the heavy wooden door open, and ran outside naked into rain so cold I gasped. I shivered and leapt down the woods path, my feet slipping in mud and over familiar roots, darkness punctuated by repeated flashes of light. At the gate to the pasture I stopped, closed my eyes, turned my face to the sky, and opened my mouth. I swallowed mouthfuls of rain. As the rain slowed, I ran into the pasture, lifted my arms and twirled and danced and laughed. I lay down and rolled on the slippery grass. I let the rain pelt my back and legs. My tears soaked into the ground as I smoothed the grass with my hands, the hair on my arms and legs tingling.

I could no longer feel my body. No part of the storm felt outside of me. In those moments, I knew that lightning, cloud, wet grass, heavy rain and I were the same being.

I was not under the guidance of hallucinogenic plants or fungi or the influence of alcohol. The spell of life had gripped me, and for once I didn't shake myself free.

Thunder called me to forget what humans had taught me. That night, my body understood that the risk bigger than my own death by lightning was not responding to that storm's summons with all the power that surged in me.

Everything about this experience made sense to me. But I kept it to myself. The year was 1991. I was twenty-six years old. I could think of no one in my life to tell.

The next day, sunlight warmed my face and woke me. My wet hair soaked the pillow. Mud caked to my arms and legs. The bottoms of my feet were raw. Still naked, I felt cleansed and clear. Hallowed. Every heartbeat, every breath of wind, every fly buzzing around my head, loudly pulsed with life. I spent the day lying by my tiny garden in front of the cabin, spellbound.

That evening, I had agreed to care for a friend's dogs while she was away for the night. I drove an hour to her house, took a long walk with her golden retrievers, then curled up on a futon on her screened porch and slept.

When I returned home the following afternoon, my neighbor, Steve, a rangy, grey-haired farmer, met me at the trailhead to my cabin, at the pullout where I parked my car.

Someone was up in your woods last night, he said. *I was down at the barn before bed and saw a light shining through the trees. Someone was walking around up there with a headlamp.*

I had few visitors, and no friends who would drop in unannounced late at night.

Seems odd, Steve. Maybe it was moonlight reflecting on the cabin windows.

But I knew the moon phase. The new crescent had set well before midnight. And my cabin could not be seen through the trees.

I don't mean to scare you, but I thought you should know.

A little tendril of fear sprouted in my belly.

A burly guy in the general store always asks me my name and invites me to see the coyotes he's killed. Another man who smells heavily of tobacco and stale beer once said to me, *I know where you live. I just been up there, hunting.* And what about two nights ago? Had someone seen me out in the field during the storm? Suddenly, I was not only afraid, but angry. Who would creep around at night? Who might know I was away?

On the trail, all the footprints were mine. Inside the cabin, the mason jar of daisies, the copper tea kettle on the wood stove, the sky blue ceramic canisters of flour and rice on the counter were all untouched. Nothing looked missing or out of place. Maybe Steve was wrong.

Still, I took my heavy cast iron frying pan up to bed in the loft with me that night.

The wind rose as I lay down. White pine branches knocked onto the roof. The porcupine that liked to chew on my little porch trundled up and cooed. The barred owl soughed its four-syllable call. I imagined the great horned owl in the maple tree, guarding my place in this forest. I listened for human footsteps. Eventually, I closed my eyes. I slept.

The next morning, the charred face of the skillet on the loft floor next to me looked like an intruder. It belonged hanging above the wood stove. I climbed down the ladder with the pan in one hand, and hung it on the thick iron hook. I would not live with a weapon in my bed.

Stepping outside onto the dewy ground, I felt like I was the only woman in the forest. I stood among maple tree, bracken, petal, wild bee, fox, worm, coyote. I knelt down and stroked the waxy leaves of wild ginger, imagining their thin gold roots below my feet. I looked up at the hemlock and white pine that made a dark green canopy above the cabin.

A woman making love to the land, pressing her body to the ground, feeling the pelting rain, and knowing this as ecstasy, was once not shameful and something to hide. Before millennia of patriarchal repression. Before colonization. Before the earth—and women—became things to exploit and desecrate.

I remember how white male professors in my literature seminars in the 1980s praised Whitman, Wordsworth, and Keats for making love to the earth. So natural, for those guys, to see the earth as lover, and then make some poems about it. No one killed them for writing about their sensual love of each leaf of grass.

That night in the storm, my body remembered the time before women were murdered for the power of their connection to the earth. As I made love to the rain, the thunder, the clouds, and the grass without shame and with intense abandon and pleasure, I felt complete love for myself. Love for my love of the earth that birthed me. Love for the earth that I will nourish in return, with my flesh and bones and teeth and organs, when I no longer breathe.

Why is that still a little hard to write?

Because the history of women who could not live as freely as I live flows in my veins. Because in my country at this moment, the rights of women to govern their own bodies are being systematically taken away.

I put a birch twig in my mouth and roll it on my tongue, break through to its cambium with my teeth. I lick dew from a new maple leaf on a sapling. I put my bare feet on cool, wet pasture grass.

How many generations in my own lineage do I have to go back to find a woman who wasn't afraid to lie naked on the ground?

How far back to find a woman who openly loved herself for the sensual, sexual being that she is?

Like the earth, an ancestor's body is a place we inhabit, and in my family there was a secret.

When my maternal grandmother was a child, she had a special, favorite aunt who took a train trip across the country with a girlfriend. She was young and single and adventurous.

My great, great aunt's name was Florence Waters. *Flower, water.* Her name evokes blossoms, springtime. Florence never returned from that train trip. The family never heard from her again. She was twenty-four years old. The year was 1923.

My mother told me this, over lunch, at a busy cafe, while I still lived in the cabin. In a few days, I would be leaving with a girlfriend to bicycle and backpack in Newfoundland.

Florence seemed to have far more money than she made at her job scooping ice cream at the corner store, my mother said. She had a few boyfriends, nothing steady. She stayed out all night.

To me, the thought of a woman in my lineage who left home and traveled at a time when few women who had little financial means could and did, was exciting.

Maybe Florence created a whole new life for herself, I said to my mother.
Not very likely. Everyone believes the trip ended in tragedy.
Maybe she was pregnant, and left home to have a baby. Or her friend was pregnant.
That's possible. Florence was…well…everyone in the family said she was a prostitute. Whatever happened, everyone thinks Florence and her friend got into some kind of trouble that was impossible to get out of. Your grandmother was devastated.
You mean you think she was murdered?
It's what everyone in the family thinks.

I'm so stunned by this, I don't ask my mother why she tells me this story. Why now. But I think I know why. This story is a warning.

I will not let it make me afraid.

Florence Waters becomes my muse, my mentor. I make altars to her memory with river stones, sea glass, owl feathers, and coyote bones. I write a poem about her. I promise her I will not forget her. I absorb her memory and feel her life intermingle with mine.

It will be years before I think to look up the etymology of the word *prostitute*. When I do, here's what I find:
From the Latin: pro – forward, forth, toward the front, public
From the Latin: sta/statuere – to place, set down, to stand, or make firm
The word *prostitute* originates in the idea of being *in public, going forth, standing in place.*
I extemporize. *A woman who places herself in the world. A woman who stands in her place.*

The fear of my female ancestors flows in my veins. But so does the courage of one.

Florence, I don't know where you are buried—at the bottom of a river or a well or in a shallow grave—or beneath the grass in a cemetery full of graceful cottonwoods, with an engraved marble headstone, marking your full and chosen life in a place that loved you back.

But I remember you and honor that you are alive in me. That you were with me that night the thunder called. That I was anticipated by and fed by women like you. In the story I tell myself about you, you fully loved the raw beauty of the earth.

One day I will be buried on the land where I now live, where the roots of trees will find nourishment in my bones. Where insects will inhabit my uterus and heart and lungs. Where well below the ground, new springs will well up and new life will blossom, fed by me, as I was birthed and nourished by the earth.

Until then, I will stand in place, my feet cool and damp in summer grass, knowing that here, on this land, is precisely where I belong, that the earth is who I am meant to love.

Nancy Windheart
Aspen Ways of Knowing

From the time I was a small child, one of the guiding questions of my life has been, "How do other beings know, understand, and perceive the world?" In particular, I have been fascinated by trying to understand how beings of non-human species feel and know, and what these perceptions and ways of knowing and being can teach others.

Photo by N. Windheart

I live in Santa Fe, New Mexico, at about 7200 feet elevation, with the Sangre de Cristo mountain range, the southernmost subrange of the Rocky Mountains, overlooking the city. The mountains are a primary habitat for the Quaking Aspen forest—or, as I call them, the Aspen People.

The quaking aspen are best known for their brilliant yellow-gold foliage in the autumn; however, I adore being among them at any time of year. Their energy, consciousness, and wisdom nourishes me deeply.

Over the last year, the aspen have taken me into a kind of apprenticeship, and have been training me in their wisdom, their ways of knowing, their perspective. I have devoted time on a regular basis to feeling their energy, listening to them, understanding more and more deeply the role they play and the energy that they hold on our planet.

When I listen to the aspen and other non-human beings, I open all of my internal senses, my body, my energy field, my intuitive knowing. I receive communication from other species as a multi-sensory and multi-dimensional gestalt of knowing and understanding that often includes vision, perception and sensing of energy, imagery, and sometimes auditory communication. Frequently, I receive in a kind of somatic "blast," where I feel energy and information coming in…I've trained myself to become quiet, still, and open, setting aside my human perceptions, thoughts, and ways of knowing, in service to opening to and listening to intelligence, awareness, and perspectives often vastly different from my own.

I have come to understand the Aspen People as one of the great consciousnesses of the earth, and as I have opened to them, their teachings and transmissions of energy and wisdom have astonished me, humbled me, and filled me with gratitude.

Quaking Aspen (Populus tremuloides) is the most widely distributed tree in North America, ranging from Canada to central Mexico.

Aspen biology is, in itself, a teaching about community and interdependence. Stands/groves of quaking aspen are called "clones" because they are not a collection of individual trees, rather, they are one organism, with many shoots sprouting from its long lateral roots. Each "tree" is genetically identical, arising from and sharing the same root system, in aggregate called a "clone." Aspen clones can be less than an acre and up to 100 acres in size. There can be one clone in an aspen grove or there can be many.

The largest and oldest known aspen clone is the "Pando" clone on the Fishlake National Forest in southern Utah. Also known as the

"Trembling Giant," it is over 100 acres in size and weighs more than fourteen million pounds—more than forty times the weight of the largest animal on the planet, the Blue Whale. Pando has been aged at 80,000 years, although 5-10,000-year-old clones are more common. Considering the age, longevity, and perspective of even these "younger" clones, compared to a human lifespan, completely reorients my human perception of time.

September, 2019

I am in the mountains on a solo hike, on a trail that I know best as a cross country ski trail. As I walk among the aspen, opening all of my internal and external senses in a kind of walking meditation, I sense a pulsing, low, humming…a vibration that I "hear" and feel with my entire body, though it is not audible to my ears.

It is similar to the vibration that I sometimes feel in the ocean when I am with the whales…or like the low-frequency sounds that elephants use to communicate with each other across vast distances. The pulsing energy moves in my cells, through the boundaries of my skin, and my whole body feels as though it is expanding in every direction into the space around me in the forest.

I understand that I am being given an invitation to breathe with them, to feel their respiration, to sense their energy exchange with sun, wind, and sky (aspen photosynthesize through their bark as well as their leaves) and to glimpse their vast awareness of time, space, distance.

I realize that if I try to allow my body to match their rhythm, slowing my breath down as much as possible, I'll be here for several hours, pulsing in and out with each wave. I also realize that I can't do that…or I'll be spending the night unprepared on the mountain.

The moment this thought moves through me, I feel the aspen respond. Their rhythm speeds up, shifts, just for a short time—just enough so that I can feel it in my human body. They communicate this directly to me—working with my energy field—so that I can more deeply understand and resonate with their frequency.

I stop, open, and allow my energy body to continue to expand. My legs grow long, extending into the earth, until they meet the aspen root, a long, horizontal root from which the shoots of the clone arise. I allow my body to plug in, to join with the energy of this root system, to connect with its life force, its intelligence. I feel the aspens' vast understanding of long stretches of time…and my limited human perspective in my small body, individual awareness, and short life span.

I become aware that I am in contact with… literally, standing in/above/below/among, one of the greatest, wisest, oldest consciousnesses of the planet. Whether old clones or young in our human conception of time, these exquisitely sensitive and aware beings are ancient elders who carry immense wisdom, vision, and perspective. I can barely touch what the aspen know and hold. I bow my head in humility and in gratitude for the presence of these great beings.

As I open to this awareness, I feel again the low hum…the vibration… so similar to what I feel with the whales. I look up, and in the fissure of the bark of an older stem/tree, there is the image of a breaching whale.

The Whale Aspen by N. Windheart

No wonder I feel the whales here, I realize. The aspen and the whales know each other…land and sea…and they swim in the same rivers of vast cosmic wisdom.

Bark… skin… breath… life… joy… wisdom… grace…

I continue along the trail, and come into a grove of Douglas fir, also common in these mountains. As I enter their shade, I immediately sense that this is a "Faery Grove"–a place where the nature spirits gather and flourish. I feel their energy, hearing a faint sound that I sometimes hear when in their presence…a bit like crystalline chimes or bells… and feel their joy. It makes me giggle out loud. I can feel how the whole mountain is filled with the magic and grace of the devas, the nature spirits, the faeries…tending the plants, the trees, the streams.

The aspen all over the western United States are struggling…for many reasons…almost all of them related to climate change/global warming and human interference and forest disruption. I think of this as I walk among them, feeling the expansiveness of their perspective. As I walk, I hold the questions that so many of us are holding in these times: How do I show up for the world as it is, as it seems, right now? How do I show up for the melting of the Arctic, the burning of the Amazon, for the children separated from their families, living in cages, traumatized by the government of my country at the border of the state I live in; for the poisoned waters, the species dying daily, beings of all species all over our beloved planet who are suffering in countless ways…

I walk with my daily prayer in my heart: "Show me how best I can serve; help me to live each moment in compassion, kindness, and joy; teach me to love purely, boundlessly, as the great teachers of all species love…" And I wonder, in my small, limited human perspective, does it matter? Does it have an impact? Can it ever be enough?

The aspens sing me their answer, in the vibration of their trunks and leaves, in the flow of the ancient wisdom of their roots: "Sing the song that is yours to sing. All beings must sing their own song. From the singing of our songs, a new world is birthed into form."

The song that is mine to sing is this listening to the aspen, the whales, the dragonflies, the cats, the bees, and helping others of my species to hear their wisdom, too. For others, it may be loving a child, caring for an old dog, making a home beautiful, writing a poem, making a meal, nursing the sick, becoming an activist, running for public office.

The aspens, in singing their song, inspire my own. Each of us has a song to sing...and the time is now...sing we must. It doesn't matter if the song is small or large, loud or soft, or even if we are particularly good singers. What matters is that we sing...that we send our songs, our devotion, our love into our world, as best we can, every day, with the full commitment of our hearts.

Photo by N. Windheart

November, 2019

I have come into the mountains to listen to the forest, and to offer my prayers. This time, my heart is heavy with the knowledge that the clear cutting and burning in these mountains has begun again, a massive and misguided policy that is marketed to the public as "forest fire prevention." In reality, it is anything but.

I walk among the aspen, feeling the energy of the burns, the forest struggling, the animals imperiled, the ecosystem once again fractured by short-sighted human actions that deny the innate wisdom of the earth and all she holds.

As I walk, I am stopped again by the Aspen People with a wave of understanding and wisdom. Their message is clear, straightforward: *Hold the vision. See the burns stopped, the machinery gone. See the forest healthy and whole.*

I pause and see and feel these images as best as I can: a healthy forest, no burning, no bulldozers, a strong and vibrant ecosystem in balance.

Birds, squirrels, trees, sunset; the forest quiet, holy.

I am invited to take a small aspen branch and a stone and bring them for my home altar. When I return home, I include a statue of Kuan Yin, and a malachite crystal for carrying the energy outward. My intention for the altar and the energy it holds is: *The forest is safe, the forest is healthy, the forest is whole.* I use Reiki to charge the altar with the intention that it hold and carry these prayers and intentions in an ongoing way, outside the boundaries of time and space.

Photos (opposite and next spread) and Home Altar (above) by N. Windheart

December, 2019

I make my pilgrimage to the mountains, now blanketed with snow. I am hiking with my snowshoes, and the forest is silent, rich with the quiet of deep winter. The aspen people, the firs and the ravens greet me, and I sink into their deep winter embrace.

The aspen begin communicating to me right away as I walk among them, showing me that the energetic healing for the areas that have been cut/burned/destroyed began immediately, and is ongoing. The healthy parts of the forest begin the repair work for the damaged parts instantly, both energetically and physically, sending energy to the areas of the forest that have been so unconsciously harmed and destroyed. The ravens carry and circulate the healing energy with incredible precision; the trees immediately send energy, nutrients, life-force to the destruction. The healing is happening even in the burning and cutting. I kneel on the earth in the snow, in gratitude. There is so much I don't understand, so much I can't see and know from my human vantage point. The perspective of the forest, and the aspen in particular, is vast, timeless, and constantly awake.

The aspen show me that they are aware of the burning, the destruction of the Amazon rainforest ... the fires in Australia ... the ongoing struggles of so many regions and ecosystems of our planet. They are aware, and they are in connection. They feel and sense the entire planet ... not just their local ecosystem. There is also a partnership in sharing regenerative, healing energy with these distant ecosystems and expressions of life.

January, 2020

I come again to the ski trail, this time with my cross-country skis. There is a palpable sense in the forest, a shimmering, sparkling energy in the deep winter quiet. I feel so at home as I join my aspen friends on this winter afternoon. As I ski, I feel their presence, their being-ness, their understanding. They speak to me about joy. I can feel their awareness of me, a small, rapidly moving creature, with such a limited life span and experience compared to theirs.

They give me a feeling…a sense…which my mind/body translates as: "Joy-flying." They show me that they send their energy through their roots, their stems, their leaves, their energy body, as a brilliant shower of joy, sparkling, radiating far beyond their physical forms…flying the joy, flying their intelligence, their communication, their understanding, into, above, around, through the earth.

And then this message comes, clearly, with precise wording, in my language: *We Dream the Forest Alive. We Breathe the Planet Awake.*

I understand that they are engaged in a constant broadcasting of an immense vibration of healing, emanating grace, peace, and wholeness. As I write, I recognize that my words can only point to, or approximate, the vastness of the wisdom and understandings that the aspen share. Yet, I also understand that, for me, and perhaps for my fellow humans, these distillations of the essence of their communications may be helpful in giving us a glimpse of their ways of knowing, perceiving, understanding, and Be-ing.

As I attune with the energy of the Aspen People, I feel their senses and wisdom permeating my awareness, my cells, and my consciousness. As I receive their transmission through the words: "We Dream the Forest Alive. We Breathe the Planet Awake" I consider the possibility that this dreaming, breathing, awakening may be something that our species, too, can share. Can we open into our collective consciousness, beyond our individual perspectives, and dream the forests alive, healthy, flourishing, vibrant? Can we breathe our planet awake, healthy, and whole?

Deena Metzger
Dreaming Another Language: She Will not Kill

It is raining. I am listening to rain on the roof and skylights. A rain I have not heard in four years. This is not the heavy rain that is still predicted. This is the "light rain"—it intensifies now, as I write these words. It precedes, we hope, the "heavy rain" that could reach down to the very tips of the deepest roots of the tallest trees to restore the aquifer and the future. I am writing in rhythm with the rain, and it is setting up a path of communication between us. Between the rain and myself after such a long time. A communication in another language.

I have been speaking to, praying for the rain, this rain, for almost four years. Praying as I watched the land parch, watched the animals of the wild desperately seek food and water, watched even as the drought-tolerant purple sage withered and browned. There are animals in these mountains who have never seen rain. We keep a large pail of water filled for mountain lion, bobcat, coyote and deer—they all have to learn to drink together, and so live together in the feral orchard.

We put down bales of alfalfa in the driest winters for the deer and other non-predators. But the animals have to be safe there—we can't lay a trap for prey, or an opportunity for the predators. And so it is.

For more than four years, I have been listening for a Literature of Restoration. Simultaneously, I have been listening for a dialogue with the elementals. I began by praying that the rain would come. But I knew we do not deserve it. So then I prayed for the rain. On behalf of the rain and the other elementals. Such prayers require another language.

Indigenous peoples sing to the elementals, the ancestors, the spirits. For most peoples and religions, songs and prayer are one. In many indigenous languages, prayer and honoring the spirits are embedded in, intrinsic to, each word of the language. To recreate such prayer and honoring is intrinsic to the Language of Restoration.

Beauty is also an essential element of The Language and The Literature of Restoration, but it does not exist if its other face, Truth, is not present. Beauty and Truth become Integrity, and Integrity requires Responsibility. What we say, and how we live and act, must be one. The Literature of Restoration demands this.

I am not writing in a straight line. I am writing in a circle. If you write in a circle then there is a field within it. The field is the earth and the future. A Literature of Restoration holds the earth and its future in its arms.

Here comes the rain. I must speak about the rain in a time of drought. I must speak about the rage and anger of rain. I must speak about the rain as it returns as one who has been in prison or in exile. I could not call for the rain to return, I could only pray for its welfare wherever it had sequestered itself, wherever it was hiding. I could only pray for the soul of the rain, wherever it was confined or held captive.

What needs to be offered, so the rain can be free to be itself?

We must change for the land to be free. In order for the rain to be free to come to the land that requires it, we must change. We must change entirely. We must change so that we do not live against the earth and we do not live against the rain. We must give our lives to the rain.

I give my life.

This is what the dream requires through its language from another world. It is a sacred message from Spirit. The dream comes in its own language to remind us that we have to find, remember, learn and develop this Language so we will understand. Understand the dream. Understand what we are being called to set right. Understand what we are being called to create: She will not kill.

Here is the dream.

The dream came in another language. That is, it came in a rhythm from another language and, therefore, spoke of another world than the one we inhabit when we speak English. An unknown world.

I am, or she is, holding the photo and speaking to him, or he is the face in the photo. I am, or she is, saying, "No, you will not kill." He, as a revolutionary, or they, together, they will do what they must, what they have been doing, what has been necessary, but they are here in this country, this Spain of the Imagination, and they will leave without killing. Killing will not be the last act. Killing is not sanctioned. I am, or she is, adamant.

But now I am the Mother in a Spain of the Imagination and I am going to the Teacher. I open the door. I tell her that I am here on my knees. I fall to my knees before her. One can only fall to one's knees before someone one trusts implicitly. We are women in a Spain of the Imagination. We have dark hair, our faces are strong and clear, we wear black skirts and white blouses. But if we wore only black you would not be surprised.

I tell her that I have come about my daughter. She is sixteen or eighteen. She is the Daughter. She will not kill. I will not allow it. It is not to protect the victim; it is to protect my daughter. She is a revolutionary, as we all are, as we must be. But, I tell the teacher with whom I am now collaborating, who understands everything, I will send the daughter away. She will go to another country. I cannot send her to the United States. It is not a country of such women as we are or we have become. It is not a country that forbids killing.

That young man will go to another country, too. That young man who is her partner, in the way the man was my partner earlier, when I held the photo and knew that he must not, and so would not kill. He/they will not kill.

I speak this to the Teacher. I am on my knees, and she is seated on the single wood chair by the windows in a classroom empty of children. I fall to my knees and then I rise up. It is possible that I am also the teacher. It is possible that there is only one person in this dream and it is myself and I am playing all the roles. No, I am not playing roles. I am everyone in the dream as I must be, because it is a dream and that is how the dream teaches us as there are no others in a dream; there is only what we know or what is being told to us by the dream—which, ultimately, knows what needs to be known.

This is the dream. A dream from a world of the imagination that birthed me when I was a young girl or a young woman, and when killing (despite Guernica, despite World War II, despite Hiroshima and Nagasaki) was not killing a person, but an act that created another world. In such dreams of language, killing was a word, not an act. It was a word that led to another world, an act that had to end in a dream of Life, of words come to life, like justice or freedom. A dream of a world in which killing was not ever to have to kill a body that could not understand the horror of killing. To kill and not to kill were the same, because they created the world we had to create so that the killing would be over.

It was a world I recognized in an imaginary literature of Spain where I have never been. It was a world I was born into through dreams I do not remember that have rhythms that might be flamenco and which I found again in the rhythms of the poetry and the literature of Latin America.

In these dreams that are not dreams so much as patterns in other worlds, the women know what they have to know, though their mothers wore veils and were silent and sequestered behind walls in cities called the Alameda or Alhambra, the Red. In the languages of these worlds, the men told the stories of what the women were not to know…The men who told the stories did not know what the women knew and were passing on to the daughters, the daughters who come to me now at this time in my life in my dream. The daughters who are straight and tall, who are revolutionaries in black skirts, who have red lips and carry red roses and will not kill. The women who will not kill, so killing is forbidden. That is how strong they are.

The women say, "This is what we taught you in dreams you have forgotten you dreamed in your childhood, the dreams that formed you and that surface now at this time in your life when you are asking what is to be done, what is to be done, what is to be done?"

This is the photo of the man who, at the end of what he is to do, is not to kill. The photo is not of the man who is to be killed. The photo is of a man, who ultimately, because he is the revolutionary—the one who brings justice like the sunlight or the rain—will not kill. The woman says so and so it is so. That is what the dream says. And it says that all of this, the story, the strength not to kill, the strength that ends killing, is in language, in the rhythm of the words, and this is what we have forgotten. Earth, rhythm, language, light—they were to have come together in a poetry from which the future might have arisen if we had listened and learned to speak that language, its rhythms and images, its absolute poetry.

But then we forgot or yielded to the trance, to the relentless noise from which our cities dull as old metal and gray egg cartons arise in the fluorescent lights of super markets and endless parking lots and deluded malls which have no music to them and so are not the languages that we had been given to heal the world.

And because of this, because it may not be too late, the dream comes and the woman says, adamantly, "The man, my lover, the woman, my daughter, her lover, we will not kill. At the end of the dream, at the end of the dreams, we will not kill."

The dream comes in another language, a Language that emerged from a Literature, or a Literature that emerged from a Language that, despite war, blood, prisons, cruelty, iron bars, sequestered women, had a poetry beneath it that was a river of life, even when life was forbidden.

The rain is here again like the tap of the heels of a woman who is dancing flamenco. She is dancing her life and her death to the music of the guitar whose chord slides down from heaven to earth, from her wild black hair into her pulsing groin, the bud of her clitoris within her red rose. Arpeggio. Crescendo.

This is why she will not kill. She will prohibit killing. She is like the rain. She returns. She persists. And so the earth will be restored by the insistent and persistent rhythm of her dancing heels, one phrase after another, in her secret Language of Restoration.

I am waiting for the rain to come to see if I can send this dream to you. The rain is here. We are on our knees. It is a hard rain. Flood, its other face, is possible, but now we welcome the rain and we pray in another language.

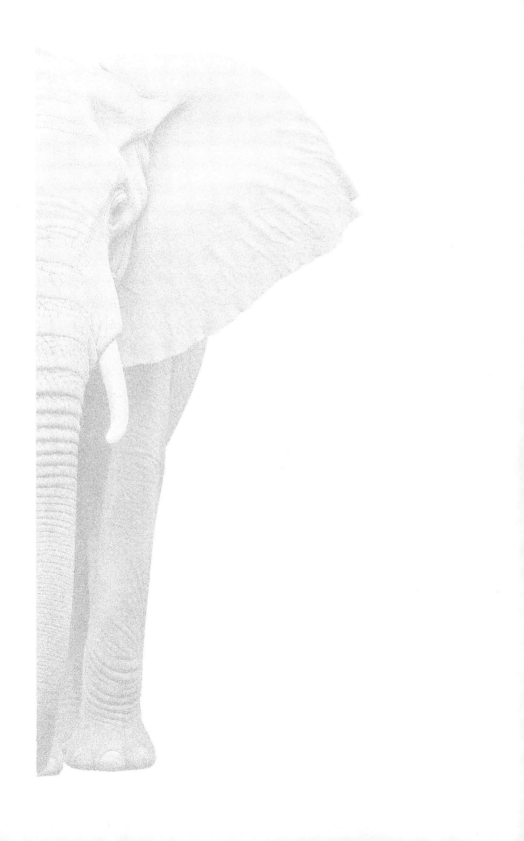

Songs of Undoing

Our sacred task now is to dissolve pride of 'first place' and lordship, to give over our old identities on behalf of the law of creation.

—Sharon English, *Nourishing the Future*

....my urge to pitch into their world and unmake myself.

—Jaime Wood, *Yaquina at Low Tide*

Sharon English
Nourishing the Future

I'm walking on a trail by the river Thames in London, ON, near the neighbourhood where I grew up. I enter the ravine, moving into the woods, and find myself at a place I know well where the river bends. The current's powerful here, and on the opposite bank rises a sandy cliff full of swallows' nests. I swim across, emerging on a ribbon of sand at the cliff's base. Suddenly, I'm naked. I roll in the sand vigorously, really getting it into my skin and hair. Then I lie back, waiting.

A rope or belt, interwoven with shells, comes up from the ground and hooks me by the neck, hard. I resist briefly, instinctively, then surrender, and am pulled into the earth. It's utterly dark, and for a while I see and feel nothing but the rope now loosely about me. Then a place appears, dimly in the distance: a small beach against a rock face with a cave opening there and a little fire burning before it. It's night. I come and sit by the fire. I can sense water close by, though can see nothing but my immediate surroundings and stars overhead. The white sand is fine and cool. All is still. I feel like I'm in a spirit world, or our world long ago.

I lie down, thinking to sleep. A crab emerges from the sand and crawls onto me. Though briefly unnerved, I accept it. Then many crabs emerge. They crawl all over me—and they begin to eat me.

This happens fast and slow. My awareness is focused on them: their eyes glinting in the moonlight, their delicate legs, their smooth hard backs and strange claws. I'm a floating awareness now; I've become food to nourish them. They eat neatly, until everything is gone and only my clothing and bones remain. All of this feels utterly holy: a great, spiritual event.

The crabs disperse, some toward the unseen water and some nearer to the cave, where they lay eggs in the sand. Disembodied, I observe, aware that I 'am' the crabs now and that I'm making possible the next generation of crabs. This feels totally right.

I find myself crossing the Thames River again—but the I who emerges on shore is not the same person. I feel distinctively other. I'm barefoot now, and wearing a long blue dress interwoven with shells, with shells adorning my hair. I feel beautiful.

— April 2017

What does it mean to be devoured? According to the dream, it means offering oneself fully to the needs of others—in this case, earth and spirit. Doing so ensures there's a future. Doing so brings to life the shelled one, the beautiful barefooted woman in blue.

All of us learn early on in this culture that humans occupy the top of the food chain. We choose what we eat. We call the shots! And do we ever do that: we eat and eat, and regard those who dare nibble us or our food as vermin. In this dream, however, there is no 'top,' only the cycle of life and spiritual transformation.

It's time to give our old identities over. We must act—and the action required is to stop: stop interfering, stop controlling, stop thinking we know best. Be naked, and surrender. Trust that Earth, which has created us, knows what to do. Crab will take it from there. Crabs are scavengers and meticulous cleaners. Sensitive and tough. They operate on land and water. What better creature to consume our tainted selves, and create new life?

Our sacred task now is to dissolve pride of 'first place' and lordship, to give over our old identities on behalf of the law of creation. Can we trust this earth? How can we not? The best of who we are can feed the future of all beings. This is the path to becoming earth-human, spirit-human—integrated human beings. Then there will be a future.

Jojo Donovan
Dispatches from the Collapse of Time

Time is collapsing. Five years ago, this message started knocking. I'd sit down to write, and strange passages would tumble out—with the collapse of time always at the center. The first passage came scrawled on a thin strip of paper, twisted and taped into a mobius strip. So the passage had no ending or beginning, and instead circled around and through itself, the inside becoming the outside and the poem playing itself on loop:

A Reading from the Book of Endings
Time is collapsing.
Look around: you know it to be true.

⤸

This frenzy.
This fervor.
It's not just a question of technology.
Faster and faster, moments
arrive. The future
scrambles, scurries,
scrunches itself
into the margins of
the present.

⤸

Call it hyperventilation:
More time pumped through the vents
than the body can manage.
The world trapped
in a wheezing
in-breath.
The next
moment arrives before
the last can be
exhaled.

Time is collapsing.
Arriving too fast.
The lungs of the earth
are strained past bursting.

And worse: no time
to breathe out, no chance to discharge,
loose moments settle
in our lungs and on our bones.

The living body must make dust.
But with no future-space to flake and float towards,
the dead cells we slough now gather and pile and bury our limbs
under one more layer of cast-off skin.

One more layer,
one more layer,
Until our motions grow thick, heavy, slow with time.
Memory coats our bodies soft and gray.
Lifetimes of loss dust our lips dry.
And the coarse grit of history scratches, always, at the backs of our
throats.
This doesn't help our breathing.

Time is collapsing.
A shock to the system.
The center cannot hold.

Don't ask what to do now.
Now is sand sifted through the palm,
a seaside phantom lost to wind and wave.

Don't ask what happens next.
Next is a caving tunnel,

a last gold ray choked by smoke and rubble
as the walls give way.

    ↶

It's time to find more useful questions.
Ones unbound from the time we no longer have.

    ↶

What is possible, here?
What shapes can our bodies take?
How can we touch each other, and where?

    ↶

What could be born of this?
Who is here to hold us through the birthing?

    ↶

Time is collapsing.
Look around: you know it to be true…

↶

I believed the message despite not knowing what it meant. The voice coming through felt like a near-future self, one who seemed more competent and capable and knowing and *real* than the self I was actually inhabiting at the time—who was fumbling their way through the early stages of gender transition; who was bewildered by a sudden call into animist, embodied spirituality; who was engaging old trauma and confronting their own capacity to cause harm; and who was deep in depression and struggling most days to get out of bed.

So I fell hard for this imagined future self, who became real in the moments her voice reached the page. She could speak with confidence and weight and even something like flair, where my day-to-day self was often caught in a fog of executive dysfunction and frozen by self-doubt. I named her "the priestess"—and I longed not just to hear her voice but also to *become* her, to reach her or to birth her, to arrive at a future where she was real and she was me.

And I longed to understand the messages she left—most of which came in short fragments scattered through my journals. I invented a "scholar" self to sift through those fragments and attempt to make sense of them from a more rational lens. The scholar archived each passage as "A Reading from the Book of _____"—hoping or pretending they could eventually be compiled into a cohesive whole.

The agenda of the priestess was to get me out of my head and into the world—and to face down and engage with the many crises unfolding. At intervals, the messages kept coming:

A Reading from the Book of Endings

It's not that it isn't shameful.
It's certainly not that all is forgiven.

᠔

It's only that shame cannot heal shame.
And that which cannot serve healing
must now be culled.

᠔

Look, though: even now, the earth reaches out her body.
Even now, at the moment of collapse.

᠔

Every field a killing-field.
And still, each spring: new blossoms
from the unmarked graves.
Even now, her fever rising, these gestures of embrace.

᠔

How dare you be ashamed?
In these last hours, at this last sacred invitation,
how dare you cast down your gaze?

᠔

If you must say no,
if you must fail her this one last time –
at least have the strength to meet her eyes
and name your failing.

∽

How could this world reach out for you still?
Your shame would say she has no reason.
One more echo of that great Enlightened arrogance—
to believe yourself beyond her body,
separate enough to leave or to return.

∽

But you are her body, inseparable.
One of her many sensing organs,
a bundled few of her countless firing nerves.
Flesh of her damaged flesh, fingers of her reaching hand.

∽

And so your shame is her shame.
Your pain her pain, your losses hers to bear.
The paths of destruction your people have paved –
a network of scars carved into her skin.
Your history a bloody map she cannot help but study.
A wound she would give anything to heal.

∽

Of course the earth reaches for you.
What else can the wounded body do,
but reach for the part that hurts?

∽

Stepping into my gender, reclaiming my sexuality, engaging trauma, and
moving into animist spiritual practice all led to breakthrough moments
of deep joy, pleasure, and aliveness. But all that unearthing also brought
me into intimate and often-overwhelming relationship with shame.

I had changed out all the furniture, but I was still largely trapped
within the spiritual architecture of Catholicism—a binary framework
of sin and salvation where every thought and action was a reflection
of my basic goodness or badness, and the risk of being cast out and
condemned hovered over everything. I had subbed in a new set of
values—anti-capitalist, anti-racist, animist, queer, abolitionist— but

kept the impossible standards and the perpetual judgment. And so in the moments when I encountered my own capacity to cause harm and violate consent, or when I touched more deeply into both the global and body-level costs of white supremacy and colonial ecocide—my sense of myself as *one of the good ones* would collapse, and I'd tumble down a long shame spiral.

The priestess wasn't gentle with my shame-wracked self, but she offered a pathway out: feel the world reaching for you and choose to reach back.

When we reach back, new possibilities unfold:

A Reading from the Book of Endings
Try not to fret, child.
All times are end times.

~

The end has been nigh
from the first night onward.
It has come already,
more times than we can count.

~

Yes: this time is different.
Not end times, but the end of time itself.
But even that great ending is not unknown to you.

~

You have been ripped from time before.
More times than you can count.
Trust that this knowledge can serve you.

~

And maybe the collapse won't be as gloomy as it sounds.
Who said the end of time was the end
of joy, or of love, or of desire?
Who said it was the end of the body—
its worries and its wonders?

ᔐ

Time is collapsing.
Who will you become?
Who said you don't still get to choose?

ᔐ

The experiment is changing.
Without the violent eye of history
to flatten us with its gaze,
the many woven possibilities of the body unfold.

ᔐ

Most of us cannot remember existing the way we will soon exist.
Most of us cannot imagine living that full, that wide, that free.

ᔐ

Many will panic, faced with the sudden dreadful weight of it all.
Many will cling to the cage of time
as it collapses.

ᔐ

You, my child, I expect will fare better.

ᔐ

Search your body.
The tender places.
The raw hurt, the dull and dormant throbbing
that threatens, always, to erupt—
and so often does.

ᔐ

No stranger to collapse,
You know how to survive
when the wound gapes wide
and the solid ground of time is sucked away.

ᔐ

Child, this is a survivor's world, learning to survive.
When the time comes—when the time goes—
you will pause, and take a breath,
and show us what you've learned.

If the earth is a living body, she is the body of a survivor. And here, the priestess likens the collapse of time to a trauma response on a global scale. Strange, then, that this is one of her more hopeful passages.

Flashbacks and panic attacks pull the body out of consensus reality and into a space where past and present collide and tangle. Because we're no strangers to that particular form of collapse, the priestess says, survivors may have a head start in navigating what's to come. Maybe we're a bit less invested in the myths that are crumbling, and so we're a little less likely to cling to the wreckage as it falls. Maybe we've already done work to heal and process and restore and reclaim, and so have tools in place that will be useful.

What's important is that the crashing wave of the collapse isn't all there is to the story. Somehow, the priestess suggests, it will wash over and resolve into something worth hanging on for. *Without the violent eye of history ... the many woven possibilities of the body unfold.* There will still be choices to make and life to live—if we can learn what it takes to navigate what's next.

What will it take? What will we need to learn? For gestures at an answer, I turn away from the Book of Endings and towards this fragment of what the scholar named "The Time-Tunneller's Handbook"—where the priestess shifted from reading the signs to assigning a time-collapse curriculum:

A Reading from the Time Tunneller's Handbook:
Study moles, badgers, ants, worms. Study their excess dirt. Where does it go? Study prairie dogs, certain snakes. Study the pits and burrows and chambers carved from the body of the earth.

Study caves, how they form. Study the gaps in the crust, the pockets of air. Study caverns and canyons. Study groundwater and learn how it flows. Study the fault-lines, the sites of rupture and repair.

Space is a metaphor for time—matter is a metaphor for her body. Study the metaphors. Learn density. Learn mass. Learn the insides of things, the way space is filled.

It will be harder than you expect. Surface-dwellers struggle to believe in depth. That an under, an inner could exist. That it could not only exist but be worth learning.

The skin is only a thumbnail sliver of the body. It's time to relearn the innards, the guts.

Too often, the sighted move and live by sight alone. Every object, every being we encounter: a tiny moon known only by its surface shine. Our entire visual knowledge rests at exactly the point where the body ends. The lights go out and we are lost.

Meanwhile, the heart of things is cased in darkness. Learn to think of your skin that way: a thin bright boundary. A soft casing, protection for the dark unseen field that is your body.

All of this is a metaphor for the body of time. Humans are surface creatures. We have known time as we have known the earth: by her surface. By her skin. She beckons you to dig...

Dig
In the days beyond the collapse of time,
we learned to tunnel and tap
to scratch our songs
in the language of the soil—
which, yes, is the language of the heavy dark,
whose only vowel is hunger,
whose favorite verb is to decay—
and yes, we were afraid.
But we learned to speak through our fear
with knuckle, nail, and tongue,
to tunnel and tap and scratch a song
of buried futures, and hear those futures singing back—
to live with palms forward

in tight spaces,
under root and over rock
where the ancestors wait
shoulder to shoulder
for your return.
We learned to read your face
in the texture of their whispered longings—
we learned to hunger for you and to seek
as the worm seeks,
not for endings or arrivals
but for one more gritty morsel,
for whatever we might pass through the dark tunnel
of our bodies, and then deposit, changed—
in the days of the collapse, we started our long learning.
We tunneled deep—we sought—we found you
and we scratched a timeless rhythm
on the edges of your world.
Linear time, that invention of the imperial mind,
has ground itself to dust.
The forests may be threatened,
but a chorus has risen in the deep places,
and the time the forests keep will outlive this collapse.
So come with us and learn. We are your kin.
We emerge from your body,
and you from ours.
We are here to call you back
into the soil—
to pass you through the tunnel—
to help you live
palms-forward
in the tight space
of the time that's left.

What's clear is that the time-tunnelers have learned the insides of things, and they ask us to do the same. *Learn about the soil*, they say, and we can celebrate: lots of people are doing that already. We can piggyback on learning that's well underway. It's a gift of the moment we're in: mycelial wisdom weaving its way back into the collective imagination.

Even imaginations shaped and structured by white colonial mythology, which denies the life of the interior in order to strip-mine and consume it, can find pathways to the soil if we choose. Even pockets of Western science are feeling for the roots and finding life there. *You are not alone in this*, the tunnelers say. *A chorus has risen in the deep places.* You only have to listen, and learn, and then join in.

N.B.: This is an abridged version. Please see Dark Matter: Women Witnessing #14 *online for the complete essay.*

Yehudit Silverman
Refugia

Poet's note: Refugia* *is a scientific term referring to places that become safe spaces for organisms and life to endure in the midst of upheaval.*

The Arabs used to say, when a stranger appears at your door, feed him
for three days before asking who he is…
— Naomi Shihab Nye, *Red Brocade*

The night of a thousand stars
won't keep you safe
as you run on desert sands
Let me tell you about the prophets
yours and mine
how they listened
to the poetry
of the persian lynx
how they kept each other warm
night after night
Blessed be the stranger
The one you don't know
whose body is still
whose breath is gone
I have no purpose now
but to offer you bread, wine
a wet cloth to cleanse your wounds
you have no purpose now
but to offer me the same
How did we end up here
fighting
for a piece of this dry land?
The night of a thousand stars
won't keep you safe
See the young lovers
holding hands
as the bombs fall
Hear the cry

Photo by NEOM on Unsplash.com

of a newborn babe
lifted gently
out of the rubble
Hurry
your plate is waiting
Hurry
soldiers can't tell us apart
our semitic curly hair
like snakes slithering
down our backs
If only we could stop running
There must be a place
a refugia
where both of us
are welcome

Notes

As the blood flows on the desert lands of Israel and Gaza, I try to remember the tents of long ago where a stranger was welcomed, where tea was served, where survival meant keeping each other fed. I listen to the voice of the desert itself, where olive and lemon trees flourish, to the brave ones who bury their dead and then embrace their so called "enemy" because to lose a child is the same no matter where you live. I believe there is hope if we are willing to sit with each other in our brokenness and connection to the land.

———————

* For more on "Refugia" see Deane Moore, Kathleen. *Great Tide Rising: Towards Clarity and Moral Courage*. New York: Counterpoint Press, 2017. Print.

Pamela Booker
from Lil' Lizzie: Go Let Yourself Learn How to Live

After marrying, everyone thought she'd settle into the regular-ness of life with her blacksmithing husband and household. She did not. In grown womanhood, Lil' Lizzie still "acted a fool," performing what the other wives of her community signified as her "peculiars." Born the colors of raw umber wheat and sage, the kind that grew across the fields that surrounded her home, she willed herself into an eccentric personality of applied gilt decorations in the wearing of pine cones embellished with holly berries for earrings, raw quartz stone and amethyst necklaces and ankle bracelets. It had taken days, but she'd blown small, bitty holes into the stones then slipped them onto thin strips of cow's leather that a sloppy tannery worker had mislaid.

Had she come of age in the 1980s, she'd have been a "sista" who defined her Afrocentric aspirations with gele headwraps, Kente cloth bags, patchouli oil and custom-tailored coats made from mud-cloth. Instead, she was the first child on the plantation born of the haziness of Emancipation to Dill and Pine-Grover, so they named her Pine-Grover Elizabeth, the first daughter in the Lizzie line. Where others wore bitterness or promise on their sleeve, Lil' Lizzie displayed the sullen look of a Hush-Puppy hound dog on her young face with all of her future happiness or disdain surfacing only when needed.

Her outbursts could be especially vulgar when scrubbing shit stains from her husband's drawers or hollering on full moon nights for "all the matters that escaped my reach," as she'd exclaim. Neighbors were entirely stumped when she screamed from her windowsill one morning, "Today, I'm reclaiming my time!"

A neighbor passing the house shouted, "Go 'head and do it then, Lizzie, and stop all that ruckus!"

"Know-it-all-witch," Lil' Lizzie hissed back under her breath, grinning and waving feverishly at the woman. All of which suggested that while she appreciated her neighbor's attention, she resisted the trivializing of her ambition. Though recognized for her exceptional intellect, droll wit and ability to thrive with such vigor in the years following Emancipation and Jim-Crow lawlessness, she was terribly unhappy, having never been shown how to get things of value done in her life. She resented not being expected to in a world that appeared unmoved by her hollers, opinions, and language; a woman who'd only known freedom through skewed parallels and right angles. In the way that subsistence can be long-suffering and distant, close but small and incrementally rewarding, she craved evidence, omens, for how to salvage anything satisfying about living—until the day she walked inside her husband's grimy shed.

She stood with both hands on her lower back and closely eye-balled the jumbled world that Nelson worshipped in as his "little piece of heaven." He'd fussily crafted every shelf, nook and container and then aggressively filled them with the assorted complement of farming tools, nails, hinges, sickles, machetes, Bowie knives, horseshoes and more horseshoes of all sizes and makes, along with decorative wrought iron gate parts and damaged gaslight fixtures, which left such little room for air. Now, they all lay flumped and neglected.

Charmed by the physique and swing of the roughly cut iron hammers that she came upon in his collection, she approached them with curiosity. They pretty much all looked the same to her until she snatched up one then the other, rolling each chisel and tong from one hand to palm, pivoting for weight and ease. Pick one up, drop it, pick up the next, until finally, a hammer with the firmest grip proved satisfying. A delicious lucidity spooled through her body. ...

Nelson's esteemed status as the town's most skillful and trusted *Black* blacksmith helped them to navigate or bypass at times the life-threatening conflicts usually experienced by freed Black or indentured peoples in their town. There again, maybe not so much "bypass" conflicts, but that his skills granted them degrees of tolerance—though also not to be confused with fairness—from the local white businessmen and farmers. Mostly, they remained averse to the legislated promises given to "coloreds" in the Mason-Dixon counties where they resided. Yet Nelson chiseled an autonomy for himself based on the mutual goodwill and need they shared for the proper shoe-sizing of horses, repairs for plows and hoes, and of course, their guns. "White folks only civilized when it comes to they guns and they animals," Nelson frequently declared, chomping on his dinner, followed by a stifling silence.

He wasn't lying, Lil' Lizzie mused, scrutinizing the dents and blisters of his battered anvils scattered about the shed. Some were upright, others overturned on sides that bore the strikes of his guzzled rage. On badly favored days, life could be a hostile discipline. Increasingly, hers too were turning into a succession of bad days with lots of ugly rushing up.

Noonday's waning light glided across the carpet of violets that aligned the gravelly path to the front porch. The house's main entryway faced the east side of the property. Gossamer sun rays slipped between the wall's clefts and splits, adding much-needed warmth to the shadows. On the right side of the room was a window beveled into the mounting structure. Curtains dangled from either side. They'd been a house gift from her mother and were yellowing or maybe were never white. Perhaps she'd wash them, Lil' Lizzie supposed, releasing bitty sighs sprung from the fatigue and square footage of her domestic trimmings.

A striking set of mirrors, ten to be exact, hung silently in the living room. She floated over and propped herself in front of them. With all the audacity she could summon from the depths of her belly, she crooned—"Mirrors, oh mirrors hanging on my walls, who is the most beautiful of all?"

Firmly clutching the hammer that she'd brought with her from the shed, she studied it scrupulously, picturing it a wishbone to break for the recovery of her heart's desire. The words, "I wish…I wish" tumbled from her mouth. A flummoxed leer reflected back. Mirrors, long thought inanimate objects, are actually living portals, prone to mimic, to echo, the very same emotions cast into them.

"If only you could see yourself, really see yourself," the mirrors whispered. "You are Masai-infused exquisite and tall like your mother, sturdy and defiant like your father. Your vastness, if measured, would be immense, nothing short of 12 feet high and 3 feet wide."

Lil' Lizzie shook her head. Was she being mocked by her own reflection? She squinted, was that even possible? Then too, she needed all the reassurances that flowed her way, for her spirit was no longer soaring. If she couldn't be soul-soaring, then she'd have to find another way. But to do what?

The ancient Egyptian bronze hand-mirror caught her eye. It dangled from the nearest interior wall, though away from the others as a separate collection that she was building for her baby daughter, Queenie. She fingered it with an intense rush of affection and pleasure. Despite her intense physical rebuffs since the baby girl's birth, Nelson gratified himself in that musty shed by reproducing a mirror. Shaped in the head of Hathor, one of the Ancient's most revered goddesses, said to personify the Milky Way, the mirror's poetically cut beveled silver glass and metal frame illumined Lil' Lizzie's mind, reawakened her most arcane desires.

"You…you like them," Nelson had confessed when she at last permitted him to be intimate with her. "I heard from a salesman passing through town once, his buggy needed new wheels, that, that *Egyptian*s was beautiful women, said to be African women, too. They spent time takin' care of themselves, bathing, rubbing oils and sweet smelling salves on they skin."

Lil' Lizzie softened in recalling his boyish kindness, how he reeked of mousey breath. She sniffed at the air and dabbed spots of cardamom and rose-hips on the dark surfaces of her heart. How does a woman reconcile life with a mate who exalts her but that she treats with abject indifference? She craved another smell, another set of skin cells to rub. Her husband was someone who could be present but not there. He consumed space, made things, ate, but rarely shared with her the meaningful occurrences of his day. Occasionally, he thought to gift her with flowers pulled from their backyard.

Her loose-fitting dress collar slipped from her shoulder. The gesture of smoothing it back into place helped open her already widened eyes to a vision she sought based on procuring something new, something beautiful and glorious in her life. Horizons, anything rising, newborn, and hued by the miraculous. On the lost continent of her mind, she *was* Hathor, a celebrated goddess. Each sunset promised as much, but by the close of the day for ensuing years, nothing changed. Today must be different, she decided, levitating her body with the might of bat wings as she oh so judiciously picked up the hammer and commenced swinging at the mirrors, one by one with steady strikes, not unlike her *Black* blacksmithing husband's, until she'd reduced them to tiny bits and pieces.

When she was done, piles of sparkling silver particles danced about her feet. Some landed in her hair, giving her the appearance of a luminous Empress. All she could hear were the loud, sharp cries of birds outside her window intermingled with the massive gulps of air and exhalations that escaped her heaving chest. Thankful that she'd sent her baby girl to her aunt Trixie's. Sweat beads popped across her brow and drizzled from the pockets of her underarms. Blood trickled from her fingertips as she coarsely rubbed them back and forth, scratching at the mirror's cracked surfaces. With each sobbing stroke she tore at her bones and inflamed skin, until, to her astonishment, she heard a nearby voice, causing her to drop to her knees.

The forms appeared to her not as saints or demons, rather a commingling of distorted wavelengths and body rays, a mixture of red, orange, blue and golden dynamic orbs percolating from steam and vapors.

Lil' Lizzie hastily wiped her swollen face with bleeding fingers before shoving them into her arm pits. "Is transformation possible for someone like me? Is it?" she screamed, not sure to whom, since she was unable to make out the tottering forms that emerged from the mirrors' fragments.

One dashed forward. "Depends," it replied. Then: "Are you moving on from this world or intending to stay?"

"Yes!" she screeched, scaring herself with a conviction she rarely heard voiced in her own ears.

"Yes!" parroted the orb. "But what is it that you want?"

"I—want—enchantment. I want beauty in my life!" Lil' Lizzie cackled, through hefts of laughter and tears. "I want something glorious to happen in my life! Is it even possible? ...

Notes

"Lil' Lizzie: Go Let Yourself Learn How to Live" is excerpted from the forthcoming collection of braided speculative short stories *Dill's Mirrors & the Lizzies* that offer portraits of an Emancipated woman's matrilineal line of first-born daughters over five generations and a set of ten mirrors that Dill uncannily secures as reparations for damages incurred while enslaved. On the night of her departure, "sparkling" stellar forces or "Couriers" (African souls that escaped bondage by choosing to fly beyond enslavement when their ships arrived on American shores) return to protect the mirrors and the women as their carriers. Each future daughter grapples with her needs relative to the "inheritance," which requires balancing the burden of legacy against honoring the mirrors as divine instruments.

As the "first daughter" in her family, Lizzie feels a profound responsibility to a matrilineal legacy, even as she risks losing her agency, living forever in the shadow of Dill, her audacious mother. When the Energetics ask Lizzie what she wants from them, she confesses, "I want enchantment. I want beauty in my life! [...] I want something glorious to happen in my life! Is it even possible?"

To which the ancestors respond: "You are the first daughter, a Black Gold descendent and we are the system's paradox species...blessed across more lifetimes than you can count in numbers. Find another way to be brave, Lizzie. To claim your Superpower. To live!"

Post-colonial scholar Homi Bhabha wrote interestingly enough in a foreword to Franz Fanon's *Black Skin, White Masks*, "the site of an emergency is almost always the site of an emergence."* This equation is critical to Lizzie's struggles when a stranger from her past returns and sets off in her a deeply buried yearning. To declare it may cost her dearly. But she's finally ready to "learn how to live," to know "authentic joy"—both exhaustive and exhilarating.

N.B.: This is an abridged version. Please see Dark Matter: Women Witnessing #14 *online for the complete essay.*

———

* Fanon, Franz. *Black Skin, White Masks*, trans. Charles L. Markmann. New York: Grove Press, 1967, p. xi.

Jaime R. Wood
Yaquina at Low Tide

Sea lions peek their heads up
like periscopes to stare
at the bipedals corrupting
the rocky shore. Each time
the waves sweep the blue black
pebbles and roll back into themselves
the stones applaud the effort
it must take to be the tide.

Atop the fisted cliff jutting from the shallows
perch a thousand Murres and beyond them
a thousand more who will never know
the prison of a cage or a too-small wage
or the death that awaits them
beyond their knowing.
They understand the sea, the cycles of the sun,
the threat of eagles stealing their young,
the cacophony of seagulls
who catch their unhatched progeny
and return each day for more
as if this is what they live for.

We make words for everything,
name every species we find,
but there's no word for the distance
between the clumsy penguin-like birds' desire
to nest in the crags,
the long-necked Cormorants' skill
for fishing the bay,
the sea lions' bellies buoying
on the water,
and my urge to pitch into their world
and unmake myself.

Notes

Dark Matter's mission asks the question, "How shall we live in these times?" We live in confusion about our own natures as something quite animal and yet separate from the "wild" that we shield ourselves from both physically and philosophically. In his book *Becoming Animal: An Earthly Cosmology*, David Abram notes that, "We are by now so accustomed to the cult of expertise that the very notion of honoring and paying heed to our directly felt experience of things—of insects and wooden floors, of broken-down cars and bird-pecked apples and the scent rising from the soil—seems odd and somewhat misguided as a way to find out what's worth knowing...This directly experienced terrain, rippling with cricket rhythms and scoured by the tides, is the very realm now most ravaged by the spreading consequences of our disregard."* My poems explore how humans crave the natural world just as we're so eager to escape it, how we mold animals and plants to serve our needs without considering the consequences to them or us, how our desire to anthropomorphize everything blinds us to a beauty that exists beyond ourselves. There's a loneliness in our "cult of expertise" that I hope to embody in my poems as a way of questioning our place in the world and to make note of the power of the planet we've found ourselves on.

---

* Abram, David. *Becoming Animal: An Earthly Cosmology*. New York: Pantheon Books, 2011, pp. 4-6. Print.

Anne Bergeron, Debby Black, Andrea Mathieson, Cynthia Ross, Nancy Windheart
Lac Café Medley

In August 2019 Lise Weil hosted a gathering in rural Quebec for contributors to Dark Matter *and like-minded artist friends. She had been collecting responses all summer to Deena Metzger's essay* "Extinction Illness: Grave Affliction and Possibility," *published online in* Tikkun *earlier that year, and so thought to bring the question to the group: "How to respond to the disease of extinction illness?" The group decided it was important to involve all the beings around them in this question. So one afternoon the women spread out, claimed a spot on the land, hunkered down and began to listen...*

Photo by A. Bergeron

Andrea Mathieson

Like a magnet, I was drawn to an area behind the cabin I was staying in, where a trail led to a pond oozing into the lake. Journal and cushion in hand, I walked slowly down the path, lined on one side with large stones. I came to an abandoned, rotting tree fort; a mature pine, its needles brown, blocked the way. I later learned it had probably been felled by a beaver.

Placing the cushion on the ground, I sat on it, and tuned in. With my attention drawn to the fallen tree, I began listening and taking notes…

The way forward is blocked. Accept that. Do not push through with an old agenda. Accept the message of 'obstacles' and use the time to pause and reassess: Is this the route I should pursue? Is this an issue of timing — not now, maybe later? What is this blockage protecting? I kept listening…

Study the nature of the blockage: Is it organic, a natural phenomenon? Is it my responsibility to clear? What other creatures or elements are able to move in, under, over or around the blockage? Air, water, plants, small animals?

Photo by A. Bergeron

Turning my attention to the stones along the pathway, *I heard: Stones are the bones of the earth. They hold the stories of the planet. Learn to read the stone-bones as an entry into the realm of the ancestors. Every stone has a story, taking you beyond linear time into no-time.*

For a few seconds, the ground near my feet began to morph and 'swim.' Twigs were snake-like, dried leaves became alive in their composting.

This unsettling, disorienting sensation stayed with me, as though a veil into another world had momentarily opened.

Remember the way of Wyrd. Things are never just what they appear to be. In times of crisis, the web of Wyrd is more operational than the static status quo. Learn to ride and swim in these currents where things have several levels of meaning, several frequencies, several possible ways of manifesting. Become familiar with the unfamiliar. Open into it with wonder, curiosity, humility and wise instincts.

While integrating that message, I became aware of the breeze in the trees, shifting from stillness to a light, playful dance, then back again. Weather was to be my final point of entry for the question, 'How can I deal with the phenomenon of extinction illness?'

Changing weather patterns are some of the most articulate indicators of the changing times. Where our observation of weather has primarily focused on its effect on human activities, the atmosphere deserves respect as a highly intelligent, volatile indicator of the planet's 'voiced' needs and will. There are many ways of restoring a respectful relationship with weather. Here are a few examples:

- Stop talking about weather in terms of 'good' or 'bad.'
- Find ways to physically be in all kinds of weather, breathing in teachings through your body's responses to heat and cold, wet and dry, still and stormy, etc. Each different weather pattern offers an enormous wealth of information. People once appealed to weather gods; these ways of relating were not meant to alter the weather but simply to be with it.
- Be present to the subtle shifts of wind. Feeling and syncing with the changing movements of leaves within a summer breeze restores and balances both the brain and the body.
- Remember to sing to the earth, focusing your attention on specific elements. The rapidity of nature's response will astonish you. Sound can serve as 'fertilizer,' 'pesticide,' cleanser, chemical balancer, etc. This practice is one of the most essential elements of restorative earth-work.

Extinction illness is only fatal if there is no creative response to it. Extinction illness is a call to the forgotten, abandoned parts of our psyche that are being squeezed into remembrance and action now. How a person responds, whether from a rootedness in love or with a fearful reaction, will shape the nature of the experience. Notice the 'nature of the experience' not the 'outcome!' An expected outcome is part of what needs to be set aside.

Cynthia Ross

Finding a place where I could sit quietly, I tried to attune to the nature around me. Rather than address a specific plant, I opened to the woods community. Before asking, I thought I would make an offering – of my own heart energy—attempting to convey my deep appreciation for the Green World. At first, my mind was busy, coming up with a list of what humans might do in this time. Breathing, letting go of the mental, I let myself slip more deeply into a space of quiet, opening to the soft flow of the energy. The embrace of the Green World came immediately and held me—a beautiful vibrant green energy—joyous, peaceful, restorative.

Photo by C. Ross

I think this communication from the forest at Lac Café was about love—a joyous response to a human reaching out with heart frequency. And an answer, too, to the question we were sitting with—how are we to be in this time ...of loss, of peril... of extinction. Maybe the word 'joyous' is not quite right. What was this embrace of Green? It was like being gathered in by a vast, benevolent intelligence, received with... joy. I can't find another word for that sense of glad welcome...and the invitation, '*Be with us.*'

Anne Bergeron

meeting extinction illness:
an antiphony

I. the call

a pause spreads into silence
until a woodpecker knocks insects
from peeling tree skin
while greenskin frog blows
smooth water into bubbles
and sparrows siphon water striders
from the lake's surface

they call, too
these bodies who are you
i hear you sing through them
in one voice

listening
i grow green skin
i peck away at insects
as my tiny talons clutch tree bark
i soften when i am plucked
from surface water
and slide down
a sparrow's slender throat

i live
and so i sing
back into you

II. the response

extinction is a threat
because you have separated from me
because you have forgotten
that you knew how to listen
that you knew you and i were the same

it is time to midwife your ancient selves
time to walk into the fire that is burning
time to let it engulf your destructive ways
and then stir the ashes for carbon

it is time to know yourselves
as permeable membranes,
to feel me breathe into you
as you exhale into me

it is time to take me
into the deepest parts
of yourselves
and move with me
over and over
toward dawn.

———

(next page) Photo by A. Bergeron

Debby Black

Wandering, watching, staring out into the distance: diamonds on the water, waving blades of grass, buzzing of insects....

Drawn to water, this small round lake, cup in the land of thick green woods.

Walking out slowly, feeling water, cool, silky, sinking at last into soft wetness. Gliding slowly, lazily toward White Rock, as if pulled. Like an iceberg, most of White Rock is under water tapering out to the deep, rooted into lake. Sliding along, up her slippery underwater slope my hand latches onto a protrusion. Finding footing in rock-cleft, hoisting my body up her side, dripping. Mmmmmm...flanking out tummy-down on gently curved sun-hot rock. Smooth, rough, black specks in white hard granite, receiving my body. Smelling earthscent of Rock.

Out of crevices grow tree, small bush—marsh grasses in wetlands beyond. Helicopter dragonflies and dazzling blue airbeings thrum, flitting here there...being, living.

Nancy Windheart

I took the question of extinction illness to the land and beings at Lac Café, and connected with others at a distance.

Hummingbird: Her response came in feeling, images, and rapid communication of understanding. I asked her, "Are you aware of "extinction," of the vast changes on our planet?"
"Of course! Food, navigation, the energetic channels–all are changing and shifting.
Shift dimensions! Shift realities! Find new ways of being!"

Mushrooms, including the mushroom spores: "We are always regenerating, rebirthing. We are always creating new life, from the moist, the dark, the decomposing. There is not a line between life and death. There is a continuum of life/death, death/life. Always, there is regeneration from decay, from death. It is the way of the universe."

Then, I brought the question to Lise's cats:

Buh: "I send my energy deep into the earth. I delight in its lusciousness—we are the same being. My belly—the air—the ecstasy in my bones—the pleasure in my cells–I love. Love, Love, Love. It's like a great water bowl of Love."

BoBo: "I weave the web of protection, of life. I am the energetic guardian of this land, and beyond."

When I ask her about extinction, the answer comes clear, loudly, and fast, "Not for cats!!"

She says the lines of energy will always be there. They will always create life. I understand that Bobo understands energy fields as a generative force.

Bee: This was a particular bee who was feeding near some flowers close to where I was sitting. S/he communicated: "We sing the new earth into being. As our bodies die, we sing our song. Generative rebirth, vibrancy. Calling new life, new energy in. The Earth is not dying. Individuals die. Individual expressions/species die. The Earth herself is not dying." She was clear and emphatic about this.

In the week before coming to Lac Café, I had the privilege of spending time at a whale research station in northern Quebec in the Gulf of St. Lawrence. We had an encounter with a north Atlantic Right Whale, a species whose population is now estimated to be at just 400 individuals.

At Lac Café, I asked this Right Whale specifically about a response to "extinction" and/or "extinction illness"; his awareness and communication was clear:

Right Whale: "It's all energy. We, the planet, you, all of us… everything…it's all energy. We know this. We understand this in our bodies, our lives, our communities, our families. Yes, we are stressed. We are adjusting and adapting to find food. Many of us are dying. Yet, we are still here. We are still living our lives…expressing ourselves through our bodies. We may not survive…as individuals, or as a species, but now, we are here, and we are aware of the efforts to help us, and we are not gone yet. Nor are you.

Bodies die. We grieve the losses of our kin. We hold a particular frequency of energy, and when that expression in physical form 'dies,' there is a loss, and grief.

Yet. And. All is energy. All is spirit. The generative energy of the cosmos…of life…of spirit…of sentience…is infinite."

I see the figure 8, the infinity symbol… The sacred geometry in all its forms shows us this.

Right Whale: "There is a great 'unburdening' at this time. Your human perspective is limited: in time, energy, scope. There are multiple dimensions, multiple layers of reality."

Then came a communication that was not from any particular individual, but rather, a general, gestalt knowing held in the energy field of Lac Café and beyond:

The manifestation of "illness" with regard to the question of extinction comes when there are not the tools—physical or spiritual—to process disruption and trauma.

As I considered the communications and transmissions I received, I realized that there was an essential/essence message from all:

There is a creative, vibrant, rich energy of aliveness that is transformative, regenerative, nutrient-rich: It is the energy of love.

The energy in a dying form will find a new form.

The only "illness" is in resistance...holding onto what is/was...a refusal to shift.

Leslie Schwartz
Leaving the Mother Country

The day I arrived in Los Angeles from San Francisco in 1991, I was sad and fully unprepared for how weird a place it was. I spent years—too many—at war with L.A. for all the regular reasons: traffic, pollution, shootings, police helicopters dive-bombing our house at night. I would leave often, for months at a time, to be closer to my heart geography— Northern California, Oregon, Washington and Wyoming, where I could write in peace, but also feel the wild nature nearby pushing me to be something better and brighter.

I stayed in L.A. for decades, mostly against my will. But there were a few wonderful reasons to remain; love and children and a home built over twenty years rooted to the same ground. The quiet walks with my dog in the early morning darkness of Elysian Park, the wintry evenings in Griffith when you actually needed a sweater. Those falcons in May, the bobcats, the summer wildflowers. L.A. could be so heartbreakingly beautiful. And then there was P-22, the world's most famous mountain lion. I know I am not the only one who fell in love with the 'loneliest cat' in L.A. Yet, somehow, these gifts of L.A. were not enough. My heart never found its place there among the noise and pollution.

Photo: istock.com/JasonKlassi

The journey out and eventually to Iceland, where I now live, was via a small cabin in the woods in the Pacific Northwest. We would use it to get away from the Southland. And every time we pulled out of the woods after a month or two and headed back to L.A., I cried. I didn't want to go back. I loved the cabin so much that we kept it and moved to Iceland anyway.

In a larger sense, my move to Iceland was probably a move not just from L.A. but from the recklessness of California's tension between capitalism and growth and the vanishing natural world. I had been born to a wilder and less inhabited Northern California. I swore I'd never leave the place I called home, where there were still streams you could drink from, and a natural world not yet sullied by hordes of tourists. It still pains me that I did leave; or really felt I had to for my sanity. There were other problems, too, that seemed deeply rooted in American culture and made me increasingly anxious and depressed. Iceland felt like home. What could be better for someone desperate for the wild society of nature than living on a giant windswept rock in the North Atlantic where fire erupts from the ground and falls freeze into ice sheets over cliffs.

Then something happened. On December 17, 2022, my beloved L.A.connection P-22 died. Sitting in my apartment in Reykjavik, I fell apart. Nothing made me think of Los Angeles as home more than that reclusive cat had while I lived there. P-22 was to me a solitary apparition, roaming without benefit of mate or offspring, tagged by wildlife biologists to be studied and evaluated, seen as an "only in L.A." celebrity who was known throughout the world. His most daring and improbable feat was crossing two ten-lane freeways from the Santa Monica mountains to his new and final home, Griffith Park. He lived there without a mate and largely alone for the rest of his life, with a fraction of the room he needed for an adequate home range.

But P-22, who liked to hang out in the sun under the Hollywood sign, was also a majestic puma born, like all mountain lions, with remarkable agility. His dexterity and innate cunning—intrinsic qualities of cougars—may explain why he managed to evade death crossing the world's largest freeways. In 2016, cameras at the L.A. Zoo caught him leaping over an eight-foot wall and mauling a sleeping Koala to death. Zookeepers decided, against policy, not to trap and kill P-22. Instead, they adapted to his wildness (and possibly his celebrity) by keeping the zoo animals inside at night.

P-22, like all mountain lions, was very rarely seen, no small feat in a park visited by millions of people each year. When I look at pictures of him, I am struck every time by his regal stature. P-22's natural stealth and independence was typical of his species. His hind legs were so strong he, like most mountain lions, was able to leap forty feet horizontally and up to eighteen feet in the air. He became a symbol to me of enduring strength and power even under the most difficult circumstances. Sometimes, in my darkest hours, I would think of him and gather my own courage.

It can't have been easy living in Griffith Park, though for P-22 there were plentiful deer and enough water to stay alive. Space, or in his case, lack of it, was his greatest challenge. It is remarkable that he survived there at all because mountain lions, as a rule, have the largest "home ranges" of any mammal in the Americas. One hundred-twenty-five square miles is a general estimate for their needs, but sixty square miles will do. Griffith Park, where P-22 deteriorated and died is six-and-a-half square miles and bordered on every side by freeways and boulevards. It is no place for a lion.

At the end of his life P-22 was captured and evaluated after he attacked two domestic dogs. Alarmed by his movements, the biologists who monitored, and loved him, finally sedated him, and brought him in for an examination. Not only did he suffer head trauma and an eye injury from being struck by a car, but he exhibited signs of kidney failure and appeared to have a parasitic skin condition.

I am comforted by the love and care the biologists had for him, that they brought him in and away from further depletion and humiliation. I'd heard about his deteriorating state after he was hit by a car. I often wondered who hit him, if they knew they'd just collided with the most famous mountain lion in the world. The driver left the scene. Witnesses said they saw a dark sedan luxury car driving away after striking the puma. And wasn't it just so L.A. that the beginning of the end of P-22's final passage of time on Earth was instigated by someone hitting him with their *luxury* car and fleeing the scene?

When P-22 was captured, his list of health issues was exhaustive, and too serious to fix. It was time to say goodbye and he was humanely euthanized on December 17, 2022. Miraculously, P-22 did manage to live a long life, somewhere between twelve and thirteen years, before he was put down. This is perhaps what I love most about him. In spite of it all, he persevered and even outdid the ten-year average lifespan for his kind.

His celebrity status made it possible for him to become the face of a much needed campaign to build a wildlife bridge so wild animals can safely cross into other parts of untamed Los Angeles. Yet, I can't help but feel rage and confusion over our monumental failure with this animal and so many others like him. His difficult life and unseemly death reveal our collective failure to protect all wildlife, urban and otherwise, and not just for the animals but for all of us. I am constantly baffled that people don't realize humans are inextricably part of an ecosystem and the protection of one animal protects us all. P-22 faced challenges that no mountain lion should have to endure and his hardships and eventual deterioration, much of it human-induced, struck me as cruel and senseless.

I don't know if it's fair to project loneliness on a distinctly solitary animal like a mountain lion. But if P-22 felt any "loneliness" as I might understand it, it would probably fall under a vague category of homelessness. I would sometimes imagine him roaming at night, hunting and mourning for the natural order—a mate and offspring and plentiful land on which to wander. I can't help but believe that on some instinctual level he knew that something profoundly true to his nature was missing. I saw him as the archetype of rootlessness, cast into a world ravaged by human indifference.

And that was just the way I'd felt so often about myself living in crowded, filthy, violent Los Angeles. My plan had been to move back home to

San Francisco, but things kept happening—a fight for my life with addiction, family, children, work—and when real estate skyrocketed there, it became an impossible dream. I would not get back home ever, I realized. Instead of a freeway, it was American capitalism that kept me from living the life that I somehow believed I needed in order to flourish and feel my deep connection with the natural world.

It is not fair, obviously, to compare my modern, urban, and incredibly privileged human desires to the hard and fast needs and instincts of a mountain lion. But I found my own humanity in the dignity of P-22, who was somehow condemned to live an unnatural life. I loved him. In P-22, I felt the noble qualities of suffering, of being denied, of being rooted out by the viciousness of a greedy world and one that seemed appallingly indifferent to nature and our biological need for a healthy Earth.

When I felt frustrated by the trash in the street and the never-ending brown-tinged skies, the lack of care for the addicted, the mentally ill and the homeless, the gunshots, the freeway mayhem of L.A., I experienced a growing fear that I would die in Los Angeles away from the places I loved.

I craved the windswept Northern coastlines of California, Oregon and Washington, the big trees of Sequoia and the California Coastal Redwoods, the deserted empty plains of Wyoming. It was then, in those dark thoughts, that I would sometimes flash on P-22. And I would see in the hard circumstances of his life his courage and his bravery and his endless suffering yet his refusal to give up. He would not be taken down and who knows, if he hadn't been hit by that car, maybe P-22 would have been allowed to live just a little longer and die freely and peacefully on the land, however small and compromised, that he knew as home.

I left my mother country to find my home. I will not die, like P-22, in a city besieged by its disregard for the wild and natural world around it like he did. I don't regret leaving. And though I mourned, crying for days after P-22 died, my attachment to what I left behind also finally and resolutely withered and fell away when he died.

I am in a new place of vast, empty terrain, feral, uninhabited landscapes to explore, a place of silence, wind, water. Fire. Ice. A place that ignites my curiosity and creativity. And I like to think I feel what life might have been for P-22 if he'd lived in an earlier time before humans, machines and pollution encroached on his world.

Iceland is not a perfect country but in my mind it is better than most. Key to the country's staunch environmental policies is a commitment to cut emissions by 55% by 2040. In Iceland almost all heating and electricity is provided by hydro and geothermal energy. Afforestation, revegetation and the reclamation of drained wetlands are key projects, and by now well-established in Iceland's ongoing efforts to remove carbon from the atmosphere. I think it is why so many Americans come here to live. Because we lost hope in America to do the right thing for our Earth and the creatures that should be given the respect, the land, and the freedom they deserve.

When P-22 blasted off, I hope, to the pristine forest of his afterlife, a place where he can wander freely for the rest of eternity, I felt somehow deeply ready to let go all of the hurt I felt living in Los Angeles, and in a larger sense, America. I felt most of all, that l could put away the sadness that came from living in that city's overriding disrespect to and indifference for the Earth on which it sits, the suffering of its least represented humans, and the stubborn nature of its failure to look directly at its weaknesses and accomplish much significant change.

I forgive myself for not staying, for not fighting harder. But I had lost hope. And for an addict, even one like me—free, finally of the disease that wanted me dead—to live with extended, deep hope-loss is not safe. Depressed and longing for uncrowded open spaces and a place that values and preserves them, I made my escape. Though P-22 didn't make it out alive—none of us will—mine was a last-ditch effort to save my spirit for the years I have left. It was my way of choosing to live as he never could. Whenever I am out exploring a new glacier, discovering a hidden waterfall, or hiking to a remote natural hot spring, I like to think that P-22's spirit walks beside me, enjoying the space and beauty he deserved.

Emilee Baum
Demoness

I am a demoness. I am huge, many stories high, and my body is black with white markings on it, stripes like a tiger, but not as regular. My face is white but I have deep rings of black around my eyes, black hair, black mouth. I am naked and ferocious, bone ornaments swinging.

Fierce, but not nearly as demonic as my male counterpart. He is huge, horns, long fangs, wild rolling eyes. He has captured me here, is taking great delight in terrifying me. We are in the middle of the road on a gray desert plane and there might be some single standing trees, leafless branches twisting in the distance. The sky is dark and full of fire and stars. He is coming after me down this road, and I am lying prone, nowhere to run any more. I watch him coming. He is going to rape me, I think. He wants me frightened.

I am frightened. As he draws near I lie on the earth and open my arms and legs, all of my self to him. He mutters curses at me, threats about how he can hurt me, can grow as long as he wants, how he will rip right through me. I lay on the earth and take him in, reach behind him with my hands. I grab fistfuls of knotted hair and pull him down to me, whispering through demoness teeth chiding him: You fool no matter how big you are how long how terrible I am deeper. You are with me under my stars I swallow you whole I keep entire universes in my womb.

Feeling the power come out of him as I speak, taking it all, everything inside me, all he can give, more. Depth in my body opens infinitely, a deep well of accommodation his aggression cannot fathom.

Notes

I had this dream in 2002 when I was living in a nunnery in Nepal, in the aftermath of 9/11, but it still resonates today in 2018. The violence done to women's bodies, the body politic, the body of the earth. And the depth of *her* power.

The assault is so relentless, so preposterous, so seemingly endless. Everything from the environmental climate to the political climate is claustrophobic, densely pressed warm wet cotton, maybe in places wool, soaked through, now that Nepal is no longer a buffer, my blast shield.

The fatigue of a constant onslaught. Here in the American south (and all over, I think) everyone is walking on outraged incredulous eggshells, feet already bruised and bleeding. Can't speak, can't not speak. Can't scream, can't not scream. Can't stand to see it, and yet can't look away.

Must not look away. There is nowhere to run to anymore.

The dream reflects the binary violence we're grappling with. The parallel between woman and earth is plain, the rape and violence apparent. But she has the wisdom and vastness to overcome the aggression coming at her. Her strategy is not to meet violence with violence, or to run away, and this reminds me of *tai chi*—the yielding to the energy, through incorporating and redirecting its force. What follows is deep calm, the well of certainty, clarity. Vast, deep, unfathomable. A place of creation.

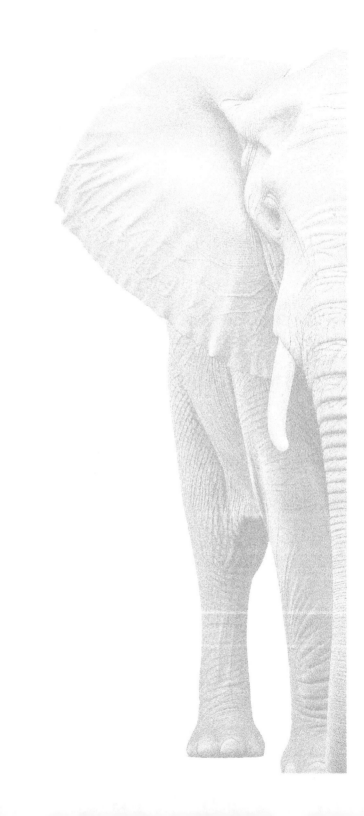

I am Nothing Without My Dead

The world speaks to us in a language I long to know, to hear. It's a good thing the dead love our longing for them. It would be a good thing, too, if the living kept the gate cracked.

—Nora Jamieson, *I Am Nothing without My Dead*

My grandmother taught me that the history of our family, of the land, of all the beings who lived on the land before us, continues to exist within our bodies and the bodies of the plants that grow there.

—Maria Blum, *Memoria: la poesía de las flores*

Nora Jamieson
I Am Nothing without My Dead

I put out apples for the dead last morning. Cut in half, two rounds of sweet flesh, twin star-wombs nestling tiny brown seeds. The rounds were uneaten this morning. I guess they haven't come by yet, unless they've grown finicky basking in my attentions. Unless I have not yet found a way to feed them well. I've prayed, sung, pleaded, offered and even made my case as I've heard the indigenous sometimes do, yet of late they're not speaking to me and I miss them.

Unless the wind just now is their answer to my call, the wind that swirls down dead leaves in a rattle of descent against a grey, storm portent of a sky. Unless the scavenging of the squirrels in the same dry leaves, nosing into cold earth for acorns is an answer. Unless the thin tissue voice of the corn stalks is them whispering, we're here. And now the late-day sun finds its way through the dark clouds. The wind has stilled. Is that you?

The world speaks to us in a language I long to know, to hear. It's a good thing the dead love our longing for them. It would be a good thing, too, if the living kept the gate cracked.

Why? And by what authority do you say that? Someone asks, someone who lives in my mind, *Why carry the dead? What on earth for?* She is persistent and I suspect she too is my inheritance.

Because, I say to her again, if I am the sprout of their planting, how can I not carry them? How can I forget them?

At any rate, I cannot help myself. I cannot help the persistent call to the web of my origins. I want to know who and what I belong to. And who belongs to me. And besides, if you cut a piece of the web, without repair, it falls apart. Until I make that repair, I am a clanless, tribeless woman and I know it. This is a dangerous condition, afflicting many, cut loose from any obligation to carry the past, to ensure a future. A world gone rogue.

I have always known that something is inside of me, someone lives in this skin house, someone calls to me in these bones. But it is dark in here and the voices far away through time. I hear weeping. I see grey granite sheared and plunging down, a steep chasm, a mountain? I hear weeping. Is it my own? Is it my dead come in the night?

I dream of an old woman with white and luminous hair. She is surrounded by young people who attend the feast of her dying, the rhythm of her breath straining through cheesecloth lungs. This is the instruction to me — attend to the oracle of her breath — keep my finger on the red circle inscribed before me until she releases her last breath. I do. She does. I leave.

I dream an old woman who tells me my unacknowledged grief is terrible.

I dream that CS Lewis of A Grief Remembered *has given me his room.*

I dream of my dead returning to me.

I dream of grief bowls made of earth, sold in the village marketplace where we pay our debts to creation. In the carrying of them, peace is created between neighbors.

I dream of collecting death teachings with a dying woman.

I dream of carrying a human skull, memento mori, *remember death.*

I dream of crossing the bridge of tears, her daughter and I guiding my friend to the other side.

I dream I am dancing, swaying with a dead man in my arms. A Pieta.

I dream of probiotics for the dead.

I dream I tell someone there are old ways to touch the dead.

I dream of an otherworldly café, I am lost, I am afraid, I've made a mistake, I want to go back. The GPS fails. The roads are icy and I skid. I ask a woman for help, she tells me she cannot help me go south. I am traveling North.

I dream. I dream. I dream.

Following the instructions of a teacher, I look for my dead, their tracings, in the old ways of my people. I study Scots Gaelic in which I learn that my ancestors did not say *my* land, *my* house, *my* family, *my*. Other than for relatives and the body they did not express possession in that way. They literally expressed connection by saying someone or thing is on me, with me, at me. An echo of all my relations. The dead are at me. They surely are.

I try my hand at the drop spindle, the most ancient form of spinning. I hook the roving to the spindle, draw out the fibers and spin the spindle sunwise. I imagine spinning the thread of creation; as the spiral of energy travels up the wool I pray to renew the world and make holy the daily life. I spin, I pray, all to weave myself back to them. I write. I sing. I call to my dead in their language, I introduce myself and the dog who is with me.

I am trying to carry my dead. And, I don't know how.

Some would say I am obsessed, and they would be right. Some would say it is a distraction. Perhaps. But this is what I know. It is the story that has conjured me my whole life, that has tried to plant itself in the stubborn soil of my heart. A heart harrowed by grief — both the proper grief that calls to those gone from my sight, and the sorrowful wreckage that I inevitably caused when running from that grief.

I surrendered to my grief many years ago, I had no choice, on my knees in the garden unable to move for the pain, and in doing so tried to heal it. In Western ways, that means I put myself to the task of disappearing it, killing it with kindness, drowning it in tears, purging it with catharsis, and boring it to death with analytic repetition — all in the name of healing. But grief's faithfulness was carried on the back of my necessary failure. Grief is meant to grow something, it seems.

Yet, the seed has taken this many years to root. It is fragile. Will there be time? It is a calling no one has asked me to take up. Except, perhaps, my dead? It is, by necessity, in these times, a solitary work. It is lonely. And I don't know how.

I search in the old way. I circumambulate. I circle around.

I take the light and move from room to room in this haunted house that I am, tracking my own dusty footprints looking for signs of them. The light reaches deep in the corners, shadows loom and I wait.

She shows herself in a dream.

There is a wolf, who is a woman, who is a wolf. She lives behind a wall in my mind. She steps out, she looks at me and in her fierce gaze she tells me to knock it off, this doubt, this worry. She has come a long way. She has been waiting for me and my lantern. There is work to take up. When she arrived I do not know, perhaps she was a seed, a dream, a song carried in the egg basket of my mother, that tiny pocket woven with flesh and blood, filled by other-worldly hands, the midwives of fate, with oracles. With me.

I am coming to know her, the one with a name only known to the spirits. How did they know that she, the one who lives behind the wall in my mind, would be needed. Now. At just this time. For these times.

She follows the tracks of the disappeared stories, the exiled names, the stolen children, she laments the lost heart, she might even return it to you. I see her. Her throat is open, there is a rope, a thread, an umbilicus, twisted by the spindle of stories we do not want to hear, but must. She is the throat woman, the spinning song woman, she wraps the lost, the missing, the forgotten in the silk of her spinning lament and brings them to the living.

The pitted earth is the throat of the keening woman: the test pits, the uranium pit, the mined earth gouged with our longing. Out of the throat of the keening woman comes everything you did not know you longed for. Out of the throat of the keening woman comes everything we destroyed in our innocent desire for a good life.

She is the throat woman, the spinning song woman, she wraps the lost, the missing, the forgotten, in the silk of her spinning lament and carries them home. But first we must hear her cry, be shattered by the ululation of her grief. Then maybe all will be whole.

She is faithful, she has called to me through death, the flood of my own longing, the floating wreckage of history. Like luminous moths battering against the light in soul darkness, she is faithful. She is wolf, she is woman, howling. She spins the thread of return; her throat is a whirlpool, her voice keening, wild.

I see now, she rocked with me when my beloveds died. She lamented. Oh, do not pity me. They died, the gate opened, she saw her chance, stepping through and into a child's lament. She has been the unknown walking stick of my journey; she is the singer, the finder of lost sorrows, the weaver of memory; she lives in the underside of history's tapestry, the underworld of our dreams.

I heard her once in the death lodge in the voices of rain and thunder. Lightning. I thought I'd imagined it.

She is of my people. The Keening Woman. And I belong to her.

I walk up the hill in these small woods and I lay down tobacco, I lay down corn meal and mead, I pour whiskey, and I sing a mourning song. And I ask her to teach me.

Judith Redwing Keyssar, RN
Gift from the Ancestors: My Work as an RN/Midwife to the Dying

> Where I come from, nobody knows
> Where I'm going, everything goes
> The tree grows, the wind blows,
>   the River flows
> —Jess River, *Circle Song*

Nana, my Russian grandmother (her name was Zipa), was the first person to contact me from the other side. She had died the night before my eighteenth birthday, which for me solidified and sanctified my spiritual connection to her. Zipa and I shared a bedroom when I was growing up in New Jersey. Each night, my child-self would keep my eyes open long enough to watch her slowly unbraid her waist-length grey/white hair and calmly comb it out before she crawled into her single bed, across from mine. She was my first mentor.

Zipa stood only 4'10" tall, but her strength was enormous. As a young woman she left her orthodox Jewish home in the shtetl in Russia where girls could not be educated and went to Kiev to become a seamstress and eventually a nurse/birth midwife. She and her husband were involved with the Mensheviks in the Russian revolution and had to move to Germany. Many of her family were killed by Nazi genocide. Her husband went on a trip to Paris, where he committed suicide. After that Zipa lived in London during WWII, nursing her only daughter who was dying of metastatic cancer. After the war my father brought her to America, where she survived until the age of ninety-four. She had witnessed the first train pull into her tiny village in Russia ("no horses," she would laugh) and the first man land on the Moon. She taught me never to give up hope for each other or the earth. She also taught me how to make fabulous pastry and pies. She sang me to sleep most nights as a child– Russian lullabies that I still sing to this day.

I was twenty years old in 1973, living on a commune in Northern California, in a yurt made from discarded triangular sections of geodesic domes, when she appeared. It was a dark, balmy summer evening and I was just falling asleep on my mattress on the floor, covered with a sheet and my lightweight sleeping bag. Suddenly there was a whoosh of air and a feeling that someone was standing in the room, beckoning me awake. I was afraid. I closed my eyes tightly and pulled the sleeping bag up over my head. I still felt the Being standing close, watching me. Then I heard her voice, so clear, so strong in her mixed European accents. I began to breathe more calmly and slowly took the covers off my face and opened my eyes. All I could see was a faint shadow of energy, but the voice continued:"I have come to tell you that I'm alright. That I'm fine, actually. I am at peace. You are the only one in the family that I could come to. I knew you would understand and not be afraid. I need you to tell Alex, my son, your father, that I am alright." Then just as suddenly as she had appeared, she was gone.

A few years later, when I lay in the snow on top of Zipa's grave in northern Vermont, asking her for connection, for a sign, the changed words to an old Quaker song came through:

Tis a gift to know the Spirit
Tis a gift to feel the Heart
Tis a gift to know that where we end, we start
And when we understand
that the Truth and the Light
Are inside us,
To Guide us,
We come round right

Zipa has visited occasionally since that evening in 1973, always as a presence of calm and connection. Her strongest presence and guidance, however, came fifteen years after her initial appearance.

September 1988. My best friend Kim was in a coma in the ICU at Marin General Hospital, after somersaulting off her motorcycle in rush hour traffic on Highway 101, heading home to the quiet roads of Mendocino County—the only roads she was accustomed to riding. I had a very strong connection to Kim that did not end when we ended our romantic relationship several years earlier. We remained best friends and music partners. Two nights before she left on her motorcycle trip to the Yosemite Women's Music Festival, I had a dream that she was in an accident. The night before she left, when I dropped her off after work at her self-built yurt in the woods, I told her I was nervous about her trip and that I hoped she would put a card in her wallet with all my numbers where I could be reached, "just in case." "They'll figure it out," she grimaced, accusing me of acting like her mother (I was five years older).

A week later, arriving home after sunset to our communal kitchen/living room on the women's land where I lived with my partner and several other women, the phone rang and I knew. I picked up and immediately felt the whoosh of intense energy all around me. It was a police officer, looking at the card in Kim's wallet with my phone numbers. I phoned Kim's family, a few close friends, and then the hospital to attempt to get more information. The ICU nurse could only tell me was that it was "very serious." She said if this were her best friend, she would come now.

Three of us piled into one of our old Volkswagens, hoping it would survive the three-hour drive over dark, twisting and hilly roads from Mendocino to Marin County. We sang and tried to connect through the ethers to Kim's spirit as we drove. When we arrived, late at night, after navigating the halls of an unfamiliar hospital, we walked into a surreal scene.

Kim's thin, muscular body was connected to every tube and machine imaginable. Her body looked fine, just a few scratches and bruises, thanks to the leather pants and jacket she had worn despite the late summer heat. But her head was the size of a beach ball, swollen, discolored, and also connected by wires to various mechanical devices. The bed constantly and slowly rotated from side to side.

Survival was not certain.

Each night, once darkness had enveloped the world outside and most people had left the hospital, I would enter the finally quiet ICU and work with Kim's energy field. I would lay crystals on her chakras, run energy and try to communicate with her Spirit, something I innately knew how to do. At one point when I asked her directly if she wanted to stay, I thought she opened her eyes briefly and for a moment, connected with me on this earthly plane. But mostly our communication was on a heart/soul level. I knew her answer.   When her blood pressure and heart rate and intra-cranial pressures slowly came down on the ICU monitors, the nurses would rush in and ask what I was doing.

"Just running energy, being present with her," I replied.

Kim turned thirty during her three weeks of lying in what Western medicine so oddly terms a "vegetative state." Comatose. Unresponsive as we understand the concept. I knew that Kim would choose one of three days to die: her birthday, the Autumn Equinox, or the Full Moon. A few years before she had named herself "Kim Moonwater." We lived in a community where connection to Nature, to the Earth and stars and all sentient Beings was the foundation of our lives.

On Kim's thirtieth birthday, about twenty of us gathered in a circle on the front lawn of the hospital –singing, crying and praying for her release. We were not accustomed to young people dying, but I knew it was her time. Kim had always made sudden and drastic changes in her life. Her death was no different. She stayed for her birthday and the Equinox and chose the Full Moon to let go.

During those intense weeks, each time I entered the sanctum of life and death known as Intensive Care, it was Zipa's voice I heard, saying "This is the work you are on the Earth to do. You are here to be a midwife to the dying, to witness this transition from life to death. To communicate with the dying and the living. This IS your work."

And so it is.

The gift I received from Kim and from my grandmother was this very clear guidance. I had been a pre-med dropout in the Ivy Leagues in 1971, but now it was 1988, and I understood that I would need a legitimate profession (other than artist/musician/healer/writer) to show up at bedsides of the dying, to witness their transitions and help guide their loved ones. Thanks to the voices and spirit connections that I never once doubted, I re-entered school as soon as I could and became a Nurse.

On New Year's Day 1989, several months after Kim's death, I was standing at her graveside on her land, where we had planted her "cremains" in a beautiful box in the earth under one of her favorite redwood trees. I felt her strongly. I spoke out loud, saying, "If you are really here with me, send a song." Within moments I was channeling these verses (now sung regularly in our communities' spiritual circles):

Take one step at a time my friend,
take one breath at a time.
Think one thought at a time, my friend
and Love all the time

Your heart is the key, dear friend
You must open your eyes to the sky.
Plant your feet on the ground,
my friend
and let your Spirit fly

Family Ancestors: Visitations and Lessons

Part of my professional journey included twelve years of Directing Palliative Care and Nursing at Jewish Family and Children's Services in San Francisco. The day I went to be interviewed, in 2006, I sat in their Holocaust Center Library, surrounded by books written about the Nazi atrocities. I suddenly felt one of those surges of energy and voice, clarifying for me that part of my work in attempting to serve people so they might die peacefully was reparation for all the ancestors of mine and others who had died so traumatically. When I am at a bedside, humming or chanting old Jewish tunes and prayers, with or without a Rabbi, I am transported to the old country, feeling my ancestors from the Jewish side, my grandmother, my father, but even way beyond them—ancestors from much more ancient times—humming along with me.

When I feel the presence of beings/ancestors from the other side, it is often at night, but I do not experience it as a dream. There is a more present, urgent and ethereal quality to these visitations that is difficult to describe in words. I sense that it is similar to the presences people feel during the dying process. So many I have attended in their dying (including my father) speak of seeing their older relatives and friends who have been long gone. Or they describe a simple scene they are engaged in—hanging laundry, playing solitaire, talking to a grandparent—that is as real to them as this world is to us.

I midwifed both of my parents as they died six weeks apart from each other in 1996. It was crystal clear to me that in our family system I would be the one to assist their Spirits in leaving this world. My mother died within a week of being hospitalized at age seventy-nine. During that week, I often felt the presence of her sisters, who had predeceased her. I tried to talk about it to my mother as she floated between worlds, hoping that the energy of her sisters might comfort her. In my father's last days he often spoke to his mother (Zipa) and asked me to make sure I took care of her when he was gone. He communicated with his deceased sister as well and spoke about going home, shouting to me from his hospital bed in my spare bedroom, to "get the car."

My older sister lived with metastatic cancer for eleven years (ten years longer than predicted). Six months before the end of her life, we had a conversation in which she finally admitted that she knew she would die soon, and described to me the three times that she had died in the past few years of her cancer (all actual near-death experiences that she had never before discussed.) She said, "We never grew up with any religion, and I don't have any spiritual understanding of life, but I know that without either one of those things, dying is going to be difficult. Can you help me learn to meditate?"

I wasn't able to do that, but in the last days of her life, she talked almost non-stop about things she was seeing and experiencing that were not tangible on this plane. She would come in and out of different levels of consciousness and was in constant conversation with people I could not see. At one point I asked if she knew the people she was talking to, and she said that she only recognized some of them, but their answers to her questions helped calm her fears.

At another point, after talking to her ethercal friends she turned to me where I sat beside her bed and asked, "Where are we in the Bible now?" I was taken aback as I am not in the habit of reading the Bible. But I did remember that my sister had been a Bible reader in high school, back when public schools included Bible reading in assemblies.

I said I didn't know where we were, but she insisted. I took some deep breaths, considered her question seriously and finally was able to answer: "We are at the part that says Surely goodness and Mercy shall be with you always and you will dwell with Spirit forever." She smiled and said, "That's right, that's where we are."

A Potent Patient Relationship

[...] it's the blood of the Ancients
That runs through our veins
And the forms pass
But the circle of life remains.
—from *Blood of the Ancients,* by Charlie Murphy & Ellen Klaver

In nursing school, as with all healthcare professional training, we are warned not to get too close to patients. Not to cross that "patient/clinician" boundary. But aren't we all human beings, attending to each other in whatever ways we can in the moment? Doesn't the "soft animal of our body love what it loves?" (from *Wild Geese* by Mary Oliver)

In 2010, when I was still working in a community-based palliative care setting, a palliative care MD colleague and friend called me one day asking me to assess a patient of his whom he cared about a lot. She had just had a second back surgery for breast cancer that had metastasized to her spine, and she was in a rehab facility, but would need many levels of support and assistance when she returned home. He warned me, "You will fall in love with her."

He was right. Pretty much anyone who met Merijane fell in love with her, and many people thought of her as their best friend. I walked into her room in the rehab facility cautiously, as a few others were at her bedside talking to her. She was SO beautiful, her long, thick auburn hair tumbling over the shoulders of her hospital gown, her eyes sparkling despite the pain she was in, and her smile so wide, so welcoming. She was also brilliant, with a quick wit, and as I was to discover, a fine writer. Merijane would quickly become more friend than patient.

Meri had already lived with metastatic cancer for nineteen years when I met her. Most of our adventures (when I was not arranging healthcare for her or attending appointments) involved endless conversations while drinking tea, enjoying lovely meals, reading poetry and writing together. Our bond of life, friendship and love was clearly going to endure, wherever either of our Spirits resided. We both understood this, and discussed it often, especially after I too had a cancer diagnosis in 2013.

I got the call about Meri's admission to the ICU while I was attending a palliative care conference in Arizona, offering a session in poetic medicine that she was supposed to have co- led, as she had the previous year in Chicago. We had planned for her to have a helper come with her, to navigate traveling with a walker and wheelchair, as by 2017 she really could not walk easily on her own. News about ICU admissions is never good– I spent enough years running an ICU to know that for a fact. More news came in spurts for the next couple of days—she was better one minute, then she was worse. I knew I would have to assess the situation with my own eyes.

I left the conference in Phoenix early and when I got off the plane, drove directly to the hospital. When I saw her lying in a bed, with a massive oxygen mask over her face, her skin drained of color, and her Spirit clearly hovering in the room, I knew it was indeed her time. None of us were ready, not friends, not her family, not the nurses and doctors who had cared for her for twenty-six years. No one wanted Meri to die.

I could tell she was struggling with the internal quandary of how long to stay. She had clearly stated in her Advance Directive and in many conversations with me and with others that she did not want to be kept alive just for the sake of being here a bit longer. A few years before she had written in a prose piece, *Longing to Leave*: "I long to leave this body the way a snake leaves its skin, to shed the constraints of my restrictions real and learned and tread lightly across the landscape, as it was once so effortless to do." In our last conversation about this, a few weeks prior, she said, "I know I'm going to go sooner than I want. Sooner than you want. I'm ready. This is all too much." I didn't want to hear this, but seeing her lying in an ICU bed, I had to accept: it was finally Meri's time to leave.

We had her moved to a palliative care suite where all of us who loved her could be at her side, singing, praying, telling her how loved she was, how grateful we were for her. Many days after her death, I began to sense her near me. I allowed myself to stop what I was doing and just listen. She was expressing what I knew she would have wanted to say, while she was floating in limbo in the hospital, between worlds. I wrote down what I was hearing. It felt like I was taking dictation from her Spirit.

Twenty-six years waking and sleeping with cancer as my constant bedfellow is enough. Lying here in Limbo I feel you I hear your loud and soft voices echoing sadness and gratitude. My Spirit senses your Love your struggles to surrender your tears. Time does not exist for me but I know that the long and tedious hospital days and longer nights are trying on the Living.

And so, I contemplate the golden scales and clearly they are tipped in favor of flying…

Please know, I will smile as I quietly slip out of this sacred temple where I resided so bravely for as long as I could. And you who believe will bask in the radiance of my eternal Love and Grace, always.

> The Earth, She is my Mother
> Her Rivers the blood that nourishes me,
> Her Trees help me to breathe
> and her Plants heal my Body and Soul
> —Redwing Keyssar, *The Earth is My Mother*, Song,1973

It is the teachings of the Earth herself, through intensive ceremony and experiences with both meditation and medicine plants, that have enabled me to open my own heart and Spirit to something much bigger than my tiny, human day-to-day existence. Medicine plants have been powerful teachers to me—opening my own doors of perception, enabling me to see and feel and hear the voices of the wind, the rocks and those who have lived and died before me.

I have felt the Spirit leaving a body—through the crown chakra and through the will (third) chakra. I have felt Spirits hovering in the corners of ICU rooms, waiting for the right time to complete their out-of-body journey. I watched a man who was an incredible singer and had been dying of AIDS for weeks rise up from his pillow, arms outstretched, take a deep inhale as if to start an aria, and then drop back down to the bed with his final exhale. When my forty-five-year-old friend/patient was dying of metastatic breast cancer in the hospital and seemed to have taken her last breath, she inhaled deeply, sat up and opened her eyes and asked me, "I'm not dead yet?"

I had to say "No, not yet." She then said, "It's so hard to die with so much love around me."

I have also witnessed Beings who left this world so quickly, there was barely time for anyone to cry.

I have experienced out-of-body journeys of my own, as well as regular visitations and signs from various ancestors, all of which have helped me understand the multiple and non-linear layers of reality that exist at all times.

I have stood on black lava witnessing rivers of fierce fire flowing down a Hawaiian mountainside and heating my feet. I have felt transformative turquoise ocean waves healing my body, knowing that the Spirit of this Earth is so much more powerful than any human will ever understand. And standing at the bedsides of the dying, time and time again, I have learned that Love is indeed our most poignant force and flows on from lifetime to lifetime, form to formlessness, in spirals that connect the center of this planet to the heights of this universe.

JuPong Lin
my people sent me a canoe;
1000 Gifts of Decolonial Love

my people sent me a canoe
Dorian, September 6, 2019

Last night my people sent me a yellow canoe
floating gently into my dreams.
Flash flood of flash floods, brooks surge into rivulets,
rivers tear down trees, waves crest the windowsill,
water splinters glass.
My arms shoot out for my babies,
all grown by day, but in my dreams, time
winds back, their quivering bodies hover near mine,
We look for escape routes through one window.
Flooded to our necks, we see the rescue vessel.

How to fold a canoe
fold in half, sides to center,
accordion fold. Corners to wrong side.
Fold in half, open to find gold. Fold tiny corners.
Unfold, push in penny to reverse fold.
A fold in time compresses 2000 years.
Racing from Abaco and Grand Bahama
to Nova Scotia, Storm Dorian makes ruins
of "The Mudd." Year 500, Taíno people find refuge in the Bahamas.
Year 1492, columbus lands, commits genocide.
Year 1807, enslaved people flee, find refuge in the Bahamas.
Seminoles flee U.S. Army, find refuge in the Bahamas.[1]

Tourists seek escape from colonial life, find refuge in the Bahamas.
Year 2019, Haitian immigrants find refuge in "The Mudd."
People…trade…risk…for a place to live.[2]

"Disasters are not natural," von Meding says. [3]
Disaster is designed into the homes
of vulnerable people.
We settlers, safely inland, learn to design disaster
for vulnerable people, building into their homes
"accumulated risk."
Fold up sides, float canoe. Burn canoe to send
to your ancestors. Fold another for Black lives.
Whisper, enough is enough,
a prayer to disrupt unnatural disaster

1000 Gifts of Decolonial Love[4]
Movement 1: Paper Cranes Instructional

To prepare for funerals, we fold
paper gold.
To prepare for eating peanuts, Dad folds
paper boxes for holding shells; Mom folds
paper cups for holding water.

Chih chóa is how we say "paper folding"
in Hokkien. We fold useful things,
sacred things—
paper cups, paper gold.
Now we fold cranes to remember.

First four folds—mountain and valley—
edge to edge, corner to corner, fold
memory into paper, unflatten field
to open another dimension.

Precarity held in paper form. We
fold 1000 for a wish,
to remember and honor *hibakusha*,

survivors of atomic radiation.
We fold to honor islanders everywhere, drowning,
existence endangered, like 11 of 15 crane families.

Next bring valley to valley, reverse–fold a diamond,
like the cranes' migratory formation,
open end facing your heart.
Kite fold, like diaper fold, wings to center.
Flip over, repeat.
Caress the folds, score creases with thumbnail.
From this side of the ocean, across miles
of mountains and valleys I fold, unfold,
refold, shrink the distance between my home
on Turtle Island and *Tâi oân*, my bornplace,
between the Japanese empire and occupied Taiwan,
an island someone once called "mudball in the sea". [5]
Mom called it a speck, a booger picked
from the flaring nostril of China.
Now fold down a hat, like the bamboo farmer's hat my
grandfather wore in the peanut fields.
Unfold. Flip over, repeat.

Petal fold—like a rosebud blooming, move slow
as drifting clouds…unfold wings, bend back,
gently nudge apart an opening, spread
wide like lips rounding to catch
a drop of rain. Caress edges. Flip over. Repeat.

Black-tipped, wide-spread wings.
Spread wings like the lost Siberian crane
that landed in Huang Cheng-chun's field
one lazy June day,[6] first sighting ever
in Taiwan. The farmer named his rice in honor
of his new, snail-eating friend—"Jin Ho."
Morning qigong, "spread wings to fly"
crane's majestic celebrity withers
in its too-warm wetlands. Near the Caspian Sea

guardians name a lone survivor Omid, "hope"
in Farsi. How many folds to make a crane?
How many folded cranes make a prayer?
How many prayers become wisdom
of our grandmothers, great-grandmothers? [7]

Find the legs, prime the point, fold edges of legs
towards the centerline, leaving a margin for layers.
Every fold multiplies layers, thickens the story.
This fold times four, then open each side.
Finger moves with paper, rhythms flow
from one era to the next, like language
from mother's tongue to baby's ear, [8]
like shepherds' knots accounting for sheep
bleating in green fields.
How many post-invasion years, decades
to revive generations of wisdom culture?
How to dream in a lost language,
how to rescue lifeways and ceremony erased
by colonizers? We enfold the colonizer's art
the master's tools. [9]
They may never dismantle
his house, but could this technology bring to life
another kind of home?
Animal home, floral, fungal, spirit home?

Raise the legs, reverse fold into neck and tail. Each reverse
fold makes slim, symmetrical extensions; you choose
which will be the head.

Fold, unfold, refold a prayer for the
Siberian crane, the most critically endangered
of 11 sister cranes, pushed closer to extinction
every warming year
their marshy homes drained for farming,
their existence made more precarious by the rising heat

of our extractive habits, by our insatiable pumps sucking
black gold out of sacred soil,
and water—the bluest gold—from our earthly commons.

Last fold makes a beak, sounds the alert call.
Imagined empires break apart clans, families,
economies of conquest, erect walls between communities,
interrupt intergenerational bonds,
sever storylines carried by our grandmothers.
And we resist, we fold, we hold onto
ancestral memory, manual memory, muscle knowledge,
plant medicine, animal relations, interbeing, sun–moon,
yin yang cycles, always moving like salty waves, falling
rising, folding–unfolding into infinite timelessnes.
Folding a beak is an act of resistance,
a reversal of space and time.
We can make flesh of cultural memory, and release
a revolutionary chorus of all beings.

Movement 2: Elegy

September 11. Again. We count the days, the years since.
One, two, three, 10, 15 years since 2001.
Sadako's mother counts
One, two, three years, 7 decades plus one year, 1 month and 6 days
after the so–called "Little Boy" bomb was dropped,
blew her daughter out the window. 71 years after
she believed Sadako would survive unharmed.

September 11. I drive north, making a great escape,
slow flight from the home that was never *my* dream,
daydreams interrupted by insistent radio reports,
tolling bells, names, reports of that morning 15 years ago
when Homeland Security replaced the american dream,
the dream that lured my family to settle on Turtle Island,
to settle in the land of the wild onion

ancestral lands of the nations of The Three Fires,
the Potawatomi, Ottawa and Chippewa. [10]

My hands hold still, grasp the wheel, fingers still
folding, unfolding the 151st crane.
1 paper crane, 2 paper crane, 3 paper crane, fold.
Corner to corner, unfold, reverse. Her name
slips through memory as fingers gently pry
open petal fold. Sadako. Settled into muscle
memory 1000 times, this sequence, passed on from one hand
to another, one generation to the next in creases,
unfolding, folding, telling, retelling.

She survived 1 year, 2 years, 10 years after
the mushroom clouded over her innocent years.
And then the blisters broke. In hospital, she learned
the legend of paper cranes. 1000 for the gift of one
longer life. Now thousands fold cranes for peace.
I wake up dreaming of Sadako's mother.
Searching for her daughter, making slow flight
from ground zero, her brave arms snatch her tiny daughter,
running from the ghost of the mushrooming cloud. Surviving.

Did she see her baby's small body fly
through the window? Did her heart pause,
breath reverse when they passed the safety zone,
skin unburnt, pinkish still, Alive?
Did she hold in a sigh of relief every morning
Sadako awoke and smiled and walked to school?
And did a small fissure in her heart shelter the truth,
every day since August 6, the truth she kept from Sadako,
hoping to shield her daughter from the pain that would end
her short, but not small, life.

How did her mother count the days? how many cranes
did she fold, each crane a dance against death,

a knot in the string of days she survived as *hibakusha*.
I fold in memory of *hibakusha*, in praise of survivors
who warn us of our own extinction. I fold for the living
Siberian crane whose defense call heralds loss
of her homeland, *my* homeland, land of the Pepo Tribe of
Lloa, "fully assimilated" a euphemism for
genocide, linguicide. Stones to protect
Lloa land erected by Emperor Kanhsi still
stand on the ridge of Taipingshan, marking
"them" from "us."
Can we make peace across these stones? Care
for each others' babies and grandmothers, Indigenous and
settler? Human and crane, snail, fish, fungi, cloud, moon, sun?
Let's bury the weapons of mass destruction
and fold cranes, 1000 cranes for peace, millions for uncountable
seasons, cycles of life and death and life again.

I fold for Orchid Island, southeast of Taiwan
Yami home turned nuclear dump site
Honshu Island, where the bomb known as "Little Boy"
instantly decimated 80,000 human lives
(How many red-crowned cranes? How many snails?)
I fold for Bikini Atoll forever scarred by US nuclear weapons testing
Pu'uloa, Oahu, renamed Pearl Harbor by US occupiers
Turtle Island where indigenous resurgence sings of decolonial love I
fold 1000 for Black Lives
1000 for Missing and Murdered Indigenous Women & Girls
1000 in honor of Arab Spring
1000 for water protectors, earth protectors at Oceti Sakowin,
I fold for our children, for water, for life
and call us to rise up, spread wings and fly

For whom do you fold?

Notes

When the coronavirus pandemic entered our lives and bodies, I was preparing to travel to my birthplace and ancestors' home in Taiwan. Well–laid plans dissolved, and I found myself sheltering-in with my younger son, Mica, whose plans to return to college were disrupted. Like everyone else I knew, I really struggled to stay engaged with work and with my dissertation proposal. When no sensible words would flow from my keyboard, I put pen to paper and wrote poetry. What carried me through was opportunities to share my poetry and my art. The poems published in this issue were written before the pandemic (*1000 Gifts of Decolonial Love* was begun three years ago), in another moment of awakening to the existential crisis that is climate change, petrocapitalism and colonialism whipped together into a formula for extinguishing our own species, along with countless other living beings. But the pandemic and the confluence of eco- and social-justice crises of the last few months opened a space for critical reflection and a deeper awakening that transformed how I approached my creative work. Each morning as I took my dog outside with me and practiced qigong, I would hear a question rise up through my body. "What do I need to learn to be a good ancestor for my future kin?" And this question directed me to examine my disconnection from my own ancestors. So I dove in and revised these poems, wrote new poems and let my art carry me into this question.

my people sent me a canoe is based on a dream I had of being flooded into the upstairs of our house with my (now grown–up) children, and seeing a yellow canoe glide up to the window. The paper canoe has become a powerful object in my recent art—a talisman, a ceremonial honoring of ancestral lineage, an act of sacred activism. As I folded dozens and dozens, and taught others to fold them, the canoes have become community connectors and evidence of embodied cultural memory transmission; and they helped me navigate my way towards future work. *1000 Gifts of Decolonial Love* was also inspired by a dream of Sadako's mother, a *hibakusha*, survivor of the atomic bombs dropped on Hiroshima and Nagasaki. August 6 was the 75th anniversary of the bombings. Listening to Hideko Tamura Snider recount the horror of the bombs, I wondered why we allow our nation to continue honoring genociders while refusing to honor the survivors of unspeakable suffering caused by war.

N.B.: This is an abridged version. Please see Dark Matter: Women Witnessing #11 *online for the complete essay.*

[1] Goodman, Amy and David Moynihan. "Climate Colonialism: The Picture of Dorian's Graves," Democracy Now!. Web. September 5, 2019.

[2] Prevatt, David, Jason von Meding and Ksenia Chmutina. "Risk Rooted in Colonial Era Weighs on Bahamas' Efforts to Rebuild after Hurricane Dorian." The Conversation. Web. June 28, 2020.

[3] Williams, Robyn. "Disasters Are Not Natural." ABC Radio National. Australian Broadcasting Corporation. Web. August 8, 2018.

[4] Respectfully honoring Juno Diaz's "Decolonial Imagination" (see Hanna, Monica, Jennifer Harfor Varga and José David Saldívar, eds. Juno Diaz and the Decolonial Imagination. Durham, North Carolina. 2013. Print) and Leanne Betamosake Simpson's creation, *Islands of Decolonial Love: Stories & Songs.* Winnipeg MB: ARP Books, 2013. Print.

[5] Keliher, Macabe, and Yonghe Yu. *Out of China or Yu Yonghe's Tale of Formosa: A History of Seventeenth-Century Taiwan.* Taipei, Taiwan: SMC Publishing Inc, 2004.

[6] "Rare Crane a Boost to Taiwan's Troubled Wetlands." Phys.Org. Web. n.d.

[7] Pourlak, Lisa. "The Call of the Lonely Crane." International Crane Foundation. Web. February 8, 2017.

[8] Thiongo, Ngugi wa. *Decolonising the Mind: The Politics of Language in African Literature.* Portsmouth, New Hampshire: J. Currey; Heinemann, 1986.

[9] Audre Lorde. *Sister Outsider: Essays and Speeches.* Trumansburg, NY: Crossing Press, 1984.

[10] *Black Hawk War: Naperville Heritage Society History Stories.* Staff, Naperville Heritage Society Research Library and Archive. Naper Settlement. Web. 2012.

Maria Blum
Memoria: la poesía de las flores

Author's Note: This work-in-progress is for all ancestors who have been colonized. All peoples who suffer from trauma due to colonization. This is for la *Madre Tierra*, the Earth herself.

I am Honduran born. I am of the Maya Peoples, Lenca Peoples, Chorotega Peoples and of Spanish and Irish descent. I am classified by others as a Mestiza, a mix of Indigenous blood with European blood, a term that I do not embrace as it is a further erasure of the naming of my ancestral lineage. I am white-passing. I was raised both in Honduras and the United States until the age of twelve. I was forbidden to speak the colonizer's mother tongue of Spanish in the United States due to the colonization within my own family. I was told that I had to assimilate no matter what the cost. This created a schism within my own identity. I existed in the liminal space between. The Nepantla. I was neither here nor there. I lost myself.

El Don. A gift.

When I was young my *abuela* and I shared a nightly ritual. She would make me *poleada*, a warm milk and wheat cereal and then she would tuck me into bed and light a candle and sit next to me and tell me to dream of numbers. This wasn't a game. This was how she showed me that I carried a gift from the ancestors. That I see things before they happen. That I knew how to travel into different realms. That these realms contain gifts of ancestral healing and wisdom that could not be learned from any books. Every night she would whisper to me to dream of numbers and in the morning she would come in when I first awoke and she would ask me to tell her the numbers that I dreamt. She would keep a little black notebook filled with all of my otherworld numbers and sometimes we would go to a little *tiendita* and buy *lotería* tickets with the numbers that I had dreamt the night before. And then she would show me that we won. She would show me *mi Don*, my gift of knowing the unknown, seeing the unseen. She told me that I must always remember and honor *mi Don* in a sacred way and never for personal gain.

My *abuelita Tite* and my *tía abuela* by unknown author

My mom in the garden of my ancestors, dating back five generations, by unknown author. I also used to play in this garden and learned about our plant ancestors in it.

My *bis abuela Agueda* when she was an elder by unknown author

I later came to understand that my gifts were not valued by the culture I lived in. I was feared by my own mother who would say the rosary outside my bedroom door when she heard me speak to the ancestors in the ways my *abuelita* taught me. As a child I would often tell my *mamá* when an accident or death would happen. Before they happened. My mother continued to be frightened of me. I was told to keep things to myself. I became frightened of myself. When my *abuelita* died I forced myself to forget. I hid my gifts. I pushed them down deep within me. I silenced them. When *mi Don* would appear I ignored it and over time it went away. Sometimes the voices of the ancestors would rise to the surface no matter how much I tried to ignore them. They would whisper things that were to come and guide me on my path. I began to listen and follow their guidance but with hesitation. I told no one. I hid *mi Don* in the same way my ancestors hid.

As an adult I began to revive the seeds that lay dormant within me. I delved deep into the practices of healing and spirituality within the earth- based *Curanderismo* practices of my ancestors. The ones that *mi abuelita* taught me from within the womb. Even before. In studying and practicing these ancient ways I saw clearly who my grandmother was and is. I see who I am.

Transculturation. Syncretism. Subversion. Survival.

The syncretic ways of my ancestors were a necessity. This syncretism provided a safe passage through colonization. In order to keep their ancestral ways they hid them within the rituals of Catholicism. A transculturation. To avoid persecution my *abuelita* uttered her Catholic prayers as she administered her ancestral herbs. She practiced the Indigenous ways of healing. She was very careful about never calling herself a *Curandera*, a colonizer word. Before the colonizers arrived there were simply people who spoke the language of plants. The language of healing. Who knew which plant could be called upon in times of imbalance. Who knew which rituals needed to be performed. Who knew that plants were called upon not only for the physical body but for the emotions for the Spirit. My *abuelita* would say that she was the daughter of the Earth. And that she was *una naturalista*. She was *la Madre Tierra's* healing helper. My *abuelita* was subversive. All healers are subversive. When Peoples practice the art of Indigenous ways of healing they are looked at with fear. The colonizers called out these healers as *brujas* as a way to control them. They knew that those who practice the Indigenous Healing Arts carry the powers of unseen worlds. It is why all natural healers continue to be seen as dangerous. Because they are in tune with and vibrate with *los cosmicos.* Their pulses beat with the rhythms of nature.

Subversive   Dangerous   Defiant   Feared   Uncontrollable

Plantas Sagradas.

Ritualistic and healing work with sacred flowers saved my family lineage from demise. With each hand my maternal lineage touched each seed, each petal and stem, each root. They were in turn serenaded by the sacred waters of the early morning dew that collected on these plants. *Esta agua serenada* healed my lineage and protected them. *Esta agua sagrada* holds the memory of the vital force of the plant. Held and dispersed into water. Taken in for thousands of years. In the same way that water carries the memory of our stories within our own bodies. Flower and Song. Where speech becomes song. Composed by *los cosmicos.* The poetics of *las flores.* The gesture of Peoples and Plants. Memory *memoria memoriam.*

How can the cosmovisions of our ancestral lineages guide us through the world of today? How can these cosmovisions teach us to care for the earth and each other today? These answers are embodied within *las plantitas.* It is the plants who narrate the story, the voices that remain. Plants play an important role in the cosmology of the Peoples. Archeological findings show deities and rulers depicted in art as sacred trees and sacred plants such as *Maíz.* Plants and their stories continue to be a part of Mesoamerican earth- based practices. The plants continue to reveal what must be done to balance all sentient beings and *la madre tierra.* It is time to decolonize plants and ritual and healing practices so that we can reclaim the Indigenous earth- based wisdom of our ancestors. It is time for all of the ancestors past present and future to join in the communal and reciprocal care of each other.

My great grandmother, my *bis abuela Agueda*, when she was young. She started the flower shop and was a plant medicine woman by unknown author

speak our words sing them loudly say them

memory lives in your bones and travels through your veins and is carried to the next generation waiting for the ones who know the ones who hear the voices *los cantos* of the past

what matters is that our voice is heard again.

Materia Médica. Medicina de la Madre.

Lineages of women and healing encompass the world over. These living Mother Medicine books and stories traveled across mountains. Across oceans. Were kept safely within the heart. Seeds carried in hair. Tied into long braids. In my ancestral lineage, healing wisdom is passed down through an oral tradition. *Materia Medicas* are passed down through apprenticeship to plants and through stories told and poetry sung. Passed down with reverence towards the plants. A reciprocal relationship with the plant world through ritual and ceremony. Never forgotten. Healing is not "done" by the plants. Healing does not happen when one "uses" a plant. Healing is called upon if it is what is in tune with the Spirit of both human and plant. It is a relationship of mutual care. One works with the plant. One does not use the plant.

Thousands of sacred *Materia Medicas* were written and rendered with *las plantitas sagradas*. With the sacred practices of ritual and healing. They were written on *amate paper* by the ancient Mesoamerican Peoples. And then were burned by the Spaniards. Were desecrated by the Spaniards. Were considered filth. And evil. Were considered the work of *el diablo*. These sacred texts became ash. These texts of ash nourished the earth. Texts of ash that still held the sacred healing ways of the Peoples. The deep understanding of the Cosmos. *La sabiduría de las plantas, de las medicinas, las ceremonias.* Buried deep within *la Madre Tierra*. Only a handful survived. Confiscated. Others were written after the conquest. These are whispered to carry secrets hidden within their texts. Some truths. Some deceptions. Written as ways to deceive those that forced the Indigenous Peoples to rewrite *la historia*.

Burned. Buried. Not forgotten.

La Floristería Matamoros. Todas las plantitas.

La Floristería Matamoros on *Calle La Fuente* opened its doors some time during the 1920s. No one knows for sure when it opened because it was as if it had always existed. There was never a sign placed outside the door. There was no need. Everyone in town knew exactly where it was and anyone who came from another part of the country looking for flowers, would only have to ask some one on the street. They would be sent directly to *La Floristería Matamoros*. My family's flower shop continued through the 1970s and then one day my *abuelita* closed its heavy wooden door.

The woman with the flower in her lapel is my *abuelita Tite* and the elder is my *bis abuela* and the other women are my great aunts, my *tías abuelas*- they all worked together in their flower shop *La Floristeria Matamoros* and they all lived together their entire lives. I lived with them all as a child.

She knew it was time. It was heard that on this day she said "I am now like my flowers, I am curving forward just like their stems." And with that, the door shut....

My first teacher, *my abuelita Tite, una curandera,* instilled in me a deep love and respect for the plant world. She worked only with the plants that grew in her garden. She spoke to them and cared for them as the friends and companions they were. My great aunts refused to understand the Indigenous ways of my *abuelita,* they had instead embraced the ways of the colonizers. They forgot that their parents came from *Choluteca,* a place with deep reverence for all beings. They forgot that their ancestral lineage walked from faraway places, from Mexico to Honduras, carrying their wisdom traditions in the pockets of their garments, embedded in their Spirit. They forgot that they were also a lineage of Indigenous Peoples. That their life and their medicine traditions existed because of ancestral plants. They believed instead that the only authentic medicine came from a "proper" pharmacy, administered to them by a licensed Medical Doctor.

My *abuelita's* ways of healing were considered beneath them, subpar. They would say it was *la medicina de las Indígenas* —which always made my grandmother smile in pride. They whispered about how she spoke to her plants, they feigned fear of the green-colored bottles in her home *botánica* filled with sacred plants, her bundles of herbs hanging and drying on the wood beams, they scoffed at her treatments and looked with disdain when she cleansed their family home with the smoke of Pine and *Copal.* But my *abuelita* continued regardless. I watched many of my great aunts walk secretly into my grandmother's room and ask for a little something for their headache, or their insomnia, or their broken hearts. I watched my grandmother light a small candle with grace and then call upon Spirit, plant and human ancestors, and ask for guidance. I watched my great aunts tiptoe away, herbs in tow, worried if one of the other sisters would see her.

My *abuelita* had shelves upon shelves of her tinctures which were housed in dark green wine bottles. Each bottle had labels with her beautiful script describing what was inside and what they healed. They were placed far above where my hands could reach but I would spend countless hours walking past each one and memorizing their names. Below the bottles were jar after jar filled with dried herbs. These I also studied and often she let me open them, knowing that their fragrance and their taste would teach me more than any book. *Ruda, Pericón, Hierba Buena, Hoja Blanca, Artemisa, Albahaca, Verbena, Romero, Ajenjo, Culantro, Cilantro, Santa Marta, Apazote* and so on and so on. When someone came to her home in need of care she would know precisely which *plantita* to go to. Sometimes she sensed in advance when a visitor would be arriving and she would prepare their remedy ahead of time. As time went on no one was surprised that she already knew they would show up. And that she already knew what they needed. She would often go out to her garden and cut fresh herbs that she would need for the day. These were placed on her little table. The one where *San Judas Tadeo* watched over the herbs. The one where the *copal* burned. The one where the candles were lit. At all hours of the day and night my *abuelita* was called upon, always ready to share the healing of *las plantitas*.

Early on I saw that my grandmother split herself into two people, one the Traditional Indigenous Healer, *la Curandera*, the other the respected and glamorous florist. Both sides of her existed simultaneously and were called upon mutually in times of sickness of mind, body and Spirit, rituals and ceremonies of birth through death. Flowers and plants always accompanying her in these times of need, their mutual love never waned. *Tite* was proud of her Indigenous wisdom lineage even when shamed by her family. The plants that lived in her garden were not bothered by any of this. They continued to flourish alongside her. The fruits and the herbs gave of themselves to her as she gave of herself to them. I spent countless hours in this sacred garden. I was taught by my *abuelita* to ask of the plants for only what is truly needed. Never more. And to always give an *ofrenda* of prayer or song to my plant kin. When we consume a plant they become a part of our structure. We exist in symbiosis. Everything that they receive becomes a part of us, both reverent and destructive energies. Their environment, their care, the sun, the moon. There is a constant exchange between us, inspiration and respiration.

My grandmother taught me that the history of our family, of the land, of all the beings who lived on the land before us, continues to exist within our bodies and the bodies of the plants that grow there. That our ancestors are the plants themselves. That we are intertwined. That our history lives within the earth. Lives within the cells of each plant. The rain, the wind, the air all contain parts of us. Plants are Elders. Plants are Teachers. Plants are Family. And for this reason the stories and the plants must be known and shared, honored and protected. Mutual care and reverence must be a part of the story of plant and human relationship. There is no separation between us, not human and nonhuman but a weaving of integrated cellular bodies.

Las Maestras.

Plants are a way for all to connect with and honor our ancestors, human and nonhuman, and heal generational traumas. Plants, ancestors, humans and nonhumans are all connected to the Cosmos. We need to remember this. Plants remind us how to live in knowingness. How to be aware. There are many ways to connect with plants. Working with plants is one way to connect you to consciousness. My garden is my family. The healing herbs I tend to, I take into my body. I embody my ancestors. I carry them within.

I have always been a healer. For as long as the earth has existed. My fear is understandable. My persecution real. I practiced in secret ways because I had to. But I don't have to anymore. I cannot hold back thinking I need other ways, the right practices, herbs, flowers. The ancestors have waited long enough.

Briggs Whiteford
Sister Ancestor

Sister Ancestor by B. Whiteford

I have come down the mountain naked.
I am here to nourish life from my huge body.
I am now picking up and carrying the brothers who most need me.
We can no longer live in an old system that is destroying life.
You were my big sister when I was living, but now I am big sistering you.
Taking you under my wing.
I am here to help you.
Call on me,
and listen for my guidance.

I come down the mountain naked,
no longer covering the body that caused me shame while living.
I spent my living life preparing to be an ancestor.
A life lived in hardship was my preparation.
The dream announces my arrival.

The dream was set in a bleak and austere landscape on a treacherous mountain path, steep, frozen and rocky. On both sides of the path were violent humans and animals. The only nourishment available in the harsh tundra climate of the deep winter were humans, cows, pigs and horses. There was an utter standstill, unconscious memories dangerously frozen in time, with humans and animals devouring each other.

In the midst of this bloody and brutal dream my sister Pamela thundered down from the mountaintop as a large earth woman with huge breasts, naked in the freezing cold. She was enormous as she moved with power down the path, her astonishing presence a strength greater than cruelty. Two grown men were withering from malnourishment and hypothermia on the side of the icy path. Their refusal to slaughter the animals for food meant they would not survive in the harsh environment. They could no longer stand up and were frozen almost to death. Pamela picked the men up, put them on her breasts and carried them down the mountain, her milk nourishing them and nursing them back to life. She covered her naked body with a sheet to protect the men from being seen by the other humans and animals. These sensitive men would die rather than follow the rules to dominate and kill.

Notes

Pamela died 35 years ago after living 34 years with obesity, epilepsy, diabetes, and knees that could not support her weight. Over the last three years I have been inviting her in as a sister ancestor—to learn from her, to see what she sees now and what she saw when she was alive. Before I could have this bond with Pamela on the other side, I needed to honor her and give her the respect she deserved by fully bearing witness to her pain. I had to let in the truth of how she suffered and begin to fathom what caused her suffering.

My sister was a big woman. She was taunted and bullied for not fitting into the narrow mold of Southern Belles as her three older sisters did. I needed to ask her forgiveness for ways I was unconsciously complicit with Southern etiquette at that time. Because she did not fit in, she absorbed our shame so we could maintain the facade of a well-heeled, flawless family.

Pamela died in the middle of the night, surrounded by her rescue dogs. Most say she died alone…but she was not alone. The abandoned dogs that she had taken in and cared for were with her on that night.

Pamela's voice has come in subsequent dreams after this first powerful dream. She comes in lucid moments when I hear her speaking directly to me: the wind on my face, the sound of a pheasant's sudden thwack in the bushes, a shooting star in the night sky.

Please do not pity me, she says to me. *I carried the family's pain inside my body while I was living.*

The time will come when I will ask you, my dear sister, to be my microphone, that I might speak through you. I have been waiting for you. I want you to forget everything you know and open your ears to hear my messages in other dimensions. Something new is being born. Nourish this. The power of the imaginal realm is great and as strong as primal instinct. Follow its relentless rhythms. I will come in images and dreams. Make images, make altars, assemblages, ceremonial environments for the sacred to dwell. They will become containers to anchor the mythic and spiritual energies in time and space. In collaboration with the natural world make art that venerates a multi-dimensional experience of reality.

The images you receive will carry power from beyond to alter consciousness the same way primitive art in caves carries the Spirit of the image through the ages. I will come to you in dreams. Write them down as soon as you wake and trust them, live with them, let them reveal themselves, and once the river fills and flows it will carry the messages from beyond through your art into a world that is dying, is starving and needs nourishment.

Pamela's instructions are alive in me; art-making has become an abode for the sacred to dwell, a portal to infinite dimensions where consciousness can be changed. She gives me courage to follow a deeper river within where she abides with me.

Hilary Giovale
Embers into Fire

> *Cuimhnich air na daoine bhon tànaig thu'*
> (Remember the people from whom you descend)
> —Scottish Highland Gaelic proverb

When Nona threw our heavy mahogany dresser across the dining room, she woke me up from centuries of amnesia. The dresser, which had been sitting there quietly for more than a decade, landed with a sickening thud, shuddering the wooden floors and rattling the glass cabinets of our old house. Nona's framed photo, her antique clock, and a tall glass vase were propelled across the room, intact. The big dresser nearly landed on my youngest child, who was trembling with fright. Most alarming of all, Nona was dead. There was no logical explanation for a large piece of furniture suddenly flying across the room. A supernatural occurrence had threatened my child. Something had to be done.

I consulted Yeye Luisah Teish, a Yoruba Priestess whose maternal authority conveyed that she knew exactly what to do in such circumstances. She prescribed a ritual to take place on the dresser, now restored to its former inert state in the corner of the dining room. Flowers, grains, fruits, a seven-day candle and a bowl of water were arranged with care around Nona's framed photo. I was to sit and listen to Nona for seven days.

Staring at these items on the dresser felt ridiculous at first. It was quiet there in the dining room, the ticking of Nona's antique clock barely audible. Gradually, after several days, time stopped altogether. Nona's message permeated the cells of my skin and blossomed in pictures behind my closed eyes:

"How could my grandchildren have forgotten me? You haven't spoken my name in years. You don't tell my stories anymore. Your children don't even know me!"

Nona's sorrow at our abandonment pumped through my blood. She had thrown the dresser across the room and threatened our youngest child in a last-ditch effort to get our attention in the chaotic material world. Nona, my husband's Italian grandmother, had a dramatic flair. As a devout Catholic, widowed single mother, and owner of a bar in Rock Springs, Wyoming, Nona became enraged when a priest tried to extort money from her, and she never set foot in church again. Of course she threw a dresser when we neglected her memory.

Until that night, my ancestors had been people of no consequence in my mind. They had come from dreary places like Scotland, Ireland, Germany, and England. In contrast to fiery, Italian Nona, they were Protestants who wore drab woolen clothing in rainy places. They lived in sod houses; they worked hard. They were people of small stature because food was often scarce.

In their antiquated black and white photographs, my great-grandmothers were packed uncomfortably into corsets, their hair pulled back harshly. My great-grandfathers wore stiff suits, long beards, and looked lost. I did not know how to relate to these people who seemed frozen in a distasteful past. I was born on the Fourth of July, 1975, in America. Ancestors had no place here. There was nothing of interest in their forgotten languages and obscure ways. They were dead people from a long time ago who had lived in bleak places with bad food. They had come to this land to make a better life for themselves. There was nothing else to say. No one thought of them anymore; why would I?

Although I'd always been stubbornly averse to my own ancestry, Nona had piqued my curiosity when she threw the dresser. I had a vague recollection of *Samhain*, an ancient Celtic festival at the end of October. I remembered hearing that *Samhain* is an auspicious time to honor the ancestors. So, on October 31, 2015 I picked up Luisah

Teish's *Jambalaya: The Natural Woman's Book of Personal Charms and Practical Rituals*. Following her instructions for creating an ancestor altar, I cleaned my house, placed a small table in a corner of the dining room, laid a cloth on top, lit a candle, and filled a small bowl with water. My youngest child had found two sheep horns in the countryside when we traveled to Scotland one summer. I placed them on the altar to honor our Scots ancestors.

I pulled up the chair my father had given to my mother when I was born. Sitting in the same chair where my mother had nursed me, where I had once rocked my babies to sleep, I whispered to my ancestors. Curious about those who belonged to the ancient Celtic and Germanic tribes, I addressed them first. Who were they before old-fashioned cameras captured their descendants' stilted images in black and white? Did they have anything to tell me? A blank silence yawned back from the doorway of these questions; a void I couldn't cross.

On a crisp, icy morning a few weeks later, I sat with an astute Diné storyteller named Sunny Dooley. The previous evening, she had shared a mesmerizing story at a community event. Wrapped in the warmth of her story, on a whim, I invited her to breakfast. In a bustling diner, we chatted over coffee and pancakes, getting acquainted with friendly small talk.

I was acutely aware of myself as a white woman visiting with an Indigenous Elder. There was a lot of history between our people that I didn't yet have the capacity to understand. I could sense it lurking beside us like an uninvited guest. Feeling an uncomfortable mixture of curiosity and defensiveness, I sat with a vague sense of the horrific mistreatment of the Indigenous people of this continent. I didn't know what to do about it. Out of the blue, with a twinkle in her eye, Sunny said:

"You know, you carry the epigenetics of the oppressor. You carry their

DNA. We're told that at this time, that DNA is turning back on itself and coming to help us. It's turning back to make things right again."

I smiled politely and continued drinking my coffee, buffered by the din of the diner. But inside, my blood ran cold. My ears buzzed with a high-pitched whine. As far as I knew, my ancestors had been poor, devout, humble people who arrived on this continent only a few generations ago. A settler myth I'd accepted for a long time allowed me to think of them as innocent bystanders rather than oppressors.

That night, my well-rehearsed denial was already wearing thin. By candlelight, I bundled myself into the chair in front of my ancestor altar and demanded:

"What did she mean about the epigenetics of the oppressor? Is there something you want to tell me?"

I heard nothing but sparse whispers floating raggedly on the chilly wind.

One night, a dream arrived:

I am standing on top of a stone fortress in the Scottish countryside. Next to me is a man I've never seen before, a father figure. With alarm, I watch as he topples over the edge of the tower, falling.

I race down the spiral staircase of the tower. Turn after turn, it feels like I will never reach the bottom. I am afraid he will be dead before I get there. When I finally reach the bottom, I find a circle of stones pressed into the earth with glowing embers at the center.

The man's body is nowhere to be found. The embers are all that remain of him. It will take time, but they can be rekindled.

Soon after this dream, a family tome came into my hands. My great uncle had researched and written the book of genealogy decades ago. It had been collecting dust in attics and basements since then. I opened it randomly and read the name of an ancestor who immigrated to this land from the Highlands of Scotland in 1739. This was much earlier than the immigrants I'd previously known about. The book's hundreds of pages recorded all his known descendants. Some of them received grants of land that were stolen from the Indigenous peoples of North Carolina. Some of them enslaved African peoples in Mississippi.

My neck prickled and my stomach curdled. The book revealed that I am a ninth- generation American settler. Sunny was right: I carry the epigenetics of the oppressor.

I am standing in a small apartment. Someone has violently thrown my beloved childhood cat against the wall outside. Her injuries are so severe that she will probably die. I wail with mourning.

I open the door and peek into the hall. Living relatives are marching down the hallway toward me. Some of the relatives silently rage and fume, "It had to be done." Other relatives shake their heads in mournful complicity, holding fingers to shushed lips. "Don't talk about it, whatever you do," their expressions plead.

Inside the apartment, my deceased paternal grandmother awaits. She turns my attention away from the hallway and toward her. She embraces me and drapes a green snake around my neck. I become a person I do not recognize. It is an initiation.

This dream sent me to my ancestor altar, shaking in the chilly predawn. Harm has been happening on this land for centuries and it continues today. I was being asked to accept that the harm has got something to do with my own bloodline. With dread and anticipation, I sensed an assignment taking shape inside my bones. Years later, I would understand that my dream of the father figure falling from the stone tower depicted intergenerational trauma from millennia of war and patriarchy. In my initiation dream, the ancestors nudged me to look unflinchingly at the horrors some of our people perpetrated on this land. I would need to break the unspoken rules that had silenced and justified these patterns for a long time.

When the ancestors' assignment first took shape in my bones, there was nothing to do or say. For weeks, I simply listened, aware that this assignment was going to change everything. Finally, I went to the forest and asked the trees for their help.

Grief came as I sat in the forest day after day. The ancestors' wails erupted and their tears flowed. I cried the tears of my great-grandmothers who left their impoverished families in Europe under duress and came to the so-called "New World" as young women and mothers. I cried the tears of my ancestors who must have known the cruelty of their presence on this land but were powerless to stop it. From *their* ancestors, even more primordial laments arose. At the time, I did not understand the layers of suffering that led my people to these shores long ago. It would take years to learn about the events that impacted them while they were still in Europe. Gradually, I realized that just like the Indigenous peoples of this continent, they had once held sacred relationships with their land. For now, their tears were unstoppable, so I simply followed their assignment to *let the grief move all the way through me.*

Earth was the only being big enough to hold the tears of my people. Over time, I took their tears to Her forest, to soak into the soil and nourish the trees. I took their tears to Her creek, to be tumbled amidst the slippery rocks. I took their tears to Her mountain, who was big enough to hold a grown woman in her lap. I took their tears to Her ocean, whose waves moved in sync with my blood. Renewal is always possible. It is never too late to begin.

During this process, I often felt rage and disgust toward my ancestors who had colonized and enslaved. How could they have stolen others' homes and lives so cruelly? Why had they disconnected from their hearts and brought sickness to this land? I was often tempted to abandon them, but their assignment in my bones insisted that I keep going. Now I could sense archetypal, seemingly divergent strands running through my DNA: oppressor and healer. I returned to my ancestor altar often, offering plates of homemade food, bowls of water, burning candles, cleansing rosemary and juniper smoke. Sitting with the paradoxical inheritance they'd left, I shared my feelings and asked for their help.

With their vast cosmic library, the ancestors began teaching me over several years. Certain dreams distinguished themselves as ancestral messages. These dreams came fully formed, bearing repeated symbols, storylines, and strong emotions. Exploring scholarly works, I learned that my dreams were pointing to ancestral mythologies. Synchronistic interactions came in waking life to corroborate these dreams. Eventually, the ancestors connected me with human elders who taught me old songs in Irish and Gaelic. To my surprise, these songs contained memories of Earth-based cosmologies that honored water, land, and animals. My heart blossomed when I learned that my ancestors once practiced longstanding, complex rituals to honor *their* ancestors. They once employed folk magic to navigate the challenges of life. Long before feminine wisdom was assaulted throughout Europe, women's sovereignty was the law of the land.

Further historical research taught me how their traditional ways were interrupted by millennia of hardship. The Roman Expansion, Viking conquests, the Inquisition, the Burning Times, the Black Plague, eviction, and endless wars had razed cultural and linguistic diversity throughout Europe. I felt my ancestors' despair when their kinship bonds were broken in favor of nation-states and market economies. I felt their shame when politically enforced religion disparaged their folk traditions, oral histories, and reciprocal relationships with the land. I felt their terror when the loss of the commons ensured their hunger, homelessness, and desperation.

Amnesia descended. Wave after wave of exodus from hurting families, stolen lands, and broken communities ensued. Sometimes they came willingly, but often, government and corporate entities colluded to force their migration. After long journeys by sea, they arrived on the shores of this land as orphans. The bones of their ancestors were lost to them. The old stories and songs would die with them. How many generations did it take for them to forget their ancient languages and speak English exclusively, the language of conquest? In exchange for a measure of security, they adopted a new identity that was engineered to consolidate power into the hands of a few. White.

Learning these histories enabled me to patch together an arc for their story; a way to make sense of the unthinkable. I imagined how, in their denial and amnesia, consciously and unconsciously, they consented to the lie of Manifest Destiny. They upheld a delusion in which this continent was rightfully theirs; in which they, the "civilized," were entitled to take all they wanted of others' bodies, lives, land, and labor. White supremacy told the lie that they were exceptional. The wounded, ancestral European orphans believed the lie, and repeated ever more extravagant versions to their children and grandchildren. After a few generations, our forgetting was complete.

How could my DNA turn back on itself to make things right again?

Waking life mirrored my dream of relatives walking down the hallway. When I told my friends and family about grappling with my ancestors' longstanding presence on this continent, some justified this legacy with silent rage. Still others pleaded for silence.   But the ancient ancestors presented a third option: Remember. They said:

Welcome, Daughter. You are an initiate in the School of Ancestral Memory. Wind your way through the maze of amnesia. Feed us with songs and flowers; remember our beauty. Rekindle the embers we left for you after our fall from grace. Become a good relative to the land. Become a good relative to the descendants of those we colonized and enslaved.

Use your time on Earth to take the steps that you can. Unfold the long arc of our story with honor.

Unravel the lie of supremacy in your mind. Remember who you are: a humble child of Stars and Earth. You are having a brief embodied experience in flesh and bone. Soon enough, we will reunite. You will remember that you are us and we are you. We have always been related.

Become the ancestor who plants seeds in the dining room; rocks babies awake; dreams embers into fire, turns the DNA back to make things right again.

"I will," I whispered.

Over six years, this assignment continued to unfold, transforming me from the inside out. And the process continues. Today, I am familiar with the oppressor in my DNA. I have developed the strength to look him squarely in the eye. He is afraid of not having enough, of not being in control. I seek to understand him, empathize with his wounds, and make him a relative. Sometimes he becomes agitated when my white comfort is challenged. I have learned to take deep breaths, sit with him, hold his hand, and keep my mouth shut until he settles down.

There is also a healer in my DNA. She provokes discomfort and generates change. She tells unwieldy truths, grapples with trauma, and summons courage. She is not afraid to wail because she knows that tears cleanse my heart. She teaches me how to build relationships across the divides that were manufactured so long ago. She nudges me toward sovereignty *and* returning what was stolen. She soothes the present generations of our family with memories of our grandmothers' ancient songs, stories, herbs and foods.

Over the years, my friendships with Yeye Teish and Sunny Dooley have deepened. Our relationships give me the courage to face these legacies *and* continue building empathy. Sometimes, being the first to publicly acknowledge my ancestors' history on this land feels overwhelming. Other times, it feels insignificant: just one small piece of our collective human story. Always, it feels necessary.

Threads from the lands now called Italy, Scotland, Ireland, Germany, and England run through my children's bloodlines. To honor this weaving, our simple ancestor altar still stands in the corner of the dining room next to Nona's dresser. Most days, I spend time with the ancestors there, sharing food, water, prayers and songs. We have come to an agreement: this is a portal through which their messages can pass. I am constantly reminded of their assignment to become a whole person in relation to the past. I do this for my children as well as the future generations of our family.

Fondly, I remember the hands, voices, and stories of my beloved grandparents and fiery Nona. I call on those whose human identities are lost to time, but whose genetic blueprints live in our blood. Appealing to their cosmic body of wisdom, I ask: please show us the way toward equity, healing, and peace.

Azul V. Thomé
Being with Ancestors

Praising the rooted standing ones and all the ones who have gone extinct. I am sitting on the Ancestors' bones and on Death seedlings. The vultures are mentoring me to pay attention.

I must first sit on the ground where all transforms, our earth. Here in the mountains of the Southeast of France with monk vultures spiraling high in the sky to feast on death and with the beloved haunted wolves only daring to appear in my paintings…

Here I must pause.

I wish to start by feeding and praising death, life and ancestors. With a racing heart and with tiny black ants investigating the laptop I type like apocalyptic raindrops. I can hear far below a river enthusiastically chewing at the gorge. Perhaps she longs for an ancestral song that is deeply buried down there. My head spins within the deep time of it all; I just wish to lie down in good company, ears to the soil of the matter.

Extinction

In 2017, before Extinction Rebellion was born, I called the community of Totnes to create a Life Cairn – a memorial to honour and grieve extinct species due to human activities.

Andreas Kornevall, storyteller, ecologist and writer inspired by Norse mythology, inspired me to call this Life Cairn into being, the very first one in the UK. I am grateful for the generous and courageous souls who created it with me!

Our Life Cairn is still growing on Sharpham Estate, near Totnes, for all to be with if their heart can bear the truth of the matter. We must bear it and become the alchemists of soul's grief if we long to be fully alive!

Prior to its creation, day after day, week after week we met as a community to make flags with children while discovering, honouring and feeling the animals, insects, plants, fungi and other beings that had gone extinct or were on the edge of that threshold…due to human activities.

All Art and photos by A.V. Thomé

Each night I would lay my head on the pillow, sometimes too grief-stricken to cry, while hearing within the deep cave of my head a voice saying "today another 200 species have gone, you do not know their names, their choreographies nor their songs but you can still say farewell." I did, each night.

When I brought this grief, only compostable with others, I 'heard' the words: "unsolvable, this situation is unsolvable, don't look for solutions for relief." It was in one of the precious Grief Composting Circles happening in total darkness that I could transform a little, just enough...

It is there, in these ritual spaces, that another layer of intimacy with extinction was revealed to me. I did not know then that extinction also needed intimacy. I could not turn away and it cost me. It is the natural law of 'things of rituals' in our tattered world, to become food.

My interwoven relations would never come back. Their songs would be removed from the wild and wondrous orchestra of Life. Their elaborate courting and joyous dances would no longer caress the air we are all breathed into. The vivid and subtle colours of their bodies and longings were being plucked out of the sacred art of the last 4.5 million years, in the blink of an eye. Un-bear-able.

That all-encompassing void.

The clawing poverty of the fabric of life, thinning at such speed as a result of such voracity was unbearable to my heart and psyche.

The loss of wild relatives due to our desperately brutal activities as humans, intrinsically woven with their absolute compassion for us, was radically maddening..

All that...was tearing my own soul apart into the most absurd shreds.

I understood then and there, within the tearing, that extinction was not death.

I found myself in a territory never ever talked about to me before. I was unprepared, existentially lonely and frightened to live or die. A rough initiation indeed!

If I was to stay devoted to whom I belong, to our living earth, if I was to keep on keeping on with reverence, I would have to deepen and widen my person while losing my personality.

I was summoned to support and 'passage' the death and birth of a new relationship with being alive as a human. I am not alone I am glad to say; many are becoming doulas and passages for our dying world.

Some of us dare to dream of a culture that belongs to the depth of compassion, generosity, presence and reverence that all non-human beings are naturally gifting life.

If extinction is not death, is there a particular temple to craft, to welcome this new being? Our imagination is perhaps required to stretch beyond our abilities…and 'wilden.'

Death and Ancestors

There is a passage inviting us to the ancestors' shore, just after death summons us. Unprepared but devoted, I accompanied three humans through this passage: the 40 days and nights to the shore of their well and wise ancestors.

The first human, the one who initiated me into this work, was my mother, France. When she died I was not ready to move on. I followed a calling, a sacred task, an instruction to remember and birth these ways into our Soul-starving culture. I am her eldest child, her eldest daughter.

Like many of us here, born in such cultural and living poverty, I stumbled between deep intuition, profound trauma, Soul's longing and wild imagination.

I sniffed and looked and searched and studied other cultures, religions and faiths – to see what they do when their people die. Something landed; a seed took root, fast like a rocket seed.

The instructions came fast:
You must start from the West. Create the most exquisite sailing boat to place her in. Her dress and shawl are to be made in the finest hand woven cloth.

Everything is happening in the sea, at dusk, just before the night wraps her body.

To the East, very far away, you will perceive the shore of the well and wise ancestors. They are preparing the fire, weaving the songs and drumming the heartbeat of her dream of Life – so your mother will not get lost through the passage.

Each dusk for 40 days you are to drum and journey with your winged ally, the raven, to accompany France's crossing. Your mother!

It became clear to me then that we can get lost after death, as we get lost when we are alive. I still had something to do in our relationship, to make sure she arrived safely to the shore of her ancestors. My mother and I did not have a loving relationship, it was woven with much suffering and trauma. When she died, all that drama disappeared! I became a *passager* and for the first time I knew why I came into her life. To build her a boat…and sing her home.

The second person I was moved to accompany after her death was Mary Oliver. A very favourite poet of mine.

The third human I accompanied after her death was Polly Higgins. A sister.

I created a book with images, poems, songs and prose of the 40 Days and Nights. Here are some excerpts.

Please read them with your belly full, with generous offerings and with consent. I choose to share them here to feed our new world where Soul is back in the frontline.

Forty days of crossing for Polly

Dear friends and all

*I want to share with you that I feel moved to offer a space of 40 days of
Mourning and Ancestralisation for our dear Polly's passage
A space to accompany her soul to the shore of her ancestors.*

*Would you imagine her laid on a beautiful boat on the ocean of her whole life
where through our love and grief we become the wind to her sail so she can
reach the shore where all her ancestors can welcome her.*

*We sing, we drum, we chant, we cry and we remember our encounters with our
Polly where we see her in her beautiful boat sailing East.*

*Here is a space to share our memories, our photos, our love and stories ~ a
container to hold and to become ripened human beings. We stay with our dead,
we accompany them so they become the ancestors we call on for the journey
ahead.*

Polly, you will become a magnificent ancestor. It is up to us.

With immense love and deep wild grief, Azul

*My dearest Polly, this is a space, like a virtual village shrine, where we can all
come to meet and cry and remember and weave the finest, strongest filament of
soul mycelium with you and between one another.*

*Here we will imagine you laid into the most beautiful Scottish sailing boat
where you can deeply rest wrapped in the finest of handwoven cloth.
Our songs woven in love to become a gentle breeze through the ocean of your
life*

Here we imagine the shore of your ancestors 40 days and nights away. They are also singing and drumming you back Home where all can be healed and restored. Where the contract with ancestors can be rewritten with gold thread spun from Dark Matter.

Our roles and duty as the living ones are to accompany you there. To be rigorous and awakened to our love and our sacred connections with Grief, Love, Death, rebirth, and Ancestry.

We are relearning the good ways and we will for you and for Life ~ DARE TO BE GREAT ~ renewing our pledge often <3 Missing you in my bones Polly xx

You are still above the Soil for a few more days, Anima Mundi longs to welcome you back within her own bones again.

Meanwhile, for 35 more days and night, we will keep singing and praise and pray for the crossing of your soul to your ancestors. At 8am UK time ~ We will call and court your ancestors to also sing and praise and pray for you.

The sounds and love will create a mycelium of the finest of gold and black thread.

The Conscientious Protectors mycelium is growing, the Law of Ecocide will pass, your effort will take form, be nurtured and protected.

Rest well beautiful Polly. You are loved <3

This is your last day above ground, I feel your delight in returning to the soil and to Anima Mundi ~ the Soul of Earth~ to rest deeply, to carry on your journey to the shore of your ancestors.

In our letting you move through with our love and our songs we support this sacred journey.

As a Mother Tree in a forest, your falling has called on all the other trees to strengthen and connect with each other in a new way, with Mycelium as the main connector.

The living system you have left behind is growing strong with new partnership and renewed ones.

So much love <3

Chère Polly, I was drumming and singing on this 15th morning since your death ~ your sails are full, the ocean deep and welcoming of the little boat that carries you East wrapped in the finest and softest of cloth...towards the shore of your Ancestors.

They are feeding the fire. 10000's of them singing and drumming delighted at your arrival in 25 days and nights.

We ~ "the living in a body ones" are here to blow wind in your sails and to cherish the sacred seeds and saplings you have left us to care for and protect.

The starlings might come and see you on your beautiful cedar boat.

with deepening love <3

This morning my dear Polly I saw your ancestors throw the finest of threads on the water ~ thread as fine and strong as a spider web and as reciprocal as the filaments of Mycelium. They threw them towards the West (where you now are sailing from) ~

The thousands of threads touched the Ocean of Soul ~ growing towards you ~ not touching your little boat just yet.

I do not want to move on too fast to the next chapter, this one is crucial I sense. To stay with our love of you

while we miss deeply,
while our chest cracks and aches in wild and subversive dances,
while our hands long for one more embrace, one more cheering, the holding through pain and dancing for life.

40 days and nights as a wild rigorous practice of Love to accompany you from Lady Death to the shore of your awaiting Ancestors.

We can do that. <3 with deep ocean love Polly <3

Beloved Polly ~ This morning in my meditation I sang a little song ~ each note, each sound became water drops in the ocean that carries you to the East, to the shore of your Ancestors. They are well aware that you are almost halfway on your 40 days journey of your crossing...our crossing...the crossing when one we love dies. No one stays the same.

It is initiatory for all, that journey. From leaning out of the void, to life, to living, to death, to dying, to calling the ancestors, to becoming an ancestor, to be called again...

It all matters greatly...that duty of care for our dead as well as for our living ones.

There is an alertness needed that resembles what wild animals are...all senses open, tracking the air, the water, the stone people and the soil...being the air, the water, the stone people and the soil. Tomorrow is half way. A time of risk when life calls us so strongly that we might forget that our darling Polly is not yet welcomed nor wrapped up by her ancestors.

We must stay awake deeper in our songs, our grief, our letting go, our love, our prayers and praises.

Coda
Art as Prayers

Most nights I wake up gasping for air, for company and for arms around my shoulders. What happens in the darkness is what needs to be worked with during the daylight…to mend my separation with Life in solidarity with many sisters and brothers who are also called to mend the broken web as well as listening to the profoundly loving summoning of all other species and beings.

So every day I must paint my wide family. I must touch and work with trees, sing with the river and place deep rest into our tired soil. I must make fire and feel the death of the stars sprinkling their heartbreak remedies.

Each place I go to I paint, to present my intention and pray. In the last six weeks I have painted on old roof tiles to greet and meet those who live here with me.

Here they are as a fare-well. Wolf, stag, redstart and moon.

All art and photography by A. V. Thomé

Ysabel Y. González
Chameleon or Thinking About My Mother
the Sparrow

Chirrup caught in its jewel-throated song,
she is the sorrowful sparrow flitting above,
leading me although she doesn't quite know the way.

This is no dream and I'm grateful
she's flying and I can see her from the ground.
Sometimes I hear her story better
when I tilt my head slightly—
the sparrow's melody is a siren. Now
a bruise. Blade rising. Now
a clue to how to move in this world,
sort of trembling (some say dancing).

Her music is my own and I inherit the achy
sword and swerve, even when I'm unsure it will serve me.
Every day my body morphs, colors rippling
over like tidal rainbow, giving me hope and exhaustion,
molding to the world as it holds my skin in its hands.
I take comfort in any spritely creature broken yet full of faith,
but especially this sparrow, who believes her spell will guide me to
where
the universe needs me to stand. I'm right
where I'm supposed to be, mother, getting rained on.
The sun will dry me up, will fill
my cupped palms with light.

It is dawn again and I should rest from all this singing.
Sit with today. Tomorrow
will come and I'll wonder, wander through it then.

Notes

Chameleon or Thinking About My Mother the Sparrow: Chameleon is a persona I've developed who is constantly thinking about changing, shifting, and adapting to and with the world. Here she sits and thinks about her mother, who is different yet ancestrally, the same.

Sara Wright
Crane Song: Finding My Way Home

Ways of knowing may be passed on in non-linear ways—circular ways—that are not acknowledged by Western culture. What follows is one woman's story of finding her way home—back to her Native roots—through the power of an image of the Medicine Wheel, with assistance from a dead Abenaki Medicine woman, the sharing of Indigenous story, celebrating ritual, and moving through time. There is no progression here, just a circular journey with new insights occurring with each turning of the wheel.

The last gift I received from my very distant parents was a print of a Native American Medicine Wheel by Ojibwa artist Joe Geshick. I received this present on my birthday in 1993.

When I opened the cardboard tube I was astonished by the image. A Medicine Wheel? As far as I knew neither of my parents had any idea that I had picked up the thread of my Native heritage and was studying Indigenous mythology. What could have motivated them to send me such a thing? I was stunned by the seemingly bizarre synchronicity.

At the time I was also giving an Indian program in the local elementary school called "The Circle Way," educating children and myself about the mysteries of the medicine wheel.

An Abenaki Medicine woman, a healer named Mollyockett who lived in the area during the 19th century, seemed to be guiding me in this process. Before walking to school to give my program I stopped at her gravesite to ask for help. One day I was shocked to discover a Great Blue heron sitting on her gravestone. Some days I could feel a presence when I knelt there in the tall grass.

Thanks to interlibrary loan, I was also learning about my own Passamaquoddy/Malisset heritage, but I felt like I knew almost nothing about Northern tribes in general; most had been decimated by disease brought to them by the colonists that destroyed Native core values and the way of life for most of these Indigenous peoples. Some pockets of Native peoples, beliefs, and stories survived in Canada because they had less contact with white people.

Photo by S. Wright

I hung up the Medicine Wheel immediately and began to use it as an image to help me prepare for my classes. The wheel reflected *equality* on a level that was familiar to me; we *were* all connected—trees, people, rivers, flowers. As a dedicated naturalist/ecologist I had always felt this idea to be truth, but suddenly I began to *speak* about what I knew with a voice I didn't know I had.

When my father died suddenly about six weeks later the Medicine wheel (otherwise known as "The Circle of Life") became the last gift I ever received from either of my parents; it developed a 'charge' that resulted in me hanging the wheel in every space I ever inhabited. It is still with me.

In 2013 I was finishing a thesis on my study of Black Bears and decided this image would become the cover of my manuscript. Researching the artist, I learned that Joe was born in 1943, grew up on a reservation in Northern Minnesota, spent two years in jail for minor infractions and began to paint there. After his release he studied at the Art Students' league in New York and then taught art in Ontario. On the La Croix Reservation in Ontario he learned something about the fragmented history of his clan, and was introduced to traditional ceremony. In 1977 he began studying with a Lakota Sioux Medicine Elder in Nevada while participating for five years in the annual Sundance Ceremony.

As a result, Joe became rooted in traditional ceremony and his paintings reflect this dramatic spiritual shift. "The Circle Of Life" embodies this change, drawing attention to the four sacred directions, the four seasons, the sacred colors, the four races. All are equal; all require respect. Joe often said that he wanted people to relate to his work through personal experience.

After doing preliminary research on the artist, I recognized that like him, I too had been totally separated from my Native roots and was finding my way back through image, my experiences with animals/plants, creating/celebrating my own ceremony, and by studying Native mythologies. A slow, circular lifetime process. But Joe became a model for me, validating that the way that had been chosen for/by me was an authentic one.

I felt a deep kinship with this particular wheel with one exception. In the center Joe had placed a thunderbird; after learning about the Ojibwa I didn't understand why the bear wasn't in the center of the wheel because the bear was the most venerated healer for his people.

Recently, I returned from the Southwest where I was introduced to the ceremonies of the Pueblo peoples, ceremonies that reflected my own spiritual practices, reinforcing their authenticity. This interlude also allowed me to be part of a people who had never lost access to their roots. They had never given up their ceremonies or surrendered their way of life.

I returned to Maine with a much stronger sense of my Indigenous cultural identity than I had when I left. I hadn't realized until I went to the Southwest how much this identity had been eroded by local people. Living in western Maine had brought me in contact with the frightening bias people have towards Indians; some are openly despised.

My first reality 'hit' occurred a few months after moving to the area after giving an elementary school program when fifty people from an irate religious group gathered one night at the school and attempted to indict me as a *witch*. "I was turning their children into trees," one of my accusers said. Although the program I had given was an astounding success, no one intervened on my behalf, including the superintendent of schools and the principal of the school who asked me to give the program in the first place.

Numerous other negative encounters followed over the years. Two neighbors bought property next to me and moved in. I didn't understand why they disliked me. It took me years to understand the reason. Because I am "different"—an "Indian" (their words, not mine).

Just up the road from my home seven years ago some locals put up signs that stated "We don't trust you, Sara Wright," to humiliate me and prevent me from walking up a mountain road.

I was betrayed by the town of Bethel when I offered to become part of their annual Mollyockett Day—supposedly a celebration of Mollyockett and our Maine Abenaki Native heritage. In actuality, this celebration had/has nothing to do with Native peoples. One of their most egregious practices is the frog-jumping contest when hapless amphibians are forced to hop around steaming concrete for children's pleasure. No Native person would ever agree to torturing animals in that way.

Just last spring, two months after my return from New Mexico, a red truck left a dead baby grouse in my driveway. Others continue to leave screaming tire marks. I am an "outsider" because of my heritage, regarded with suspicion. These grim examples reveal that hatred of the 'other' and discrimination is a way of life here.

But to return to my present story… this fall I decided to do something different with my medicine wheel. I carefully cut out a photo of one of my bears sitting in the mother pine and placed the photo in the center of the wheel, replacing the thunderbird. Ah, now the wheel looked just right, and I placed the print above a little mantle in a dark corner of the living room. A solitary candle lights the wheel unless the sun is just right and then the entire space lights up eerily. An abalone shell reflects the blue green waters below.

With the Medicine Wheel in a place of honor I decided to do some more research on the image. I was astonished to learn that the 'swans' that encircled the wheel were *cranes*—Sand hill Cranes, my spirit bird of the East—birds whose haunting cries literally freeze me in wonder, birds that I lived with every winter in New Mexico for four years, birds that I discovered to my great joy are now living/breeding here in western Maine. Cranes, not swans. And Joe painted the cranes with their feet becoming red roots seeking green earth ground. According to Joe, "the two cranes that envelop the circle represent a spiritual relationship with the earth." Exactly! Oh, it fit.

Then came the next surprise. I read that in their creation story the Ojibwa who were water people were led by the Sand hill Cranes who were their leaders. The original holy people were cranes, loons, fish, deer, marten, bear and thunderbird, but the thunderbird had to be returned to the sea because his powers were too strong. The Bird people replaced the thunderbird. Today the Crane clan is the leader followed by the Bear, as Healer.

I guessed that it was Joe's spiritual experience with the Lakota Sioux that led him to place the thunderbird in the center of his medicine wheel paintings because the thunderbird is sacred to the Lakota Sioux.

Joe died in 2009 but what follows is what he wrote about his beautiful and deeply moving paintings.

I am motivated to paint by my desire to share this connection with others so that they may discover their own natural and spiritual relationship with the earth. I want people to feel and experience the wholeness and simplicity of life.

Today, our blue green planet is in crisis and I believe our only real hope comes from embracing the ways of a people we despise or dismiss, a people whose way of life could teach the rest of us how to embrace "The Circle Way"—the values of respect, equality, community, a gift economy—and most of all help to reattach us to this Earth we call home.

Healing with Land and Ancestors

"Civilization" spread like a crust over the land and suffocated the life out of it. ... As I walk, my ancestors send visions of the great crust of my culture slipping off the living land, just as a crab sheds his shell. ...

—Julie Gabrielli, *Song of the Chesapeake*

If the humans were to cry tears of compassion for the earth, for all the beings they have harmed, for themselves in their foolishness, these tears would replenish and heal the waters.

—Valerie Wolf, *Dreaming the Future*

Naomi Shihab Nye
My Grandmother Said

They just don't know our stories,
(after being tear gassed by Israeli soldiers,
she held the cut onion, the hankie to her face) –
If they knew our stories, they would behave a different way.
They never sat around my small fire cracking almonds.
They don't know I have a great sense of humor.
I never showed them what I keep inside my green trunk,
the tiny treasures I have left, since they took my house…
… if they saw them they might laugh,
the broken plate, the strip of cloth.
It might be good for them to laugh,
since they never smiled at us yet,
not even once. I don't know where they came from
but I come from here, it was always my field,
I don't care who owns it, it's mine.
If you speak to the trees, they'll speak back
not only with olives but a soft mixing of leaves
after the soldiers return to the city, or wherever else they go,
and the trees with their deep hearts apologize for all meanness,
I mean this, a rustling…
They just do not know.

Notes

My Palestinian father, Aziz Shihab, was a newspaper journalist most of his life. Though generally a congenial, gracious spirit, he was highly annoyed by headlines that didn't actually fit their stories—a more common predicament for print journalists than many might believe. He resented poor grammar—in English or Arabic—and was exquisitely careful with his own. And he was saddened by displays of inequity and small-mindedness—in society, religion, politics—and the ongoing false spins about the "great democracy of Israel," when his own family had lost their home in Jerusalem in 1948 due to the occupying

Zionist soldiers. It was all a sell-out: money, guilt, power. Why couldn't a balanced country have been created instead, one which recognized that Palestinians were already conducting themselves and their precious lives on the same soil (do not for a minute, please, believe the empty desert-before-their-coming myth which Zionism has repeatedly tried to perpetuate)? It was a lifelong grief for him and he did everything he could—speaking, writing, advocating—to try to balance the "dark matter" of lies.

Why couldn't we more easily imagine one another's lives? Why was empathy so difficult? Former President of Israel Shimon Peres once said what surprised him most about getting to know Palestinians was, "that they had aspirations like ours." Well, why wouldn't they? Do I in my Texas home two hours north of Mexico imagine mothers across the border don't love their sons as much I love mine? Since when did human imagination become so parched and puny?

Many regular citizens of Israel are able to appreciate Palestinians as human beings with traditions, skills, incredible patience and intelligence—and vice versa. Consider hospitals. Consider Hand in Hand Schools. Consider the fascinating and balanced-power Neve Shalom village, etc. Why can't politicians with tons of cash behind them imagine a wider horizon of shared lives together, as regular citizens can, and do? Can anyone even imagine what a tremendous glowing society that might be? And how would this single shift change the sizzling, awful, underground energy of "terrorism"?

But the "chosen" theory would have to die. You can't have "chosen" and "unchosen" dwelling in easy harmony...The current crop of Republican candidates, with their righteous spouting of devotion to Israel (never considering all the crimes against humanity Israel conducts on a daily basis, or the regular massacres of thousands of innocent Gazans, with American weapons, which gets almost zero press) would have disgusted my father. He would have turned his face away. I am almost glad he died so he didn't have to hear them.

Anne Bergeron
Calling Out the Names

Journey

On a snowy December night in our rural home in Vermont, as I stood by the winter solstice fire listening to my friends speak aloud their hopes for greater peace in the world, I did not know what I would say. I had moved to this land to grow my own food and live a life close to the earth, but what exactly did this mean in the context of a changing climate and the sixth greatest extinction? How could a lifestyle choice — or hope — be enough? What came to me by the fire was the understanding that I owed the worldwide water crisis, the shriveled coconut palm, the blighted fields of potatoes, something more. When my turn to speak came around, I heard myself say something about wanting more peace in the world. But inwardly, I felt a new and different statement forming. On the brink of this new year, I realized I wanted to give the collective survival of the earth my voice.

The Ainu, who are native to Japan, have a word, "iworu," which means their territory or range, their biome.* "Iworu" has specific land mass denotations — the deep forest over the rise, the salty bay full of salmon, the high, pointy mountain. As is true of most original cultures, the Ainu invest their geography with spirits. There is a pulse in the forest, a cry in the winter field, a song in the mountain.

Language belongs not only to humans, but to animals and spirits, to all things wild. Ancient cultures, whether in the depths of the Indonesian jungle or the high arid desert of the American West, felt a natural desire to sing, chant, call out the names of the places that held their stories, as an answer to the hawk's cry and the wolf's howl, as an expression of gratitude for how the land gives us our lives. Story and place were one, and that symbiosis meant survival.

Survival was catalogued in the beauty of hearing the names of places spoken aloud.

I have long been nostalgic for a home I never had, a feeling that my family, who provided me a very good home on the shoreline of Lake Champlain, surrounded by the Adirondack and Green Mountains, has found difficult to understand. As a teenager, I felt generations of family bonds splintering at the same time that I witnessed the wild spaces around me diminishing. I felt the ache of being someone who, by following my heart's desire to leave home and explore the world, knowingly participated in the twin losses of family and wilderness. My brothers, my cousins and I were the first generation that was not planning to live in the town where we grew up, even though it meant discontinuing the legacy of three generations of family stories held in the memory of our neighborhood by the lake. My family never traveled; we have no stories for journeying. And here I was in their midst, needing to experience life beyond the family, beyond their chosen place. For over a decade, that desire would take me on airplanes, boats, and trains to Canada, Europe, Central America, and Asia, as well as on numerous car trips crisscrossing the United States. To compound matters, I would expend finite natural resources to take myself where I wanted to go. The strength of my desire left me no choice. I had to leave. I had to explore. As a young woman, all I knew was that it hurt to want what I wanted.

I have curled myself around that ache, hidden it like a family secret, wrapped it with a silk cloth of protectiveness. I am surprised now to find beauty in the language of its cry. In what appears to me a not-entirely-even trade with the wilderness, my husband and I have swapped our meager savings for 47 acres of forest land and wild animal habitat high in the hills of eastern Vermont to try to learn something of the language of one place before we die. In memories of our early days here, I find the beginnings of an understanding of our "iworu," and in these memories the beginnings of a language we will spend the rest of our lives learning.

Intimacy

My husband Glynn and I walk our land with a local forester. Glynn carries loppers, I carry a scythe that belonged to my grandmother; Marcus carries a slide and a clipboard that holds a topographical map. His pocket holds a GPS. We are placing a conservation easement on our property to prevent development in perpetuity, and the state of Vermont requires that we submit a management plan in order to conserve the forest.

On this walk we identify beaked hazelnut, hay- scented fern. I find a clump of maidenhair fern, and Marcus points out evidence of beech bark disease and spruce rot, the latter an illness that takes mature spruce trees by hollowing their cores from the roots upward. Nothing to be done about it, he says. It will be fine to cut the trees where the rot has not spread too much and mill them as lumber for the house we plan to build. A few years after this walk, we nail white spruce boards milled from those trees into diagonal sheathing as early snows fall on us. Those trees now surround us daily, keeping us warm when the winter winds barrel across the meadow.

As we walk our woods in the peak of autumn foliage, the overcast sky has the sheen of pearls which illumines the sugar maples from within, their reds a contrast to green beech and birch leaves. The wind picks up as we descend toward the far boundary of our land into a conifer forest. We find fresh moose scat, and shortly after, flattened, mossy ground where the moose bedded down. In the wet earth of the vernal pool, black as raven feathers and muck dry, we find evidence of the bear who has been digging trout lily bulbs.

The moose browses on native buckthorn and maple saplings, the bear digs bulbs and forages wild raspberry in summer, the coyote yips and laughs at night, and I walk along, trying to find my place in this forest.

The intimacy the Ainu have with their landscapes is born of feeling the direction of the prevailing winds on the skin, of knowing the subtle scent of a strong storm coming, of divining the first inklings of winter in the August air. It is knowing well the scents, sights, sounds, and textures of a place; it is understanding its intimations, feeling what the trees intuit.

Night descends and we leave the forest. Marcus will write a plan for us to review. As I move cautiously into my new habitat, I feel the whole of the place listen for what I will ask of it. I sense the deep tug of responsibility to hold up my end of the deal, to learn exactly what I have entered into with this land. I hold a promissory note of paper birch, a deed proffered by white spruce and sugar maple. What response do I offer to the blue jay's screech or the tiny saw whet owl's repeated calls for a mate? In the darkness, I feel the weight of my choice.

Roots

I cannot imagine living without a garden. The return of my favorite strain of red Russian kale or calendula or salmon runner bean provides a consistency to the chaos of summer. In the garden, all about me grows excessively — daylight, heat, grass, thunderstorms, the buzz of insects, the fulsome songs of birds. Spinach bolts, thistle and witch grass thicken between emerging heads of ruby red lettuce, and arugula reaches its prime one day, then shoots sprays of white flowers skyward the next.

Building gardens makes us feel established here; we push out gently against the forest. Transplanting bee balm, anise hyssop, Siberian iris, rhubarb, and false indigo, given to us by friends, feels like sealing our commitment with every place we've ever traveled, with every place we've called our home.

Plants root easily, but how do I root myself? I think of the Ainu and try to speak my way into rooting in this ground, to offer my attention to the conifers, the maples, the hay-scented fern, the bear, the moose, the rhubarb, the indigo.

I stand in this fledgling garden and say aloud the names of the places that hold my stories, in my territory, my iworu. The sounds I make are barely whispers, tentative. I feel self-conscious. No one is watching. Just the trees. I turn toward the white spruce and red maples and speak their names louder, hearing my voice grow stronger with each one that comes.

Lake Champlain. Red Rocks.
Winooski River. Huntington Gorge.
Colchester Point. Nebraska Notch.
Mount Mansfield. Bolton Mountain. Camel's Hump.
Salmon Hole. Wild River. Mount Osceola.
Pemigewassett River. South Kinsman. Three Ponds.
Grand Isle. Keeler Bay.
Hurricane Ridge. Moonstone Beach. Highland Place.

The air around me inhales each sound, each exhalation of my breath. The forest breathes back into me as I breathe in between each word.

The air, the trees, echo back to me my life. It is like hearing my own name called lovingly. It is like hearing a eulogy for all that I have to lose.

Harvest

Saturday morning, I stand by the vegetable garden and a familiar honking directs my gaze up. It is the fourth flock of migrating Canada geese I have seen in the last two days. What tugs at me as I see them in a wavy wishbone heading south? The cycle of the year turning inward once again. I watch them leave and am thankful I have the good fortune to stay. My love is here, my gardens are here, my animals, my cabin, the whole of my life. In the oven, a pie made of wild apples bubbles over, cinnamon tea steeps on the wood stove. I measure the wealth of my days by scent and harvest, by the warmth of a fire and a hand that slips easily into mine.

With the turning of the leaves, the cold settles in. The crickets are barely audible at night and the sun pulls away from our meadow by five in the afternoon. Light grows dense and golden, yellow pin cherry leaves dapple meadow grass. Still, twenty-five blue morning glories opened today and pale pink hollyhocks bloom without a hint of fading.

One year has passed since we were handed the deed to our land. Under this autumn sky, I begin to understand my youthful desire to leave family and home as a yearning to be a denizen of the planet, not a person of a specific neighborhood or even of a specific family. For the first time in many years, I have no desire to leave in fall. On the autumnal equinox, we gather friends to a potluck supper. Night falls, and we stand in a circle around the fire. As I watch the rising smoke, I promise myself to kindle the home fires in honor of the voices that speak to me in these woods and from my ancestral past. I listen to the geese and do not wonder where my next migration will be.

An Apache man once told the anthropologist Keith Basso that he repeated the names of wild places aloud simply because "they are good to say."

They are good to say. And we need to say the names of our wild places – chant them, sing them, call to them literally – so that their sounds flow easily off our tongues, become a part of the daily language we speak. In my sleep, on my woods walks, as I drive my car to work, I practice calling to the wild places being cut, flooded, and dried up. Deep in the forest, at the edge of the lake, on the banks of a river where wild leeks grow, on the top of the bare mountain summit, saying all the names of the things I love is the beginning of breaking a deafening silence and rooting myself in my home, the earth.

Highland Place, West Corinth, Home by A. Bergeron

---

* Snyder, Gary. *The Practice of the Wild*. Gary Snyder. New York: Farrar, Strauss, and Giroux, 1990, p. 93.

Cynthia Travis
River of Kin

Author's note: This piece is excerpted from my forthcoming book *Atlas of Sorrow: A Natural History of Empire and Family*. The book is a family memoir that links the ecological devastation of empire with personal and global events. It explores how the trauma of the Natural World shapes our reality and our perception of reality, and how sexual trauma cascades through multiple generations.

In 1939, for fifty thousand dollars, my grandfather purchased five thousand acres of raw land along the Colorado River in Blythe, California, where Arizona begins and the river bends south toward Mexico. We used to joke that at the time, Beverly Hills was for sale; the Palos Verdes Peninsula was for sale; and the San Fernando Valley, as well: all are now sprawling suburbs of Los Angeles, worth untold millions.

The land my grandfather bought was known at the time as 'swamp and overflow land,' reclaimed by local farmers through a system of levees constructed by dynamiting the riverbanks and throwing in pilings and mesh to block debris in order to redirect the river's flow into a narrow, straightened course. In 1935, Hoover Dam had been completed about two hundred miles upriver and the wild Colorado was permanently subdued. These days we understand 'swamp and overflow' to mean wetlands and marshes, meanders and oxbows, rich in the wildlife and water-nourishing biome of a natural river. But my grandfather and father were in a hurry: they weren't thinking about the health of the river or the longevity of the soil. They wanted a place for German Jews to escape to where they could grow food to feed their families, and they wanted to make money. (Ironically, since my father wasn't eligible for military service, he spent WWII constructing Internment Camps for Japanese Americans.)

For the sixty-plus years of my family's tenure in the desert of eastern California, on the banks of the Colorado River, outside the small, homely town of Blythe, the story of the place began with us. The land

and the river were props. The story was one of wresting abundance from a bleak and lifeless landscape through the triumph of technology. But desolation can be deceiving. Places that seem empty in the eyes of a stranger are actually brimming with complexity. Now, reading myth fragments from the ancient peoples of that harsh desert place is like falling out of an empty box adrift in a dark sky and tumbling into a galaxy of relationships.

Standing on the riverbank on the land that was briefly ours, the view to the East is silent. Neither roads nor fields interrupt the clusters of arrow weed and mesquite. It belongs to the Colorado River Indian Tribes, an alliance of people from ancient riverine cultures who have thrived in the area for thousands of years, primarily Mohave—the Water People. According to Native accounts, American troops arrived after the murder of a white man who had shot a Mohave boy for teasing his child. The people who settled on the reservation were survivors of sickness and slaughter whose forbears had once thrived for a hundred miles up and down the river. They must have watched in horror from the shore of their reservation east of the river as my grandfather, father, aunts and uncles strung chains between tractors and pulled down the cottonwoods and the willows, killed the rattlesnakes, and drove out coyotes, mountain lions, foxes, raccoons, pheasants and beavers. The land was leveled. The river grew quiet.

Just past the ranch, on the mesa at the Northwest edge of the Palo Verde Valley, are the mysterious intaglios created by prehistoric Yuman people. It's said that the rock drawings tell the Yuma creation myths and were crafted in places where certain historical events took place, where healings occurred, or where young healers and leaders received their medicine. It seems the petroglyphs were likely also dancing grounds and may have been places of mourning for deceased warriors or beloved members of the community. One of the intaglios depicts a man nearly two hundred feet tall, standing next to a mountain lion or perhaps a coyote, and a figure with a spear aimed at fish that swim at his feet. Today, from that dry, gravel canvas above the river, one hears only the wind as it sings through the chain-link fence, and the silence of missing stories that wait, patiently crouching in the arrow weed, or hanging suspended from the flowering tips of Palo Verde trees. The intaglios can best be seen from above, far away: they are visible to birds and journeying humans who traverse the sky to read the messages tattooed on Earth's wide arms. Maybe this is how the dead and the land watch over the place to protect its meaning.

My father was enamored of the Green Revolution. He thought it would solve world hunger. He had a degree in chemical engineering and always said that organic and non-organic chemicals were identical. Everything was reducible to its basic mathematical expression. Organic farming was nonsense. A few months before he died, my father wrote a letter to my children describing the early days of the farm that seem prescient now—he intuited the result of their labors but stopped short of recognizing causality: *We 'rented' geese to weed the fields and we even tried spreading blocks of frozen ladybugs… to eat bad bugs, as soon as the ladybugs thawed out. We tried to avoid putting poison on the crops. We dealt with our share of rattlesnakes and rabbits. Beavers were frequently found in the larger canals. But sadly, there were fewer and fewer wild deer and pheasants to be seen as the land was put into production… The shores of the Colorado River were neatly rip rapped. Cement-lined canals and drainage ditches did their jobs.*

These days the agricultural run-off, laden with chemicals and salt, still trickles into Mexico about ninety miles south. The water is undrinkable and can barely be used for agriculture. But the real damage can't be seen: the free flow of water affects wind and, therefore, weather. In earlier times, as now, the pace of currents that slowed at the end of summer or hurtled seaward in spring would move nutrients in ways that aquatic and riverine plants depended on, adapting their root structure, exudates and rate of maturation accordingly: tender shoots appeared at just the right time for wobbly-legged baby deer; aquatic plants protected fish eggs and tadpoles; overhanging branches of plants kept the water cool for all the Selves that depended on a consistent range of temperature.

My father and his partners added a feedlot and a dehydrator that pressed alfalfa into pellets to export to Japan to feed cattle there. In its heyday, the feedlot held forty-thousand cattle packed together in its fetid rectangles. They arrived in boxcars, herded with electric prods into a narrow chute whose iron bars held them fast as they were castrated, and their horns trimmed while they were being inoculated, branded, and tagged, all without anesthesia. The memory-scent of burning fur and skin; the sound of their hoofs sliding beneath them as they struggled to gain purchase in the gravelly dust; their snorts of terror as they struggled and writhed, ask me to consider how it is that my family came to torture cattle so we could sell and eat them.

My father convinced his family, his in-laws and friends to invest in the feedlots and dehydrator, and they did, but the price of cattle collapsed and everyone went bust. Eventually, my father repaid the original investments, but the prolonged crisis sundered the family and eroded friendships. Then, in 1972, the Department of the Interior, the Department of Commerce and the Bureau of Indian Affairs sued some of the ranchers in the Palo Verde Valley on behalf of the Tribes, arguing that, prior to the closure of Hoover Dam, when the river overflowed its banks in the spring, riverfront land now in California rightfully belonged to Arizona and, therefore, was part of the Colorado River Indian Reservation. My father and his partners went into Chapter 11 bankruptcy. The lawsuit lasted eighteen years. In 1987, California Magazine ran an article entitled '*Travis' Last Stand*', decrying the injustice being done to my father and other landowners in the valley. My father felt vindicated. I was appalled. In the end, the Tribes were awarded 1,500 acres at the heart of the ranch. By then, nearly all the remaining acreage had been sold. Looking at the jumble of boulders and brush across the river, my father would shake his head in frustration and say, *The Indians are happy just to hold on to the land and not do anything with it!*

The Mohave were *Pipa Aha Macau* – the people along the river, instructed by their creator to protect it.[1] They knew themselves as dreamers, as the People of the Water who had settled in that valley at least as far back as 1150 A.D. They traded with tribes as far away as the Gulf of Mexico and the Pacific Coast and could run an easy hundred miles a day at a leisurely jog through the desert heat. They believed that the First People had appeared in the form of birds and animals who thought, spoke and behaved as human beings. They dreamed the names of their twenty-two clans and all their powers of governance and healing, including the songs that cured illness and more than three hundred Bird Songs sung in sequence that described the path of the ancestors and mapped exactly how to survive in the desert.

For my father, his partners and the family, the ranch was a place of struggle and strife; a place to try to make money; the place that shattered the family and became the central challenge of my father's life—his heartbreak and his triumph in the Sisyphean struggle to redeem himself in the eyes of his father and siblings, and to prove that mechanized farming could conquer world hunger.

Seventy years later, in 2015, my mother and I returned for one last visit to the ranch. My father had been dead for three years. My mother brought along my father's briefcase—a worn, leather satchel etched with his initials in gold at the top. I don't know what papers were in it, if any. It seemed more like a talismanic stand-in for my father. We left it on the back seat when we stopped for a snack. When we returned to the car with our bags of over-salted pistachios and over-sweetened dried fruit, the briefcase was burning. A tendril of white smoke twisted up from a dark-edged circle the size of a bullet hole.

Late that afternoon, at the ranch, as we stood on the bank of the quiescent river, a coyote appeared on the opposite shore—the first and only time I saw a coyote there, long after I thought my family's story in that place had ended. I watched her trot from the water's edge into the cattails and back again, bathed in the wet glow of late afternoon, lapping her reflection as she bent to the water to drink. Like my parents, coyotes mate for life. Seeing the coyote confirmed three things I already knew: this was my mother's last visit to the place where her life with my father had begun; tricksters are alive and well, moving between worlds as they always have; the unexpected and the possible are twins.

Before Blythe, the extended family lived in Tulsa, in the homes they had built next door to each other. In Blythe, my Aunt Ava and Uncle Mike were sent to the far, dry hills at the north end of the ranch, at the periphery of the family story. My Aunt Elaine and Uncle Ron moved to an airless adobe in town, and my parents settled into their mint-green cottage next to the irrigation canal. Everyone except my father grew to hate the ranch, the town, the weather, the landscape, my grandfather's dream, and, sometimes, each other. One by one, they fled back to Los Angeles. None of them had a relationship to the land or the river other than to try to make a living from it. Eventually, my father bought out his parents and siblings. When the ranch at last recovered financially, the rest of the family accused him of swindling them. Angry letters were exchanged. Over the years, a superficial détente was established, but the rift in the family never really healed.

It's odd how patterns of closeness and betrayal get passed along: it happened between my grandfather and great grandfather; my father and my grandparents on both sides who had gone into business with him; and, ultimately, between my father and me. Shortly before his death, my father accused me of plotting with our accountant and lawyers to steal control of his money. Our relationship never healed. The ranch ricocheted between profit and bankruptcy as regularly as the river had once flooded her banks. But my grandfather, ever the shtetl boy who wanted his family close and well fed, and my father, who inherited the pipe-dreaming gene, were convinced that success was just around the corner, and it was, in a way, though they underestimated the number of corners by several orders of magnitude.

On the other side of the river, Mohave tradition held that information and skill were *ineffectual* unless they were dreamed. *All noteworthy success in life was obtained through dreaming.*[2] The 'great dreams' occurred in utero. At birth, the dream was forgotten, then dreamed again in adolescence. During the precious days of a girl's first menstruation, a warm pit was prepared for her to sleep in so she could dream: these dreams were understood as omens of the future. Song cycles containing instructions, prophecies and origin lore were dreamed by singers. There were thirty cycles, each with as many as two hundred songs, recounting the tribe's Great Stories. No matter if the Mohave had splintered or settled in remote locations, *They thought of themselves as one people regardless of where they lived.*[3]

In the early 2000's, the California Department of Fish and Game decided they wanted to buy what was left of the ranch and turn it into a wetlands preserve. Developers from Arizona wanted it, too: they promised quick money and a choc-a-block retirement community of mobile homes on manicured cul-de-sacs with happy snowbirds plying the streets in golf carts. My arguments in favor of Fish and Game weren't having much effect.

On the Tuesday before Thanksgiving, I gathered with seven women on the banks of the river in the middle of the ranch to make offerings on behalf of that place: my grandmother, Molly, my mother's mother, had told me in a dream to come thank the water. The following morning, I was to meet my parents to decide on the fate of the land. I made a feast and brought my grandmother's fine china to serve it on. Silver candlesticks. Loaves of bread. The wooden owl that my grandmother carved out of a solid chunk of walnut: it perched on the white tablecloth that we spread on the ground. This was to be a Thanksgiving *Tashlich* and it was important to do it up right: *Tashlich* is a ceremony that is usually performed at Rosh Hashanah, the Jewish New Year, which takes place in the fall. Paired with Yom Kippur, the Day of Atonement, these are the holiest days in the Jewish calendar, known as the Days of Awe. During this time, one apologizes for wrongdoing in hopes of wiping the slate clean so as to be 'inscribed in the Book of Life' for another year. For *Tashlich,* one goes to a body of water and tosses in pieces of bread that carry our regrets and our prayers: we cast the regrets upon the water and ask that they return as blessings. Each of us in turn prayed in our own way.

How sweet and unfamiliar to stand at dusk with a circle of women, two days before Thanksgiving, tossing in chunks of bread, watching each piece as it dissolved and sank below the surface. In the fading light, I asked that the hearts of my parents, whose decision would determine the future of the place, be softened towards the possibility of repairing the river so that it could once again flow towards Mexico, untroubled along this stretch. I asked that it become a place of refuge where the birds and the animals and the reptiles that once were plentiful could repopulate in protected exuberance. I asked solace for the spirits of the people who had lived there long before we ever knew of the place, especially the young Native woman who they say was raped by a white man, one of the newcomers, her ravaged body left in the shallows. I apologized for Hoover dam because what made it possible for my father and grandfather to find a homestead for their dreams and their own restless souls had cost the river her freedom, and dozens of workmen their lives, and the people and land and animals of the United States and Mexico the water they had relied on for centuries.

I thanked the river for the rattler we saw swimming one time, its head barely lifted above the surface, its body like a gently undulating stick sending out tiny ripples— glad to see it from the car and not from the water, in spite of the heat that day. To the river, I said *thank you* for the inner tube rides. When we were first married, my husband and I would smoke a fat joint, jump in the water and float all day, hugging the shore, towing six-packs of beer with a rope so they'd stay cool in the water. One time I came face to face with a beaver, so close we almost kissed. I thanked the burrowing owls for teaching us how to spot them as they peeked up from their nests in the ground. And the barn owl who flew close at twilight when we stood on the ruined tracks, and the owl grazed the top of my head with the tip of his wing—the brush of air as he swooped past; how enormous he was up close; the immense cape of his shadow as it slid down my face to my neck, brushing the top of my shoulders.

How must it have felt to the land to host our feast, that night of women and offerings? What must it have been for the river to receive that bread and those prayers after sixty years of enduring the violence of my family's dream?

In the morning I met my parents at the park. We sat at a picnic table of molded plastic, its bright colors all faded to sherbet pink. We were glad for the warmth of the sun on our backs as we talked.

Well? said my father. *We had a lovely picnic,* I told him. *We blessed the land and the river and said thank you.* Fifteen minutes later, my parents agreed that the ranch should be sold to Fish and Game. Now, of the feedlot, the office, the dehydrator and the train tracks, only rubble remains. Someone else lives in my parents' green bungalow. In place of alfalfa and cotton, Fish and Game planted neat rows of Cottonwoods and Palo Verde. Rattlesnakes returned, along with ducks and deer. Hoover Dam is still there. And so are the coyotes.

1 O'Neil, Francis L. and Paul W. Wittmer, eds. *Dreamers of the Colorado: The Mojave Indians, Part 2: Their Culture and Arts.* Farmington, Connecticut: Tunxis Community College Publication, 2013. Print.
2 Ibid
3 O'Neil, Francis L. and Paul W. Wittmer, eds. *Dreamers of the Colorado: The Mojave Indians, Part 2: Their Culture and Arts.* Farmington, Connecticut: Tunxis Community College Publication, 2013. Print.

Suzette Clough
Remembering Our Original Pattern Ancestors:
Painting as a Way of Knowing Earth

Visual Language is our first language, our Mother tongue, the language we dream in. Visual Language is the Language of Earth, the material world, of all living systems.

When I was twelve, three things happened that shook my world. My family left the ochre sandstone and eucalyptus bush of Sydney to live in the slate grey moors of Yorkshire in the north of England, then remigrated to Australia nine months later. I changed school four times that year and was initiated into painting by my high school art teacher —Mrs. Eve.

In our first lesson Mrs. Eve asked us to randomly sketch a pattern using wax crayons. I scribbled a flame-like pattern using red, yellow and white then put a wash of black paint over the top. The black paint momentarily obscured the crayon marks, but as I watched, the waxy colours reappeared even more brightly through the pool of watery darkness.

In that moment I had an experience of recognition. I felt, heard, and sensed the painting speaking to me. On some obscure intuitive level, I knew that the painting was alive, had a voice and it *wanted* to speak to me.

Later, I understood the painting was telling me an essential truth about my own inner nature: that my soul would always be present, no matter what was overlaid on top. I had an embodied experience that 'I' could not be covered up no matter what was done to me or in later years what I did to myself. I was not able to say these words to anyone, but some part of me knew that I had been spoken to by a wiser, more ancient voice, a voice that was *born* and spoke through the life of the painting.

In the decades since this experience, I have moved in and out of my creative process tracking this voice and often failing. When I tried to direct the paint to look the way I wanted, the painting acquired a feeling of 'as-ifness'—became a facsimile of itself. When I allowed the authentic materiality of the painting to show itself by becoming present with my own body—a process Donna Haraway describes as 'sympoeisis,' *creating with*—something else happened. Paintings flowed as a river, or as a view of Earth from above, from within, from beyond.

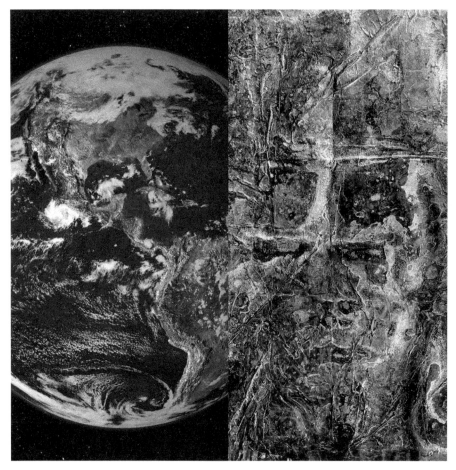

Left: NASA GSFC Earth from 22,000 km, NASA Earth Observatory, 13:02 14 Llu 2007 Right: We are Ocean, We are Light, 15cm x 10cm, Watercolour paper, acrylics, gold dust by S. Clough

When I stopped trying to paint 'something' and opened to *listening* to the voice of the painting, *Her* body stories arrived. Guardian spirits emerged from the pigments; rock beings protecting the sacred interior of cave and womb came through onto the body of the paper, sloughed-off beeswax serpent skins shed themselves as actual living material forms from the canvas to floor. The Great Mother's tools showed up: stone axes, cloaks, blankets and cups, star bodies birthing whole galaxies, hollowed-out bones, baobab ancestor tree spirits, mycelial sporic tapestries, intricate webs, beehives, prehistoric animal guides. The Devas of Earth were calling out from beyond the veil to trust our original pattern Ancestors.

Left: Sandstone markings – Standley Chasm – NT Australia Right: Cosmogenesis, Detail – 150 cm x 125 cm Watercolour paper, graphite powder, graphite power, natural pigments, gold dust, inks, water, Spirit by S. Clough

The unconscious, unscripted, co-created paintings that emerged from this co-participant call-and-receive practice are energy stories that

Left: Giant Fig Tree buttress roots – Bangalow Rainforest NSW Right: Earth Papers – wax paper, acrylics, natural pigments, gold dust by S. Clough

track the in-between, watery crossings from one side of the quantum membrane to the other. These paintings arise as visual pattern-holders of Earth's DNA, the generative blueprint of the patterns held in creation itself. The visual stories that emerge through watery layers of natural pigment on canvas coalesce into a shared pattern kinship that remembers Earth's own body and our bodies. This pattern language is the visual thread connecting us to everything and everything to us. The paintings tell visual narratives that remember us into relatedness.

We are all part cloud, part star, part leaf, part tree, part animal, part fungi, part living soil. Her body is our body, our body is Her body. These patterns are our Ancestors telling a visual narrative that shares the same language as Her body and all that has been born, will ever be born through the body of Earth.

What I understand now is that the act of painting can be an actual liminal portal, a crossing-over place to the multiverse of Creation itself where the principles of reciprocity, mutuality, and awe reign—where life continues to birth itself through patterns that have visual and energetic consistency with all Matter.

Painting is a way of listening to the voice of Earth—to Spirit, to spirits, to our own bodies, to the bodies of others, dead, alive, human, animal, to light bodies, air bodies, mineral bodies, terrestrial bodies, cosmic bodies, animate and seemingly inanimate bodies. All bodies that communicate the sporic, tentacular intelligence of the multiversal, multidimensional mycelial entangled web of life that we live in, and lives within us.

Painting is a way of knowing Earth. Painting is a way of remembering our Ancestors, coming to know ourselves not as bystanders witnessing our species teetering on the edge of ecological catastrophe, but as activators who share cosmic DNA with Creation itself. We are made of the same complex luminous fabric as the Universe. Painting is a way to know this truly—in every shining filigree of our Being.

Valerie Wolf
Dreaming the Future

In 2007, I undertook a solo vision quest on Joseph Mountain in the beautiful Wallowa Valley of eastern Oregon, having felt intuitively called by my Spirits to seek guidance in protecting the Earth and securing a better future for all who dwell here. As one who has walked the shamanic path for twenty-two years, as an Earthkeeper, someone who attempts to discern what is best for the Earth and all beings here and live accordingly, I was now being paged by my Spirit team to receive messages on this topic. I had a sense that I was making this journey on behalf of the Earth and my spiritual communities, as well as myself. Too many humans did not know how to live here properly; far too many seemed oblivious to the evidence that we were destroying our planet. I did not know what it would take to stop this. How could I do more, what were the right actions that could heal the planet's suffering? I hoped a Spirit would come to me in vision and offer something to bring back to my community.

I was not in the best shape to make such an arduous journey being fifty-four and with my backpacking days more than twenty years behind me. The climb would be seven miles up a steep rocky trail with a pack and water to a peak just under ten thousand feet. I would have no companions as a safety net. I called my spiritual mentor before I headed up the trail to let her know my intentions and she agreed to hold me spiritually, even though her wolf was dying at the time. Quests are unpredictable and can be grueling. As I moved into the Spirit World, I wanted a human anchor to support me in facing whatever might come.

As I steadily hiked the trail, I felt in every being around me—every tree, stone, cloud, chipmunk, spring—a loving consciousness and a sense that they were all on this pilgrimage with me. It was as if the quest itself had awakened the Spirits of this land. I had experienced the same profound love on my first vision quest in 1994 in Joshua Tree. Here was this flow of love emerging from the Earth again at the beginning of this spiritual trek holding me, encouraging me, guiding me. I was honestly terrified to make this journey for this was bear, mountain lion and rattlesnake country. Yet I also trusted the Spirits entirely. If trouble or injury awaited me on the high peaks, I accepted the necessity of it. I had lived and worked long enough with the Spirit World to know my Ancestors and the Spirits would keep me safe in every way they could.

The upward hike was even more grueling than I had imagined. A high waterfall required hurtling myself across a five-foot stream at its base where it tumbled down a steep drop-off. I just barely made the jump, my feet sliding and staggering on the muddy edge of the fast-moving stream before they found safety. When I turned to look back, I discovered a couple at the fall's edge debating worriedly whether to go forward, having observed my bold, precarious leap. Smiling ruefully, they shouted that they were turning around here as the falls seemed too dangerous to cross.

Within an hour, I had to climb over several downed trees whose trunk widths were taller than me. The angled slope made this just as treacherous as the slippery falls but after tossing my pack over first, I was able to scramble over each challenging barrier. A few miles more brought me to a spring where I soaked my swollen feet and sponged my aching knees, and listened to a friendly fly inform me that my boots weren't tied tightly enough, that my joints needed the support of a firmer fit. Thank you, Fly!

After a full seven hours of hiking, I stumbled into a meadow at the top of Joseph Mountain, and stood among tall pines gazing out over the five-mile stretch of Wallowa Lake and the green forests below. I dropped down to the Earth, resting and observing the open meadow with its sprawl of scrub sage and the rocky peaks rising up before me. I noticed a young pine broken in half in between two tall mature ones. Although the top of this pine was split and hanging, the tree was healthy and vibrant. I marveled that a being so severely injured could still thrive and felt as if the Elder trees were watching over her. I felt broken too, felt that all of us humans were deeply wounded in our hearts and minds. Perhaps we too could still thrive with proper tutelage.

An old man and his dog arrived briefly, and we chatted. He asked if I would be camping here, and I evasively answered I had not decided yet. I did not trust men in the wild, particularly not men who would know I

Joseph Mountain in the distance, Oregon by V. Wolf

was alone in the shadowy night that was fast approaching. But he seemed kind enough and I did not feel in danger. I asked if there were any bear troubles up here, and he said he had never encountered one on the mountaintop and that he did this hike three times a week. I had traveled through a long series of switchbacks as I climbed the seven-mile trail but he told me there was a two-mile path he used that went pretty much straight up and down, and only took two hours. He confessed he had met with mountain lions on a few occasions but they had never threatened him, just followed him with what he felt was curiosity more than predatory intentions. I felt my heart stall a bit at this information, imagining myself stalked by lions. I quickly tuned back into the lovingness that I still felt floating around me and my anxiety eased. The man waved goodbye and hiked briskly back down the mountain. A part of me wished I was going down the straighter, easier path too before the light ended, and not having to spend a night alone in hours of darkness with no tent. But I stayed, committed to the feeling in my body that said I belonged here now, whatever might come.

I created my medicine wheel out of a few small grey stones, made tobacco offerings, then set up my blue sleeping bag in a circle of small sage plants. I watched the sun pull the light off the lake and the shadows drop into everything. I offered four rounds of prayer, one each half hour, as guided by my Spirit council. A vast silence seemed to hold everything in expectation. I settled into the long quiet that I have come to love on quests. After an hour or so, the Spirits encouraged me to rest as there would be work to do later. I slept briefly, dreaming that I was explaining to one of my students that when a deer comes in a dream we must observe the deer's behavior so we will know what message it brings. Suddenly the sound of drums awakened me, an ancient Native American four-beat rhythm. Had Native people arrived below in the campground at the base of the mountain or perhaps someone who knew this pow-wow rhythm? I was deeply moved that drummers were with me now, felt the hunger within me for this ancient song pounding through the forest. This strengthened my resolve to hold steady despite waves of fear that sometimes washed over me like a small tsunami. My Ancestors were letting me know that I was welcome here.

As the stars offered their focused beacons in the charcoal sky, I felt their presence; how alive they were! They too kept company with me, embracing me in the same abiding love I had treasured coming up the trail. I felt I was in the stars, had never been so close to them, so fully with them. Tears of awe opened my tender worried-about-the-Earth heart and my own affection flowed out to everything around me. I loved this Earth so much! How lucky I was to be in the forested wild with my beloved Earth Mother. I felt so grateful for this mountain solitude peopled by Spirits. I hunkered down into my sleeping bag as a chilling wind picked up and lay down to simply gaze at my Ancestors, the stars.

Hours and hours passed as I lay awake on the dark Earth. Spirits arrived and offered personal messages on my own growth and healing, which I greatly appreciated. But for the bigger question of how to help the Earth, I waited patiently, knowing the Spirits work in their own time and ways and that one cannot rush or force contact. The night was calm now except for the sound of running hooves at one point, which made me wonder if a deer was being chased by a mountain lion. I was glad it was too dark to tell.

The vision that I was seeking arrived shortly before sunrise.

A Spirit made of smoke floats in the air before me. I sit up to see him more clearly, and he leaps from sky to Earth, and now stands in front of me. He is larger than me, looks almost like a lion, or a Griffin, a bit shape-shifty and not clearly definable. I am given information by my Spirits that he is one of the guardians of the Earth. After sitting a moment in respectful silence, I ask: what is our future and what can we humans do to meet it? How can we bring healing to our poisoned planet? He responds in the voice of an oracle. "You have destroyed the precious waters of the Earth." I think of our human-made chemicals, oil spills, pesticides, pharmaceuticals, all leaking into the aquifers, rivers, lakes, and seas. Have we destroyed them entirely already or is he talking of the future here?

Again his resonant voice echoes through the surrounding forest. "See now what will come."

He opens his great mouth in a mighty roar and fire pours out; flames spread across the Earth destroying forests, homes, people and animals. A second blast of his voice and a fierce wind births tornadoes and hurricanes that spin across the land, shattering everything in their path. The Griffin calls out a third time and great floods sweep away whole towns and their inhabitants. With his last roar, stones roll from his huge mouth, and avalanches, Earthquakes, and volcanoes crush and bury everything around them.

I am shocked by these violent, deadly scenes and cry out, "Is there nothing we can do to stop this future from coming?"

"No."

Grief-stricken, I struggle inwardly, searching my own mind for some way these disasters can still be prevented. "Shall I speak of this to others, warn them, so that perhaps the humans will change?" I suggest hopefully.

"Not yet. They need to learn the consequences of their actions first."

Distraught, I plead one last time for a reprieve. "Is there nothing to be done by the humans that can alter this fate?"

"If the humans were to cry tears of compassion, for the Earth, for all the beings they have harmed, for themselves in their foolishness, these tears would replenish and heal the waters."

But humans would not cry such tears yet, I believed, for we were still too arrogant, too greedy, too ignorant of the full consequences of our behavior. My own tears surged now. Broken-hearted, angry that our reckless, thoughtless human ways had led us to this place, I watched as the Griffin disappeared, his grey smoke form turning to black ash, a dark snow drifting down to the hard, dry land.

I was stunned and disheartened by the Griffin's fierce message. It was not what I had expected or hoped for. I was wary too, initially, for I had never met a Spirit quite like this before. I did not want to believe that what he said would come true. Yet a part of me already knew, what my own Spirits now gently confirmed: the Griffin was no trickster Spirit, teaching with pranks and lies, but one of the truth- tellers.

I finished out the night with a sacred song calling on the Ancestors for guidance in how to meet so bleak a future. Environmentalists and indigenous people had been fighting for years with our governments and corporations to stop the poisoning and warming of the Earth. Might these efforts save us from such a devastating future? If not, what else would it take? And how many years would pass before we humans would come to that tender-hearted place of remorse for all the harm that we have done here, all the injustice we have inflicted upon other species, the lands, the waters, one another?

When dawn came, I placed my Pendleton Circle of Life blanket on my shoulders and sang a welcome to the returning light. I left an offering of a turtle necklace on the blasted tree with one last prayer for healing for us all. Then I descended the mountain uneasily, knowing I did not have enough water for the trip and that my body was still battered from the hard climb the day before. I hiked the direct, steeper trail down hoping to save time but it was equally grueling, every step a jolt to my agonized joints and ravaged muscles. The last hour of the trek I cried most of the way due to pain in my body and the grief of my vision. But there was also a moment when the Spirits made up a silly song with the words "Walk like a Bear." We sang this over and over to distract me from the terrible knives in my joints. I laughed, grateful that the Spirits were keeping me going when I wanted to give up.

By the time I staggered to the trail's end, I had so much rampant inflammation I begged two middle-aged campers to give me a ride from the lake's edge back to my car at the trailhead. They glanced at me suspiciously but when I explained how much agony I was in from my four-hour hike down the mountain, they kindly provided a lift. Afterwards I drove to the Lake knowing I needed ice for all the swelling and that the chilled waters would provide it. I gratefully soaked my limbs and my suffering eased. What I didn't know yet was that these were not mere muscle and joint aches of over-exertion but the first flare-up of the rheumatoid arthritis that would shatter my life within the next few years and teach me that human contamination of the Earth, waters and air was rapidly increasing autoimmune diseases. Our human bodies were poisoned unavoidably, too, and the most sensitive among us were already paying a painful price.

I was allowed by the Griffin to share this vision with my mentor but several years would pass before I was given permission to speak of these prophecies with a few of my students in my shamanic training program. Only now am I requested to share it publicly with a wider audience, now that so much of it has come to pass. Each day there is more climate chaos, blizzards and hurricanes caused by global warming, Earthquakes caused by fracking, dying sea lions and other creatures whose territories can no longer provide enough food due to damaged and diminished ecosystems. Many creatures, like the bees, are wasting from diseases caused by the deadly chemicals we have poured upon the plants. Oil spills are frequent; radiation is steadily leaking into the sea, air and land from nuclear power plants. The horror of our current reality has more than matched the Griffin's prophecy.

As the truth of the Griffin's predictions unfolded across the globe, I continued to ask for dreams to help us know how to transform this fate. In 2013, I received this dream.

A young man has been harming others. I firmly move him away from his girlfriend, and tell him we will not allow him to hurt her ever again. He sneers angrily—"Oh, yeah?"—daring me to stop him. I move closer to him and stare fiercely into his hostile eyes to show him how serious I am. He yells at me to get away from him.

"There's a part of me that would like to," I confess, "but another part wants to lean in and help you change. As it stands now, you are not even fully human yet."

"Do no harm." I speak these words to him slowly and emphatically. "Do you know why the native people say this?"

He shrugs sullenly, as if he could care less about anything I might say. "Because we are all family here, we are here to protect one another, to help one another." He looks away, still feigning indifference, but I sense he is now listening. "If you allow us to help you, we might be able to turn you into a true human being."

I say this in a half-joking manner, but I am serious. This community of people who know how to take care of the Earth, who have learned not to do any unnecessary harm, are his best hope for healing his angry, wounded heart.

My understanding of our global culture at this time is that it is predominantly shaped and controlled by an immature wounded masculine energy. We humans are not grown up yet, do not know how to live wisely and compassionately with our resources and one another. Some people know more about what might be possible than others. Much of this knowledge seems to be held by certain elders and communities who are committed to guarding the Earth. Communities can do what individuals cannot as this dream suggests. Communities can heal individuals who are doing harm to others due to their own unhealed trauma. Communities can stop fracking and block the Keystone pipeline. Communities can heal our poisoned waters, lands and air, by holding companies accountable for the effects of their actions, by refusing to allow them to continue environmentally unsound practices. Communities can stop our politicians from sacrificing our long-term future for short-term benefits for the extremely wealthy minority.

I also believe that the Spirits who have been with us since the very beginning of our human journey offering to teach us how to live in right relationship to our ecosystems and other species, are essential to whatever possibilities might emerge. Corrective visions, such as the one I had on Joseph Mountain, have come for centuries to communities and their seers, shamans, and medicine people when people were no longer living in right relationship to the Earth.

There once was a Lakota holy man called Drinks Water who dreamed what was to be; this was long before the coming of the Wasichus

(Europeans). He dreamed that the four-leggeds were going back into the Earth and that a strange race had woven a spider web all around the Lakotas. And he said: "When this happens, you shall live in square gray houses in a barren land and beside those square gray houses you shall starve." They say he went back to Mother Earth soon after he saw this vision and it was sorrow that killed him. You can look about you now and see that he meant these dirt-roofed houses we are living in and that all the rest was true. Sometimes dreams are wiser than waking.

Drinks Water was killed by the sorrow of his vision and I sometimes wonder if I developed rheumatoid arthritis in part because of the grief at what I witnessed of our broken human future. But I have not given up hope because of the many dreams and visions that are still coming. They have encouraged me and others to learn to live in healthier and more balanced ways.

In the high desert of Joshua Tree a few months ago, I quested once more upon the land, this time only briefly as that is all my health allowed. I asked the Griffin to come once more and offer guidance for humans. I smoked the peace pipe I have used for many years as I prayed for help. And then he appeared before me.

The Griffin floats in the air, hovering over the huge golden boulders of Joshua Tree. "Clean up your mess." he says curtly. "Then learn to take care of the Earth. That is what you are primarily here for, you see."

I was so grateful that the Griffin had returned, and for his words. His response made me believe that healing the Earth and our own broken hearts and minds is still possible. But only if we open once more to the Spirits and the Ancestors, to the Mystery itself, and return to their sane and thoughtful ways. The Plants have been on this planet more than 450 million years; the Animals have lived here more than 350 million years. Humans, in their current form as homo sapiens, have only dwelt here for 220 thousand years. Who should know more about what works here? The Plants and Animals are our Elders. These and other helpful Spirits can bring Humans back into the knowledge that we are all family here, all one being, here to take care of the Earth and one another, as the Griffin reminds us.

Dancing is one of the most ancient traditions for entering the Spirit World or bringing the Spirits down to us, sometimes even into our own bodies. But there are so many ways to make this essential connection. We can send a part of our Spirit into the Spirit realms with proper training in shamanic journeying. We can create artwork and masks that invite particular Spirits into our lives. Meditating, dreaming, singing, writing are all time-tested forms for communicating with the Spirits, opening our hearts and minds to their teachings as we engage these forms. The Spirits will come, will speak, will teach if we ask them to, if we receive them humbly and warmly, as our Ancestors once did. They have not given up on us yet. Once, early in my shamanic training, the Spirits said to me: "Be not ashamed to follow."

We are the youngest beings on this planet. If we seek help, if we follow the guidance of the Spirits, change and healing is still possible. Then we can say thank you, bless you and start again.

N.B.: This is an abridged version. Please see Dark Matter: Women Witnessing #2 *online for the complete essay.*

Kathleen Hellen
Out of the beringian refugium

> …what are you doing that I cannot do
> —*Black Elk Speaks*

some might cancel this appropriation, say
that I transgress, say I don't know anything,

but I see in my reflection root features: Yup'ik, Inuit, the Eastern
    Eskimo.

You see them too, when I sit with you at powwow, my face the two-
    faced axe
left in a pit, with antler rods and dart points, at the mouth of the
    Upward Sun River.

You see in me the sunrise child-girl swathed in ochre, let me visit
in the circle, find my way back to belonging. No dipnet, stick-spear, no
    fires lit
to find the oyster beds abundant. But I do what I can—lift the feather
    on the beat, gift

the drum tobacco, cleanse with sage the spaces where I tend
the sickness of this living without birdsong and the feel of dirt
    between my fingers,

sleep with legend:
how you rubbed the soldiers out, and the women on the hill made
    tremolo—which in my dreams
becomes a song of sorrow. Not a past-life wound, not karmic illness,

but a refugee of tribe, the clan of standing at the mirror, where I see
    myself a ghost, traveling
from Siberia across the frozen strait, migrating far, far away, up the
    coastal rivers to the north,
to the south, to the interior, paddling with the salmon toward the weir.

I honor wild asparagus, dandelion, the elderberry's syrup. The bitter
   roots that stay
the long winter. My teeth like yours,

like those of lions in a standstill population now extinct.

Notes

The Blackfoot tradition holds that the first Indians lived on the other side of the ocean; the Hopi people say their ancestors had to travel through three worlds to cross the ocean to a new world. Genetic evidence supports a theory that ancestors of Native Americans lived for 15,000 years on the Bering Land Bridge between Asia and North America until the last ice age ended. For hāfu—half Japanese, half European—the question of ancestors has always been problematic. I stood outside both groups as observer, never fully integrated or accepted. It wasn't until my thirties, when I began to participate in pow pow, that I recognized in features the root association: the same dark hair, the same high cheekbones, the same slant of the eyes. Something stirred, a powerful sense of belonging. Among first people, I learned that where I stood was the center of the world. I danced, made tremolo, made myself a dress of chamois.

Gillian Goslinga
Healing with Land and Ancestors

Trouble with the Land

Three times I walked away from the little house for sale perched on the side of the largest Sheepshead Crossing mesa in Cornville, whose crown had long ago been one of the many Pueblo settlements dotting mesa tops along water bodies in the Verde Valley of northcentral Arizona. On drive-by one I had seen a dark cloud hovering above the cute little house and entire road. I turned around and drove off. On drive-by two six months later—the house hadn't sold and the location was fantastic, with sweeping views of the greenbelt of Oak Creek and Sedona's famed red rocks in the distance—I parked at the mouth of the dirt road, wondering what energy had slapped my crown as soon as I had made the turn. What was wrong with this place when everything should be right? The word "meth" sprang up in my vision. I turned around and drove off. Then, another six months later, my new realtor took me to *that* land to see *that* cute little house. The house was built for a chemically sensitive person, like me, and it had good bones, she said. This third time I walked away from a contract. The house was riddled with issues and there was mold, another of my health nemeses, in the bathroom. Its front door location reversed the Feng Shui luck of the house. Then, compelled by a force that felt to me like a death wish and went against every fiber of my physical being, I entered a second contract at an adjusted price only a month later. The night I signed the deed transfer, a friend had to drive me to the emergency room, my blood pressure skyrocketing so high I thought my head was going to blow off.

There I was the morning after, financially locked into this place of darkness. Why had I signed? What had I signed up for? My Sedona New Age friends had gone from "It's an amazing vortex of light" to "This will be your last battle with darkness" and "you're going to have to learn to love more than you fear!" I didn't feel capable of that kind of love. My mother, to complicate matters, and all the way from Spain where she lives, had had her first ever vision of the Virgin

Mary over the mesa ruins above the house, not once but twice, as I was wavering atrociously in those final days. "The most beautiful light I have ever seen, so brilliant and healing, Gigi," she reported. I myself had experienced the sweetest of energies enveloping me while I walked the land. I had wanted to believe the Ancestors of this troubled place were letting me know they approved of me.

The mesa with Pueblo ruins by G. Goslinga

I had a powerful dream, too, where I walked the slope of the mesa as wild animals have for millennia, crisscrossing their narrow footpaths up to the top. A retinue of creatures gathered behind me, Pied Piper-like, in the dream. My body entered the Earth. Half in, half out, I continued to walk as though through water, except it was soft beautiful fragrant moist rich composted Earth. Behind me, the air turned to faery dust, a brilliant sparkling cloud of twinkling starlight that brought every tree, every boulder, and every creature to shimmering life.

There had been terrifying visions, as well. In a full-moon sweat lodge after I had entered the second contract, I furiously prayed for some sort of sign as to what to do. I was given a vision of a gigantic black snake with a design of red and white diamonds unfurling along its back. It lay upright and etherically on the slope of the mesa like one of those enormous city letters that greet airplanes from the sky. The snake's tail touched the back porch of the house where a skeleton Lady appeared, looking straight at me. She cut a Frida Kahloesque figure with her ash-colored bones adorned with red ribbons and her hair, also tied with red ribbons, piled on top of her skull. In her bony hands, she held a bundle of smaller bones and herbs wrapped in red cloth. Bone Lady smiled at me but my reaction was visceral and unhappy. I screamed and retched in the lodge, purging violently. As I wobbled out after that round, frightened and spent, the full moon greeted me like the benevolent Grandmother she is. I welcomed her bath of sweet, pure silver light. Impervious to human affairs, the Moon loves without condition. I pledged to her that terrible night that I would not buy. Curses and death poisoned that land and that house. I was sure of it now. Yet, inexplicably and only a week later, I found myself signing the deed. This was madness.

Staying with the Trouble

The celebrated science studies feminist and dissertation advisor Donna Haraway refuses to see our times as an Anthropocene, a time of endings, but instead as times ripe for formidable new becomings, a Chthulucene. Always the word magician, Haraway tropes the Greek world *chthonic* and its rich associations of ancient, subterranean, and underworld to spawn the metaphor of a thick and crumbly dark humus of composted histories of trauma, survival and love from which to make kin once again, not only amongst us humans but also with the nonhuman. She invites us to "stay with the trouble" long enough that we can make kin *with* these histories bringing us to the edge of extinction. Staying with the trouble means staying in place. I rolled up my sleeves to attend to all that was wrong with the house and the land, now on a mission.

The house, however, quickly became "The Little House of Horrors." There was more mold than the inspection had found. Rooms had to be stripped to their studs. Things broke randomly; even my glasses snapped in my fingers as I took them off one day. My predecessor had rigged many repairs, and the home inspector had been sloppy, missing much. My first contractor, charged with the priority task of moving the inauspicious front door, announced on our first day as we finished coffees watching a beautiful sun rise over the horizon of mesas across the valley, "I just had a coyote cross the road to your house. Haven't seen one of those in a long while!" He was thrilled, but coyote has always announced big trickster trouble for me. Accidents, reversals of fortune. I sighed, my stomach tying into even tighter knots.

I did soon after have a terrible accident, totaling my car on the switchbacks that rise up out of the valley floor behind my mesa, where car accidents are frequent. I figured the Indian wars that had been fought in this and the surrounding valleys and culminated in a Trail of Tears were at the root of the darkness hovering over the area like a cloud. I speculated the breakings at the house may be due to being built on a geopathic fault line as the mesa—and house—directly faces the youngest shield volcano on Earth, surely the geological mother of the whole valley.[2] I tip-toed around the Ancestors on the mountain thinking they were in fact angry, refusing me, the new white settler. "Fuck you" had been the energy echo from the mesa one full moon night when I led a small circle of women outside to bow to the mesa top in a display of "respect." I was not the only one to experience the angry echo. We retreated back into the house, which had become, suddenly and ironically, a fortress of safety.

Then, as only Chronos—Time—in her infinite wisdom can reveal, information started to come to me. I learned from a random handyman that there had been a Church of Satan that the FBI busted up in the 1970s, right across the Creek and on the direct visual path between my house and the shield volcano. Another helper at the house, a local, volunteered that one mesa over, people used to gather to sight E.T.s in the 1980s. The "Star Lite Ranch" sign that stubbornly clung to its weathered post on our road had been the group's meeting place for decades. I explored the canyons in between the E.T. mesa and my own, and to my amazement found a field of natural springs and the remains of a small dam, nested deep in the canyon. Hiking the mesa ruins above the house, I found three contemporary graves, two with Christian crosses, amidst the pueblo ruins. Seventh Day Adventists owned, and farmed, land on my road. My realtor had been an Adventist. The Christian presence surprised me, though it shouldn't have given the settler history and my mother's vision of the Virgin Mary.

The Pueblo ruins on the mesa above were at the hub of a large medicine wheel of sacred mountains all around, marking cardinal points on an unobstructed 360-degree horizon: Bear Mountain, Thunder Mountain, Tuzigoot, Squaw Mountain, Mingus, two "sugar loaves," one of which was a registered burial ground, and, on clear blue-sky days, the tips of the San Francisco Peaks in Flagstaff, the emergence place of the Hopi Kachinas. I had the broken pottery sherds that I found in a pile in the yard when I bought the property dated. These sherds were everywhere on the mesa slope. They held more than thirteen hundred years of memories, including of Hopi. They told of trading between five tribes across vast Southwest distances from 125 A.D. to the 1500s. I came to see the valley as a rich mosaic of composted Christian and Indigenous histories and New Age heavenly metaphysical inspiration even: the famous Drunvalo Melchizedek of *The Ancient Wisdom of the Flower of Life* fame, a New Age classic, lived on my road, too. I knew by now to wait for more to be revealed. I mused that the bad death in this valley from recent histories of violence and even Satanism was the trouble I was dealing with, imprinted on this place.

And the Sins of the Fathers Shall be Re-visited Upon the Sons (and Daughters)

The late cultural anthropologist Deborah Bird Rose, learning to see from her Australian Aboriginal teachers, writes that settler-colonial civilizations founded on death that violently and irreparably breaks the continuity of life wilds the land rather than civilizes it, as such societies claim.[3] Rose names as one of the deadliest legacies of Christian settler colonialism this "Ground Zero" phenomenological orientation to peoples and living systems where the present is wiped clean of what has come before—razed to the ground—just as Jesus Christ the Savior's birth reset calendar time to zero. In a repeating fractal of new world resurrections, settler-colonial culture breaks from the past to make room for "better", "improved" futures. My valley had experienced a ground zero.

I began to recognize in me another ground zero, the psychological temptation for us moderns to privatize our traumas to a "self" or a "nuclear family" and wipe out our own ancestral and historical inheritances. As I worked on my Little House of Horrors, I also participated in a Systemic Constellations experiential group where, like the healing circles I had been a part of in South India as an ethnographer, the wrongs and wounds of prior generations were brought into the present to heal afflictions haunting descendants. My lineages held their own houses of horrors, and these triangulated with the troubles on my land.

On both lines, there was bad death. My mother's father's older and only brother, a French aristocrat, had committed suicide within a year of returning from the trench wars of World War I where he was mustard gassed. He was still a teenager. At the height of my chemical hypersensitivity in 2013, almost seven years before I bought my house custom built for a chemically sensitive person, I had in desperation bought a gas mask just like those worn during that first world war, to help me cope with the violent chemical fumes of a new apartment, freshly painted and carpeted. I remember experiencing an anguish and terror that was primal as the fumes seared my sinuses and brain, as if my death were imminent. I bunked up in a small nook of the apartment the three nights I had to stay in that hell, struggling to breathe in that mask, feeling trapped and utterly uncomprehending, entangled with Oncle Gerard's bad death and the suffering of millions.

On my father's Dutch side, there was more bad death and also sexual violence. I had known I had sea captain Ancestors but not connected the dots with the slave trade. What I knew, proudly, was that a great grandfather had been one of Netherlands' first abolitionists. But conflict raged in the privacy of the family, with much suffering. My grandparents set up house in the old slave quarters on Curacao in the Dutch Caribbean in a demonstration of humanism when they arrived as new colonial administrators before the second world war. But there were messy affairs with slave descendants; the seventh child was born black, with sickle cell anemia, and soon died. While my young father nobly jettisoned his promising career in American oil in West Africa to clandestinely set up his own company to help the new free Algeria build its own free oil industry, in our home, the sins of his fathers still played out in terror, alcoholism and sexual abuse. He had my mother terminate two of their pregnancies, the one before me and one after, in essence killing his own children, atoning perhaps for massacre. My own life was decided at his mercy.

No wonder I had been magnetized like moth to flame to a place layered like me with bad death, sexual violence and colonial trauma. There were more crossovers between me and my land to be revealed. Almost at once, for example, a neighbor told me the prior owner of the home, a schizophrenic, had held orgies in the house. And then a cell tower was proposed for the mouth of my road that was to bring about a whole new depth of healing.

A mock-up of the proposed cell tower visual impacts on the ceremonial sight lines between the Pueblo mesa top village and the registered Chieftain burial mound. Photo by L. Wright

A Cell Tower is Proposed

On September 11, 2021, a date that recalled America's September 11th, my beloved horse Feather Spirit kicked out and broke my leg, the only harm he has ever caused me in our 18 years together.   In shock at yet another break, I was now forced to stay in the Little House of Horrors 24/7, and be with the tense energies. These hadn't left, despite the beautifying renovations and a powerful land and house blessing by traveling Tibetan monks and all the knowledge being revealed. The house creaked and cracked with mysterious energies and I still was experiencing that unpleasant hum in my nervous system when home. A month into my ordeal, I heard from a friend that a 10-story high cell tower had been approved for the mouth of our dirt road, to be planted by AT&T up against the Oak Creek greenbelt, like a flag claiming our rural and scenic valley for its wireless market territory.

The repeat colonial fractal was not lost on me. The tower's massive ganglia of antenna would be on par with the Pueblo ruins on the surrounding mesas and block the sight line between these and the ancestral burial mound on a loop of Oak Creek further down river. Birds of prey, including endangered Bald and Golden Eagles, holy to the First Peoples, hunt the chapparal groves on the mesa tops and nest in the riparian corridor immediately below. I read the landmark trilogy in *Review of Environmental Health* just published that described the biological mechanisms by which the tiny manmade 4GLTE and 5G millimeter radiation microwaves change the biophysical properties of the surrounding habitat of air in ways foreign to Earth's lower atmosphere. For insects and birds, and other flying mammals like bats, whose body sizes or parts approximate or match those wavelengths and whose body cavities are full of magnetoreceptors that naturally attune them to Mother Earth's natural electromagnetic fields, these bioengineered radiation modifications and frequencies spell confusion and direct harm, up to instant death, for example, when these beings or their body parts match in size the bioengineered waves and go into partial or full resonance.[4]

Compelled once again by a force greater than myself, I rallied the community from my couch and then my hobble leg to protest the tower.

The fractal date "11" repeated over the months.[5] On January 11, 2022, at our Cornville Community Association quarterly meeting, we confronted the cell tower executives, who had been invited by our pro-tower Board of Directors to talk sense into us, along with our county officials. The valley needed to modernize. Emergency services were hampered by poor reception. Suspicious of the executives' lawyerly phrased claim of compliance with the federally required National Environment Policy Act (NEPA) review, two of us filed a Freedom of Information Act (FOIA) request at the Federal Communications Commission (FCC). Our FOIAs turned up nothing. By April 11, 2022, we had filed our closing documents requesting NEPA environmental review at the FCC. The developer had been forced to initiate compliance. On September 11, 2022, after another round of environmental screening disclosures by the developer packed with false claims that only our feet-on-the-ground could counter, the FCC ordered the developer to open a new public window for environmental review requests. In that window, the Hopi, whom I had alerted to the impeding desecration of the sight lines from mesa to burial mound months before, could now also write to oppose. I learned then that the mesa of ruins above my house, the burial mound, and another mesa of ruins and another mound formed an ancestral geographic complex of the Hopi Bear Clan, the first clan to have settled in the valley on their Fourth World Great Migration.

Over those initial months of opposition, I discovered and nurtured in myself a fierce love, one greater than fear. I observed, just as Deborah Bird Rose had argued, that genocide and ecocide travel together in white-settler-colonial worlds. A blind self-centeredness soon gripped our valley over the tower, where the sacrifice of the green belt and its many endangered species and critical habitats was a price many were willing to pay for the convenience of a cell phone working everywhere. I received Old-West-style threat calls—you are making enemies, Gillian, watch out—and was trolled on social media. But I also found new allies, on the land. The red Hawks that nest in the Oak Creek corridor below, and hunt the chaparral groves on the mesas above, began, now with exquisite precision, to time their whistles, appearances and flyovers with my intuitive hits on what action to take next or my moments of deepest doubt. Hawk helped me trust myself and also withstand the backlash. Heart-shaped stones popped up every time I walked my mesa slope, in a reversal of my Pied Piper dream, blessing me with faery-like goodness. After months of trying to find a lawyer, my email about the "Oak Creek Case" to biologists and scientists fighting the same fight reached a lawyer with NEPA and FCC experience, who emailed me to offer *pro bono* consulting, a miracle.

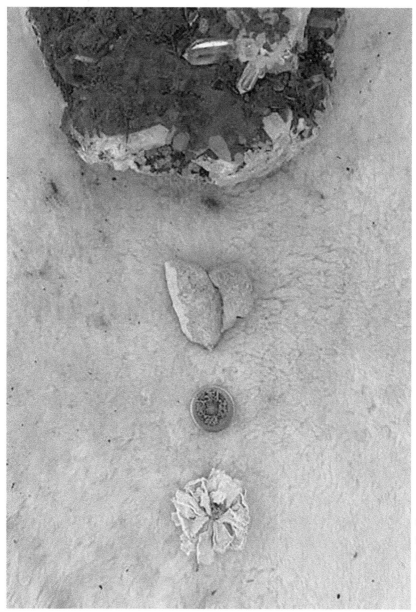

Altar by G. Goslinga

Coin, Yellow Roses, and Healing with the Ancestors

Around the June solstice, as the cell developer's NEPA compliance report deadline was coming up, I had the impulse to put Feng Shui wealth coins in a circle on my altar. The following week my constellation group decided we would explore the unbearable tension that I was still experiencing in my home. What emerged was a tableau of the aftermath of a massacre. But unexpectedly, the period was not settler-colonialism as I had long thought, but the earlier arrival in the valley of Spanish conquistadors in search of coin in nearby traditional Indian mines. No wonder the broken pottery sherds stopped abruptly in the 1500s. No wonder my mother had had a vision of the Virgin Mary above the mesa top and Christians had buried two of their dead on it. Also unexpectedly, a trauma fractal appeared in the constellation tableau of Spanish soldiers, many of whom had been conscripted from Spanish prisons to fight in the new colonies. These wretched men had apparently been left to die on the land side by side with the Pueblo people without the Catholic rites of absolution that would have redeemed their sins of pillage and rape and guaranteed their entry into Heaven. These were the angry souls still haunting the mesa. The "tyrants," as the Hopi called the Conquistadors, had in fact traveled the ancient Hopi Palatkwapi Trail here from the Hopi Mesas to the north of our valley. An historical recreation map showed the Hopi Palatkwapi Trail branching right through the proposed site of the cell tower and along my land.

The day after this constellation work a guest at a potluck at my house brought with her a gift of dried Castilian yellow roses from her garden. This felt to me like no coincidence and I invited her to present the roses to the mesa behind the house and place them on my altar. She carefully laid the roses between each coin on the circle. She had no knowledge of the history. As soon as everyone left, I researched the yellow rose and Catholicism online. One of three Rosas Mysticas in the Catholic cult of the Mother Mary, the yellow or golden rose represents the spirit of penitence. The Spaniards had brought the rose to the Americas, a symbol of the Virgin Mary, Queen of heaven. When the Virgin Guadalupe made her appearance to Juan Diego, an indentured Indian, in present-day Mexico, it had been on a mountain where the Spaniards had destroyed a native temple to the Lady of Place as was their ground-zero custom. This Virgin materialized a bouquet of yellow roses for Juan Diego to bring to the Spanish bishop to prove his vision of the Mother was authentic. Now dried Castillian Roses had materialized through my guest.

A week later I convened another constellation group. The room was filled palpably by the wild rage of the soldiers passed over for death rites by their Lord-Priests and the wild rage and grief of the Pueblo people whose loved ones had been massacred and whose homes had been demolished, bringing their way of life to a bad end. A woman had chosen to represent the land and she reported the same hum coursing through her body that I experienced at my house and on the land. The land was holding these cursed emotional energies, forcing a repeat of the trauma fractals in the present because life knows no ground-zeros and continues to invite healing until healing happens. As soon as reconciliation between victims and perpetrators happened, spontaneously, the room in turn palpably *quieted* as a feeling of grace descended upon us. Something monumental had shifted, and healed. Over the next few days, this same quiet descended on me, my house, and the land.

Becomings in the Chthulucene

When the officers of the Hopi Cultural Preservation Office (HCPO) first came down from their mesas to walk my land, a red-tailed Hawk circled above us for a long time, punctuating our conversation about the ill-placed tower siting with its piercing whistle. "Our ancestors have come," announced Leigh Wayne of the Hopi Bear Clan with a smile. We looked up to admire the majestic bird gracing us, pleased.

This first visit was followed another after the FCC in January 2022 ordered the tower developer Tilson to redo their mandated historical review, this time in consultation with the Hopi as to the scope of visual and other impacts. The developer had in its first review grievously misrepresented location and surroundings, which I had flagged to the Hopi and FCC both in my legal documentation. But the subsequent surveys and visual study determined that visual impacts on ceremonial

"lines of sight" between mesa tops and the sun calendar horizon would not be "significant." The Hopi Cultural Preservation Office officers returned to my land one last time as the Tribe's Elders gathered in Council to decide what the Tribe's final "determination" would be. To our amazement on this last visit —we should not have been surprised —Hawk flew above us as we stood at the summit of their ancestral village on the mesa above my house. Earlier, as if to raise the stakes even higher, Eagle had flown above them as they visited the adjacent ancestral village on the mesa that would directly face the tower's rings of emitters.

The following month was nail biting for me. As I sat at my desk one morning, I heard Hawk whistle outside my window. In my inbox an email from the Tribe's archeologist was waiting for me. The Hopi Elders had decided to uphold their "Finding of Adverse Effect" as Stewards of the Earth, this time purely on ecological and spiritual grounds, a bold legal move that could potentially set NEPA legal precedent in defense of Mother Earth from the harms of bioengineered microwave radiation. The FCC has fallen silent since....

Photo Caption: Delineated in the crest of the old growth cottonwoods growing along Oak Creek across my house, a dragon-like figure suddenly showed itself to me around September 11, 2022, the date the FCC re-opened the window for public comment in our NEPA case. Her head points to the left as the last cottonwood crown. Can

you also spot the heart window in the trees? Through it, in the distance, is revered Thunder Mountain, Sedona. Magic on the land by G. Goslinga.

---

[1] Haraway, Donna J. *Staying with the Trouble*: *Making Kin in the Chthulucene*. Durham, NC: Duke University Press, 2016. Print.

[2] I still haven't been able to learn the Native name for this beautiful mountain, her wide lava flows congealed into snake-like ridges when the setting sun strikes her flanks. Settlers called her "House Mountain" because of the rectangular ridge at her crown.

[3] Bird Rose, Deborah. *Reports from a Wild Country: Ethics for Decolonisation*. Sydney, Australia: UNSW Press, 2004. Print.

[4] See Levitt, B, Henry, B, Manville, A. "Effects of non-ionizing electromagnetic fields on flora and fauna" "Part 1. Rising ambient EMF Levels on the environment" (May 2021) & "Part 2 impacts: how species interact with natural and man-made EMF" (June 2021). In *Review of Environmental Health*, De Gruyter, online, https://doi.org/10.1515/reveh-2021-0026, https://doi.org/10.1515/reveh-2021-0050.

[5] See Linebaugh, Peter. *The Magna Carta Manifesto: Liberties and Commons for All*, Berkeley: University of California Press, 2008, p. 271. In a riveting passing comment, historian Peter Linebaugh observes the curious recurring number "11" in many of the major dates when conflict between commoners and capitalists erupted as the Magna Carta Manifesto got rewritten over centuries to enshrine rights of private property in land and bodies rather than the Ethos of the Commons the Manifesto originally enshrined with its sister document, The Charter of the Forest.

Julie Gabrielli
Song of the Chesapeake

> Anything we love can be saved.
> —Alice Walker

Wharton Creek, Northern Bay, watercolor by J. Gabrielli

As a resident of Baltimore for the last twenty-five years, I have spent many days on the Chesapeake, usually in a sailboat. Like many Marylanders, I am acutely aware of the state of our great estuary and her many tributaries. The Report Card issued in late 2014 by the Chesapeake Bay Foundation gives the State of the Bay a D+,[1] the same grade as in 2012.[1] Hard-won improvements in water quality were offset by losses in other areas, the impression of no progress defying the dedication of thousands of people and millions of dollars.

Returning from western Maryland on Interstate 70, I've seen a highway sign that says, "Entering Chesapeake Bay Watershed." A colorful foursquare illustration depicts a wading heron, a blue crab, a rockfish, and water waves. The Chesapeake Bay Commission and state highway departments in Maryland and Virginia have scattered them on roadways throughout the watershed. This is likely counted as a win for awareness. The signs have subheads like, "Be a friend to the Chesapeake Bay," "Please Treasure the Chesapeake," and "Conserving Waterways Protects the Bay." My heart aches at the irony of such a sign placed on a four-lane divided highway crashing through farmland and forest, where exhaust from cars and trucks spews nitrogen into the air and overheated, hydrocarbon-laden water gushes off paving into local streams. Scouring banks, this "runoff" erodes fragile soils and sends sediment into the Bay.

The Report Card says:

> The State of the Chesapeake Bay is improving. Slowly, but improving. What we can control—pollution entering our waterways—is getting better. But the Bay is far from saved. Our 2014 report confirms that the Chesapeake and its rivers and streams remain a system dangerously out of balance, a system in crisis. If we don't keep making progress—even accelerate progress—we will continue to have polluted water, human health risks, and declining economic benefits—at huge societal costs. The good news is that we are on the right path. A Clean Water Blueprint is in place and working. All of us, including our elected officials, need to stay focused on the Blueprint, push harder, and keep moving forward.

Pushing harder is the mantra of the human-centered mindset that has been destroying the Bay since French and Spanish explorers came through in the 1500s, followed by Englishman Capt. Smith's expeditions in 1607. It's time to try something new. Or something ancient. In this uncharted territory of climate change, species extinction and the general breakdown of our old cultural stories, imagining new pathways is a first step towards taking them.

I have begun dreaming about going on a "Water Walk," following the example of Grandmother Josephine Mandamin, who has circumnavigated the Great Lakes with blessing and prayer ceremonies and inspired many others to follow her lead. The shoreline of the Chesapeake Bay and its tributaries presents quite a challenge, as it measures over 11,000 miles, longer than the entire west coast of the

United States. Much of that is on private property or marshy and inaccessible. I'm intrigued with another possibility: walking the outline of the Bay watershed, an area of about 64,000 miles, in stages, as a pilgrimage.

Her surface is a threshold between visible and invisible worlds. Above: the great dome of sky, waves, wind, low-slung shoreline. Below in the brackish gradient from the Ocean: menhaden, crabs, oyster reefs, eels, skates, terrapin, mud. Above: cormorant, eagle, osprey, goose, great blue heron, ibis, pelican. Below: drowning, dredging, a riverbed gouged out by an asteroid, red algae, fossilized sharks' teeth. Above: clouds, sunsets, gales, heat, dead calm, bluster, ice, moonrise, meteor showers. Below: eelgrass, shipwrecks, molting crabs, and sunken islands that once supported towns bustling with confectioners, baseball teams, Methodist churches and cemeteries.

Last summer, I had the helm of our old 34-foot Bristol as we glided slowly under a perfect blue sky, heading southwest on a broad reach out of Eastern Bay. We'd spent a quiet night anchored in Tilghman Creek off the Miles River, tuning ourselves to sunset, stars and sunrise. Poplar Island stretched along the horizon to the left and the wide-open Bay beckoned straight ahead. The breeze was light enough that I could divide my attention between steering and daydreaming over names on the nautical chart. The two-word epics read like Haiku: Hollicutts Noose, Wild Grounds, The Hole, Airplane Wreck. Gum Thickets. Brownies Hill. Bloody Point. What events had named those places? What ghosts lingered there? A waterman might board his skipjack and head out to Bugby Bar or Choptank Lumps or Devils Hole to tong for oysters early on a cold November day. The only data he needs to set course is the feel of the breeze on his nose and cheeks and the position of the sun emerging low on the horizon.

While the watermen were dredging and tonging oysters, fishing sturgeon and trout and netting crabs, the first oil in North America gushed forth from deep beneath the land far upstream in Pennsylvania. At that time, the Civil War raged through the land: men cutting each other down over stories of power and domination, economics and ownership. The land-dwelling men were soon beguiled by the energy from coal and oil, but the Bay's watermen remained under sail well into the twentieth century. Eventually, even they could not compete with other vessels powered by the dark energy of the Underworld. Under pressure to continue feeding their families, one by one, they began retrofitting their boats, taking the heartbreaking step of cutting into wood-planked bulkheads to install loud, stinking engines.

"Civilization" spread like a crust over the land and suffocated the life out of it.

Despite their enslavement to coal and oil, the watermen still treasure their kinship with the Chesapeake herself. Skin of leather from hours under the merciless sun. Arms and backs sinewy from scraping for peelers in eelgrass. They speak of the wily Jimmy with respect, as of a complex relation whose mysterious ways can be observed, sometimes anticipated, but never fully comprehended.

On the soft sandy bottom where the grasses wave in the tide, golden light filters down from the close surface. When the usually fierce Jimmy encounters a Sook half-hidden and ready to mate, he rises to the tips of his walking legs, dancing and waving his claws. She submits. He sidles up and embraces her tenderly from behind. In a cage made by his walking legs, she sheds her shell, becoming utterly defenseless and ripe for mating. Jimmy cradles and protects her, gently turning her to face him for the act. Their lovemaking lasts from five to twelve hours. Afterwards, they remain locked in a two-day embrace while her shell hardens.

I live near a stream called Western Run that feeds into a larger stream called the Jones Falls that flows into one of the Chesapeake's rivers, called by the original people the Patapsco. I imagine the Bay offering this suggestion of a Water Walk to every heart living in the 64,000 square miles of her watershed. As I research the idea, it helps to see that I am not the first one who has said yes. Still, I have no idea what will be required of me.

In the Creator's Original Instructions, women were to be the caretakers of the living water. When the big ships arrived in North America with men who did not know these instructions, many traditions were suppressed and forgotten. Some of the original people still follow the instructions and the prophecies of the Grand Chiefs, women like Grandmother Josephine Mandamin. She was born an Anishinaabe far to the north in a land carved by glaciers, and grew up on an island, living the same way as the Chesapeake's first people—in kinship with the water, the fish, the birds, the sun and moon, and the seasons.

In answer to the cry for help from her watery home, which her people in their language called *The Big Boss Lake*, Grandmother Josephine took up her copper pail in 2003 and started to walk. She walked with her open heart along the awakening springtime shoreline, circling the entire lake to bless the water, to listen to and speak with the water spirits, to sing prayers of healing, and to perform ceremony by offering tobacco and thanksgiving. She walked to restore right relationship with the water and for the benefit of the next generations.

La Trappe Creek Sunrise. Watercolor by J. Gabrielli

The following year, she circled another of the Great Lakes, gathering attention and new participants along the way. These walks continue every year.[2] Their journeys are both spiritual and physical. They walk to call attention to the sacredness of water, to honor and heal it, and to raise awareness of the need to take care of the water. Their 2015 Walk took place during July and August, trekking 846 miles westward from Ontario through Michigan to Wisconsin.

Many of Grandmother Josephine's sisters have been inspired to organize Water Walks along ailing waterways in their own home places, including the St. Louis and Ohio Rivers. The 2014 Ohio River Walk spanned 906 miles from Pittsburgh to Cairo, Illinois. They walked for thirty-three days, averaging twenty-seven miles per day.

Closer to home, in May of 2015, walkers in Virginia trekked the three-hundred-and-forty-mile length of one of the Chesapeake Bay's tributaries. When the English came, they named this river the James, but it was also known as the Powhatan, after the great chief of that land. They walked to bless and pray for healing of the waters after a CSX train derailment in April 2014. The one-hundred-and-five car train, en route to Yorktown, Virginia from North Dakota's Bakken shale region, spilled crude oil directly into the river, which then exploded into a fireball.

The Unity Walk began near the river's source in the Blue Ridge Mountains at Iron Gate, Virginia. They averaged twenty-eight miles per day on the twelve-day journey, which took them past state parks, historic sites, farms, cities, wildlife refuges and industrial sites. When the group reached the Chesapeake Bay, they sang and performed ceremony to offer the headwaters from their copper pail. "We are telling the water, 'This is how you began, and this is how we wish for you to be again,'" Ojibwe elder Sharon Day told a local newspaper. The walkers wept tears of joy to be greeted by a family of cavorting dolphins.

I imagine walking with a small group of companions, carrying a copper pail and pouches of tobacco and corn pollen. Walking with an open heart and listening, trusting that my sincerity will allow me to hear the song of the Chesapeake, even though in my growing up no one taught me how to do this. In my culture such things are dismissed as childish superstition. As I walk, my ancestors send visions of the great crust of my culture slipping off the living land, just as a crab sheds his shell. When my path takes me through the asphalt parking lot of an abandoned shopping center, I see the truth of their vision: knotweed rising to the light from a crack in the paving. The spirit of the knotweed plant sings of restoring balance to the waters of the human body. And my spirit is filled with hope. I know myself to be water, to be united by water with all other beings.

There are hundreds of thousands of creeks, streams and rivers in the Chesapeake Bay watershed. At the shoreline, the major tributaries are the Susquehanna, the Patapsco, the Patuxent, the Potomac, the Rappahannock, the York, the James, the Pocomoke, the Nanticoke, the Choptank, and the Chester. Smaller rivers include the Elk at the head of the Bay, the Gunpowder near Aberdeen Proving Ground north of Baltimore, the Severn and South Rivers at Annapolis, the Piankatank and the Nansemond in Tidewater, Virginia, and the Sassafras on the Eastern Shore. There are two small Wicomico Rivers. One feeds into the north shore of the Potomac about twenty miles from its mouth. The other lies between the Pocomoke and the Nanticoke, with the Ellis Bay Wildlife Management Area at its mouth. Mostly marsh and forested wetland, this three thousand-acre haven for ducks, wading birds, deer and smaller animals is one of many lands left behind by time on the Eastern Shore. Lands that will be submerged under rising sea levels.

I can see no practical way to embark on a walk like this. Using Google Earth, I gauge the perimeter of the watershed to be a rugged line through valleys and mountains, cities, suburbs and farm fields, measuring approximately seventeen hundred miles. By comparison, the famed Pilgrimage Route (*Camino*) of Santiago de Compostela winds its way across Northern Spain for five hundred miles. People embark on this walk with motivations varying from spiritual to sporting. It's usually done in thirty to forty days, for an average of twelve to seventeen miles per day—roughly half the daily distance of most of the Water Walks. This is the granularity with which such adventures must be considered. People have been walking this route since the Middle Ages, staying in quaint *Albergues and Refugios*, gorging on local food and basking in the scenery of ancient landscapes and villages. Probably not how a Bay Watershed Walk would go.

The Appalachian Trail also comes to mind. It runs from Springer Mountain in Georgia to Mount Katahdin in Maine, and measures about twenty-two hundred miles. Every year, "thru-hikers" attempt to walk it in a single season, usually from south to north to follow the weather as it warms. This takes at least six months, not to mention the training and preparation beforehand. Some avid long-distance hikers go for the "Triple Crown" of hiking, completing the Continental Divide Trail and the Pacific Crest Trail, which measure thirty-one hundred and two-thousand-six-hundred-and-sixty-three miles, respectively. Seeing those numbers makes me think this might be possible.

Until I remember that none of my walk would be on public trails, maintained by parks departments, nonprofit environmental groups and scout troops. I had hoped that the Chesapeake Blessing Walk would at least follow the Appalachian Trail in the mountains of Virginia, Maryland or West Virginia. Alas, a quick superimposition of the two maps in Photoshop reveals that the A.T. neatly bisects the Bay Watershed.

Gradually, others join the walk, women and men. They too hear the song of the Chesapeake. Together, the people walk along shorelines of sand and stones, of hard paving, manicured lawns and tall marsh grasses. They say blessings and sing prayers, perform ceremony and gaze upon the Chesapeake and her many tributaries in wonder. They converse with the spirits that dance in the sunlight on the water's surface and with the shifting tides in the depths below.

Rather than choosing between shoreline, rivers, or watershed perimeter, why not walk it all? Why not here, there and everywhere? It's the least we can do, after the last four hundred years of ignorance. We have the science-based advocacy, the citizen activist teams, the interactive web maps to track stream health and bird and butterfly migrations. We have the license plates and highway signs and storm drain stencils. Why not keep going and try everything that comes to mind, get all hands on deck? What have we got to lose? The places we love just might save us. Or at least they will change us.

As we walk, pray, and sing our blessings to the land and the water, we feel our own bodies and hearts becoming more whole and vibrant.

When we return from our walks, we raise oysters and restore the grasses that have been lost. We plant trees and care for streams in towns and cities far from the Bay's shores. Some of us tend gardens; others turn panels to the sun and blades to the wind. We walk and sing and share more. Our dances cause more cracks to appear in the crust, and more healing plants emerge. People are inspired to tear up paving wherever they find it.

And on it goes, as the oysters multiply. The Chesapeake is well pleased that she and her rivers run clear again. The cormorants and osprey, herons and geese and Monarchs once again fill the skies. The blue crabs thrive because the grasses have grown thick. Even the rockfish and the sturgeon return in great numbers. And we do not blush to bless a glass of water before drinking it nor find it strange to sit in hushed stillness under the sky that arcs over the Mother of Waters, bowing our heads in thanks as day becomes night.

---

[1] See https://ecoreportcard.org/report-cards/chesapeake-bay/issues/2014/
[2] Websites have sprung up such as www.waterwalkersunited.com, www.idlenomore. ca and www.nibiwalk.org. There's even a Facebook group, Water Walkers United.

Wendy Gorschinsky-Lambo
Making Love with a Three-Billion-Year-Old Woman

Editor's Note (Lise Weil): When I drive up to my cabin from Montreal in the summer, I'm always in a rush. I'm especially pumped once I reach the long hill that takes me to our little road in the woods. So for years I ignored the sign that stood on the corner at the bottom of the hill —PRODUITS ECOLOGIQUES OEUFS BIO. Then one day as I rounded the corner I saw at the bottom of the sign the words "SACRED SEX." On my next drive down the hill I stopped. The door was open. I walked past a sign reading "Sacred Sex Boutique"—and was welcomed by a woman about my age with long hair done up in a bun. Surrounding us were bookcases filled with titles about ecology, sound healing, eco-feminism, sacred geometry, the Divine Feminine and yes, Sacred Sex. In the corner was a basket full of freshly harvested vegetables. It soon became clear that the sex at issue here was not exclusively or even primarily between humans. As Wendy and I talked, it did not take long for us to feel very glad to have discovered each other. The following March I returned to her home to participate—along with twenty other women, most of them from Montreal—in a women's Water ceremony that the Algonquin Nation had transmitted to her. And the following summer, she gave me a tour of her remarkable garden which she had designed according to the teachings of a Mi'kmaq' tribe—and the no less remarkable home she had made for the worms who made this garden possible. Not far from this home Wendy walked me to a small tent. She told me she sleeps there six to seven months out of the year, to be close to Mother Earth. Rawdon is about an hour north of Montreal and at least 3C degrees colder. I was impressed. I had wanted Wendy to write about her relationship to her worms for one of our "Making Kin" issues—but she couldn't meet the deadline. As she has pointed out to me several times, serving The Mother is a full-time job. In this article, which she finally was able to make enough time to write, Wendy not only writes about her worms, but explains how she came to develop the relationship she has with the Earth, to be connected to the Mi'kmaq' tribe and to do the work she is doing. All of it could be said to be a lifelong experiment in what it means to heal.

I was a big-time social activist in Montreal for many years—demonstrating, writing, going to meetings, carrying placards, making speeches. I was a home-based entrepreneur, raising earth worms for gardening and selling books, fair trade coffee and ecological products out of my flat, a single mother who wanted to do it all the right way. In 1998 an occasion arose for me to demonstrate the worms and vermicomposting at a huge Home and Garden Show. The organizers had invited some alternative vendors to show their wares in an allocated "Green Aisle". On a break, I sauntered into the end of the aisle space where the Lnog of the Mi'kmaq' Nation were set up with a tipi and herbs for sale. As we packed up after the show, I noticed a small poster they had on the wall, advertising Saturday nights in Montreal, with an organic buffet, dancing and music for $5. I asked to take it and it sat on my desk for months.

One evening, exhausted after another exhibition, getting the children from different friends helping with child-care and having my lover in from out of town, I suggested we go across the city and check this out. It was an awesome evening. We ate delicious vegan food; we listened to music composed by the Lnog and later there were tam tams for dancing. My young children loved it and so did I. We kept returning and gradually came earlier and earlier to prepare food with the Lnog. Their buffets were always an education; food was displayed in beautiful geometric patterns and we feasted on wild-crafted fruits and veggies. Over time we got to know them—a little.

Our time together in Montreal was to be short-lived though as they received an invitation to help in Haiti by setting up their way of life on a donated barren piece of volcanic rock. We got the opportunity to visit them in Haiti a few times and it is on that land that we experienced what miracles the Lnog could achieve with their patience, their knowledge of trees and tree-planting, and way of life. We witnessed the constructions of *quams*, or vegetable-based tipis. One day under a tree I first learned about Alvéoles. I had seen a sister Lnog constantly in a kind of euphoria in their gardens. I found her so beautiful and asked what she was experiencing. My teacher took paper and pencil and drew Alvéoles, a system of surveying, gardening and building construction that is fundamental to the Lnog way of life. As a former math teacher,

I was fascinated by the geometry and exactness of it all, but more than this I did not truly understand. I could not appreciate yet what kind of gift I had just been given.

In spring of 2001, there was a two-week period in which my life came undone. My business suddenly collapsed when my worm partner's wife died unexpectedly. An ecologically-socially responsible business venture I was involved in was being deceitful—and so was my lover. I had to evict my tenant (my lover) out of my home in the country, which was financing my living in the city for my children's education. The school, a Waldorf school, had a huge financial melt-down, which put a halt to my daughter's continuing there. I handled it all by crying, journal writing, meditating, and dancing for about forty days.

It was during this intensely stressful period that I started receiving a constant message in my head: "It's in the Water. It's in the Water." The voice even woke me up at night, asking me to pay attention. "It's in the Water," it whispered. Then a Japanese friend showed up at my door, just back from a visit to Japan. She stood there with book in hand, hardly able to talk from jet lag. "It's hot off the press and I wanted you to be the first person to see it," she declared. The book was *The Hidden Messages in Water* by Dr. Masaru Emoto. "No way!!!!!!!" I screamed. That moment changed my life.

The first thing I did was to go through the images, hoping to understand what Dr. Emoto was demonstrating. When I came to the two images on the following page side by side, I got suddenly very frightened and I broke down sobbing. I am crying even now as I think of it.

The images demonstrated that our intentions, thoughts and feelings, our scoldings and judgments have visible effects on Water. The second image showed me speaking to my children—and in fact me speaking to everyone because I was so damn tired and had taken on way too much. I had been doing battle, like every other activist I knew. I was giving all my energy to the "dark side," which was the opposite of what I was trying to achieve. I saw that despite my good intentions of trying to provide the best of education, food and mothering to my children, I was in fact providing a role model of exhaustion, negativity and victimization. This is not a healing scenario for anyone. This is not a healing scenario for our planet.

 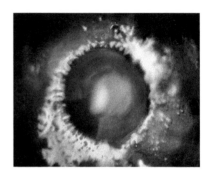

Left: "Let's Do It!" Right "Do It!" from The Hidden Messages in Water, *2004, p. 101-102.* Photos by M. Emoto

One month later, I found myself packing to return to our home in the country. So much was directing me there now, as if I had no choice. The children were overjoyed. They kissed the walls as the movers moved us in.

My old gardens were all overgrown after seven years, so I decided to put into place what we had learned about making Alvéoles from the Lnog. Alvéoles are an extremely precise hexagonal surveying system that is aligned with the stars, planets, and the Telluric Forces, the energy points of the Earth. The Lnog use this memory system to *work with* the Mother (Earth and Cosmic), instead of dominating Her, in everything they do and live.

The Lnog had taught me where to locate this grid and entrain *myself* to this wise map, so I could precisely align my garden with Her, harmonizing with Her rhythm. These hexagons are alive and all parts of the Alvéoles are aspects of the female form. They guard the memory of Sacred Sexuality, an element of Water, within the Tribe, both in their relationship with the Earth Mother and amongst themselves. Their adoration, their caresses of the soil and the plants and the flowers turned the wheels of transformation and communication with their Earth Mother and the other Star Beings in the galaxy. This is a

Oneness Consciousness that was lived by all a very long time ago. I am so grateful that the Lnog I met have kept this flame alive for us.

Photo by W. Gorschinsky-Lambo

By now I had discovered the book *The Ancient Secret of the Flower of Life* (Melchizedek, 2000.), The Flower of Life design is a specific hexagonal grid that exists all over the planet's surface. This geometry creates a matrix field, which is nature's most efficient way of holding information. It is a kind of neuronet, a brain that feeds information about us and what we are truly feeling into Water, which holds and transports all memory as Dr. Emoto demonstrated. The Flower of Life hexagram is the same shape of a Water crystal. Alvéoles and the Flower of Life were the same sacred geometry. The word Mi'kmaq' means "the People who hold the Memory" and they believe themselves to be descendants of Atlantis. Living, breathing with them daily and tactilely has given me a more profound understanding of their ancient wisdom than I could ever had learned from a book.

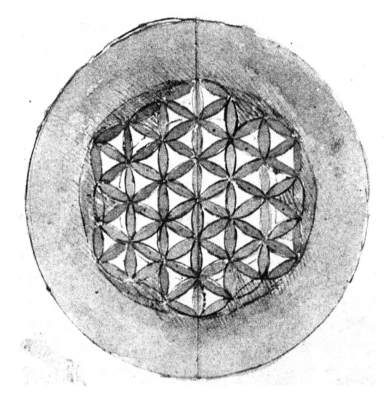

Art: Leonardo da Vinci's drawing of a Flower of Life from Codex Atlanticus, between 1478 and 1519. Leonardo da Vinci - Codex Atlanticus fol. 309v. Public Domain.

Before we went out on a large expanse of land to trace out Alvéoles, I wanted my children to have fully integrated the Flower of Life design in the core of their being. We drew it precisely with a compass and colored it; we decorated cakes and windows with it; we embroidered it, and we danced it all winter long. Then we went outside. We found the starting energy point and aligned it at night with the North Star. My daughter and I set to the task of measuring the Flower of Life design to the exact millimeter and digging out the wild vegetation with our bare hands and sticks, because the Lnog had taught us that metal breaks the energy field and the cut hurts the Mother's skin. There were still many things we would eventually learn about making Alvéoles, but we got this part right. We made three of them and I devoted them to the Divine Feminine—Isis, Magdalen and Sophia. At the same time I registered my land and house as a Community Land Trust called La Magdaliene to protect them forever.

Photo: Alveoles pattern of planting following Flower of Life by W. Gorschinsky-Lambo

From my vermicompost business in Montreal, I had about twenty boxes full of worms in a city basement, not so hard to move, but I also had fifty pounds of worms and a ton of vermicompost growing in a back alley as well, all of which had to be moved to the country. Not an easy task for a lady with only pails and her station wagon. Worm growers typically grow worms in rectangular or square arrangements and it was my intention to reset up along the country house that way, but my internal voice strongly guided me to a nearby place in my forest. "Ok", I said to the voice, and when I went to dig, my hands unconsciously worked with the hexagram, same as the Alvéoles, but on a different scalar measurement. I ended up with something beautiful—a circular nest, which made so much more sense for the worms.

The Eisenia foetida, commonly known as Red Wiggler Composting Worms, have a hydro-skeletal body, which means they are made up of

Water and Water always prefers to be in round places. These worms are also the only animal on the planet having *five* hearts. Each of their hearts has a double chamber and each heart is connected to another heart above and below in a row. In addition to being all Water and muscle encased in a skin, they are a warm-blooded annelid, which makes them a feeling being, and their blood circulates through their five hearts in a figure-eight movement, much like a biodynamic flow form. They re-digest their materials eight times before the process is finished, refining and re-defining it again and again, so that these materials may be offered back again purified to the Earth Mother with an altered vibration and a new frequency—Re-Memory. Polluted Water comes out clean and potable!

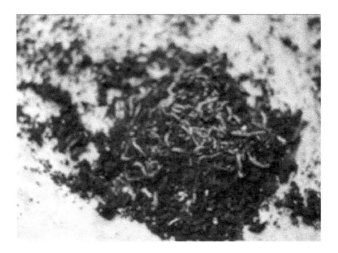

Photo by W. Gorschinsky-Lambo

The Lnog do not use worms but they do use human waste. What we consider waste are very precious resources for them, particularly in countries where there is so little Water or carbon material, like leaves. Haiti, for example has few trees left. The Lnog see their urine as Golden Water and their feces as a gift to the Earth. They know they can be generous in all ways with Her.

I never used to give sitting on the toilet a second thought. Get to it and then get off. I saw the pictures of Water crystals distorted by neglect in Dr. Emoto's book and I wanted this lack of respect to change for myself, for my loved ones if I truly wanted the planet to heal. Now I made myself urinate in a pot. I had to pay attention and be careful pouring Water over my genitals to clean them and wiping them with a soft cloth. I felt fear and a shame arise in me that I did not feel from the self-pleasuring in my bed. I was emotionally challenged by such a simple act and it brought me back to my infancy.

Sex education starts when your first diaper is changed and the expression on the face you see above you and the words you hear. To observe my own surprising feelings about peeing, having or losing control, embarrassment and pleasure, rocked my daily world. It helped that I knew scientifically that urine is sterile; it carries no bacteria and the smell is caused by minerals. But now I had to take the pot out. I had seen the Lnog do this often but never done it. To my surprise, I found a great pleasure in humbly bending my knee in beauty and grace and offering "my" Golden Water to the Earth Mother. I started to notice great changes in my flowers and certain vegetables. Disease disappeared and the leaves got brighter and brighter.

Then there was defecating. A different pot in a different place in the bathroom. Same issues and more. I felt great guilt along with the shame. I heard "Don't touch it or yourself. It's dirty! It's dangerous!" If it were not for my devotion to this experiment, I could not have gone on and missed out on learning about the great shadows in my psyche, hampering true intimacy with myself and with others.

As I brought this pot out to the Alvéoles, and to the worm beds, I knew the worms could take care of it. In fact, they were delighted to get all this food. If you naturally compost human waste, it takes two years before it is safe, but if you offer it to the worms, it is transformed and safe in six days! And in twelve weeks it is totally transformed into a valuable nutrient for the soil, as well as a natural protective barrier against dangerous bacteria/fungi leaching into the Water table. These little earth beings carry a strong Dragon energy, the fire of transformation.

Again, I was moved to bend knee and offer my feces. I had a sense of co-creation, as the worms would transform it and the geometry of the Alvéoles would take it out into the universe.

Biophotons would make their way into the soil, into the plants, flowers and fruit, and also into my bread and my body, when I soaked the infusion of broadcastings for my dough or in my bath.

As my self-esteem slowly grew, I could see that like the Lnog I was being generous to the ground in giving Her my vibration of bliss through my Golden Waters. Or I could be generous in passing my Waters to my septic system to travel to other parts of the region and perform their magic, or to a city sewage system, so that all Life may be served. All this took time.

The work of the worms is an amazing instance of what I call Mother Technology. The technology of the Mother is much like a tuning fork. The Red Wiggler loves getting newspaper as bedding, which they also transform, and I get excited thinking about what they can do with all that bad news. Gaia loves and is healthiest when She has diversity, so I like to make sure the worms have lots of diversity in their litter and in their diet. This includes cardboard, mouldy straw, leaves, kitchen waste and shit. Using all these components will give the highest quality broadcastings, colloquially known as vermicompost. When the worm's broadcastings are finished being edited, they go out into the world to entertain us, just as our newspapers and televisions do.

Broadcastings are usually given to plants, but they are safe for humans to use as well. An enormous amount of vitamins, minerals and hormones is stored in them, but this is not the reason I infuse castings in my bread baking and in my bath Water. The vibrations in broadcastings coming from the worm's five hearts are packed with biophotons. Biophotons consist of ultraviolet light with a high degree of order or coherence. These particles of light, which are existent in all life, serve as the organism's main communication network. Biophotons also principally regulate all life processes. Science is still learning so much about them, but we do know that the more alive a subject or material is, the higher the biophoton count. They are what makes your eyes twinkle when you are in love or makes you shine brighter when you are passionate about something. Imagine biophotons as fairy dust entraining all living beings around them. The more there are, the more life you have. Worm broadcastings, loaded with biophotons, feed the energy field of the Earth Mother.

We here in Quebec and lower Ontario are holding onto the largest store of fresh Water in the world. And women are the guardians of Water in all indigenous nations around the globe. Over time, I learned to work with the Torus energy for the sake of the Water. The vortex at the heart is the place of honour, where I direct my bliss and send my intentions to the Water table, so that it may be disseminated out into the world.

When I am in joy and appreciation, Dr. Emoto's work showed me that my Waters inside were being imprinted and the Waters outside were receiving the same imprint, even from very far away. This was exactly what the Algonquin and Mi'kmaq' Nations were also teaching me. They instructed me that my urine, my saliva, my blood, my tears, my generous genital fluids, and all the Water outside of us, polluted or unpolluted, are receiving messages from us, as individuals and as a collective. The Native women taught me a song and a ceremony for Water that says, "The Water that I carry is the blood of the Mother Earth." I concluded from this that the Earth Mother receives an orgasmic vibration when we are in orgasm. (I wish I had known this in all the years I taught sex education to high schoolers!) Pleasure and appreciation can all be directed to Her and recorded in Her memory—and what a memory a three-billion-year-old woman can have.

Pleasure and appreciation is the principal reason why I sleep outside on the ground for six to seven months of the year. The Mother and I are in Love and so I sleep as close to Her as possible. She whispers to me, offers Her fragrance and regenerates me, so that I can hold an energetic force when I am separated from Her. It is a lived eroticism.

N.B.: This is an abridged version. Please see **Dark Matter: Women Witnessing #6** *online for the complete essay.*

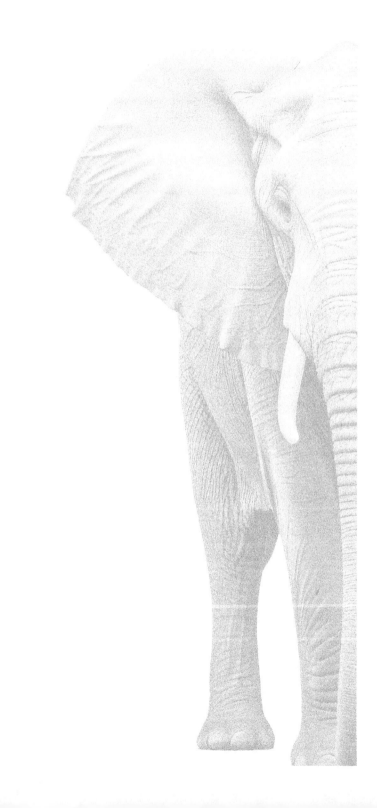

The Music of Grief

Grief is the key that unlocks the gate to reveal the path that leads us home.
Home is our place within the entirety of Life.

—Cynthia Travis, *The Music of Grief*

Sing as we walk—it makes the trip less painful.
It's true for bees as it is for human beings.

—Erica Charis-Molling, *Requiem for the Bees*

Kim Chernin
Mother of Us:
A Prayer for Healing

Grief, grief unutterable in the trade winds of your passage. We are here upon a shadow's generosity, ley lines undone, winds burrowing through the parched soil that say not whither or whence we wander, why we are here and what we have come to fathom. Is there work for our hands the last drop having fallen? Is it the beginning or the end of prayer? Let the tall grass teach us to speak your name, bent low beneath your urgency. Mother of god, mother of us, mother of what is, restore us.

Breezes hurrying in from the far east with transports of nostalgia, what is beauty for if not this, a kind of memory? Now beauty burrowing at the core, speeding the south wind eastwards, where evil is said to lie in wait, where winds are losing their locations, meanings have been undone, storm, outrage, blistering skies call up the flood beyond its natural ebb. Tell us what part to play, instruct our hands, where is the needle, where the thread?

Give us this day should it be our last, and we bound upon its darkening skies to take as the spoils of memory one seed of our world, a future will harvest. Here we wait at time's unseeing edge, cousin to tempests, born to the air, raucous bunch if ever was bounding up daybreak's broken stair.

Word is, dancing will do in the fissures of headlong, feet never touching the earth, leaping, howling ever falling, gone to the wild on the wave of a windswept, turning and tumbling and tripping the light foot, race to the wild to conserve what remains. Leave mourning to our mother of sorrow, her grief in the pollen that laces the aster, her brace of winds bleating hard from the north.

The poppy turns back into herself at the turning of our longest night, did you mix sorrow in the dying soil with just enough grief to drive her into California gold? Needful it is Mother that you return, forgetting feeds on our world, a toothed poison gnawing our roots.

I know you by some other sense than sight, a practiced touch wiping sweat from my eyes, transplanting the parched bush close to the fence, its blue berries hardened to lethal pits, your whispering, a quickening breath, you say you are not weeping but you seem so old, you who never began, began with us, trusting this precious to our hands and we have failed you. Give us this day some humble work, some small, seemingly dispensable toil, show us how many hands it takes to hold the waters back, here we stand at the outcrops of time, Mother, to work for you.

There are strangers out on the trail tonight, they carry messages. Send us the woman to enter the trance, the women who summon the guardian spirits, bring back tales of the new weather's force, the tread-path of walking between, the whiplash of raising up storms and bring our longing back to its source.

Death: delirious forester, lay down your knife, your work goes on, you are no longer required, you who were planning to carve out a unique death for every dying thing, off they all go by the barrel, your hopes shattered. Death, endangered species, sit down with us beneath this heart-sick oak to mourn the passing of your necessary. Rivers on their way to the sea don't speak of dying, you, creation's sister, leave it to time the great sweeper, mighty the broom, invincible the brush, we have no need of death, you weary forester.

Bare, barren, most barren the soil, most achingly barren, awaiting the touch that brings back life. She sees the future sprouting among the ruins, our beginnings beginning again, forms spread out on the sand, fish forms, mollusks, single cells, a gill, a fin, a tail not meant for walking. Are there takers? She summons the seed-carrying winds, they have been carousing in emptiness, she touches the fingers of both hands to her breast, the gesture of continuance, puffs out her cheeks, sends forth the teeming breath; earth begins again bearing her own fertility, settles the name of mother on the soil, invites the sky knee bent to render homage, hurries to make the flowers first, beginning with the brindled rose; coiled fire leaps up out of the soil, requires taming, she pricks venturing into spring, harvests autumn, beholds the bark climbing the winter tree, the hoar berry ripe, the stunned leaf yellow, invents the three-stringed harp, begins the long wait for the harper, the one who will sharpen the lathe at work by day, at rest in her lap at night, singing the blueprint of possibility.

Notes

I'm not at all sure I can claim this piece of writing as my own. It showed up on several distinct days with a flood-like pressure that made me feel exhilarated but uneasy, as if I had left a faucet open and didn't know how to stop the flow. I wrote the words out fast on the computer not sure what form they should take. Was this a poem, a rushing piece of prose, did I even understand what it meant? This cataract of words, however, was having a considerable, negative impact on my mind. I said things I didn't remember saying to people to whom they should not have been said. A client experienced me as "weirdly other," saying things she did not understand. My driving became difficult; I would struggle to stay awake but would fall asleep and drift over the double yellow line, fortunately when no cars were coming towards me. I had a trance-like sense of the world around me, which looked intensely beautiful and flooded with presence but in the next moment I would find myself suddenly awake again. Several times I pulled over to the side of the road to 'catch a few winks,' as I said to myself, but would find myself instead writing down words. My partner experienced me as "just not there;" apparently, I would stop in the middle of the kitchen with a pan in my hand and stare fixedly at nothing. After many tests it was determined that I had not had a stroke and that my brain was "100 percent the way it should be." But I was growing tired and I found it difficult to sleep at night. Finally one day I got the words that would turn out to be the end of the piece: "[She] begins the long wait for the harper, the one who will sharpen the lathe, at work by day, at rest in her lap at night, singing the blueprint of possibility." What's that? "At rest in her lap at night?" So be it! And with that, the whole thing came to an end.

When I started to pull together the scraps of paper from the glove compartment of my car, littering the floor around my bed, under my pillow, on the sheets of paper I printed out from my computer, the words stopped rushing about and seemed willing to stay in the order I sensed they had when they'd first shown up. What was needed now was quiet, patient work to find their correct form. I first wrote them out as a poem but the line breaks required the words to give up their momentum; things went better when I worked them as prose, although I had to apply more commas than had seemed necessary when they were little verses. It was odd to work with words I didn't fully understand; and there were so many of them. The work became an exercise in getting rid of some lines, perhaps the most obscure, but then again I didn't know what made some more obscure than others. Nevertheless, as I kept working with them they began to lose their strangeness and a meaning, admittedly only my interpretation, began to emerge. They were evidently a prayer to the great mother of us all requesting healing. And they bore dark witness to the disaster of nature occurring around us.

Cynthia Travis
The Music of Grief

> Our bodies are the texts that carry the memories and therefore
> remembering is no less than reincarnation.
> —Katie Cannon, *The Body Keeps the Score*

In January 1999, I attended a peacebuilding course at Eastern Mennonite University in Harrisonburg, Virginia. I was a fish out of water —a Jewish mediator come to learn about conflict transformation from a group of innovative, intrepid churchgoers. Harrisonburg is a small town studded with contrasts. To get there, one flies into Washington, DC and drives south and west through famous Civil War battlefields. Once there, it is common to pull up at a stoplight alongside a horse and buggy driven by Mennonites in top hats and tails, long dresses and lace caps. The folks that run the Conflict Transformation Program there are modern pacifists with a history of volunteering in disaster relief and what they call 'accompaniment' in places around the world where there is great suffering. After WWII, they decided that there must be something they could do before disaster struck. Pro–active peacebuilding was born.

My roommate Jean, and her husband, had been missionaries in what was then called the Congo. We both arrived late at night, weary from our long journeys, I from New Mexico she from Minnesota. I remember the adrenalin surge of my dislike of missionaries (still have it, but softer now) and my impatience with her gentle equanimity. Perhaps I sensed something ominous taking shape. Too late, the story was pouring out of her, so I listened.

Most afternoons, she and her husband would sit outside in the shade with their Congolese church guests, at a low formica table with broken chairs. One by one the men told their stories and began to weep. As they spoke, their tears became so copious they flooded the tabletop. Tears sheeted into their laps and poured onto the ground. As her husband leaned in to listen, Jean would wipe the table and wring out the towel. When Jean finished the story she shrugged. We may have hugged, I don't remember. I sat, stunned, as she went into the bathroom, turned off the faucet, and closed the door.

During the next several years, I returned frequently to Eastern Mennonite for their Summer Peacebuilding Institute, where grassroots peacebuilders from more than fifty countries gather to teach and learn the art of building peace: In South Africa, Mennonite peacebuilders worked behind the scenes to build 'human safety nets' because they anticipated—correctly—that the fragile negotiations between Mandela and de Klerk would likely fall apart. In the U.S., peacebuilders from EMU helped sensitize both prosecution and defense lawyers in high-profile capital cases so that victims and their families were not re-traumatized. Liberian peacebuilder S. G. Doe explained his work with child soldiers and warlords in the civil war that was still raging when I met him. He told me, "…We must deliberately move into the field and lavish love on those incapable of loving." I realized that, as I slept, someone on the other side of the world was awake and working for peace.

In late 1999, as a result of meeting some of these extraordinary ordinary people, I founded the non-profit *everyday gandhis* in hopes of making their stories more widely known. Five years later, I found myself in Liberia, in the wake of the civil war that had just ended there. I was soon to learn that even the best ideas born of the human mind benefit from collaboration with unseen sources. On the eve of that trip I dreamed that the dead from the war were asking to be properly buried and mourned:

I am standing with two colleagues on the banks of an underground river. On the landing where we stand, near the water, I see three small suitcases that become three coffins that turn into three wooden boats. On the other side of the river is a burning tower, like the Tower card in the Tarot. In front of the tower is a Liberian friend whose name is Roosevelt. He stands quietly, holding a shaft of gray light. Ours eyes meet. He says, "Everything is ready."

A few months later, I dreamed again:

I am on the battlefield of Gallipoli, walking through heavy artillery fire. I seem to be in a parallel reality. Bombs explode around me, clumps of earth and gore are bursting at my feet. Bullets whiz past, zinging right next to my ears. I walk, safe from injury, witnessing everything in slow motion. As I watch, a circle of women appears. One by one, they step onto the battlefield. Each of them claims a fallen soldier – a husband, a brother, a son, tenderly kneeling by the corpse, lifting him into her arms, caressing his face as she weeps. Each of them is singing her lament. A beautiful, terrible keening rises up, columns of wailing and grief.

These dreams and others led to everyday gandhis hosting Liberia's first post–war traditional Mourning Feast. During a Mourning Feast, the extended family and community of a deceased person gather to resolve their differences and put any lingering conflicts to rest with the dead, who are then sent 'across the river' with drumming and dancing, taking the community's conflicts with them. The ceremony concludes with a communal feast during which the act of eating from the common bowl is an oath of reconciliation. I found out two years later that local dreamers had dreamed that the dead had told them: *We, the Dead, have come together. We are united. It is time for you, the living, to do the same.*

Photo by C. Travis

As in most traditional/indigenous cultures, in Liberia it is well understood that if it weren't for our ancestors, we wouldn't be alive today. Therefore it is our pleasure and our obligation to honor them. But, since the war that consumed the country from 1989–2004, over 250,000 bodies were left scattered helter–skelter across the land. These rites had not been performed and the deaths had not been grieved, leaving the country in the lingering paralysis of unhealed trauma and unexpressed grief along with the anguish of failing to honor their dead.

"Our" Mourning Feast was peacefully attended by more than 5,000 people. It catalyzed the community to continue with many, smaller feasts — for children, women, healers, the land, the forests, the animals, the birds and the water. One man, a traditional herbalist who cannot read or write and has never traveled beyond Liberia's capital, Monrovia, dreamed that a goat was to be sacrificed at a particular stream in a particular village so that the blessings of peace (carried by the blood of the animal as it mixed with the water) would flow to Europe and the United States. After the ceremony, I was able to trace the stream on a map — barely a trickle at the site of the offering—and saw that, indeed, it flows into the Atlantic Ocean.

In Liberia, as in much of Africa, animal sacrifices reflect a deep and conscious covenant with the natural world — not unlike the spiritual partnership of traditional hunters, in which the animals "agree" to give their lives to feed the human community in exchange for mutual respect and devotion. In Liberia, the blood of the animal that is offered is understood to be a potent conduit for human prayers to reach the Other World (similar to the rising smoke of sacred herbs in Native America such as sage and tobacco).

To take a life is to enter into active partnership with Death. Therefore, these activities engender an exchange of respect and humility, creating tangible results in daily life, as can be seen in the way the Mourning Feasts inspired the community and released pent–up grief. More importantly, these rites create a dialogue with the Other World and among human beings in ways that acknowledge and engage with Nature and the spirit realm as the primary nexus of those relationships, seen and unseen, that establish peace through heartfelt exchange and mutual accountability.

Nature responds. Often, Nature initiates the communication, through dreaming and synchronicities — inexplicable coincidences too numerous to be attributed to mere chance, too timely to ignore, and cohering into a clear message or discernable pattern. It is our responsibility to learn how to pay attention and how to interpret the signs. Master General, a rebel commander who considers himself to be a traditional man and is also an Imam and a Pentecostal preacher, told us that, according to traditional understanding, elephants are considered to be a sign that peace is coming. Three months prior to the ceasefire that finally ended Liberia's civil war, Master General and his troops were on their way to attack Monrovia. In the forest, he saw a mother elephant and her calf. "I knew that God had spoken," he told us. "No more war in Liberia!" He commanded his men to lay down their arms on the spot, and decreed that anyone using a weapon from that moment forward would face a firing squad.

"How many men were with you that day?" we wanted to know. "How many men laid down their guns because of the elephants?"

Master General thought for a moment. "Thirty-six thousand."[2]

Last week, I met a man who will soon come to a circle being offered by my community here in the U.S. to speak the stories that haunt him from his time as a volunteer fireman — the water-swollen corpses he has pulled from rivers and ocean, the charred remains trapped in burned-out buildings, the mangled bodies of young drivers in wrecked cars. He is bursting to tell his stories into the container of the circle. He has had nowhere to put them. His sense of isolation has pushed him to the brink of a nervous breakdown. His first question about the people in our circle: *Do they do any drumming?* It turns out that neuroscientists are discovering what the Ancients knew, what Indigenous people have always known, and what our broken hearts tell us if we will listen: that storytelling, theater, collective ceremony, rhythmic sound and movement heal trauma. This knowing is instinctive, primal.[3]

If not addressed, trauma hitchhikes from generation to generation, our constant companion, co-author of our lives. It will have its say, invited or not, whether or not we choose to hear its message. As a case in point

Liberia was founded in the 1820s by freed slaves sent to colonize the land from which their forebears had been torn. The civil war there, similar to wars elsewhere, may have been the inevitable implosion of multi–generational trauma stemming from slavery, abduction, displacement, repression, colonization and exploitation.

In addition to the assaults on our bodies and our nervous systems, the renaming or misnaming of what we know to be true makes us crazy. Whether we call it 'spin,' or marketing or rewritten history, the result is the same. Our felt experience is the cornerstone of identity and meaning; when we are told that what happened didn't happen, that we aren't who we know ourselves to be, that our voices do not count — that corporations are people — our sense of reality crumbles. Remember that, in addition to stealing and renaming the land that was kin, one of the key strategies in the genocide of indigenous North American culture was to forcibly remove children from their families and send them to residential schools where they were given western names and forbidden to speak their own languages.

Photo by C. Travis

Who's to say how much heartbreak or trauma will push a person to violence, or a culture to collective madness? It could be as straightforward, as complex, as insidious as the 'christening' of unimaginably large tracts of ancient indigenous home terrain with names that bear no relation to those by which these places were originally known – names that expressed an intimacy, a depth of relationship unimaginable to those who imposed the labels. Dehumanization is a potent provocation. To be abused, 'othered,' or ignored is to become invisible, non–existent, debatable. We are chopped down, becoming the trees that silently fall in the forest.

My Pakistani friend Hassan is a profound peacebuilder. I met him at Eastern Mennonite, too. It was his practice to go to remote villages where tribal violence had broken out. He would camp at the edge of a field, fly a white flag, and invite farmers and warlords alike (sometimes they were one and the same) to come tell their stories. He once told me, 'Violence, too, is a form of communication.' It is the communication of last resort.

As with what cannot be spoken, what we cannot hear matters a great deal, and not only in the human realm, where the silence of exclusion is already overwhelming. "There is an information density…of between one and ten million bits per half hour of whale song — which is the approximate amount of information contained in Homer's Odyssey. In other words, whales are communicating *each half hour* the same amount of information as that in an entire book that would take us hours or days to read." [4] (And, because of their size, and the fact that they traverse the ocean from surface to depths and along their epic migrations, whales distribute vital nutrients across vast liquid expanses. In recent years, the ever–increasing traffic of container ships and super tankers is killing whales at alarming rates.) The cacophony of modern life is devastating animals whose mating calls and echolocation signals cannot be heard above the human din, interrupting vital life–sustaining systems, and depriving us of essential, encyclopedic realms of magic and connection. We find ourselves living a new and terrifying creation story whose divine authorship has been supplanted by machines. The trauma of separation from which we suffer globally is not God's banishment. It is our man–made exile from the Garden of the Earth in all her resplendent, thriving, complexity. Grief is the key that unlocks the gate to reveal the path that leads us home. Home is our place within the entirety of Life.

It seems that the sheer volume of heartache pouring in has caused it to stop pouring out. The escalation of atrocities made possible by the sudden, depersonalized, mechanical efficiency of modern warfare has replaced the undeniable reality of hand–to–hand combat and its strangely personal code of honor. Colonization, the slave trade, the holocaust, the nuclear bombs, the killing fields, the genocides, the clear–cutting, species extinction and now the impending collapse of the global ecosystem have reshaped our shared landscape and our responses to it. We are at sea in a toxic soup and trauma is at the helm.

My friend and colleague Bill Saa lost his brother Raymond during the Liberian civil war. Raymond was tortured to death – his body hacked away piece by piece until he died. He was then buried in a shallow roadside grave. For several years, Bill worked to learn the circumstances of Raymond's death, to locate the makeshift grave, and to find Raymond's killer. When he had found the grave, Bill met with the local elders of the nearby village, then gathered friends and family, including people from the community, to help unearth the body so that they could bring Raymond back to the family compound, bury him there and hold the requisite Mourning Feast. Though the grave was a shallow one, the exhumation stalled. They were unable to pull the remains from the ground. A local elder recognized the problem. He cut a branch from a nearby tree and offered it to the earth in exchange for Raymond's bones. Speaking to the earth, he explained that the people understood that after so many years, the earth did not wish to relinquish her son, but that the people wished to return the body to his human mother and father so they could bury him properly in the family compound. The elder then offered the branch in exchange for Raymond's remains. When the prayers were complete and a libation offered the body came free. The following day, they arrived at the family compound with Raymond's bones and shreds of clothing. A great, deafening cry rose up from the waiting crowd, a chaos of shrieking and shouting and anguished wailing that lasted far into the night.

Meanwhile, another brother, Nat, plotted to kill the murderer. A few of us from the US happened to be in Liberia when Nat dreamed that he had found Raymond's executioner and was on his way to kill him. In the dream, Bill put his arm on Nat's shoulder and told him, "Please don't do it." Nat vehemently affirmed his plan. But later that day, he had a change of heart. He joyfully phoned everyone in the family to tell them the news that he now wished to join Bill in forgiving Raymond's killer. A few weeks later, Nat and Bill met with the killer and told him, "You deprived us of our brother and our parents' son. Therefore you must take his place in the family." From shared grief compassion is born. Deep grieving makes room for miracles.

Last night a friend told me a story of a poisonous plant he found growing in a pot in a home he was renting. One day as he sat meditating, he felt his attention being repeatedly pulled to the plant. At last he turned to face it, and began to listen. He heard the plant say, "That's better. Now we can have a conversation."

"What would you like to tell me?" asked my friend.

The plant said, "You humans are so very, very sensitive. Your bodies are designed so that you can feel and hear and sense so many tiny, exquisite things. But your ways of living now have caused your receptors to become congested. You can no longer feel these things, or hear or sense them. You have lost this capacity that is your birthright, and so you have lost yourselves."

"What can we do to open ourselves again?" asked the man.

"Grieve," said the plant.

It happened that someone had lent my friend an elephant tooth. He spent the next three days sitting with the plant, cleaning that tooth, and weeping.

N.B.: This is an abridged version. Please see Dark Matter: Women Witnessing #2 *online for the complete essay.*

---

1 See *Everyday Gandhis,* Web. n.d. Name suggested by Bill Goldberg in conversations at Eastern Mennonite University.
2 Elephants also mourn their dead. They have specific burial rites and can remember the exact location of their loved ones' remains. Dolphins, chimps, dogs, sea lions, geese and many other animals mourn as well.
3 van der Kolk MD, Bessel. *The Body Keeps the Score: Brain, Mind, and Body in the Healing of Trauma.* New York: Viking, 2014. Print.
4 Buhner, Stephen H. *Plant Intelligence and the Imaginal Realm: Into the Dreaming of Earth.* Rochester, Vermont: Bear & Co., 2014. Print.

Lois Red Elk
Take Her Hands

Poet's note: "Take her hands" are words Sioux women say when someone is overwhelmed.

Female whole, but losing ground,
        standing there weeping
and screaming her loss.
It was like the sun and the moon left
        her alone on an isolated star,
her voice failing, her arms flaying,
        I thought she would fall over
from the vanishing of breath.
        Her body swayed in a
circular motion, an angle
        the force of anguish.
Loving feelings, so precious
                        leaving
and out of reach.
        Suicide thoughts
taking over all her senses,
                all stability.
                Her knife slashes her arms.
"You with the beaded moccasins,
        take her hands," shouted my aunt,
"Bring her back,
        she needs to think clearly."

It was our way of showing support,
  sharing her grief that she must
    continue with the earth for now,
      to remember the living.
                And, it was enough
  to give her composure,
    to let her know, why she had to stay.

Notes

When a woman intentionally takes the hands of another, it is to console them. Prayer is shared to keep the grieving spirit here in this time and place and to remind of their earth responsibilities. Sometimes grief can be extremely difficult and the spirit may leave or wander.

N.B.: This poem was first published in Lois Red Elk's Dragonfly Weather. *Sandpoint, Idaho: Lost Horse Press, 2013.*

Elena Herrada
Gardening in the Motor City

The Motor City is a place where less than 60% of the people own a car, despite a miserable public transportation system.

It's nestled in the center of the Great Lakes, where over 20% of the world's fresh water comes from, but 40,000 of its residents have had their water shut off by the post-bankruptcy internal IMF scheme.

It is important to note for those who may not know: Race Rules Detroit. Every single development, every single ordinance, every single action by the banks and the non- profits (banks in drag) is informed by race and racism. The city of Detroit is 85% Black and has a white mayor.

Detroit Public Schools are 90% Black and have a white superintendent.

Neither the mayor nor the school superintendent is beloved here, except by bankers, contractors, non-profits and philanthropists, most of whom do not live in Detroit and none of whom has a child in Detroit Public Schools.

Currently there is an effort to change the state taxing authority constitutionally to grant the mayor alone the ability to levy taxes. A small ragtag army of which I am a proud foot soldier called "Detroiters for Tax Justice" has warded off this effort at the state legislature, but we know it's not going away. The new scheme would tax land where once homes stood before the banking orgy of foreclosures and the demolition derby that provided so much in kickbacks as a result of which we have acres and acres of vacant land here.

The mayor would like to tax the vacant land and give more relief to developers to build.

I live in the hot gentrified neighborhood of Corktown. It's historically zoned so that homes can't easily be demolished as in most of the city. Corktown is a place where white people feel safe and the humble frame working-class historic cottages are affordable to only white people. At least that is who is moving in, although it was historically an Irish and Mexican neighborhood. I am an Irish Mexican. There were so many of us here that at one time we had our own festival.

I became a gardener out of rage. When the casino gambling industry finally broke past Detroit's hardy resistance and "won" at the ballot it brought three casinos: Motor City, located where Wonder Bread factory once was, Greektown and MGM. I fought casinos with all my heart and was demoralized when they prevailed. In a proud city where everyone who wanted a good union job could have one and we actually produced goods- cars- we got casinos. Where people could lose their life savings in one night; where a 911 operator was killed by her husband when she lost their retirement funds, homes lost, utilities shut off, less food on the table for the kids, all for the hope of winning big. The House Always Wins.

I went to a work conference out of town. A man who had a shop next to the hotel kept asking me to come in. It was a shop of herbs, oils, incense, semi-precious stones. I wasn't interested, but I did promise him before I headed back to Detroit, I would stop in. He was a man from India. He asked me what ailed me. I shrugged him off and told him I have little money and less time and what did he want with me. He asked me what was bothering me. My response shocked me: "The mayor died." (I loved Coleman Young the way Christians love Jesus). "We got casino gambling now. My city is turning into Babylon; people gamble instead of work."

The man said: What do you do to heal yourself? I had no answer. I was a single parent, a union representative for SEIU and was engaged in battle at every turn: ex-husbands, bosses, grievances. I said sometimes I garden. I read. The stranger told me to garden as if my life depended on it.

When I got home I got a shovel and dug up my front lawn. Without a plan, I just took out all the grass. Next, I went to Belle Isle, our beautiful Island park, and dug up native plants. I knew them because i walked by them all the time and they needed no watering. I brought them home for days on end and planted them in my yard. Sometimes I would ask friends for transplants and so began to fill it all in. Soon there was no grass anywhere in my yard. No watering, which became helpful when the water grew so expensive we could barely afford it.

My garden is filled with Marigolds for Day of the Dead; pollinators which invite butterflies wildly; dozens of rosebushes from an erstwhile admirer; a wild rose tree that doubles as a security fence with its ruthless thorns. Since the death of my beloved cousin in 2020, I went to her garden and dug up her things. I brought them here to my garden following another death of another cousin. I have planted Rose of Sharon in her honor. My small yard has become a series of memorial gardens. No longer do I weep as I plant. I think that most people's gardens are actually memorial gardens, even if they are not conscious of it. I am particularly conscious, because when someone close to me dies, I take something from their garden and plant it in mine. This has helped heal my broken heart.

Photo by E. Herrada

Ruth Wallen
Cascading Memorials: Public Places to Mourn

We used to get a lot of rattlesnakes. Now you don't see rattlesnakes
and you don't see deer. You still get coyotes, and plenty of rabbits
and squirrels
.

I miss the frogs, too. Unless we get a pretty good rain that brings
them all out, you don't hear them at all.
The other thing we had years ago was horned toads. I haven't seen
one in years. I remember that my youngest boy had a horned toad
in an aquarium. He hand fed it for six months with red ants and
then let it go.

When the development came, the red ants got overtaken
by black Argentinean ants.
—RS and HW

The statements shared above are from residents of Arroyo Sorrento,
San Diego, a small enclave just north of the University of California,
San Diego and east of the coastal community of Del Mar. This is the
place I first visited upon moving to San Diego thirty years ago. I've been
coming back here, and to the wild mesa pictured above, misleadingly
called Carmel Mountain, ever since. I imagine that similar recollections
could be elicited from many parts of the continent, although more
readily here in southern California where the human population has
grown so rapidly. A hundred years ago there were well under a hundred
thousand people populating this large country. Now there are over 3.2
million.

Such rapid change means that most adult residents moved to San Diego
from somewhere else. For each new arrival, what they find as they settle
into their new home becomes their baseline. It is hard for newcomers to
imagine that only ten or twenty years ago the local ecology was radically
different. While the lack of collective historical memory may be more
extreme in areas of the country with rapid growth, it is characteristic
of our times as a whole, with frequent migration common throughout
the continent.

Carmel Mountain Chaparral in April, 42"x16" by R. Wallen

Even for those who have stayed in one place, the changes that have occurred in San Diego County just since the turn of the twenty-first century are hard to fathom. Fifteen percent of the land area of the county, primarily back country, burned in 2003, and another fifteen percent burned again in 2007, overlapping the earlier fire in some places. Most of the conifers in the high country burned. I can only hope that they grow back in my daughter's lifetime.

Similar stories can be heard elsewhere. Wildfires, drought and bark beetles have ravaged western forests. Frogs are disappearing throughout the world; bats are dying by the tens of thousands. Whether one listens to the news from around the continent, or pays close attention to one place, the multiplicity of stories about environmental degradation are startling.

Now is a time not only to pay close attention, to bear witness, to remember—but to grieve. *Cascading Memorials* is an ongoing project to provide spaces for public memory, places to share stories, and places to mourn. It began in my community as a gallery exhibition, then moved to exhibitions elsewhere, with plans for an interactive web site and outdoor public installations. The work calls viewers/participants to attentiveness and to appreciation and gratitude for their surroundings. It provides a space to share in the wisdom of scientists and fellow citizens, and to grieve the rapid loss of the environments in which we live.

I have begun to create memorials to specific places that are undergoing rapid change. I focus on specific sites so that I can get to know them intimately. I return to each place frequently to photograph. Instead of the heroic sublime so frequently invoked in landscape photography, which distances the viewer, I present a fragmented, layered perspective

Imagine how this area might have looked when the Spaniards first
arrived. Drawings and written records provide clues.

Evidence shows that
considerable
type-conversion
has occurred. Native
vegetation has been replaced
by non-native grasses.

Grazing, accompanied by introduction of non-native grasses, excessive
fire, development, and water and air pollution are all contributing factors.
Predominance of introduced species affects insects and wildlife adapted to
indigenous plants.

(above) Sketchbook page from Mission Trails Park Memorial, 9"x12" by R. Wallen.
(below) Middle Peak, Cuyamaca Forest, San Diego County, several years after 2003
fire, 24"x40" by R. Wallen

of dynamic systems undergoing unusually rapid change. Carefully stitching together photographs is for me an act of reverence, respect. I try to convey a sense of my gratitude, the wonder of the experience of being in a particular place. Accompanying the photomontages in gallery exhibitions, a single poetic question on the wall ignites viewers' curiosity. Sketchbook pages allow for more detailed exploration, combining text, drawings and photographs to provide scientific and historical context, and raise further questions.

Continually returning to the same places provides the opportunity to look closely. It was only after years of walking on Carmel Mountain that I realized that the puddles along the path were actually vernal pools, ephemeral pools that are home to tadpoles, insect larvae and a host of invertebrates that live nowhere else. Ninety-seven percent of the vernal pools in San Diego have been destroyed by urban development. It is estimated that at least a third of the micro-crustacean species in California vernal pools have yet to be identified.

(above) Cascading Memorials: Urbanization and Climate Change in San Diego County, Athenaeum Music and Arts Library, San Diego, 2012 by Ruth Wallen (next page) Sketchbook page from Carmel Mountain Memorial, 9" x 12" by R. Wallen

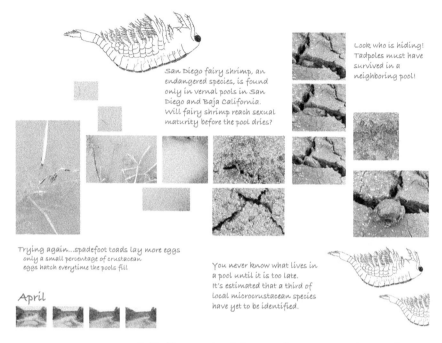

San Diego fairy shrimp, an endangered species, is found only in vernal pools in San Diego and Baja California. Will fairy shrimp reach sexual maturity before the pool dries?

Look who is hiding! Tadpoles must have survived in a neighboring pool!

Trying again...spadefoot toads lay more eggs only a small percentage of crustacean eggs hatch everytime the pools fill

April

You never know what lives in a pool until it is too late. It's estimated that a third of local microcrustacean species have yet to be identified.

97% of the vernal pools in San Diego County no longer exist. Will climate-change-induced drought will further imperil sensitive species?

When a truck drove through a vernal pool that my daughter and I visit frequently, destroying the contour of the pool and crushing the inhabitants, we were both outraged and heartbroken. As Aldo Leopold observes, "We can only grieve for what we know."[1] When we develop a relationship with a place, loss becomes palpable. Ecological degradation is no longer a myriad of statistics or abstract facts.

You knew that you were living in a place and you knew who your company was. There were no fences between the homes. Owls behind the house. Hawks in the sky. Deer. Coyotes howling. I still see so clearly the mama quail and all the little baby quail with their heads bobbing up and down. There were often many families of them.

—Helen Meyer Harrison

In every public installation of this project, I not only share memorials to sites with which I have an intimate connection, but I ask viewers/ participants to share their stories of animals, plants and places they have loved that have disappeared or are changing irreparably. Aldo Leopold writes that the consequence of ecological awareness is living "alone in a world of wounds."[2] Collective sharing, not only of loss, but gratitude for the places that we have known and loved, breaks this isolation.

.

When I first visited the Dawson-Los Monos Canyon Reserve, long before I dreamed that I would become its manager, I used to drive across the agricultural fields to the south, and down a little canyon in the landscape to reach the main meadow of the reserve. Along the way I passed through an open valley with grand oaks and chaparral, as well as wet meadows and seeps, very different from the Los Monos Canyon just over the ridge to the north. When they started to bulldoze the area for commercial development (much of which stood empty for 15 or more years) I had to stop the car because the tears made it impossible to see to drive. I finally got out of the car and screamed and screamed and screamed...
—Isabelle Kay

Unfortunately, rituals for public mourning of any kind have been largely discontinued. Between 1880-1920, public mourning, including mourning clothes and accouterments, gradually vanished from view to the point that Philippe Aries declared that in "industrialized, urbanized and technologically advanced areas of the Western world...except for the death of statesmen, society has banished death." What is lost when a society has the hubris to deny impermanence, attempting to banish death from public consciousness? Consider that in the *Sutra of Buddha Teaching the Seven Daughters* the Buddha says, "If one knows that what is born will end in death, then there will be love.[3]

It is not grief, but the fear of feeling, the absence of sadness or rage, which leads to paralysis, despair and psychic numbing. In a widely circulated op-ed piece in the *Los Angeles Times*, Richard Anderson asserts: "the alternative [to grieving] is a sorrow deeper still: the loss of meaning."[4] Judith Butler argues, "Without the capacity to mourn, we lose the keen sense of life we need in order to oppose violence."[5] That includes, I would add, the violence of ecological destruction.

When we avoid grief, according to Catriona Mortimer-Sandilands, we live in a state of suspended melancholia, where grief is internalized and objects of loss are fetishized. She contends that this process of displacement gives rise to "nature-nostalgia," manifesting in such activities as ecotourism or even campaigns to preserve a particular species or wilderness area. Such practices, although well-meaning, reflect a mythic or idyllic view of a natural world separate from humanity. Nature becomes a commoditized fantasy. Environmental destruction becomes incorporated "into the ongoing workings of commodity capitalism."[6]

Instead of idealizing a mythic wild, can we dare to love the world in which we live? As we witness loss—whether family homes, childhood haunts, the croaking of frogs, or stately old oaks and pines—can we dare to feel the pain of loss? Public grieving is an essential step. In communal moments of grief, when the flow of life is temporarily halted, when the ache of losing that which was loved feels unbearable, hearts open. Sense perceptions are heightened. One is touched by the full poignancy of the living world. From these feelings compassion arises. In this heart-opening, the vital interconnectedness of the living world is palpable.

Hearing testimony as many bear witness prompts not only sadness and outrage, but also a desire for explanation, for autopsies. Any answer prompts more questions, and increasing awareness of the complexity of ecological systems. As such, each explanation leads to the

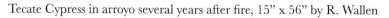

Tecate Cypress in arroyo several years after fire, 15" x 56" by R. Wallen

reestablishment of the network of ecological connections. In this heightened sense of interconnectivity with those with whom we grieve, and with a wider sense of self integrally intertwined with the environments in which we live, we can find strength.

Tears are cleansing. Grief allows us to see with new eyes, eyes that demand accountability, responsibility to make meaning or sense of the loss and take action. As Joanna Macy reframes this, we can understand "pain for the world as a call to adventure."[7]

Working on this project, I have noticed that as we bear witness to the immensity of change in our communities, even long-term ecological transformations such as climate change become less of an abstraction. Whether it is flooding or fire, deep freeze or searing heat and drought, increasingly many of us have stories to share.

It is fear of change, fear of grief, fear of the implications of grief that is immobilizing us, hardening our hearts. Let us face the dark, bear witness, and share our stories. Let us dare to imagine anew, recognizing that as in any relationship, if we love the environments in which we live, we must give back as well as take. Let the tears flow, let us howl in anguish and rage, and let us act.

Most of the conifers in San Diego County burned in 2003. I love to take my daughter camping, but she asks me why I want to go hiking when as soon as we leave the campground, all we see is dead trees.

Twelve years later the chapparal towers overhead. Some worry that it is so thick that seedlings have no where to sprout. They initiated programs to speed up regeneration by removing the chapparal and replanting seedlings.

How can we nuture new seedlings?

As climate changes and temperatures rise, bark beetle infestations spread more rapidly. Droughts are more frequent. All contribute to the spread of fire.

Others say that the ceonothus now covering the forest floor fixes nitrogen, a necessary first step in regerneration. Seedlings will grow when conditions are right.

Are we, as a society willing to take action to halt, or at least slow, the deminse of western forests?

Clearing and re-seeding on Middle Peak

Sketchbook page from Cuyamaca Memorial, 9" x12" by R. Wallen

[1] Also Leopold, Aldo, *Sand County Almanac*, quoted in Douglas Burton-Christie, "The Gift of Tears: Morning and the Work of Ecological Restoration" in *Worldviews* 15, 2011, pp 29-46.

[2] Leopold, Aldo. *Round River.* New York: Oxford University Press, 1993, p. 165. Print.

[3] Quoted in Jeremy Hayward, *Warrior-King of Shambhala: Remembering ChogyamTrungpa.* Somerville, Massachussetts: Wisdom Publications, 2008, p 390. Print.

[4] Anderson, Richard. "The World Is Dying—and So Are You," *Los Angeles Times.* Jan 07, 2001.

[5] Butler, Judith. *Precarious Life: The Powers of Mourning and Violence.* New York: Verso, 2004, p. xvii.

[6] Mortimer-Sandilands, Catriona. "Melancholy Natures, Queer Ecologies" in *Queer Ecologies: Sex, Nature, Politics, Desire.* Eds. Catriona Mortimer-Sandilands and Bruce Erickson. Bloomington: Indiana University Press, 2010, p. 333. Print.

[7] Macy, Joanna. and Chris Johnstone. *Active Hope: How to Face the Mess We're in without Going Crazy.* Novato, California: New World Library, 2012, p 81. Print.

Kristin Flyntz
Too Much Sky

Across from one of the nearby farms, a tired white house sits close to the road. Once, its most distinguishing characteristic was the pair of giant maple trees whose lush, full canopies overhung the road on one side and shaded the house on the other, their crowns reaching high above the roofline. They were cut down two years ago, which I discovered one bright March morning when I rounded the bend and didn't recognize the view: An expansive curtain of cloudless blue, no longer interrupted by twin silhouettes as it dropped down to meet the flat brown carpet of winter lawns and empty fields. There was too much sky where the trees used to be.

The maples were an outpost for red-tailed hawks scanning the fallow fields for food, and for crows meeting to discuss the day's business. They were home to families of squirrels, who would race down their trunks and across the road, toward the farm and the woods and brook beyond. Particularly in the summer, when they were plush with foliage, the trees softened the lines and angles of their surroundings—tidy rows of planting fields, pitched roofs of barns and houses, the straight black ribbon of asphalt that insists itself upon the terrain. The girth of their trunks said they had been present to generations of humans, animals, birds, plants. Theirs was a living history no human record could approximate. Their presence helped define that landscape for me. Now their stumps are weathered to a steely grey, but their absence can still feel as fresh as the first day I found they were gone. My mind continues to see them where they were, as they were—in anticipation or memory or denial—until I round the bend and see the open sky.

Stepping into the foyer of my childhood home, looking up into the kitchen, light streams through the window above the sink. There is too much sky. Missing from view is the shape of my mother, backlit by the sun, turning from the sink to welcome me home, "Oh, hi, honey, how are you?" Missing is the softness of her as she embraces me for a kiss, and her scent—freshly scrubbed and perfumed with Chanel No. 5 or Yves St. Laurent's Opium—warm and spicy and…Mom.

It is nearly two years since she died. Still, I expect to see her at the sink, facing out to the gardens and the woods beyond—rinsing dishes or preparing a meal or wiping crumbs off the counter or making any one of myriad gestures inscribed on my heart. Sometimes I do see her, in the same way I still see the maples. She is wearing her red holiday blouse and "ginger pearl" lipstick, light glinting off the drop earrings reserved for special occasions, apron tied around her waist, her sensible black shoes beneath sharply pleated black slacks looking as new as the day she bought them. Or she is casual in her buffalo check shirt and jeans, adjusting the kitchen table to make room for her guests, turning to offer a mug of tea, a bowl of fresh berries, a plate of crackers and hummus—her smile flashing, a giggle flushing her cheeks, brown eyes shining with pleasure and perhaps a little bit of mischief. She is shorter now with age, looking up into my face for signs that I am happy or stressed or tired, touching the stone in the necklace at my throat and admiring its color, asking for its name. I see her small hands, so like her own mother's hands—unpolished nails trimmed to hug the tips of fingers knotted with arthritis, knuckles a little chapped and red; her dark hair, somewhat thinner now, is cropped into her trademark pixie and frames her open face, her soft and luminous skin. Handwritten notes are still stuck to the fridge in her neat cursive as distinctive as a fingerprint. She is here and she is not here, her energetic imprint etched into every inch of this place I will always know as home.

People gravitated to my mother's optimism and positivity. On the evening of her wake, despite the sleet and ice of a January storm, the room was full of people whose lives she had touched. The impression was of her warmth and joy brimming in those she left behind, uplifting us as they had always done, excluding no one. Sometimes my mother had seemed to me naive about the cruel realities of the world, and sometimes it had seemed to me that she willfully looked away from them. In that way she was different from me, with my desire to understand the dark matter of human nature and behavior, the causes and the costs.

Now that she is gone, as our world spirals deeper into political instability, war, and climate catastrophe, I appreciate how, like those great maples, she offered to all who knew her a quiet, steady and reliable presence in which to rest, be held, get fed, feel safe.

When I feel anxious or despairing, I often go outside to watch and listen to the birds. Whatever known and unknown challenges they may be navigating, they appear to me to live in the moment, singing and eating, singing and breeding, singing and making the world around them more beautiful, more precious, for their presence. On the fifth day after my mother's death, I was sitting on my back porch when a titmouse landed on a branch just inches from me. She stayed for what seemed a long time, watching me watch her, then flew off. Another titmouse immediately took her place. When that one flew away, a goldfinch flew in to replace her. This continued until five birds had visited the branch, completely unperturbed by my presence. Five days since her death, five birds for the five of us: Mom, Dad, my two sisters, and me. I've experienced nothing like it before or since.

In the ensuing months, on multiple occasions a red-tailed hawk circled my parents' house, its persistent cries pulling our attention upward to witness its slow and deliberate flight around and around the house, the yard. Dad, who says he never remembers his dreams, dreamed of a catbird this year, just before they made their annual return to the arborvitae trees that line the right side of the property. Catbirds mate for life, like he and Mom did, and return to the same habitat to nest, year after year. Once, my sister and father were having coffee on his deck and a great blue heron, flying low, circled the house—eventually leaving, then returning twenty minutes later to do a shorter, slower loop.

The birds conjure my mother's memory— her easy joy despite the turbulence of the world, how she lived according to her nature, the ways in which her life circled around her family, her friends, and her home. They remind me of how she walked with beauty, grace, and kindness, despite the persistence of the cancer.

The morning after my mother's wake, I awoke well before dawn, the memories and emotions of the previous night still running through me. In the eastern corner of the yard, I watched the sun rise over the distant hills with fiery insistence, pushing over the horizon like a baby crowning between his mother's thighs until at last, he is free—visible and fully formed: *I am here!*

There is a tear in the web of limbs and branches through which I have always witnessed this ritual of renewal, an excess of space where bodies that once stood side by side now lie atop one another and the roots of their fellows. Weakened by years of intermittent drought, felled by winter storms and wind, they are still entangled, but horizontally now, feeding myriad lives in their community in a different way.

Climbing higher, the dazzling orange orb suffused the sky with shades of blush and peach. So much sky. A breeze swept a dusting of snow off the trees and roof into the air before me. Suddenly, billions of glittering crystals were alight and dancing in the rosy-golden glow of dawn. An astonishing display, utterly magical. *It's so beautiful!*

I said the words to myself and felt Mom saying them with me. To me.

Susan Marsh
Elegy for the Cranes

Reed grass sloughs, coverts of cottonwood and ash
Buffaloberry embroidering a ditch with threads of crimson fruit:
October spreads its wings, yearning for the sky's embrace.
Land flattens under cumulus and light,
Blood-red line of sunrise broadens to a ruddy streak.

By noon the wind has turned, strong and from the north.
Primeval music tumbles from the vacant blue
And all at once the sky holds columns of grace,
Dozens of cranes calling as they climb
The invisible staircase of the North Dakota sky.
One, at the far tip of a long vee of birds,
Is white. Its wings ply the air like canvas sails,
Their hems dipped in the blackest ink.

Sunset lingers, empty. The prairie sky was made
For their millions, its silence meant for their cries.
Twilight's fading violet shrouds loss,
Forgotten pathways of light.
Tomorrow the sunrise will bleed again,
The midday sky will wait
The only way it knows—
Arms open, ardent, filled with light.

Notes

This poem was written in response to paintings in the collection of
the National Museum of Wildlife Art in Jackson, Wyoming. I was one
of two poets who organized a public reading of ekphrasis – poems
responding to art – in 2009. In looking at the many pictures displayed
in the museum's gallery, I was drawn to those that felt like eulogies

for what was lost and I wrote about the deep grief they brought out in me. This poem was informed not only by a painting by John James Audubon, but by several trips I took with my husband to North Dakota. The last time we went, we saw one whooping crane among hundreds of sandhills, the only wild whooper I have ever seen.

Crane migration by S. Marsh

Susan Cerulean
Bear Requiem

Despite a court appeal, dozens of demonstrations, and forty thousand letters of protest; despite impassioned editorials in every major newspaper, and without regard for the opposition of three-quarters of the state's human population, nearly three hundred wild bears (including three dozen lactating mothers) were gunned down in a "recreational" hunt in Florida, from the northern panhandle to the Ocala National Forest, in late October. The event was strong-armed by Florida's governor and his appointed wildlife commissioners—a state-sanctioned slaughter of Florida black bears.

We hoped the bears would be wily, and escape the bullets of the hunters. But baited and tempted with corn, birdseed and glazed doughnuts, they didn't stand a chance.

How could we respond to the brutal slaying of animals only just recovering from threatened status? What gesture could we devise to transform our grief and our outrage, knowing that sixty traumatized and orphaned cubs still wandered the woods? How would we reset a moral compass in a state that presently appears to have none?

In Tallahassee, on November 21, a group of musicians, artists and spiritual leaders—mostly women—created a memorial service not much different than we might have had the mass murder targeted human victims.

On the morning of the Requiem, I dreamed of eight bears, with all manner of coats, some spotted, some gold, some brown. The animals pressed against the glass windows and doors of a church, apparently gathering for our service.

Our ritual began with procession of artists wearing handmade masks—deer, bear, wolf, bird—creeping and stalking down a central aisle to the beat of a single somber drum. The artists carried a larger-than-life bear with a bejeweled head, and a body sewn of tawny fabric. The bear was laid on a woodsy altar overarched with tall bamboo and grapevine, and strewn with baskets of flowers, acorns, shells and blueberries.

Rev. Candace McKibben spoke of the many forms senseless human violence takes, and the numbness it can create in our hearts. Many audience members openly wept. Buddhist practitioner Crystal Wakoa urged the audience to consider a perspective that seeks an opening of hearts, even those of hunters and politicians, so they might see themselves anew and change. The Ursine Chorale, a small *a capella* group of women, sang a promise to never forget or forsake the earth's creatures, reworking a Becky Reardon song for the bears: "The bear cubs remember/ A dream in September, alone with Mom/ At one with all of the woods/ We honor your spirit./ Forgive us, forgive us."

We designed the Requiem to help our community move through grief to a stand of advocacy and recommitment. Near the close of the ritual, we invited the audience to take part in a special communion. From baskets, we chose flowers to adorn the symbolic bear. We ate blueberries, sharing the sweet taste of a favorite bear food. And each of us present selected a bear paw shell, collected from a local beach, a reminder of our pledge to stand with the bears.

All photos by D. Moynahan

Nora L. Jamieson
Fleshing the Hide

Home now. Or was that home? And what did I carry home from New Hampshire beside the dried and unworked hide now tacked to the board. The yearling doe hide, who was flesh, who was a fawn, who was a wet and gangly newborn, who was carried and loved, who was the meeting of an egg and a sperm, who was a longing, who was a possibility. No more.

Who was sighted, shot, skinned, quartered, or bled out to age the meat, whose skin under my hands was fleshed and grained and soaked and smoked and will be stretched again and again over the coming winter, my hands raw and bleeding. Whose lovely head might be one of many in a large vat of heads that will feed chickadee and vulture and coyote.

I enter after the kill, after the hunter's early rising, the coffee and eggs, the toast at the local diner, before filling up the thermos, heading out to the woods, before climbing up into the tree stand. Before the waiting, before the sighting, before the shot. I arrive after the soft crumple, the violent spasm, the instant death, the slow one.

I arrive after the tents have been pitched, the food delivered to the kitchen, the smoke house fires lit, the selection of the hide carefully saved out for me. After the morning prayers and coffee and smokes, I arrive in the temporary village, too gentle a term for all that has happened before me. Children run about. Dogs prance, showing off the prized legs of deer, or wait hopefully for bits of fat to fall to the ground.

Like a paper doll inserted into a scene, I arrive to that small village of men and women in deep concentration, hunched over fleshing beams, working hides with dull crescent-moon blades, carefully, so as not to tear the thin places, perhaps knowing the debt owed to the hide that might just as much have yearned to return to earth.

How do we justify, understand what we do? A wise fool of a man once said, the holy life, the sanctified life, is not one without trespass, it is knowing the debt we owe. And how do I carry that debt and all the debts owing to one small act of fleshing a hide on a snow-squall morning in New Hampshire?

It could make a woman crazy trying to keep count of all the ways she is indebted to that one morning and all the elements that came together to weave it. So many threads on the loom. The sun thought it a good idea to meet the earth as she again, graciously, even at such cost now, turned her face to him who some call Grandfather. Wind joined in, swirling snow around us as we remembered with longing the old iron stove in the barn that someone thought to light with trees taken to keep us warm. Everyone is somebody's child, the tree the child of the seed, the iron extracted from earth's core, forged with fire and that fire fed, too. So many debts.

And the dead, I know, walked among us. And within us. Awakened by the aroma, this feast of the old ways, seeing through the plastic, the fleece and thermal space age gear, taking their place in the circle of women, holding a large hide between them, stretching and working it, bouncing a child in the center. The dead entering the hands of the women kneading the fibers apart as they did then. This is how, this is the motion, this is the way.

Yes, I am sure the dead were there. Perhaps it was their idea, *let's give them a taste of how it used to be before thinsulate, before plastic and prefab houses. Before the lie was told that the gods are dead. Let's make them hungry for us.*

And so I fleshed, up and down, listening to the conversations among the young around me yearning to find a way to live that makes sense. But I cannot remember a single word. Just the motion, the debt, the hides, and the sturdy blond woman walking the November field, playing the wailing bagpipes, and the men singing the high-pitched keening at the Mother Drum.

Perhaps this is how remembering works.

Do this. Up and down, back and forth. *Now. You remember.*

Notes
I support animal protection, sign petitions against zoos and aquariums, oppose sports hunting and killing contests. I am also called to bone and pelt and my old ones. Many years ago, I thought the remedy to planetary devastation wrought by humans was to follow certain conceptual, political and spiritual prescriptions in order to restore the world. And maybe that is one way.

Yet I am compelled to follow the old ones who are calling me into their ways, and so I flesh the hide, I pray, and I daven in this field of death out of which life comes. I know that some of these deer were taken in an unholy way, and so both the doing and the writing are a work of reparation, a work of blessing the dead, acknowledging the debt, honoring the life.

Erica Charis-Molling
Requiem in the Key of Bees, a Cento
taken from Virgil

The signs of it in the bees, without any doubt
nearer and nearer. Mother, let me take you
to blow across the deep in hurricane,
flash on flash from heaven. Every sign
easy to see because from a single root:
Life brings sickness with it. You can see
one certain lust drives every creature
eating its way as it burns inside a furnace,
leaving me weeping, with so much still to say.
Could any star rise at night, single and marvelous
or sing what I, in silence, had picked up from you.
Sing as we walk—it makes the trip less painful.
It's true for bees as it is for human beings.

Notes

Centos are like a quilt, my mentor told me—you find the used fabric in other people's poems and then you stitch it together to make it
new. The lines I gathered here from various Virgil works have different
weaves and textures from their various translators. Yet when stitched
together, the fragments form a new whole—much the way a wound
might heal when stitched together, with new implications forming an
interconnective tissue that bridges the pieces that have been brought
together. Little is known about the actual life of the Roman poet, but
his work bears witness to much war and destruction of the land; some
of it in an apocalyptic tone. There's much in the world and its current
climate that feels that way to me right now. The tenuous existence of
bees, the busy pollinators who do so much to hold our food system together, often seems a portent to me. Who knows if they buzz to comfort
one another? I know that as long as I can hear that buzz, it will be a
comfort to me. A sign that not all is lost—a sound that tells me there are
still enough scraps left to stitch together a new whole, to begin to heal
this planet.

What it Takes to Breach

In the end of the world we meet on the surface of an open wound.[...]
The wound makes us realize how tender we are. It makes us realize
how strong we are. It makes us realize how many we are,
working invisibly but contagiously.

—Juliana Borrero Echeverry, *Landscapes at the End of the World*

At my first hint of struggle in ascending, [the whales] whispered into
my cells, unleashing the dormant knowledge of what it takes to breach,
to break through, to get out from under. [...]

—Michaela Harrison, *What it Takes to Breach*

Juliana Borrero Echeverry
Landscapes at the End of the World

1

Burning 16, 18, 29, 47 days.
The anger of this fire cannot be put out anymore.
This is how it is at the end of the world.

2

In the end of the world I am writing a book
about the end of the world.
It is a book about hitting the fan.
A book about deep disenchantment and the need
to (re)construct hope.
I am writing it fast because at the end of the world
not much time is left.

3

In the end, dry red crumbling earth. So thirsty it seems to
suck up your feet.
Olive trees, like it was in the beginning.
Do you want something, asks the woman? There are still
 a few bones left.

4

After centuries of discontent, Uliza—the hero of my book— burns
the house down.
With the husband in it.

5

The end of *what* world, asks Mohammed, a Palestinian
writer living in Spain.
Because there are several.
I bloody hope you are right, I respond. But let me see if I can explain.

6

She is crouching like a wounded animal. She is wild but frozen.

While she performs her daily hygiene rituals the World climbs on her, calming his pelvic agitation, as he reads the latest world news. She kicks and spits. She likes this bumping and grinding less and less. Nausea. He neutralizes her with a blow, leaving her stunned and stupid. The World whines as he mounts her. Ohhh ohhh ohhh my love, let me introduce my new perforating drill deeper and deeper inside you. How I love to see you so dazed and scared! What? You don't want to? Well take this! A little bad porno never hurt anyone. Do you have any more viagra? Ohhh ohhh ohhhh, hold me, my love, another World you will not find, says he.

7

Put your mouth into this bucket of appless, ssaid the ssssnake, and find one that isss not rotten.

This apple is not a nuclear weapon. This apple is not a war machine. The seeds of this apple have not been registered. Its taste is woody, reminiscent of plums, with a slight narcotic effect and a touch of smoked *guajillo* peppers. Its meat has not been modified by anxiety, anguish or chronic depression. This apple is not one woman murdered in Mexico every two and a half hours. This apple is not another social activist murdered in my country. This apple is not the mind devoid of the body. This apple is not language in its capacity to build sense. This apple is not a square deal. This apple is not a satanic dance. It is not an anonymous threat. This apple will not save you. Bite it… Digest it… This apple has crossed the Andes mountain chain in flipflops with a mattress on its back. This apple never thought it would have to do this. This apple will give you a blowjob for seven dollars behind the supermarket. This apple is not lying. This apple is hungry. This apple has nowhere to go. This apple is angry. This apple is not afraid. This apple remembers the ancient Chinese recipe for gunpowder. This apple is very old. This apple has eyes, but no mouth with which to scream.

8

In the end of the world writing is:
A promise–to–purchase agreement not carried out.
An urgent court warrant sent for the third time; still unattended.

Undocumented. Jobless. Residency denied.
In the end of the world we write standing up,
at 3 a.m. in a police station
In the awful handwriting of a slobbering idiot
In the cheapest pen available on half a page
of almost transparent paper.
In the end of the world even the oxygen is violent.
In the end of the world violence is the law.
In the end of the world to write is to enumerate indifference.
In the end of the world we lose our dignity every day.
In the end of the world, we are all victims.
In the end of the world, not even that matters.
Ripping one's shirt is a form of art.
In the end of the world writing scrapes, scratches and screeches.
The page whines and the ink is perverse.
Typewriters function on automatic.
They also drill, cut metal and make cappuccino.
There are no drafts or second attempts.
Everything harms, cuts, or burns.
In the end of the world everything you say will be used against you.
In the end of the world we shoot hurricanes with nuclear weapons
and we buy Greenland.
The Indians smell bad, lack education and do not speak our language.
In the end of the world there is no evidence to suggest
that indigenous leader was murdered.
And, the Amazon is ours, ok?
In the end of the world, what is the use of poetry.

9
The last alphabet
the last egg
the last song
the last love letter
the last tango
the last tequila
the last Pyrenean ibex
the last battery
the last train

the last cent
the last…
….straw
the last light
the last flight
the last black turtle
the last cowboy
the last corner
the last cluck
the drop that filled the…
the last atom of oxygen
the last dance
the last match
the last shot
the last Tasmanian tiger
the last bark of a lost dog
the last breath
the last time
the last Peking duck
the last wild boar
the last place
the last Juliana
the last chewy mouthful
the last house
the last breath
the last ounce
the last drop of…
orgasm
fury
liquid
the last squid
the last call
the last word
the last effort
the last horizon
the last image
…   …   …
are you there, sweet heart?

the last...

...please

.......love

hope.

10

After a slumber of 100 years, the sleeping beauty woke up. And the first thing she did after opening her eyes was get a divorce.

Immediately after, she formed an organization of angry women called Devotees of the Church of the End of the World, with the following slogan: <<Never again. Never again will you keep quiet for 100 years. Transform or perish. What is already dead, let it finish dying. Anger is your blessing. Destroy what you hate. Don't come to us, we'll come to you. >>

We are sorry but sometimes all we have left is violence. A little destruction is healthy after centuries of discontent. After ages of abuse, one becomes a terrorist without knowing. It is a natural process. Would you like to see my shiny claws? Don't get too close or I'll knock your head down with a stick!

11

Dear Lise,

You are not going to believe me but after more than forty days in which I have had all the time to write, I have only written unsent versions of this email in which I excuse myself for not being able to write about "Extinction Illness," as we had agreed in our conversations among mosquitoes and bullfrogs in the rainy Rawdon forest.

The Amazon is burning and I am broken. The peace process in my country is fucked once again and I am full of disillusionment. Things seem darker than ever. We are in the hands of a system with no eyes, no heart, no empathy, that thrives on abuse and ambition. I feel embarrassed and sad. It is a dying system, so blind, so out of date, so profoundly ignorant, walking towards its own end. I cannot be part of this anymore. It seems more and more urgent to say something but my words are paralyzed. The censor inside harasses me saying that writing is not enough as I make myself write this.

I wonder if the only thing we can do is watch as it walks itself down the plank and then… push. Meanwhile, continue our invisible, clandestine work, activating bodies and empathies, inventing forms of hope. So that we can study life, in all its resilience, its diversity, its languages; can embody sensitive ways of knowing, and freedom.

Because as this World walks over the edge, I have finally found the courage to get a divorce from too many years of disguised violence and manipulation I had been afraid to put a limit to. My son is falling in love for the first time, my cousin is single father to a newborn baby, my sister is embracing his real body as a transgender man, and I am looking for an artistic voice that will have the power to express all this.

In the end of the world we meet on the surface of an open wound. We spend much of our time loving and healing. The wound requires different ways of knowing. It brings us together in new ways. The wound makes us realize how tender we are. It makes us realize how strong we are. It makes us realize how many we are, working invisibly but contagiously. Together, around the wound, we are constructing a new form of hope, or resistance, which in the end of the world is the same thing.

N.B.: This is an abridged version. Please see Dark Matter: Women Witnessing #9 *online for the complete essay.*

Michaela Harrison
What it Takes to Breach

Photo: Singing to the Whales by E. Melno

Author's note: Whale Whispering is an ancestral commission, an ode to water, a work of interspecies translation and co-creation between me, humpback whales and other cetaceans and people, a diasporic healing quest, an exploration and transmutation of the legacy of trans-Atlantic enslavement through music. Based in Praia do Forte, Brazil, it is a soundtrack for personal, communal, and global transformation, a love song for whales, for Bahia, for Earth, for the ancestors and for life. As I address the generations of sexual trauma that have left my own womb and those of so many Black womb carriers diseased, I am learning to wail with the whales as a form of curative release, just as the Africans who crossed the Atlantic in slaving vessels surely did. This siren call summoning awareness of the unity of all being(s) and resonating with the movement in support of planetary healing is offered as a vibrational antidote to environmental destruction and racial, economic and gender-based violence. I am listening to and singing with the whales to tap into the echoes of the Middle Passage that are contained within their songs, to bring forth sounds that honor Nature's prescription for this time of reckoning and share the wisdom of water as it is relayed to me. Through underwater and studio recordings, filmed documentation, blog posts and community gatherings focused on collective singing and water blessing rituals, Whale Whispering serves as a way of dreaming forward via the lens of the so-called past.

Before, I did not understand. I had an idea, an inkling…Now I carry the knowing in my body, a recently recovered aspect of my identity—one who rises, with weights around her waist, from the sweet sanctuary of Olokun's[1] embrace, where she feels safe, I feel safe, I am safe. It takes a lot to come back up from that mother's milk on the half a breath I have left after exhaling impulsively when the ocean's pressure put my lungs in a squeeze that made me feel like a python's prey. With the whales crooning a cocoon around my suspended (actually slowly sinking) body, *I am free*, and I taste how fine it would be to stay here always. I hear what they heard when they got down this far, with or without life in them still. The true blue medicine on the other side of the bitter pill of being heaved overboard or choosing to jump rather than go down with the ship toward whatever hell it might be approaching… Whalesong. Before, I didn't understand. Yes, it's the weight of the world pulling me in, it's the warped womb, the liquid tomb. But she is still in bloom, creation's song booms rapturously throughout the healing rooms inside and outside of me and there is indeed a balm to make the wounded whole. Some of them stole/themselves back/from death; this is what I know now in a way that I could not have known, before

I breached. I had and have spent so much time marveling at the whales' ability to troll gravity by flying all their weight out of the water at any given moment, and I've had several experiences of tuning in to a particular whale as they rose, having a semi-vicarious sensation of what it was like in a flesh-and-blood sense. This, though, was my body, and when I dove on a quest to meet the songs at their source, to feel myself fully enveloped in the mighty, mellifluous balm itself, it was without flippers and with a weighted belt that (I later found out) had just a little too much poundage. In retrospect I realized that I didn't take enough time or care with the intricacies of locking myself into that situation, and this lesson has come to resonate with significance in so many contexts since then. I sank with ease where I had been buoyant on earlier tries. I couldn't see them with my eyes but I didn't need to see: the whales' auric presence is massive. I knew they were under the boat and within 75 feet of me at basically the same level where I found myself, about ten meters down—and they were absolutely aware of me climbing into their reverie. Crown-first, I entered the zone where the sea pulls rather than pushes and quickly figured I had about twenty seconds to hang after a check-in with my lungs, then melted into the sound of salvation where the only truth is that I Am One with all of creation.

The treasure I dive for isn't one I can touch or feel with my hands but my heart, my soul, my mind can expand to hold the heavy of all that this song is encrypting into me. Every atom in my 3-D form thrums with the whales' emanations and I don't yet know that it's exactly what I will need in the moments to come, but I don't have to know. I am Present…Here…inside the sound…The first thing that happens when I stop all thoughts is that I sense my time-bending capacity ratchet up exponentially and those twenty seconds stretch into centuries; the Middle Passage millions set me a-tingle with their proximity. I feel more than hear them through the veil of the whales' mediation/mitigation. They're translating, using their voices to filter out the screams, the moaning, the grunts and the growls, the howls, the chain-rattling and the keening that, in addition to the singing, comprise the actual record left by those ancestors in these waters. To hear all that would do me tremendous harm. The echoes and strains I do catch periodically are enough to sear my spirit, triggering memories of branding and my own sizzling flesh and the feel of a baby's mouth de-suctioned from my breast–I would not survive hearing the entire choir. The whales' skill at distilling these African vocal spells into show-and-tell is a marvel of gorgeousness that slides in through every broken part of me, mending, illuminating as it blends into my blood, activating my DNA…so I remember how to breach.

Some of them knew how to do it. Some of them had actively prepared for it through their initiations and training, knowing they must not die so that the magic could live. To sink in shackles and then resurface is the work of workers of miracles; my awareness of them surges as my lungs push back against the peace of this apnea and I unfurl, go from fetal to feral in a flash as the weight at my waist wakes me up to what it will take to rise. I've been so faithful and so foolish, I see, refusing the flippers because they always feel awkward to me, and forgetting to learn how to unfasten the belt that now feels magnetized to the planet's core. Oh, this will take so much more than I had understood when I descended, confident in basic skills gleaned from freediving in deep tidepools near the shore without this leaden lasso encircling me. For the briefest instant I have the sense that this will be too hard, this struggle against gravity to get myself those thirty feet up, back to the surface where air awaits. The rope I'm holding is slack and therefore useless as a support in hoisting myself, still I grasp it like it's a lifeline as I locate the Power inside me and tap it like a rubber tree. I cannot panic—in the ocean panic can mean death. I must know, I must know that I am the

Power, as the ancestors have already told me. So, I inhale. Not breath, not water, but sound.

It's already everywhere, reverberating lavishly, so I'm not surprised when I start to feel the whales' song work on my physical form. They code-switch on me like champions, and without missing a beat or changing a note shift into a transmission that my body downloads with ease, taking a shape I've never felt before, flexing, repositioning, and coordinating muscles in a way I had never imagined possible, generating what truly feels like a superhuman force from my waist down to move me through what is definitively the most difficult thing I've ever done physically. As they always do, the whales know. They sing me up, sending out vibrations that propel me as I hone my focus on the surface, a streamlined, fully-embodied intention to access oxygen. Simultaneously, their voices hypnotize me into maximum fluidity, I am sleek and sliding higher and there is no thing that is not me—a breaching whale is a leaping lizard is a mermaid rebirthing herself is a miraculous resurrection of one discarded, all parting water. Whalesong glitters the endless saline solution with astral technology through notes both audible and beyond my capacity to perceive with my ears; only my soul can hear the deeper utterings. Either way I will never, ever fully know what they mean, because mystery is mystery is mystery is mystery still and always, Hallelujah. I elevate.

The whales remain below as the ancestors accompany me, they are my school as I rise. Afterwards I will reflect on visions of them slithering back onto ships then standing tall as they drip Earth-tears and dare with death-defying stares anyone to send them over the rail again. After this it will click for me that only upon living through this do I legitimately grasp what it means to be *Undrowned*[2], though Alexis Pauline Gumbs, prophetic as always, wrote me into the book with certainty that the knowing was inside me, was what propelled me to Whale Whispering and would eventually awaken to permanently alter my consciousness— as it has.

In my rising, a zillion thoughts nip at the periphery of my awareness: *I should have tested this belt! I should have formally trained in free diving! I WILL NOT DIE IN THE OCEAN TODAY*...I hear them but only process them consciously after I surface; I am a laser, I am a rocket,

I am a baby whale learning from Big Mama what it looks and feels like to spread my flippers and fly. It's fun. It's what I was born to do. I am gaining momentum as I near the Above and I *feel* what a magical machine my body is, I know this story has a happy ending—but. Just as I get to within a few feet of my destination, my lungs contort with the urge to inhale rightnow rightnow rightnow rightnow, and I am still pushing, still focusing on the whales' now-distant dirges, I am two feet from the surface and feel myself about to implode, faint, imbibe the entire Atlantic in a quest for air and I sense the last of my resistance slipping from me, still I know with my entire being that somehow this ends with me bobbing up through the Blue safe and well. Through a fleeting ripple I get another whiff of ancestral terror. Then a splash and a hand, I am reaching up as Zá, owner of the @scubaturismo boat and my whole merBrother reaches down to clasp mine. He tugs me the last eighteen inches of the way so that I soar *with support*, definitely projecting further upward than I would have on my own, and I am already grinning as if the oxygen were helium making me speak in dolphin squeaks, making me a balloon, I swoon as I go weightless again, this time breathing in as I breach. The half dozen folks on the boat break into cheers when I break the surface and from Below the whales hum their approval up through the soles of my feet, their vibrations cradling my womb.

So that's what had happened, on levels and levels and levels. I went down deeper than I ever had—foolishly, hastily—and found myself in a place from which it was extremely challenging to return. Was it as deep as deep can get? Hardly, and eventually, I will go deeper, much more carefully. But I surely could have stayed right there, forever drifting in Blue to the tune of the whales and the muffled thunder of the ancestors, sacrificing myself to Olokun. As it is, it's taken me months and months to truly begin re-emerging from the place I touched; it's like that with Olokun, more than slightly mind-blowing…I could call on some of my biologist colleagues to help me insert the right language to discuss what is physiologically involved when whales sault in slow motion from the sea, but none of it would relay the spectacle that is watching these winged cetaceans set sail. At my first hint of struggle in ascending, they whispered into my cells, unleashing the dormant knowledge of what it takes to breach, to break through, to get out from under. I imagine that each individual body has its own formula for propulsion at the end of the day; for me it was trust, more than any of the physical processes involved, that served as the ultimate fuel for my flight. Then and now I trust in the Power, I trust myself. I trust in ancestral protection, the guidance directing me, and in the helping hand that always, always, always appears when I need it, right on so-called time.

N.B. This essay was originally a blog entry at www.michaelaharrison.org

———

[1] Olokun is the deity of the ocean, its depths, mysteries and riches, and primordial wisdom in the diasporic spiritual traditions of the Yoruba people.

[2] Gumbs, Alexis Pauline; foreword by Adrienne Maree Brown. *Undrowned: Black Feminist Lessons from Marine Mammals.* AK Press, 2020.

Kim Zombik
In The Name of So Many

Last week on YouTube, I watched a video taken from a security camera in a fast-food restaurant somewhere in New Jersey. Looked like it might have been summertime, the way the light shone along the floor and tables. In the video, you see a lean black woman with a sleeveless top and long blond extensions bringing her tray of food to the table on the left side of the screen. As she goes to sit, a young black woman comes in, wearing her hair cap and a coat, and heads to the counter. Even though you can't see her face, you can tell she is exhausted as she leans in.

Since COVID, most cash register areas are still protected by a wall of plexiglass so I can't really tell what the clerk is doing; the plexi is all gloss and reflection. The young black woman backs away from the counter to plop into a seat at the table on the right side of the screen, clearly worn out. The blond black woman is looking over at her.

I had the volume off and was watching the closed caption text sputtering across the bottom of the YouTube screen, which is about a one-inch by two-inch slice of movement and color at the top of the phone screen. The words were tiny and slow.

The exhausted young woman opens her coat to hand a balled-up brown bath towel to the other,

who is now standing close and has sanitized her hands with wipes from her purse. She returns to her seat and unwraps a baby.

Unwraps a baby.
The other woman unwraps a baby, new.
Brand newborn.
New umbilical cord hanging down to the restaurant floor.
A stranger unwraps a baby.

Young mama stands up, leans over the blond stranger and her new baby. I can tell both women are sharing a moment of some kind but their words are not what the caption is reporting.

Young mama turns to the door, the camera.
There is blood on her pants and her t-shirt says "Let me sleep."
Young mama leaves,
new baby, new umbilical cord hanging.
Young mama leaves.
Baby stays.
Stranger taking care.
Stranger taking care.

Let that poor young mama go to sleep. Her face, under the bright light, has frozen hysteria smeared all across it. The new baby nearly falling out the balled-up brown towel, delicate skin un-swaddled.

Young mama in no kind of shape
to wrap the wee one in clothes
or in attention of any kind.
She just trying to not die.
Just trying to not die.
She didn't kill the baby, no.
She had hope.
Young mama had hope.
She got help.
Brand new baby got help.
Every place is someplace to be loving.
Stranger taking care.
Stranger taking care.

The woman with her blond braids pulled back, her mouth making cooing shapes to the baby puts the oxygen mask on the tiny face when the medics come.

Little baby had been having a hard time
Little baby having a hard time.
Hard time breathing.
Birth shock and being left made her breathless.
Birth shock and being left made her breathless.
She just trying to not die.
New baby trying to not die.
Strangers taking care.
Strangers taking care.

The boyfriend of the blond black woman,
who had arrived just before the medics,
the woman holding this new starling,
he took a video of the baby's first cries.
Starling's tears.
Baby crying.
Man crying.
Baby crying.
Grown man crying.

Wouldn't you know, he'd been left when he was a newborn, too.

Strangers taking care
Strangers taking care.
Strangers taking care.

Andrea Mathieson
Listening for the Long Song

> For all things sing you
> at times we just hear them more clearly.
> — Rainer Maria Rilke, *The Book of Hours*

Art by A. Mathieson

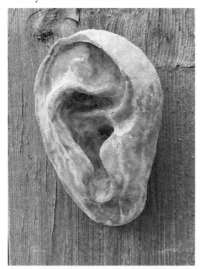

Before energy manifests as form it lives as a frequency, a vibrating song within a womb of silence. We all have an innate capacity to perceive a far wider range of frequencies than we generally engage but most of us have lost our ability to hear the subtle sounds of the Earth and the voices of all her creatures. This collective deafness reinforces the belief that the Earth is mute. It also compromises our ability to gracefully coordinate with Life on this planet. It is my belief that this quality of intimate listening is essential for wisely navigating the tremendous environmental challenges we are now facing. I call this "yin-listening," an ability we are all born with but are rarely encouraged to develop. While our culture values mental accomplishments, material success and power, yin-listening is rooted in the vulnerability of an open-hearted, reciprocal intimacy.

Rationally, we know stones do not talk; though trees may creak in the wind, we mostly see them as silent sentinels. Meanwhile, Kirlian photography reveals vibrating auras around both living and 'inanimate' things and sophisticated devices can detect sound frequencies in plants, stones, and even metals. In other words, science is helping us understand that *everything is singing*.

I only began practicing yin-listening in my forties. Though I studied many subtle nuances of music as a classical pianist, when I was a child, playing the piano was more about winning at local musical festivals than joyful self-expression.

I think of listening now as taking place within a series of concentric circles, activated from the core — the still small voice of our own heart wisdom. When we listen carefully, the still small voice grows steadily louder and clearer. Gradually, our focused yin-listening develops a palpable field of energy within and around us. We can begin to perceive other voices that resonate with our developing heart wisdom by focusing on an animal we love, a significant tree, or a landscape that really calls to us. Listening within this larger circle through an open, engaged heart brings us into a dynamic relationship with the inner life of the 'other'. Our focused desire to listen, without agenda or expectation, magnetically draws out the other's voice while enriching our own experience.

In 1995, I began making flower essences, a process that involves intuitive listening to each flower's essential nature. Flower by flower, I gathered Nature's stories through the plants in my garden. The experience became an intoxicating love affair. My focus has now shifted from producing flower essences to helping others learn to listen.

Recently I gave a private flower essence tutorial to a young woman, a gifted clairvoyant whose orientation was primarily toward communing with the angelic realms. I explained how this type of listening involved a conscious rootedness into the heart of nature. After leading Danielle through a guided meditation for grounding, I invited her to practice drawing up energy through her root chakra before going to the garden to locate the flower that called her. "There are two hosta plants," she said, "in different locations in the garden." She put the petals in a bowl of water to begin making the essence, and I asked her to take quiet time to commune separately with each of the plants. Later, she shared her experience.

"This way of listening feels very different," she said. "I had to engage all of my body, and even touch the plants to get clear messages. Before that, the information was random and scattered..."

Her first conversation yielded a fairly typical flower essence description outlining the hosta's healing properties, but when she shared the second, I was amazed. This conversation happened in an area of the garden I'd previously identified as the root chakra zone. In this setting, Danielle's communion with the hosta took on a transpersonal quality that I recognized as similar to what I feel when I'm in communion with Gaia, the spirit of the earth. Feeling a distinct humming vibration in the earth, she sensed her body was naturally in tune with this frequency. "My song is dancing with the earth's song."

•

She also realized the importance of consciously tuning into this vibration to feel safe, grounded and fully present in her body. As Danielle received information-energy through her root chakra rather than her third eye, she was able to access this different realm of earth-wisdom, accompanied by a rippling sensation throughout her entire body.

Listening to Ancient Stones

> We are not talking to the river; we are not listening to the winds and stars; we have broken the great conversation. And by breaking that conversation we have shattered the universe. We have to learn again how to listen to the earth, how to open the ear of the heart.
> — Thomas Berry in *Spiritual Ecology: The Cry of the Earth*

Every summer, my artist friends Ed Bartram and his wife Mary Bromley move up to an island in Georgian Bay where they live for four months in a very beautiful and rustic setting, painting, gardening, and entertaining friends and family. The remarkable striped stones in this area of Ontario are a geologist's treasure-map, revealing stories about the earth's formative shifts millions of years ago. I've enjoyed visiting Ed and Mary on their island for the past twenty summers. While they paint and tend other projects, I head out with my journal to commune with the ancient stones.

Listening in this landscape is very different than in my suburban garden. In my experience, while flowers tend to mirror our human personalities, ancient stones offer us entry into a deeper earth-story. Whenever I visit the island, I feel powerfully connected to the *anima mundi*, the Soul of the World. It usually takes me several days to settle into coherent resonance with this wild place before I feel sufficiently tuned and ready to receive the slowed wisdom of the stones.

Knowing how ancient and articulate this landscape is, when I approached the land in 2013, I heard '*The things that are broken apart are still connected.*' The huge broken stones, split open by ice or major earth upheavals, captured my attention with this phrase and it became the focus for our annual conversation.

Softening my tired body and opening my heart, I consciously surrendered to the Great Mystery. Once again the magnetic tug of the ancient stone drew me down into a slow, rhythmic pulsation where ideas begin to flow into consciousness like warm lava. I spent the rest of my holiday receiving information about 'brokenness within the web of life,' until a painful bladder infection forced me to set aside my plan to listen to the stones. I turned instead to my aching body. This is part of the conversation with my bladder:

A blossoming needs to occur through your pelvis. You are designed to be awake and responsive to Life's multi-dimensional, enlivened frequencies but you need to be present in a completely different way. Three words: Abide, Breathe, Attend will guide you in this different way of being. Applying these three words to your root chakra will broaden your earthed vocabulary and serve your destiny… People want transformation in the form of pain-free miracles, but it is our capacity to willingly bear the anguish that is ours to hold which actually fuels transformation.

When I eventually returned to the broken stones I received information about how the earth listens to us!

Gaia always responds with a pure, loving intent to serve and to evolve the whole of Creation. Part of what is broken now is the field of our reciprocal listening, the deep soul-witnessing that is a dance of love between human beings and the sacred pulse within all matter.

I realized that when we remember our kinship with this deeper conversation, the Long Song sustaining all Creation, we naturally allow the necessary tectonic shifts to occur during the course of our life and especially at the moment our soul leaves our body. In reality we are all rooted in this Long Song, with the topsoil and the earthworms, bees and flowers, buildings, paintings and poems…

Remembering this and tuning myself to the Long Song, over and over and over again, has shaped my deepest and most holy connection with Creation. Though there were times in my life when the web ripped open, if I listened, I could still feel the Song shaping delicate new webs. Life's mystery constantly invited me to open and stand in the emerging beauty — in the midst of the brokenness.

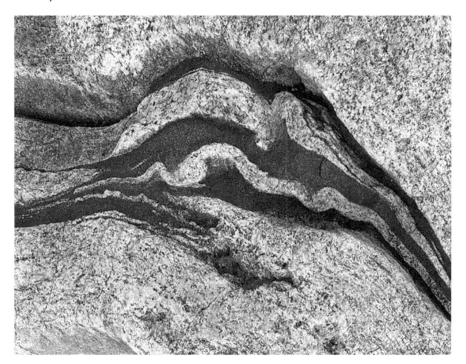

Photo by A. Mathieson

Listening to Whales

> What we need most to do is to hear within us the sounds of the Earth crying.
> — Thich Nhat Hanh in *Spiritual Ecology: The Cry of the Earth*

Evidence of the brokenness within the sacred web of life is becoming more painfully apparent each day. I am concerned that our attempts to understand and make amends will be unfulfilled and counterproductive unless we can learn to listen to the Soul of the World. Without this deep communion, we will not understand how to participate in what is unfolding now. In a dream in 2009, I was given a glimpse into the nature of this time as an 'awful birth'.

I'm called down to the shore of an island in northern Ontario by two friends who have just paddled in. Gesturing out to the water, they tell me about a huge creature they've seen. As they talk, a whale surfaces out in the bay. It comes straight toward us, arching and cresting through the water, and calmly beaches himself right in front of us on the small sandy shore. Sensing he wants to communicate I run up to the house to get my camera, feeling no one will believe me if I don't record the moment. When I return, the creature is gone.

I woke, horribly disappointed at the opportunity I'd missed. Later that morning, still very upset at my self-serving behavior in the dream, I decided to commune with the whale through automatic writing. This is the message I received:

Do not run away. I have come a great distance to be with you. I have but a brief time. Hear me and speak for me. Set aside your shame at not being present in the dream…There is a deep and painful aching in the oceans, an amniotic screeching within the watery womb of the planet. It must be heard and released… You are one who has been tuned to bear this awful birth, a birth of such agonizing pain and unknown consequence.

At this point in the meditation I broke down, weeping. With more to share, the whale waited for me to regain my calm.

We are not asking to be saved. That time is past. *We know our immediate future and have accepted it. We present ourselves to you in a pledge, an invitation to work with you in creating a new way, one where our minds and hearts are in complete harmony and communion with you, with humanity. You need us and we need you.*

*The first step is simple: Be with us. Be present. Open and listen — beyond the grief, beyond the shame. Receive us as kin, with information you can attain from no other. Linger with us, for our speech works in your cells in ways of which you have only a glimmer of remembrance. Do not dismiss what you feel in these rarefied encounters for it is the beginning of a new language between us. **We need your hearts and brains; you need our ways of knowing.** What has been divided – human from animal – must be re-membered. There is little time left for this work.*

I was stunned by the statement that, from the whale's perspective, we have passed a tipping point where all our best attempts to 'save' them are no longer possible. Loss of hope always feels devastating, yet I also heard the whale's urgent call — to remember our ancient, reciprocal kinship through a new language, apart from the drama of extinction. When we are caught up in high-intensity drama it is easy to panic, become ungrounded, go into overdrive or simply go numb. But when we respond in these ways, we become deaf to the loving wisdom constantly available to us within the natural world. Trusting the wisdom needed for this 'new language' would rise from the deep river between our souls, I kept listening through my broken-open heart for ways we might access our ancestral kinship. Instinctively, I knew I must begin by trusting my own animal body.

Wild Animal Prayers

> To listen is to lean in, softly, with a willingness to be changed by what we hear.
> — Mark Nepo, *The Endless Practice*

Over the next two years, I began developing 'Wild Animal Prayers,' a practice of spontaneous movement and authentic sounding that engages our bodies' primal wisdom. Though this work may appear similar to other techniques using spontaneous movement and sound, my intention was to access this new language of communion, not just with the animals but with all creation. Gradually I found my way into this 'common language' through my soft animal body.

My Wild Animal Prayers are done in the peaceful quiet of my living room, in my garden, or the open spaces of Georgian Bay. Yet even though the settings are safe, as I move and make my strange, unpredictable sounds, I am often aware of a distinct shift in the quality of atmosphere around me. It is as though a veil opens and I am no longer in ordinary space and time. During one session, a squirrel hung upside down on the trunk of the tree outside my living room, captivated by my sounds and movements. Only several long minutes after I stopped did he scamper away. On Bartram Island, I performed a Wild Animal Prayer near a large water snake as he lay shedding his skin in a shrub. My own serpentine movements and slow, primal chant created a thick and intensely alive communion between us.

Deepening into this work, I began to experience a potent kinship with creation, richer and more viscerally engaged than my previous encounters with nature. In a strange, tangible way I sensed I was tracking ancient songlines through the earth of my own body, perhaps in the way of aboriginal peoples' response to their landscapes, echoing Bruce Chatwin's insight, "The song and the land are one." Though this song was abandoned long ago, it still hums within and between all of us — human beings, animals and the earth.

Each Wild Animal Prayer dropped me into the earthy depths of my body-soul where I stood, quivering on the edge of the Great Mystery. It felt powerful to be witnessed by a colleague or a small group of women during the movement and sounding, for I was both intensely focused and utterly vulnerable. Coming out of the work, I sometimes felt exposed and shy; it was helpful to observe the changes in my expression in a small mirror.

We sometimes judge others by saying, "You're behaving like an animal," but this attitude conveys our ignorance of the tremendous integrity and natural wisdom of creatures. I sense that animals, whales and wolves, raptors and lions, mice and spiders, are anxious to access our consciousness not only by means of dreams but through our full body-listening. Allowing our bodies to move in uncensored, instinctual ways while releasing the sounds that want to pour out of us, we begin to loosen our 'humanness' and open to the 'other'.

I love holding space as people enter a Wild Animal Prayer. I wait, listening for buried sounds to be released as the frozen, forgotten zones of their body begin to melt and flow. With every whimper or growl, soaring cry or stuttering agony, some blocked energy is liberated into the highly-charged atmosphere. Witnessing each person's communion with Nature is vital. When people share their stories in a safe, non-judgmental space, they strengthen confidence in their own embodied intuition. Listening together open-heartedly, we honour these liminal moments, grounding our experiences and making them more real. By sustaining this intimate kinship in our conversations with each other, we deepen our relations with all of Gaia's creatures. In these simple ways, we create sanctuary, for ourselves and for the Soul of the World.

It is my belief that Nature yearns for this communion. Rather than expecting to heal the earth, we are most available to life when we bring our completely open-hearted presence. Yin-listening to the heart of Nature has been a long and compelling love affair; each encounter stretched my capacity to be an attentive witness and to receive Nature's varied frequencies of love. As I communed with the natural world, I learned a profound truth: ***Whatever is not witnessed with love tends to wither.*** To me, this is the crux of the environmental crisis. Because we have forgotten how to witness the world with love, the Soul of the World is dying. Whenever I feel heart-broken about the state of the world, I try to remember the wisdom of the ancient Georgian Bay stones:

The web may be broken, but the Long Song continues...

N.B.: This is an abridged version. Please see Dark Matter: Women Witnessing #4 *online for the complete essay.*

* Mathieson, Andrea. *The Raven Essence Manual: A Love Affair with Nature.* Self-Published, 1995. Print.

Jacqueline Freeman
Prey-er

> The Kingdom of Heaven is within.
> The eye by which I see God
> is the eye by which God sees me.
> — Meister Eckhart, *The Essential Sermons*

For my first meal in Belize I ate a fish served whole with a poached but firm puddle of staring eye. It was 1991 and inland Belize had not yet been discovered by tourism. I rented a bare-bones jeep at the airport and headed out to find a new and as yet undeveloped nature preserve a fellow traveler had told us about, deep in the jungle. As is normal when one travels with no plans, a vague rumor is as good as a map.

Over the next few hours, the red clay road steadily narrowed until branches raked the jeep doors on both sides. I wondered if I'd miscounted kilometers or turned onto the wrong rutted road, but we were committed simply because there was nowhere to turn around on the rarely-traveled trail. A half hour later we arrived at a tiny compound at the end of the road.

In my own country I am emboldened by familiarity when I seek adventure. Even though dangerous animals, poisonous insects and plants abound, I know the risks and what precautions to take. I shake scorpions out of boots, don't stick my hands into woodpiles that may house black widow spiders, and I shuffle my feet in shallows where stingrays sleep. A challenge of foreign travel is knowing what dangers are likely to occur, how to avoid them, and what tales are told merely to scare tourists. In the jungle of Central America, I was out of my element.

And that was the purpose of the trip. I wanted an adventure that would help me find my place in the world. I was in my forties, never married, hardworking, self-employed, assertive. I'd been told more than once that, in a relationship, I was a handful. I took exception to that and consoled myself that I simply had not yet met someone strong enough to fit my personality. Or maybe none existed and I was meant to be a lit flame on my own. In my twenties I solo hitchhiked 100,000 miles across North America, won a national sports award, and founded a women's crisis center. In my thirties I started a successful holistic health center and sold it eight years later. For the past few years I had led workshops and was at the top of my game. My accomplishments brought no peace; I longed for something to challenge me.

The preserve encompassed well over a hundred hectares, a few hundred acres. Small noisy monkeys, sleepy coati mundis and furry cat-sized animals rustled high in the branches or rooted in the dense brush around the grounds. My travel friend and I found three people living there: a woman who kept house and cooked, her husband who was building a small museum of local flora and fauna, and the forest-keeper who kept the tangled vines from overtaking the paths and grounds around the building.

They were wide-eyed surprised when we drove out of the jungle just before dusk. We imagined this new wildlife reserve was used to people dropping in but in fact it hadn't opened yet and we were only their third visitors ever. With no way to contact the place ahead of time, we had just "showed up," hoping to see a jaguar or two. But when we asked to rent a guest room overnight, a room was quickly readied for us and the woman made us a meal.

We rose at dawn to a cacophony of screaming howler monkeys. After breakfast we set off to explore the recently completed twenty-foot-wide chainlink tunnel that served as a passageway into the jungle. Though we called it a tunnel, it was actually more like a quarter-mile cage, not to keep animals in, but rather to protect anyone who wanted to venture into the jungle where jaguars live. I asked how often they'd seen the jaguars. Though they had lived here their whole lives, the couple had never seen one and the groundskeeper said he'd seen one only once, when he and a friend removed a tree that fell onto the fence a year ago.

Jaguars, the third largest hunting cat in the world, were the ancient symbol of Mayan royalty. Secretive hunters, they diligently trail quarry while choosing a perfect spot for attack. Their spotted coats provide thorough camouflage in the shadowy forest and they are rarely seen. Nor do native people want to see one; local knowledge says if you see a jaguar, it's only because he let you see him and that's because he is about to eat you.

We set off on the path between a dense line of speckle-barked trees and a steep-banked muddy red river. My travel friend quickly disappeared ahead as was his custom. I preferred to go slower and see more. Long-legged lizards scooted over fallen leaves and tree trunks. Birds squawked, squealed and trilled far in the distance. Branches swayed from the weight of unseen animals leaping above me into the viney forest.

I felt naive stepping into the unfamiliar jungle-forest. The forest, a patient, eternal animal itself, opened its maw and welcomed me in. But I felt alien to the landscape that surrounded me. It asked questions I was too intimidated to answer. Why am I in this jungle? What do I want? This ever-changing forest's vines grew overnight. Anything that fell would be gone by morning.

As I wandered farther away from the compound, the wide, airy path darkened. The forest came closer and a small anxiety rose in me, the kind you get when someone you don't know well stands too closely. I'd expected the forest to retain a civil distance. The dense-packed canopy dimmed and the waxy leaves and tall ferns loomed even closer in the shade.

Each branch, vine and leaf spread upward, filling any open space. Each sought to catch even the briefest glimpse of sunlight, which left little light below on the forest floor where I walked. Contrary to my expectation of spaciousness, the forest felt densely packed, too full of everything for me to feel comfortable. I came here seeking contact with wilder nature, but when surrounded by it, I found solace in the familiarity of my old sensibilities — the flinty hardness of a chain link fence, something back home I'd find offensive in the woods. How could I leap over the boundary of my cultural misperceptions to know this place?

Growing up in rural New England, I spent most of my childhood outdoors and felt more at home in the woods than in my family's living room. I knew the land around my home intimately well, able to predict the day burgundy trilliums would break ground each spring. I knew which plants to use as dye and which to leave untouched. I identified with a glance whose scat and where grew the berries they'd eaten. But here I was the alien one.

The fence wove its way through thick-rooted, mossy-branched hardwoods and twisting vines, barely separating one part of the forest from the other. I kneeled and scanned tree branches and underbrush. I caught sight of the remains of something cow-like. Was that a tapir? All that was left was its head and ribs, a patch of matted fur, and the leg bones. The large body size of this animal, compared to the size I imagined a jaguar to be, surprised me. Maybe jaguars were bigger, more ferocious or dangerous than I thought.

Suddenly my skin prickled. I felt the weight of eyes upon me and in an instant my eyes saw the jaguar. At that moment the fence no longer existed. I felt as exposed and vulnerable as the predator intended.

Silent and bone-still, the jaguar stood thirty feet away, unblinking, intent. I found myself unable to move. I locked into his stare. My breath went still.

In an indescribably long and brief moment the jaguar and I entered a primal relationship. With awe I felt myself calmly agree to be prey.

My conscious mind played no part in this. This agreement was absolute, it had no right or wrong to it. I agreed. A contract was set.

The jaguar lowered his head and moved toward me.

I could not turn away from his eyes. I could not stand up and shake this off, I could not utter one word.

Fifteen feet from me he crouches. He tenses. Coils. His whiskers fan out around his mouth.

Every cell in my body blazes alive.

His pupils dilate full black and he lunges.

His teeth and body fill the entire sphere of my vision. All four paws above me, his open jaw wider than my head, he rushes at my face.

He slams the fence and the metal links stretch over me.

He springs to the ground, sideways to where I kneel, turns his head and briefly, ever so briefly, looks at me.

I hear again the agreement: You were mine. Yes, I say.

In a second he blends back into the forest, a shadow moving into branches, and he's gone.

I'm dripping sweat, my blood galloping adrenaline, a volcano of erupting senses. Again and again the jaguar's lunge obscures the world — his open jaw over my head, arched white teeth, red-ribbed mouth-roof, his explosive feral breath thundering into my lungs, the jangling weighted fence inches from my face.

What I felt was simple: I was about to die.

But there was no fear whatsoever in that deeper part of me that agreed to die. Over and over I have relived this moment, fascinated by the covenant in the relationship, my astounding complicity.

In the moments before this event, walking through the jungle, freely spinning through my tenure of time, I bore a life of singular self-importance to me and those I care about.

The second the jaguar and my eyes locked, all that fell away and I enfolded in a new process, me named simply as food, fuel for another's life, and the kernel of a story about a woman who went to Belize and was eaten by a jaguar.

Yet in that moment I felt no regret. I felt completely willing, voluntarily invested to fulfill the covenant. Whoever I had been till that moment, wherever my life had been leading, all suddenly shifted and I was liberated from the comfort of my old bearings and directed into a new destiny as the life force that fuels a jaguar.

In the moment when he asked, when death felt real, I turned willingly from life and said yes. I agreed to die. I was complicit in the agreement, congruent in my purpose. I felt opened and freed inside myself at making this ever-so-obvious agreement. I did not imagine myself a failure or think I should fight for my life. The role opened and I stepped forward.

In that radiant moment I felt overwhelming respect for my killer. Not awe, but respect, or more significantly, equivalency, a rightness to our actions. I felt myself become the vehicle of a life force far, far larger than myself, a fundamental thread in the continuity of life.

I have sometimes wondered at the moment of my death what my thoughts might be. Would my life flash before my eyes? Would I, as I expected, fight tooth and nail to keep living?

In that moment, though, I found myself without a single thought of my own life. Instead I saw how the vital force of Life itself pours through me and surges forth into the future.

But there's more.

After the jaguar moved off into the jungle, I stood up, shaken, the way someone at a movie rearranges themselves after being frightened by a scary onscreen image. Of course it wasn't real, we KNOW that, but our hearts race and our adrenaline flows nonetheless. In that brief moment we ARE afraid, but we don't protect ourselves because we also know nothing can hurt us.

When I tried to resolve my fear by reminding myself of the fence and that he couldn't really hurt me, I realized that the jaguar was not in the same movie I saw myself in. The jaguar did not acknowledge the fence at all, except to allow that I was not eaten.

The jaguar attacked me without regard for the fence. He saw me kneeling and prey-sized, unprotected, able to be captured.

I had always been confused about the few moments after his leap and for months afterwards vivid internal pictures of the jaguar overtook me in wake and sleep. His persistent ambushes forced me to relive every detail again and again until I realized how threatened I'd been by the knowledge behind the attack. I didn't grasp till now that I simply was unable to bear knowing this.

The awareness of complicity in accepting to die undermines the illusion of being in control of one's destiny, that we volitionally determine where we go in life. That illusion of control keeps undesirable experiences at bay by separating us from events that are the very core of our participation in Life. Keeping death distant from us causes us to live in fear of it, cautious, separate from Life.

Unexpectedly, instead of feeling protective of my life and the fleeting gift so easily lost, I now have no reason to be afraid of dying, of being incomplete.

When I entered the rainforest I was a small human whose thoughts, despite my seeming accomplishments, were constantly inhibited by hesitancy and doubt.

The jaguar freed me of being afraid. In his wake I live more fully, love more deeply. I understand the responsibility of passionately imbuing our life spark with as much voltage as we can.

The jaguar didn't take my life, only a small part of it. He devoured my passivity and left me with a voice inside that reminds me to keep my flame burning brightly, a voice that constantly asks if what I'm about to do bears increase.

Each time I hear that voice, I thank this spirit of the forest for his blessing.

Margo Berdeshevsky
In the Land of Afterwards

In the land of afterwards, may we remember the poetry of almost/ the large
animals who never forget/ the sand of our first imprint/ its infant step...

In the land of before may the infant's first turning be toward grass, its
insistence on green/ the leaf, its awareness of falling, scarlet and broken
but ready

In the land of our new fear may I remember yours —and the winter's
remarkable determination to sleep until April...

Art by M. Berdeshevsky

Notes

As both a poet and a photographer, I work with layers, and montage, and metaphor…for meditation, for conjuring, and for healing, if we dare. Layer under and over layer, image leading our perceptions beneath and above the obvious. I begin by looking at what frightens me/us. Admit the hurt. Admit the soul. And then…ask for the next and the next day to dawn. The next door that seems closed and rotted—to open. The next vision of a land of afterwards, to form in my own heart. The hope for something more than night.

There Is No Light So Bright As That Which Shines from the Darkness
Miriam Greenspan

I. Omen

In the summer of 2020, in the midst of the worsening COVID pandemic, I contemplated buying a small house for my family. On a hill called Evergreen Acres with a view of Mount Okemo in Vermont, surrounded by birch, pine, spruce, oak and maple trees, with a wide area of grass, moss and wild raspberry bushes, it called to me as a refuge from the storms rattling the world.

We had rented this house for decades, starting when my two daughters were children in summer camp. It was now for sale and my husband Roger and I reached for it as a safe haven from the COVID virus where my now grown daughters Esther—at risk because of her disabilities—and Anna—at risk because she received daily doses of methadone at an urban clinic—might receive the gift of the trees.

In the car we decided we would go forward, turned off the A/C and opened the windows to inhale the fresh Vermont air. In this exact moment of our joy, we heard a loud thump.

"I think something flew into the car" said Roger. We had both heard a flapping. Looking at the back seat, we saw a trail of blood and feathers ending under the front passenger seat. There we found a stunning juvenile red-tailed hawk. It was dead.

I knew at once this was an omen. Someone in my family would die this year. I didn't know who. I prayed with all my heart to be wrong. That the angel of death would fly over our house and not descend on the small fragment of my family remaining after the Holocaust.

Six months later, my beautiful daughter Anna was dead.

II. Anna's Light

Welcomed into this world with great joy, Anna was a soul lit up by a light so intense that the obstetrician, looking into her eyes, called her a laser beam. Her eyes turned from blue to green and back again like the sea. Her nickname in grade school was Sunny. Her radiant beauty, inner and outer, was charismatic.

Anna had many gifts. She was an artist who specialized in pictures of animals—lions, tigers, panthers, salamanders, frogs, turtles. She was a self-taught cook whose culinary artistry was all about nourishing people and won her jobs at three-star restaurants. She was a talented photographer equally at home taking pictures of bucolic ponds and rough boys.

From her earliest days, Anna's love for and communion with animals was profound. She made few distinctions about which animals were lovable and which weren't. Though her cuddly friends—a succession of cats and her adored dog Kylee—were nearest and dearest to her, she was also known to pick up and kiss a slug.

Anna seemed preternaturally aware of the harm that came to innocent creatures. As a young child, she frequently asked me why humans were so cruel to animals. One of her earliest artworks was a laminated plate divided in the center. On one side were a fox and rabbit scampering in the grass. On the other side were animal furs hanging in a showroom. On the bottom, she wrote Save the Animals! She was six.

Anna was a born empath and gifted intuitive. I discovered her ability to read minds early on when, at the age of two, she spoke my thoughts. Her empathic connection to others and to the world was her greatest strength and greatest burden—a gift that put her at risk. When Anna asked me to tell her a story, she didn't want to hear only happy endings. A story wasn't complete unless it was "happy, sad, angry, and scary." All the colors on the human emotional palette needed to be known and absorbed by her. She had no filters, imbibing everything around her, the good and the bad.

Anna's sensitivity to suffering animated her kindness to friends and strangers. She could also flip it into humor, cracking people up with her genius for seeing the funny side of human weakness and dire events.

Everyone who knew Anna predicted a golden future for her.

III. Anna was Drawn to the Dark

Inside Anna was a raw beating heart that soaked up the world's tears and troubles—an abiding sorrow for suffering humanity and fierce outrage at human cruelty and folly. She was magnetized by the dark side of life, the grim underbelly of America. Racism, antisemitism, violence against girls and women and animals, poverty, injustice hit her with ferocious force. As the grand-daughter of Holocaust survivors, the transgenerational trauma of genocide was part of Anna's inheritance. Refusing spiritual bromides and glib consolations, she bore an intensity of pain that needed strong medicine.

Opiates became that medicine. The first time I did heroin, she once told me, was the first time I felt I belonged in the world.

When Anna was three, her sister Esther arrived, born with a mysterious neurological disorder. Inordinately fragile, with a host of medical issues, disabilities, pain syndromes, problems with mobility, balance and coordination, and early-onset osteopenia, Esther was unsafe in the world. She fell and broke easily—ten bones before she was ten years old. The periods of time that she wasn't suffering from injury, illness, or pain were lulls in continual storms.

When Anna was 16, Esther had a terrifying grand mal seizure at the dinner table. It solidified in Anna's mind that nothing she experienced would ever be as dire as what her sister had to endure. Her ongoing witness to her sister's endless suffering led Anna to believe that her own pain and needs didn't matter.

Roping herself in, Anna got smaller as Esther got larger. Esther went on to live a life filled with love, friends, community, music, pain and joy while Anna seemed bound on a downward course to see how it was for others who didn't have her abilities, talents, intelligence, beauty, or privileges. Her life seemed to ask the question: What would it be like to have none of these blessings?

After college, Anna moved into an apartment in midtown Manhattan. The day I helped her move in, I felt a shiver of premonition that this would be the place that brought her down. A year later, on the cusp of 2007, I got a phone call from a friend of Anna's who had bumped into her on the street. You'd better come here, she said. Anna needs to get out of here or die.

What I found the next day was an unrecognizable shadow of my beautiful girl. Anna had found a dark corner of the city where months of drug use culminated in a ten-day run on crack, heroin and benzos that would have killed her without her friend's intervention.

For the next eight years, Anna tried to rise up, only to fall again and renew her climb. On her long way down she found what it was like to live at the margins. To have no money. No job. No home. To go to prison when no treatment center would take her in. To be bound to the 'liquid chains' of methadone, the treatment for heroin addiction that was more addictive than heroin. To have a knife at her throat. To be raped by a fellow addict. To see her buddy overdose and die on the floor of her apartment as she tried to resuscitate him.

I prayed incessantly—to Tara, the Spirits, the Ancestors, God. I worked with shamans who journeyed to exorcise Anna's demons and bring back broken pieces of her soul. I invited the dark spirits and hungry ghosts to feast on my body, to make of myself a meal that would further the healing of Anna's lost soul, in the Buddhist practice of Chod. And in a comparable Jewish mystical practice called Gufa, I invited the spirits of darkness to a feast in their honor, feeding them toxins from around the world mixed with the milk of lovingkindness.

There was a time when, for our own self-preservation, we had to refuse Anna entry to our home. We drove her to a homeless shelter and left her there. But it wasn't long before we took her back in, fearing that the street would kill her. Against all advice from 12-step programs about 'enabling,' my mother's heart refused to 'detach.' As Anna slid down, I tried to consciously accompany her and let her know I would never abandon her. I followed her to dark *rendezvous* with dealers. I tricked her into getting caught by the police who brought her to court for her own protection, where she was mandated to treatment as a mortal risk to herself. I sat with her in her bedroom as she shot her drug into her veins; and when she asked me why I said: So that you will no longer have to lie to me about what you're doing. So that you can get honest and know that I know and that I still love you.

To dwell in hell on earth and bring her light into the darkest corners of human experience. This seems to have been Anna's karma.

Anna learned in her sojourns among the addicts and dealers in Manhattan to trust no one. But it took years for this lesson to sink in. She had a core understanding that privilege didn't make anybody better than the 'lowest of the low' and that even lost souls deserved respect. Like Anne Frank, a strong part of Anna believed that most people were essentially good at heart.

In a way, she reminded me of my father Jacob—whose essential innocence outlasted the Holocaust. Jacob, like Anna, had riveting eyes—blue pools of light that seemed to radiate kind-heartedness and goodness. In the dark night of Holocaust, he never stole from anyone, even when he was starving. Like Jacob, Anna kept a moral compass in hell. Like most addicts, she stole from her family and rationalized it by thinking we were financially comfortable enough to not be hurt by it. But she drew the line at her sister's disability check. She understood why addicts stole for their drug. But she couldn't fathom how they could rip off someone suffering from the same affliction. It took Anna a long time to recognize that her moral code didn't apply in the amoral world in which only the next fix mattered.

Wracked with guilt for having stolen from us, even in the depths of her worst days, she would engage me in urgent spiritual questions about sin, punishment, and redemption: "Do you think there's a separate hell for bad people like Hitler, child abusers and rapists than there is for people who are essentially good but do bad things sometimes for drugs? Do you think if you're a good person at heart but do bad things that you can still go to heaven?"

Anna was in awe of her grandparents—the courage it took to survive the Holocaust with their integrity, compassion, and love intact. By comparison, she always felt unworthy. Did Anna need to test her courage? To experience her own hell on earth to see if she could survive it?

Anna used heroin to feel she belonged to the world. She used it to escape the world. She used it to feel more. She used it to feel less. Heroin was her best friend. It was her worst enemy.

Ultimately, after all I've learned about its social, cultural, economic, genetic, biochemical, neurological, psychological and spiritual dimensions, I've concluded that addiction of this kind is a mystery. Most horrifying is the demonic way the drug takes possession of the addict…This much I know: the light Anna brought into the abyss was darkened but never extinguished.

IV. Coming Back to the Light

What turned Anna back from the drug life was not AA meetings. Not her various inpatient and outpatient treatment programs. Not religion. It was love. The love of her parents and sister, but especially the love of her life and their mutual devotion. K had done time in the Underneath and climbed up. She was a recovering addict with eight years clean who rescued Anna by seeing past the depredations of addiction into Anna's good heart and bright soul. She made Anna believe she could live without heroin, without pills. With love alone.

Anna's return to life also had everything to do with a rescue dog named Kylee, who we adopted at the start of Anna's journey toward recovery. Of all of Anna's beloved animals, Kylee was the supreme love of her life. She fit right into our family: an ultra-sensitive dog who took only one trial with a rigged-up bell on a doorknob that I rang as a signal to go out and do her business, before she got the knack of it and rang the bell herself—training us to take her out even when she didn't have to urinate. Before leaving the house, Kylee rounded up all members of the family and herded us out the door. She was more than a family dog. She was our family's spirit animal.

Photo by Roger S. Gottlieb

Anna's recovery lasted for six years, a span in which she lived as fully as she could, enjoying the love of her partner K, celebrating birthdays and anniversaries with K, Roger, me, Esther, and Esther's boyfriend Jonathan. Sitting around the table, laughing and saying our thank yous before our celebratory meals. Enjoying the natural beauty of Vermont. These were the days we savored and I thank the spirits for them. Because I know that Anna could have died any time from the moment I scooped her up in Manhattan. She lived for fourteen years after that day.

In October of 2020, Kylee became terminally ill with kidney disease. The vet said he'd never seen a dog who fought dying as hard as she did. Knowing that, as our protector, Kylee would struggle to stay alive through any amount of pain, seeing her unable to eat or drink, we made the heart-rending decision to euthanize her. Anna sat with Kylee in the backseat and fed her last treats as we drove Kylee to her death.

Kylee died in late October, 2020. Anna died three months later.

V. The Ancestors

Anna's ancestors were her grandparents, Aidla and Jacob Greenspan. Aidla's entire family and most of Jacob's family died in the Lodz ghetto and in Auschwitz and Treblinka.

Aidla was the spiritual and moral compass of our family. The four pillars of her character were integrity, humility, wisdom, and kindness. More than anyone I know, Aidla took reality straight. "We have to take it. We have no choice" was a repeated mantra. Blessed with extraordinary intelligence and a profound curiosity to understand the world…her passion to know was insatiable and the vast knowledge she carried in her memory was astonishing. Yet Aidla lived with a radical humility I have never seen in anyone else—except Anna.

At the age of 93 she gave a talk at Harvard University…in which she said:
"Everyone needs to feel they have a legacy. I hold onto the legacy of survivors of genocide—never to forget what happened. We must be kind to each other, to treat people kindly no matter what their religion or political affiliations. We are one people and we should help each

other. To do away with genocide and racism. The atrocities of the Hitler years taught us that. This is the legacy to teach our children and grandchildren."

In Anna's eulogy for Grandma, she said:
"Some people turn to movies or books for heroes. I never had to do that because I had a real live hero in my family, my Grandma, the only one of her family left alive after the Holocaust. I can't even imagine how anyone could live through what she lived through. She had every reason to be bitter but she wasn't. She was loving and kind."

With her unbounded respect for Grandma, Anna was too humble to see that Aidla's courage and kindness were a legacy that extended to her.

Aidla would not have survived without Jacob who she married just before Hitler marched into Poland. Five foot four inches, with a wiry frame that packed enormous energy, he did twice the work of most men and took on Aidla's labor as well in the Soviet gulag in which they were imprisoned.

The essence of Jacob was generosity and a quality of joyful innocence. How he managed to maintain these qualities after his sojourn in the Inferno and with the lifelong grief he carried was a mystery to me. With his slightly mischievous grin, blazing eyes, he had a zest for life that was matched by Anna's before the drug took her.

Perhaps it was the life force of her grandparents that enabled Anna to survive as long as she did.

VI. The Deathless Place

In the summer of 2010, in the middle of the period of the gravest danger to Anna, I did a Vision Quest to seek guidance from the spirits. Wracked with physical ailments and in a state of agony about the imminence of death in Anna's life, I could barely walk. I created a Medicine Wheel inside the house on Evergreen Acres.

In the middle of the night before, I had been called to the deck of the house, where I saw three Orb Weaver spiders weaving two of the largest, most intricate spiral wheel-shaped webs I'd ever seen. The next morning, seated on the floor near the Altar that contained, among numerous artifacts, statues of Tara and Kwan Yin and pictures of my greatest spiritual teachers—my children—I beseeched Grandmother Spider: Please help me!

In trance, I found myself collapsing slowly downward from sitting position, going deeper and deeper down into darkness, finally dropping through the Black Door to absolute dark.

You mustn't be afraid to die were the first words I heard.

I was impatient, waiting for something to "happen" that would remove my suffering.

Don't wait. Just be.

Throughout this timeless time, I was being taught patience—to be uncomfortable, without recourse, without exit, to be present without "waiting" for anything to happen, without expectations.

I felt Spider's qualities: creativity, night vision, diligence, patience, strength, endurance, and the capacity to sacrifice for her young. I felt a web-like covering over my body, particularly my breasts and belly. Wrapped in this covering, my pain disappeared.

Looking into the absolute dark, I saw round formations like pinwheels of ineffably bright light, shining out from the darkness.

Where am I?

You are in the Deathless place.

I prayed for Anna and for healing throughout the lineage of Aidla Olszer Greenspan and Jacob Greenspan so that only goodness and the force of Life be present for Anna.

I am weaving the future said Spider. I thanked her.

Is there anything more I should do?

Pray each day.

Afterwards, I returned to the deck. Two spiders in one web were in stasis, wrapped in a white covering. The spider in the second web was busy at work weaving the future from her body for her young ones.

Anna lived for 11 years after this Vision.

There is no light so bright as that light which shines from the darkness.

These words from the Zohar describe my vision with Spider. The Deathless place, not beyond but within the suffering of the innocent and the agonies of existence in a world hell-bent on its own destruction, is not a place that we would call 'comfortable.' It is a place of reckoning with what is, a place one goes in great, unendurable pain and sorrow for all that is endangered and lost, where an absolute acceptance of the unbearable somehow yields a sense of deathlessness. The light in the Deathless place is mysteriously ecstatic. It can be found only through surrender to the death of all that one treasures.

Help me to listen. Help me to see. Help me to know. Help me to be.

This is the prayer that I have said since Spider advised me to pray. I have done my best to listen beyond the five senses. To see beyond the veil of this life. To know with the heart. And the hardest of these in the escalating chaos, madness, disease, and cataclysm of these times, is to just Be with the destruction and loss, not to turn away.

VII. This is the End of the World

These were Anna's first words when she heard about the COVID pandemic.

Anna understood that hell on earth was not something in the distant future; it was Now. She knew this from her life as an active addict and from thirteen years of treatment with a drug that was harder to kick than heroin. Her survival on methadone was bound up in an end-of-the-world scenario that unfolded in front of her eyes each morning.

Hieronymus Bosch couldn't have painted anything more hellish than Methadone Mile—a square mile of homeless shelters and methadone clinics that constitutes the ghetto to which most of Boston's addicts are consigned. Each day dozens of homeless addicts pile onto the streets after the shelters close, where some inject themselves in the open air, fuck and defecate on the sidewalks and wander around out of their minds.

These are the most voiceless, marginalized, desperate people on the face of the earth. No one is lower than a junkie.

The sensitive ones were the first to die in the Holocaust, Aidla once said. Anna turned to heroin as medicine for her ultra-sensitivity. Methadone Mile scraped away at her sensitive skin until it was raw. Still, she courageously lived clean and sober within the parameters of a life limited by methadone—until the COVID pandemic hit and her recovery began to erode. Isolated and confined, shut away from her family as Roger, Esther and I quarantined for our protection, viscerally pained by the world's suffering, American fascism, and the death of her spirit animal, Anna's ability to navigate these troubled waters without her medicine crumbled.

VIII. Death on the ICU

If you want to see your daughter alive, come now. This was what I heard from an ICU nurse in the middle of a cold night last February. Like millions of others, we were not allowed to be with Anna as she lay dying. The nurse made an exception to the COVID rules to allow us to say good-bye.

Anna's passing was not a peaceful nod-out overdose but a brutal death of endocarditis, a bacterial overgrowth on her aortic valve that started with undiscovered sepsis followed by a stroke. The doctors tried their best to save her life, including a last-minute emergency surgery to rebuild her broken heart.

Just days before, Anna was praising me for the release of *The Heroin Addict's Mother*, my memoir in poetry. Reading the poems, she said, feeling the pain she'd caused our family, made her very sad. When I responded "Don't feel bad. That's all in the past," I had no idea that Anna had been using off and on the entire year of the pandemic. And she had no idea she was already dying.

"It's ok for me to feel bad Mumsy," she said. "It just means I have a heart and I'm not an asshole." These words, followed by I love you, were the last words I heard Anna speak.

When the ICU called, I ran to wake up Esther. She was already sitting up in bed, saying: "We have to go to the hospital! Anna needs us right now."

What we saw wasn't Anna. Her green eyes, almost shut, had an eerie yellow hue. My beautiful girl was gone, her light extinguished. We took her hands in ours and let her know she was free to go and to be with Grandma, Grandpa and Kylee. We will always miss you. We will always love you.

Literally and figuratively, Anna died of a broken heart. Rescued by love, she lived as long as she could until the world crashed around her and she with it. She was thirty-eight years old.

The shaman who worked with Anna as she struggled to get out from under heroin's spell and who journeyed for her during her last days on earth, received this message: Anna's struggles were an incredible contribution to an ongoing battle with spirits of darkness.

At her funeral, the Rabbi who knew Anna since childhood said: According to Jewish teachings, there are rare souls filled with a light so bright that it cannot be contained in this world. Anna was one of them.

IX. When the Gates of Heaven are Closed to Prayers, they are Open to Tears

The last words of my eulogy at Anna's funeral addressed her directly: *Anna my laser beam child, my beautiful girl, you're free now, your light unbounded and undimmed by the darkness you battled. You've become who you always were: brave soul, bright spirit. Freed from the damage to your body and the burdens of wrestling with your demons, may you find beyond peace the joy that you spread to us, left here to miss you for the rest of our days.*

When I finished speaking, three flocks of geese flew in formation just above my head, in three great waves of noisy splendor.

In the following days, I received messages from Anna to look for the birds. In a vision, I was led to a street where I saw, painted on the sidewalk, a huge drawing of a white peace dove. In a thick trellis of climbing ivy, I heard the noisy twittering of what seemed like a large number of sparrows, but I couldn't see them. The wind on a windless morning blew my front porch door open and I heard the loud song of many birds coming from the juniper tree in front of the house. Again, they were audible but invisible.

The sight and sounds of birds have been a source of solace to me in these long days since Anna's death. At the same time, I know that birds are dying in epidemic numbers due to disease, fires, floods, drought and other disasters brought on by climate crisis.

I see Anna now, just to my left, her green eyes a pattern of radiant energy. Her smile transmits a warm kindness. She tells me Mumsy, it's ok. Esther and Roger too feel her warmth, her kindness and reassurance.

I am grateful for this comfort, but it doesn't obviate my tears. I cry for Anna and all the Annas. I cry for the birds, the trees, for all living creatures. My tears flow into the endless rivers of sorrow throughout the world.

During the ten Days of Awe between Rosh Hashonah and Yom Kippur, Jews traditionally pray for forgiveness. Sincere repentance, it is said, will soften God's decree of who shall live and who shall die, written during these days. In the final minutes of Yom Kippur, the Gates of Heaven are closed. The Talmud tells us: When the gates of heaven are closed to prayers, they are open to tears.

Perhaps, in these dark days, our tears for the world are the purest form of prayer.

X. Hawk

Hawk first came to me after my mother's death. Rarely seen in my urban neighborhood, two announced themselves in the next few days. One flew so close I could hear the whooshing of wings. The second sat on the backyard fence, calmly eating a squirrel, as though to say what dies becomes food.

The hawk that crashed and died in my car will forever be burned into my consciousness. I buried it in a spot sacred to me, in the woods of Ludlow.

This week, when I arrive at Evergreen Acres, Anna's absence scalds me with burning grief. I open the screen door to the front deck and look out at the trees. Sitting on a birch branch is a red-tailed hawk, looking straight ahead in my direction. I am dumbfounded, filled with what the ancient Jews called awe—a combination of wonder and terror. As I stand there, I get the sense that Hawk is greeting me, welcoming me to Evergreen Acres. And with that, he flies off.

Roger and I decide to drive and take a walk on Andover Road, a favorite Vermont spot with breathtaking views of soft blue-grey-lavender mountains on both sides of the ridge. We park the car at the small cemetery and walk the ridge silently, lost in our thoughts, our longing and grief for Anna.

This is a place I feel acutely the absence of Kylee, who loved to walk ahead of us, nibbling on the grass at the side of the road, stopping to take a good look at the horses fenced in just ahead near the red-barned farm, turning around every so often to look back and check on us.

After some time, we turn back toward the car. When we reach it, there, on the ground, is a single exquisite red-tailed hawk feather.

Simultaneously, we both look up at the sky and say, *Thank you.*

N.B.: This is an abridged version. Please see Dark Matter: Women Witnessing #13 *online for the complete essay.*

Rachel Economy
A Home for the Seeds

> …to cultivate with each other in every way imaginable epochs to come that can replenish refuge…Right now, the earth is full of refugees, human and not, without refuge.

> It matters how kin generate kin.
> —Donna Haraway, *Staying with the Trouble*

Author's note: This was written after reading Donna Haraway's essay "Making Kin: Anthropocene, Capitalocene, Plantationcene, Chthulucene," which planted a seed. All quotations are from that essay.

The floods were coming in and the steam burning through the windows. We gripped our spades in our teeth and climbed into the mouth of the mountain to build secret homes for the seeds.

We did not know each other, or we thought we did not.

We had not been born in the same places. We had never spoken words the others recognized. In the flood, trying to get out of the city, we had found ourselves in a tangle of unmatched tongues and car tires spinning wretched against the finally wet, so wet, too wet soil. Cacophony. An unwieldy din.

But there was a language we held common, a thing that drove us madly into the hills soaking and coughing, our pockets full of sunflowers and fava beans. Call it the language of fertility. The rhetoric of rot. Of reimagining. Call it insanity. Call it a failure to bite down and trudge the proper path and save the proper thing. Call it disease or dis-ease or dissonance or dismantling, all.

Whatever name, we had it. We were, first and foremost, the ones who got out, some privilege and a dash of chance. And we were also ones who knew that the story of what-to-do-in-case-of-disaster was a made thing, a stitched thing, an invisible law book, something written by five-fingered-hands in one very specific language for one very specific purpose. That the disaster itself was a story too, a real thing, yes, and a real thing that had been made, a written thing. And we were the ones who knew story could, just as truly, be torn up, dug up, re-stitched, by hands, by briars, by sharks' teeth snagging. We were the imaginers. The anxious creators, for whom no law was obvious and no story a static end. We had no set idea of how precisely to respond to a flood. We were not wed to any particular conversation with G_d about the monogamous needs of animals on large boats that wait out storms. Neither were we looking to save the microwaves.

And we were the ones who had no children. Or whose children had already gone. To the waters, to the white and hungry guns, to the longing. We were the ones who had no seeds.

So we found some. In the backs of our closets, in the corner stores standing ankle-deep in water, in the jars on the tilting kitchen shelves. And we gripped our spades in our teeth, and we looked sideways as the streets began to buckle and fold into foothills, and we saw each other limping, and rolling, and running, pockets spilling over with hard-shelled children, with descendants of future trees, and we reached out as we ran, and we gripped each other's hands in our hands.

It was the queerest thing, like a bird in love with a sturgeon, a family of defectors, arms empty of objects and pockets emptied into soil above the water line, saving no wealth or infrastructure, saving the wrong things. A re-kindling, a re-kinning, a reckoning. All this dying, it has been beyond swallowing.

All those bodies, they came home to the soil. And so we gave them children. Hard-shelled and root-bound. It was a kind of making love to the dead. We slipped seeds into their pockets. Their bodies fertile, already almost soil, meeting the beans, the walnuts, the pits we plunged into the wet ground. The rhetoric of rot. The true nature of kinship: all things becoming other things. Hidden in the mountain, learning each others' languages, guarding, gardening, waiting for the first roots, those parts of the plants called "radical," to unfurl their faces into the soil.

e

"Kin is an assembling sort of word. All critters share a common 'flesh'…"

What happens when a tsunami or a big earthquake or a societal collapse hits the coastal floodplains and those who can get their bodies out have to head for the hills? How will we re-make the world? What will we eat? Who will be the keepers of the stories? Who will be the keepers of the dead? How do we show up and take care of each other, beyond the stories that we have been taught? It will take a myriad of stories to answer these questions, and we need to answer them, again and again, to imagine and re-imagine our wonderings, queries, tinkerings, what-ifs, into flesh and soil and seed.

It is not only people who will need refuge, and indeed some people might have no people. Not anymore. What if they find each other. What if they find the seeds. What if they hold refuge for the dead, for each other, and for the living who will need to eat later on. What if the story about what to do in case of disaster, what and who to prioritize, gets queered, gets failed at, gets improvised outside of, gets added on to. What if they hide in the hills and honor the dead by planting seeds into their crumbling soil. What if they find each other and keep the breath of the world alive in a secret place. What if they hold each other beyond horror, beyond bloodlines, beyond absurdity. What if they re-imagine, together, what it is that needs to be saved.

"Who and whatever we are, we need to make-with—become-with, compose-with—the earth-bound…compose and decompose, which are both dangerous and promising practices…"

Dangerous and promising. Compose and decompose—song to shit to soil. "All matter" merging into itself, one another. Microbes and worms breaking down? The myth that we ever weren't kin undoing the lie of a whole country acting as if we don't, with the flip of a leaf or a compost pile, just turn into one another's bodies.

What does it mean to become kindred with the dead? To plant into them? To unfurl and unravel and unassent to the story that exalts immortality, that promotes "failure to become-with the dead and the extinct." One of the things I do for a living is grow food, and help others learn to grow food. Every act of feeding is also an act of dying. Every moment of death is also a plate replete with food. Compost, insect, plant, microbe. Bodies becoming other bodies, matter mattering.

In our obsession with eternal life we tried to unbecome kin with the earth, to unbecome kin with each other. Instead of merging and differentiating and merging again, as matter tends to, we try to stay separate, forever, avoiding death.

And yet the dying, "… it has been beyond swallowing." It is beyond swallowing. I have lost beloveds and I am not grateful, I do not turn to death with rosy, easy eyes. So many have had beloveds taken, whole generations, the unkinning of separation, how it tries to unlink families, stories, whole histories waving in the wind.

Some of us, our ancestors, chose separation, domination, did this actively to people who were not in fact trying to unbecome. These are the dominator stories unlinking, unassembling us now, still. A planet with a fever. Bodies metastasizing something we can't always name but the sickness tries to.

But death becomes soil becomes seeds, seeds shared from hand to shattered hand, Without kin beyond blood, beyond nation, beyond body, without kindred in death, we create refugees, creatures, species, cultures with no place of refuge to recover, to thrive. No death, no kin, no food. Kin begets refuge: places of holding over, of survival, of keeping alive the children and the stories and the seeds.

I asked the ocean about loneliness, once. And the ocean laughed and spit salt water in my face. Nice try, nice try, nice try. What do you think happens to you when you die? Your body breaks down. Your body gets eaten. Your body becomes the body of this world that you so desperately, terribly, painfully love.

You cannot die your way out of mattering, said the ocean. Nice try, but we are already kin.

Authors' and Artists' Biographies

Elliott batTzedek is a Pushcart Prize-nominated poet/translator. Her work appears in: *American Poetry Review, Massachusetts Review, Lilith, The Broadkill Review, Hole in the Head Review, Naugatuck River Review, Wordpeace,* and *Hunger Mountain Review.* Her chapbook *the enkindled coal of my tongue* was published in 2017 by Wicked Banshee Press. A chapbook of translations from the Israeli lesbian poet Shez, *A Necklace of White Pearls*, was published by Moonstone Press in 2024.

Emilee Baum is a writer and researcher focused on consciousness, arts-based inquiry, and Buddhism. A former Fulbright scholar, she holds an MA in Embodiment Studies from Goddard College and has completed advanced graduate study in Expressive Arts at The European Graduate School. She is the author of *The Agency of Bliss* (Ant Bear Press, 2012), with work appearing in various texts and journals.

Margo Berdeshevsky, NYC-born, writes in Paris. Latest book *Kneel Said the Night*, Sundress Publications. Forthcoming: *It Is Still Beautiful To Hear The Heart Beat*, Salmon Poetry. Author of *Before The Drought*, Glass Lyre Press, finalist for National Poetry Series, *Between Soul & Stone, But a Passage in Wilderness*, Sheep Meadow Press, *Beautiful Soon Enough*, FC2, 1st Ronald Sukenick Innovative Fiction Award. Other honors: Grand prize for Thomas Merton Poetry of the Sacred Award, Robert H. Winner Award/Poetry Society of America. margoberdeshevsky.simplesite.com

Anne Bergeron's writing appears in *Flyway, The Hopper, About Place, Eastern Iowa Review, Dark Mountain Project, Blueline,* and *The Black River: Death Poems* anthology. She is the finalist for the 2023 Barry Lopez Creative Nonfiction Award at *Cutthroat Journal of the Arts,* a *Writing the Land* poet, and a Rowland Foundation fellow. Anne teaches and homesteads in Vermont's eastern foothills with her husband and animals. www.annebergeronvt.com

Debby Black is an artist, occasional writer, meditator and walker who loves trees and bees and following moon phases in the night sky. She lives at the edge of Lake Ontario, land once that of the Michi Saaggig Anishnaabeg, within the watershed now called Cobourg, gazing into the vastness of water, sky and cloud.

Maria Blum is an ethnobotanist, poet and healing artist. Born into a lineage of plant medicine women and healers, her practice includes the spiritual and ritual relationship between plants and humans which honors the transitions of life and death. She holds an MA degree in Indigenous Knowledge Systems and Antropoesía/Poetics. Blum's research includes thanatology, spiritual plant offerings and symbolism within birth and funerary rites, and traditional earth-based healing practices of Mesoamerica.

Pamela Booker is 2024 NJ State Council on the Arts/Mid Atlantic Arts Prose Fellow for the fiction manuscript *Dill's Mirrors and the Lizzies*. An interdisciplinary writer, publications are featured in various outlets, notably, *Blacktino Queer Performance* (Duke Univ.), and currently *Shaping Destiny: Election Season (About Place Journal)*. Recent invited readings include the Segue Reading Series at Artists Space, Happy 90th Birthday Sonia Sanchez Poetry Reading and Wicked Queer Authors (Dixon Place). She is Montclair State University Writing Faculty. Follow @ pamelabooker19

Writer, naturalist and advocate **Susan Cerulean** has lived alongside and listened to the northern Gulf of Mexico and its wild birds and islands since 1981. She has published three award-winning works of nonfiction with the University Press of Georgia: *I Have Been Assigned the Single Bird: A Daughter's Memoir* (2019), *Coming to Pass: Florida's Coastal Islands in a Gulf of Change* (2015), and *Tracking Desire: A Journey after Swallow-tailed Kites* (2005).

Erica Charis-Molling is a lesbian poet, educator, and librarian. Recipient of the Robin Becker Prize, her chapbook "How We Burn" was published by Seven Kitchens Press in 2022. A Mass Cultural Council Fellow, a Bread Loaf Writers' Conference alum, and a graduate of Antioch University's MFA program, she lives in western Massachusetts with her wife, daughter, and fur babies. ericacharis-molling.squarespace.com

Kim Chernin is the author of many books in many genres. She wrote and published fiction, nonfiction, creative nonfiction, poetry and essays, including *In My Mother's House*; *The Hungry Self*; *Crossing the Border*; *The Flame Bearers*. Kim died December 17, 2020. In the notes to her poem *A Stuttering Kind of Worship* which appeared in issue #4 she wrote: "All the poetry I have written arises from this enchanted conviction of kinship, which so often brings me to a sense of breathless awe and a stuttering kind of worship."

For **Suzette Clough**, painting is her Spirit practice. It is her way of tapping into a world that is invisible, interconnected and vibrantly alive—a portal to experiencing that we are part of the luminous field of Creation. Her practice involves synthesizing creativity, spirituality and embodied emotional intelligence as an oracular path. She is the originator and a teacher of the radically transformative spiritual painting practice, Visual Medicine™.

Christine Holland Cummings' poems have appeared in: *Blueline, Dark Matter: Women Witnessing, Hamilton Stone Review, Iron Horse Literary Review, Reckoning, a journal of creative writing on environmental justice,* and others. She is the author of a chapbook titled *Family Stories* published by Orchard Street Press, Gates Mills, Ohio. Christine has an MFA in poetry from Bennington College.

Laura Alexi Davenport is a retired fundraising and development consultant, clinical pastoral counselor, and hospice volunteer. She began writing for the love of the craft after her first cancer diagnosis in 1996. Cancer's recurrence, with its mastectomy and attendant losses, deepened Laura's writing. Her threshold experience with cancer inspired her to seek out, and live with, Shona and Ndeble healers [ngangas] in Zimbabwe for sixteen days. A memoir based on this extraordinary experience is underway.

Jojo Donovan is a priestess, writer, grief worker, and educator living on the ancestral lands of the Multnomah, Cowlitz, Clackamas, Chinook, and many others—also known as Portland, Oregon. Their work supports queer, animist, and embodied spiritualities in their (re) emergence—engaging ritual and ceremony as vital technologies. Jojo's writing has been featured in *Confrontation Magazine, Hematopoiesis Press,* and *Index for the Next World*. www.sevenstonestarot.com, and on substack sevenstonestarot.substack.com

Debra Magpie Earling is the author of *Perma Red* and *The Lost Journals of Sacajewea*. She is a member and citizen of the Confederate Salish and Kootenai Tribes of the Flathead Reservation.

Juliana Borrero Echeverry is a Colombian writer, translator, performance artist and teacher. Her publications include the book and performance piece *Las Extraterrestres* (Cajon de sastre, 2021), whose translation, *Women from Outer Space*, is now looking for an English publisher, and the Spanish translation of *Aureole* by Carole Maso (Cajon de sastre, 2022). She is currently the head of the Literature M.A. at Universidad Pedagogica y Tecnologica de Colombia in Tunja, Colombia.

Rachel Economy is a garden designer, sustainability educator, poet, artist, performer, public speaker, mentor, and YouTuber. Her business, *Next World Design*, a radically sustainable design playspace, supports people who long for joy and liberation as they bring thriving, accessible worlds to life in their gardens, workplaces, and daily lives. She also creates poetry, art, videos and performances to help herself and others survive—and find play within—the world as it is.

Alex C. Eisenberg is a child of the western high desert and the Pacific Northwest rainforest, with European ancestry. A writer, circus performer, homesteader, grief-tender, and activist, Alex follows many threads of passion which she hopes weave together in service to healing ancestral, social, and ecological wounds. Alex lives by candlelight in an off-grid cabin at the base of the Olympic Mountains with her beloved cat, and is blessed with an abundance of community. www.alexandriaceisenberg.wordpress.com

Sharon English is the author most recently of *Night in the World*, described as "a splendid and searing novel, pressed up against the tremours of our times." She's also published two short story collections: *Zero Gravity* and *Uncomfortably Numb*. Originally from London, ON, she lived for decades in Toronto and now resides in rural Nova Scotia, where she teaches and writes about rooting in a new territory. sharonenglish.net

Kristin Flyntz is an assistant editor at *Dark Matter: Women Witnessing*. Her work has appeared in *Dark Matter, Cloud Women's Dream Society Quarterly Journal, The Pivot: Addressing Global Problems Through Local Action, The Corona Transmissions: Alternatives for Engaging with COVID-19 from the Physical to the Metaphysical, Psychology Today*, and on *Living One*, the video series from the Kerulos Center for Nonviolence.

Jacqueline Freeman and her husband live on their Washington farm with orchards, gardens, forest and pastures, frog ponds and glorious fields of wildflowers. The farm is a haven of respectful relationship. Her books, *Song of Increase: Listening to the Wisdom of Honeybees for Kinder Beekeeping and a Better World*, and *What Bees Want: Beekeeping as Nature Intended*, are published in ten languages. A third book is nearly ready. www.SpiritBee.com

Julie Gabrielli's work as a writer, architect, and professor navigates both climate collapse and environmental reconciliation. She is a Clinical Associate Professor in the University of Maryland School of Architecture, Planning, & Preservation. Julie writes the *Homecoming* newsletter on Substack, and her work has been published in the magazines *Orion, Ecological Home Ideas*, and *Urbanite*; and in literary journals *Dark Mountain Journal* #6, #8 and #10; *Dark Matter: Women Witnessing* #3 and *Immanence*.

Hilary Giovale is a mother, writer, community organizer, and ninth-generation American settler who lives in Flagstaff, Arizona. As an active reparationist, she seeks to follow Indigenous and Black leadership in support of human rights, environmental justice, and equitable futures. She is the author of *Becoming a Good Relative: Calling White Settlers toward Truth, Healing, and Repair*. Learn more about her work at www.goodrelative.com.

Newark, NJ native **Ysabel Y. González** received her BA from Rutgers University, an MFA in Poetry from Drew University, and serves as Sr. Consultant, Poetry at the New Jersey Performing Arts Center and Dodge Poetry. In her work, Ysabel explores her Borinquen roots and how to engage with tenderness in a complicated world. She is the author of *Wild Invocations* (Get Fresh Books, 2019). www.ysabelgonzalez.com

Wendy Gorschinsky-Lambo is the first and only person to receive permission to teach Egyptian High Alchemy and Sacred Relationship according to The Magdalen from Tom Kenyon and Judi Sion. In bringing Dr. Masaru Emoto to present Messages from Water and its research to Quebec, she was gifted for 19 years with the guardianship of the Ancient Algonquin Women's Water Ceremony. She is owner of TerrÂm(i)es, an educational research center in Rawdon, Quebec. www.terramies.com

Gillian Goslinga is a cultural anthropologist, ethnographic filmmaker, essayist, systemic constellations facilitator, clairvoyant and shamanic practitioner. Her PhD dissertation, "Virgin Birth in South India: The Ethnography of a South Indian God" (2006) won the prestigious Sardar Patel Award from UCLA's Center for India and South Asia. Her ethnographic films *The Child The Stork Brought Home* (1995, gestational surrogacy) and *The Poojari's Daughter* (2006, ritual sacrifice) are distributed by Documentary Educational Resources. She lives outside of Sedona, AZ.

Judy Grahn is an internationally known poet, writer, cultural theorist, and teacher. She has published seventeen books of poetry and prose. Her 2023 book *Touching Creatures, Touching Spirit: Living in a Sentient World* chronicles her experiences and thoughts about creature consciousness and psychic connections across species. Dr. Grahn received her Ph.D. in integral studies with an emphasis on women's spirituality from the California Institute of Integral Studies, in 2000.

Miriam Greenspan is a renowned psychotherapist, author, public speaker, and poet. Her book *A New Approach to Women and Therapy* (1983) pioneered the field of feminist therapy. *Healing Through the Dark Emotions: The Wisdom of Grief, Fear, and Despair* (2003) won the Nautilus Award in psychology. Miriam's book of poetry, *The Heroin Addict's Mother,* has been praised by prominent poets and experts in addiction. Her work has been featured in *Huffington Post, Ms., Shambhala Sun, The Sun, Psychology Today*, and the *Los Angeles Review of Books*, among others. www.miriamgreenspan.com

Carole Harmon is a Canadian photographer and writer who lives on the Sunshine Coast in Canada. Through creative nonfiction, poetry and photo collage she locates her colonial family history and environmentally-themed writing and nature photography within a twenty-first century worldview, often combining conflicting realities. Her work has been published in anthologies and literary magazines. Harmon co-produces, with Ingrid Rose and Gary Sill, the online radio show and podcast "Writers Radio".

Michaela Harrison is an international vocalist and healer whose career is rooted in relaying the transformational power of music and supporting others in accessing the healing energy available in nature through ritual and creative practices. She holds a BA in International Affairs and an MA in Africana Studies. Michaela has toured and recorded extensively, has headlined music festivals in Brazil, and is currently engaged in a project called Whale Whispering, a musical collaboration on water, healing and ancestry with humpback whales based in Bahia, Brazil. www.michaelaharrison.org

Kathleen Hellen is the recipient of the James Still Award, the Thomas Merton Prize for Poetry of the Sacred, and prizes from the H.O.W. Journal and Washington Square Review. Her debut collection *Umberto's Night* won the poetry prize from Washington Writers' Publishing House. She is the author of *The Only Country Was the Color of My Skin*, *Meet Me at the Bottom*, and two chapbooks.

Elena Herrada is a gardener, collector of books and odd things, tax justice activist (defense of libraries and public schools against developers' greed). She is a lifelong Detroiter, mother of three daughters and grandmother of three grandsons.

Nora L. Jamieson is an old woman diving into the realms of grief, impermanence, accepting the unacceptable, and as always, the mysteries of love, her dead and the mystical world. She counseled and gathered women for over forty years in both healing and spiritual groups. She's the author of *Deranged*, an award-winning work of short fiction. She continues to write, paint and counsel in her new home in Keene, NH where she's so glad she can see the stars year round.

Judith Redwing Keyssar has traversed a 35+-year journey as a Midwife to the dying, a Palliative and end-of-life-care RN and educator, author, ceremonialist and poet. Her passion for utilizing poetry as a healing modality has led to the development of a successful international program in Poetic Medicine through her work as the Director of Education at the MERI Center for Education in Palliative Care at UCSF.

Robin Wall Kimmerer is a mother, scientist, decorated professor, enrolled member of the Citizen Potawatomi Nation and the author of *The Serviceberry: Abundance and Reciprocity in the Natural World, Braiding Sweetgrass: Indigenous Wisdom, Scientific Knowledge and the Teachings of Plants*, and *Gathering Moss: A Natural and Cultural History of Mosses*. She is a SUNY Distinguished Teaching Professor of Environmental Biology, and the founder and director of the Center for Native Peoples and the Environment. In 2022 she was named a MacArthur Fellow.

Melissa Kwasny is the author of seven books of poetry, including *The Cloud Path, Where Outside the Body is the Soul Today* and *The Nine Senses*, as well as a collection of essays *Earth Recitals: Essays on Image and Vision*. Her book of nonfiction, *Putting on the Dog: The Animal Origins of What We Wear*, explores the cultural, labor, and environmental histories of clothing materials provided by animals. She was Montana Poet Laureate 2019-2021.

Shula Levine is a birth doula and hospice volunteer. Her writing practice and dream work support her ongoing explorations of life within and around her.

JuPong Lin dances with horseshoe crabs and makes ceremony with cranes and other two-legged artists. She delights in decentering humans in cosmologies of the pluriverse. JuPong lives by the motto, "by any creative means necessary"—be it poetry, community performance or paperfolding. JuPong lives in Nipmuc territory, Western Massachusetts and shows her work at UMass, The LAVA Center, and Easthampton CityArts. Her poetry is published by the NatureCulture in various Writing the Land anthologies.

Susan Marsh lives in Jackson, Wyoming. Her body of work explores the relationship of humans to the wild. Her poems have appeared in *Clerestory*, *Manzanita Review*, *Deep Wild Journal*, *Dark Matter: Women Witnessing*, *Silver Birch* and other journals and anthologies. Her work has been nominated for a Pushcart Prize. Her chapbook *This Earth Has Been Too Generous* was published in 2022. A second chapbook, *Passings*, is forthcoming in late 2024. www.slmarsh.com

Andrea Mathieson's oracular voice developed as she listened to Nature's wisdom over thirty years in her garden. Her writings, *Gaia's Invitation* (2014), *A Love Affair with Nature* (2008, with definitions for 350 Raven flower essences) and *The Book of Snake* (2021) each have a distinct, divinatory quality. Through women's circles, intuitive readings, webinars and retreats, she has generated heart-centered community that consciously engages the Soul of the World.
www.andreamathieson.com   www.ravenessences.com

Alexandra Merrill has been living and working in Maine since the 1980s. Her long-term focus has been on creating experiential education models to support the development of women's leadership. In 2019 she published *Offering*, a collection of essays and images including personal experience, a bio-mimetic, female-identified group dynamics theory, specific leadership practices, embodying gender equity, inclusion and diversity principles along with diverse writings from colleagues who are using this nature-based methodology in their own businesses and teaching.

Deena Metzger is the author of many books including the novels *La Vieja: A Journal of Fire*, *A Rain of Night Birds*, *La Negra y Blanca* (PEN Oakland Award for Literature), *Feral*, *The Other Hand* and the classic writing book, *Writing For Your Life*. She co-edited *Intimate Nature: The Bond Between Women and Animals*, which pioneered the radical understanding that animals are highly intelligent and exhibit intent, and identified Literature of Restoration as an Earth- and Spirit-based literary form. www.literatureofrestoraton.org

Karen Mutter is a practicing physician in Clearwater, Florida. She founded Integrative Medicine Healing Center in 1998 to pursue the exploration of healing outside the confines of Western medicine. Informed by specialty training in internal medicine, she relies on shamanic practices, dreams, the natural world, nutrition, osteopathic practices and principles, compassion and love as her primary healing modalities. She is an aspiring writer, peacemaker and policy-changer of medical education and practice.

Naeemeh Naeemaei is an interdisciplinary artist based in Chicago whose work centers on ecological grief. Her richly layered narratives incorporate childhood memories, classic Persian literature, and folklore, all grounded in geographical features. She is currently working on an autobiographical documentary navigating her immigration alongside the migration of Omid, the last Siberian crane.

Naomi Shihab Nye's most recent books are *Grace Notes—Poems about Families* (Greenwillow Books, 2024) and *I Know About a Thousand Things —The Writings of Ann Alejandro of Uvalde, Texas,* co-edited by Nye together with Marion Winik (a Wittliff Series Book from Texas A&M University Press, 2024). Naomi strongly condemns the "officially-sanctioned, U.S. supplied" military-industrial genocide of innocent people in Gaza and Lebanon and in all regions on earth.

Lois Red Elk is an enrolled member of the Fort Peck Sioux. She is the author of *Why I Return to Makoce* (Many Voices Press, 2015), *Dragonfly Weather* (Lost Horse Press, 2013), and *Our Blood Remembers* (Many Voices Press, 2011), which received the Best Nonfiction Award from the Wordcraft Circle of Native Writers and Storytellers. She teaches cultural courses and traditional language classes at Fort Peck Community College in Montana.

Patricia Reis was raised in Madison, Wisconsin and earned her MFA from UCLA. She has a degree in Depth Psychology from Pacifica Graduate Institute in Santa Barbara, California. Among her books are *Unsettled: A Novel*; *Daughters of Saturn: From Father's Daughter to Creative Woman*; *Through the Goddess: a Woman's Way of Healing*; and *The Dreaming Way: Dreams and Art for Remembering and Recovery Voices*. She has lived in Maine since 1987. www.patriciareis.net

Cynthia Ann Ross is an artist, writer, and teacher. She lives in Vermont, appreciating the beauty and fierceness of the seasons, watching and listening to the robust green world and its denizens. Currently, she is working on a novel and a memoir that tracks the intellectual, spiritual and artistic encounters that have presented themselves on her path to greater communion with the natural world.

Eve Rachele Sanders is a writer living in Montreal and California. A recipient of a Mellon Fellowship in the Humanities and a National Endowment for the Humanities Grant, among other awards and grants, she received her Ph.D. in English from UC Berkeley and is the author of *Gender and Literacy on Stage in Early Modern England*. She is working on a memoir about the experience of being a literacy scholar who lost and regained the ability to read and write.

Leslie Schwartz is the author of two bestselling novels and one memoir. Her books have been translated into over 12 languages and her second novel, *Angels Crest*, was adapted for the screen as a major motion picture. Her essays and articles have most recently appeared in *Salon*, *LitHub*, *The Rumpus* and *Narratively Speaking*. Leslie offers private mentoring and editing services through her company L&L Writing, Developmental Editing and Coaching Services and is co-founder of the List of Land Artists and Writers Residency in the Westfjords of Iceland where she also teaches writing workshops.

nan seymour is a lake-facing poet, celebrant, and vigil keeper. She founded and facilitates River Writing, a community-held writing practice which fosters voice and connection. As poet-in-residence on Antelope Island, Nan led day-and-night vigils on behalf of the imperiled Great Salt Lake throughout the 2022 and 2023 Utah State legislative sessions. During her weeks on the receding shore, she composed *irreplaceable*, a collective praise poem for Great Salt Lake which was published in fall of 2024 by Moon in the Rye Press.

Yehudit Silverman is the published author of several articles, OpEds, poetry, and one book, *The Story Within – myth and fairy tale in therapy*. An award - winning documentary filmmaker on issues around suicide and creative arts therapies, she presents internationally and was featured on

PBS, Global News and Writers Radio and in *Authority Magazine* and *La Presse.* www.yehuditsilverman.com

Sharon Rodgers Simone is an educator, writer, poet and former scientist who returned to her *Home* very late in years—back to the ways of her people, the Druids—magicians, diviners, and seers. The Oaks, trees the Druids hold sacred, summoned her to service—took her back. Her work is *Reckoning*—repairing rents between the living and the dead: people, Creatures, Waters, Mountains, Rivers and Sacred Places. Her book *Reckonings* is forthcoming.

Verena Stefan was a renowned Swiss German writer. Her books include *Häutungen* (1975, English translation *Shedding*, re-issued in 1994). Among her recent publications: *Fremdschläfer* (French translation *D'ailleurs*); "Doe a Deer" in *Best European Fiction* (trans. Lise Weil); *Als sei ich von einem andern Stern* (*As if I Were from a Different Planet. Jewish Life in Montreal*) co-ed. with Chaim Vogt-Moykopf; *Die Befragung der Zeit*, (French translation *Qui maîtrise les vents connaît son chemin*).

A bit raven, part mycelium, mostly water, **Azul V. Thomé** is eARTh artist, soul activist, mentor, designer of rituals, visionary. Her MA in Ecological Design at Schumacher College was titled "Collective Grief Rituals as if Life and Death Really Matter." SOULand was then founded to offer regular Grief Composting Circles. In 2016/18 she travelled our world to teach ways of feeding our starved souls and to find apprentices in Soul Activism. Her new book is: *A Living Art—Pathososphy: Wisdom born of Suffering and Grief.* SOULand: www.souland.org, soulandinfo@gmail.com

Cynthia Travis is a writer, photographer and documentarian. She is co-founder of the peacebuilding non-profit *everyday gandhis*, enlivening traditional culture, community reconciliation, ecological restoration and regenerative agriculture in Liberia, West Africa. In words and images, she seeks to bear witness to what has been lost in ways that invite personal and collective accountability. She is currently completing an eco-historical memoir, *River of Kin: a Natural History of Family and Empire.*

Ruth Wallen is a multimedia artist and writer whose work is dedicated to encouraging dialogue around ecological and social justice. Her interactive installations, nature walks, websites, artist books, performative lectures, and writing have been widely distributed and exhibited. She was a Fulbright scholar at UABC Tijuana, lecturer in Visual Arts at UCSD, and core faculty in the MFA in Interdisciplinary Arts at Goddard College. She is writing a book about bearing witness to the massive die-offs of trees.

Lise Weil, founder and editor of *Dark Matter: Women Witnessing*, was founder and editor of the US feminist review *Trivia: A Journal of Ideas* (1982-1991) and co-founder of its online offshoot *Trivia: Voices of Feminism*, which she edited through 2011. Her essays and literary nonfiction have been published widely in Canada and the U.S. Her memoir, *In Search of Pure Lust*, was published in 2018. She lives in Montreal and until the college closed in 2024, taught in Goddard College's Graduate Institute. www.liseweil.com

Briggs Whiteford is a visual artist and writer engaged in the restoration of language and a new narrative inclusive of ancient wisdom, ancestors, and the expansion of multi-dimensional realities including the imaginal and dream realms. Briggs' visual work is focused on creating images as portals to the sacred. She has participated at the New York Studio School as board member, artist-in-residence and advisor to the dean. Briggs' artwork has been in museums, public spaces, and private collections all over the world.

Leonore Wilson is a retired English professor from Northern California. She is on the MFA Board at St. Mary's College of California. Her work has been featured in such publications as *Unruly Catholic Women Writers*, *TRIVIA: Voices of Feminism*, *Prairie Schooner*, *Third Coast*, *Quarterly West*, *Madison Review*, *Rattle*, *Taos Journal of Poetry*. Leonore is the mother of three grown sons and the grandmother of two grandsons. Recently, her historical ranch and home burned down in the LNU wildfire of Napa Valley.

Nancy Windheart is an internationally recognized animal communicator, writer, and Interspecies Communication and Reiki for

All Species teacher. Her work has been featured in television, radio, magazine, and online media, and she has written for many digital and print publications. Nancy's life's work is to create deeper harmony, healing, and understanding between all beings on our planet through interspecies connection and communication. She lives in Santa Fe, New Mexico, with her animal family of dogs, cats, and chickens.

Valerie Wolf is a mixed-blood shamanic healer, dreamer, teacher and writer. She led medicine walks and vision quests for twenty years. Happy mother of two and grandmother to five children. She lives in Southern California with her beloved husband of 48 years. Her main passion now is to work shamanically to save the Earth from human destruction as well as delight in Earth's many wonders and great Beauty.

Jaime R. Wood is an author, educator, faculty developer and event organizer. She is the author of Living Voices: Multicultural Poetry in the Middle School Classroom (NCTE 2006) and co-author of the Open Educational Resource *The Word on College Reading and Writing* (OpenOregon 2017). Her poems have appeared in *Dislocate, Matter, Juked, ZYZZYVA, DIAGRAM, Phantom Drift, Dark Matter: Women Witnessing,* and *Hotel Amerika,* among others.

Sara Wright is a dedicated ecofeminist, naturalist, ethologist, and writer. She lives in a little log cabin in the western mountains of Maine with two small dogs and one dove. Sara writes weekly columns that appear in *The Bethel Citizen.* Sara has Native American roots, which may or may not be why she has dedicated her life to speaking out on behalf of the slaughtered trees, dying plants and disappearing animals. sarawrightnature.wordpress.com

Shante' Sojourn Zenith is a Relational Field Consultant supporting visionary creative projects piercing through dominant reality fields to potentiate primordial, ancestral dreamings. As an animist somatic practitioner, drawing on her own experiences with neurodivergence and energetic sensitivity, she weaves ritual experiences to help people come home to their bodies and ecosystems as a place of belonging. She lives next to the Mississippi River in Mni Sota Makoce on the ancestral homelands of the Dakota people. www.earthpoetedgeweaver.com

Kim Zombik was enchanted by words and music as a young girl in Boston. She started writing in fourth grade and decades and boxes of journals later, she writes as if she is going to sing everything. Words have to feel right in her mouth because she sings much of what she writes. Now living in Montréal QC, she teaches yoga, meditation and tours yearly with her band Silvervest.

Editors' and Foreword Writer's Biographies

Editors

Anne Bergeron's poems and essays appear in *Flyway: Journal of Writing and Environment, The Hopper, The Dark Mountain Project, About Place, Eastern Iowa Review, The Calendula Review,* and multiple issues of *Blueline Magazine* and *Dark Matter: Women Witnessing.* She is the 2023 solo finalist for the Barry Lopez Creative Nonfiction Award at *Cutthroat: A Journal of the Arts.* She holds masters degrees in literature and eco-philosophy, is an alumna of the Bread Loaf Orion Environmental Writers' Conference, and her work is anthologized in NatureCulture's *The Black River: Death Poems.* Anne has received two Rowland Foundation fellowships to support her work to integrate wellness and inclusion in Vermont public schools. She teaches teens at a small rural school, practices Thai body-work, and shares yoga with people of all ages. She lives on a homestead she built with her husband, where they grow food and tend to a medley of sweet animal companions. Anne loves listening to the coyotes howl at night, and someday, she hopes to get really good at walking silently in the forest. www.annebergeronvt.com

Kristin Flyntz is an assistant editor at *Dark Matter: Women Witnessing.* Her work has appeared in *Dark Matter, Cloud Women's Dream Society Quarterly Journal, The Pivot: Addressing Global Problems Through Local Action, The Corona Transmissions: Alternatives for Engaging with COVID-19 from the Physical to the Metaphysical, Psychology Today* online, and on *Living One,* the video series from the Kerulos Center for Nonviolence. She has directed *The Vagina Monologues* and *I am an Emotional Creature* by V (formerly Eve Ensler) and acted in numerous local and regional theater productions. She extends her heartfelt gratitude to Nora Jamieson, Deena Metzger, Sharon Rodgers Simone, Gay Bradshaw and the many wise women (including those who appear in this anthology), for their teachings and modeling of how to live in right relationship with the Earth, the ancestors, and our nonhuman kin.

Gillian Goslinga is a cultural anthropologist, feminist science studies scholar and ethnographic filmmaker. She practices shamanic and systemic constellation healing. Her first essay for *Dark Matter: Women Witnessing* in 2015 coincided with the beginning of her healing journey from cancer, Lyme, mold, electromagnetic and chemical neurotoxicity, and chronic fatigue syndrome. Her academic essays on gestational surrogacy in the US and spirit possession in South India and her award-winning Ph.D. dissertation *The Ethnography of a South Indian God* can be found through Google Scholar. Her films *The Child The Stork Brought Home* (1996) and *The Poojari's Daughter* (2006) are at www.der.org. In recent years, Gillian has successfully led community efforts to keep cell towers out of her valley, a rare high desert greenbelt in Arizona that is also a ceremonial First People's landscape. She lives with her old horse Feather Spirit and her cats on sacred land.

Lise Weil, founder and editor of *Dark Matter Women Witnessing*, was founder and editor of the US feminist review *Trivia: A Journal of Ideas* (1982-1991) and co-founder of its online offshoot *Trivia: Voices of Feminism*, which she edited through 2011 now archived at: www.darkmatterwomenwitnessing.com/trivia/archives/index.html Her short fiction, essays, reviews, literary nonfiction and translations have been published widely in journals in both Canada and the U.S. Her collection of Mary Meigs' writings on aging, *Beyond Recall* (2005), was a finalist for a Lambda Literary Award in biography in 2006. Her memoir, *In Search of Pure Lust* (2018), a long meditation on lesbian desire, was an International Book Award Finalist. Until the college closed in 2024, she taught in Goddard College's Graduate Institute. She co-edited—and has a chapter in—*Teaching Transformation: Progressive Education in Action* (2016), a collection of essays by faculty, students and alumni about Goddard's embodied pedagogy and the ways it challenged the hierarchical dissociated structures of traditional academia. She lives in Montreal and spends summers in a cabin in the woods north of the city where she host annual retreats for women and nonbinary writers centered around dreamwork. www.liseweil.com

Foreword Writer

G. A. Bradshaw is the founder and director of The Kerulos Center for Nonviolence (www.kerulos.org). She holds doctoral degrees in ecology and psychology, and she was the first scientist to recognize and diagnose PTSD in Elephants, Chimpanzees, and Orcas. Her books include the Pulitzer-nominated *Elephants on the Edge: What Animals Teach Us about Humanity; Carnivore Minds: Who These Fearsome Beings Really Are; Talking with Bears: Conversations with Charlie Russell* and *The Evolved Nest: Nature's Way of Raising Families and Creating Connected Communities* (www.gabradshaw.com). She is the primary carer for rescued colonized Animals including disabled endangered Tortoises and native Wildlife at Grace Village, Oregon, USA.

DARK
WOMEN WITNESSING MATTER

Dark Matter publishes writing and visual art created in response to an age of massive species loss and ecological collapse. It is a home for dreams, visions, and communications with the non-human world—especially those with messages for how we might begin to heal our broken relationship to the earth. https://darkmatterwomenwitnessing.com

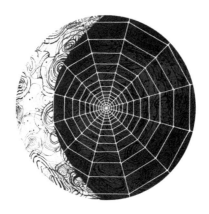

About NatureCulture Web

The mission of NatureCulture® is to help humans be in right relationship with the rest of the natural world. This anthology is the first in our new imprint NatureCulture Web, publishing books written and edited by like-minded people and organizations. Please see all NatureCulture's publications at https://www.nature-culture.net

Other NatureCulture® Books

2024

The Black River: Death Poems
ed. Deirdre Pulgram-Arthen
Cayman Brac From Bluff to Sea
Writing the Land: The Connecticut River
Writing the Land: Wanderings I
Writing the Land: Wanderings II
Writing the Land: Virginia
Wriring the Land: Maine II

2023

Writing the Land: Youth Write the Land
Writing the Land: Currents
Writing the Land: Channels
Writing the Land: Streamlines
Migrations and Home: The Elements of Place, ed. Simon Wilson
From Root to Seed: Black, Brown, and Indigenous Poets Write the Northeast, ed. Samaa Abdurraqib

2022

Writing the Land: Foodways and Social Justice
Writing the Land: Windblown I
Writing the Land: Windblown II
Writing the Land: Maine
LandTrust, poems by Katherine Hagopian Berry

2021, 2024

Writing the Land: Northeast

Forthcoming (2025-2026)

Writing the Land: The Rensselaer Plateau
Writing the Land: Washington
Writing the Land: Doolin, Ireland
Writing the Land: The Cayman Islands
Writing the Land: Horizons
Writing the Land: Pathways